International Communications

The International Telecommunication Union and the Universal Postal Union

FRANCIS LYALL
University of Aberdeen, UK

Routledge
Taylor & Francis Group
LONDON AND NEW YORK

First published 2011 by Ashgate Publishing

2 Park Square, Milton Park, Abingdon, Oxon OX14 4RN
711 Third Avenue, New York, NY 10017, USA

Routledge is an imprint of the Taylor & Francis Group, an informa business

First issued in paperback 2016

British Library Cataloguing in Publication Data
Lyall, Francis.
International communications : the International Telecommunication Union and the Universal Postal Union.
1. International Telecommunication Union – History. 2. Universal Postal Union – History. 3. Telecommunication – International cooperation.
I. Title
384'.0601–dc22

Library of Congress Cataloging-in-Publication Data
Lyall, Francis.
International communications : the International Telecommunication Union and the Universal Postal Union / by Francis Lyall.
p. cm.
Includes bibliographical references and index.
ISBN 978–1–4094–0869–7 (hardback)
1. International Telecommunication Union. 2. Telecommunication – International cooperation. 3. Universal Postal Union. 4. Postal service – International cooperation.
I. Title.
HE7700.L93 2011
384–dc23

2011016675

ISBN 978-1-4094-0869-7 (hbk)
ISBN 978-1-138-26087-0 (pbk)

INTERNATIONAL COMMUNICATIONS

For Heather

Contents

Preface

We phone across the globe and electronically interrogate remote databases. We still 'wire' or 'cable', though that language is atrophying. We listen to the radio or watch television. We put a stamp on the top right-hand side of an envelope and a postman in a foreign country delivers it. We buy from a US bookseller and in due course it arrives in the mail. We take these abilities for granted, but they only exist because of two international organisations. Working without apparent fuss, modern communication services are undergirded by the International Telecommunication Union and the Universal Postal Union.[1]

This book has several origins. First, I am indebted to Ivan Vlasic, Professor of Law at the Institute of Air and Space Law, McGill University, Montreal, who in 1963 suggested the then emergent space telecommunications as a suitable topic for a term-paper. That developed into an LL.M. thesis of 1965 and eventually into a book.[2] The ITU was fascinatingly recurrent in all three efforts. Second, through space telecommunications I met David Leive, then Legal Counsel to the Communications Satellite Corporation (COMSAT), and thereafter Counsel to the International Telecommunications Satellite Organisation (INTELSAT). David's 1970 book on the radio side of the ITU remains a classic.[3] I used to ask him when he was going to do a second edition and maybe cover the whole ITU. He would laugh and say that he would leave that to me. So here is my attempt. Third, out of the blue I was asked to contribute to a set of essays on the UN system that was being planned to celebrate the fiftieth anniversary of the United Nations. Edward Ploman had died unexpectedly,[4] and someone was urgently needed to write about the ITU. A friend suggested my name. We were asked where appropriate to refer to the structure and operation of other UN Agencies. However, nowhere in the initial allocation of chapters could I find mention of the Universal Postal Union.

---

1 'No-one notices something that works too well.' *per* Lu-Tze in T. Pratchett, *Thief of Time* (London: Doubleday, 2001) 115.

2 F. Lyall, *Law and Space Telecommunications* (Aldershot, Hants: Dartmouth, 1989). See also the ITU section of F. Lyall and P.B. Larsen, *Space Law: A Treatise* (Farnham, UK: Ashgate, 2009).

3 D.M. Leive, *International Telecommunications and International Law: The Regulation of the Radio Spectrum* (Leiden: Sijthoff; New York: Oceana, 1970).

4 E.W. Ploman, *Space, Earth and Communications* (London: Pinter, 1984) (a translation of *Kommunikation durch Satelliten*, Mainz: Hasse & Koehler, 1974); *International Law Governing Communications and Information: A Collection of Basic Documents* (Westport, CT; Greenwood, 1982).

Dr Schachter's amused response to my query was 'Ooops!' and to ask me to deal with both the ITU and UPU in my contribution. So I did.[5]

This book is not equally balanced in the treatment of the Unions. That reflects my involvement with the ITU over the years, and I am grateful to those who over many years have discussed ITU matters with me. I do not identify them individually since some spoke subject to confidentiality. For the UPU I have relied on written and electronic materials.

As will be seen from the citations, I would particularly acknowledge and praise the work of the late George A. Codding, Jr. Written from the point of view of politics and international relations his books on the ITU[6] and the UPU[7] were ground-breaking. His mastery of the detail of many meetings of both organisations is exemplary. I am sorry, relieved and pleased that I have had neither the time, nor been allowed sufficient wordage, to seek to emulate his efforts. I would also thank David Leive again for his encouragement, and for that 1970 text.

I believe that you do not understand the present without knowing the past. Where we are depends on where we have been. Both Unions arrived early at basic principles and appropriate legislative devices. Detail may have changed but not the fundamentals. In citing early material I have imposed one modern tool. The first international agreements frequently did not number or otherwise denote the subparagraphs of articles. I have taken the liberty of introducing numbering where that is useful, e.g. Article 61.3 would therefore indicate the third paragraph of Art. 61, and so on. I should also note that the early treaties and conventions were often in French. I have usually quoted from English translations in Bevans, Malloy or elsewhere. Some of these translations are oddly phrased.

Sourcing data has become easier even during my research and writing. Both Unions publish much, a good deal of it electronically, and much is now free.[8] The ITU History Portal is uploading documentation which otherwise would be difficult to find. By the time this book is published more will be available there. The commentaries by the UPU International Bureau on the UPU materials have been invaluable, though I should note that I have been unable to find a copy of the pre-1991 versions to which the current documentation occasionally refers. Heinonline affords easy access to the Bevans, Hudson and Malloy collections, to the United States Treaty (UST) and the Treaties and other International Acts

---

5 'Posts and Telecommunications' in O. Schachter and C.G. Joyner (eds), *United Nations Legal Order*, 2 vols. (Am. Soc. Int. Law/ Grotius Publications, Cambridge UP., 1995), vol. 2, 789-824.

6 G.A. Codding, Jr., *The International Telecommunication Union: An Experiment in International Cooperation* (Leiden: Brill, 1952; New York: Arno Press, 1972). See also G.A. Codding and A.M. Rutkowski, *The International Telecommunication Union in a Changing World* (Dedham, MA: Artech House, 1982).

7 G.A. Codding, Jr., *The Universal Postal Union: coordinator of the international mails* (New York: New York UP, 1964).

8 ITU PP-10, 'Free online access to ITU publications', Dec. 12 (Guadalajara, 2010).

(TIAS) series. It has also recently uploaded the British and Foreign State Papers (BFSP), a very extensive compilation.[9] For those tracking League of Nations Treaty Series (LNTS) material I may say that http://www.worldlii.org/int/other/LNTSer/ often affords easier access than the UN database. As with other of my writing I am grateful to the University of Aberdeen for electronic access to the Hein, Lexis, Westlaw and other databases.

Although this is a book about law, it is not a manual for solving telecommunication or postal problems. Those with particular difficulties should consult the appropriate regulations. Even so there is much detail in the following pages. Doubtless there are errors, and it would be charitable to let me know in case correction becomes possible.

I have used material that has come to my attention down to 1 January 2011, though it has been possible to include some later data. There will be further change and development. Both Unions now operate on a rolling programme between regular plenipotentiary conferences. The last ITU plenipotentiary conference was held in October 2010, at Guadalajara, Mexico. Users of this book after 2012 should note that world conferences are scheduled for Geneva in 2012, one to consider the Radio Regulations and another to revise the International Telecommunication Regulations. The next UPU plenipotentiary conference, its Twenty-fifth Congress, is scheduled for Doha, Qatar, in September/October 2012.

Finally, for those who discern truths in fiction I would recommend the novel *Going Postal*, by Terry Pratchett, first published in 2004. Though an invention anent postal and tele-communications occurring somewhat elsewhere, it has much to teach. *Res ipsa loquitur*.

Really finally, as always my wife has been very patient and encouraging, giving me time and space to browse, burrow and write. Thank you, Heather.

Francis Lyall
Aberdeen, Scotland

Postscript

Ivan Vlasic died, aged 84, on 20 April 2011. These pages had been sent to the publisher and I had hoped to send him a copy of the book. Croat by birth, Ivan was one of the Yugoslav partisans that fought the Nazi occupation in the Second World War. After an undergraduate Law degree in Yugoslavia he gained an

9 The BFSP is a treasure-house of fascinating material, ranging widely from stuffy speeches by sovereigns to debates on what to do with Napoleon, from data on (then) remote areas to arrangements as to the succession of monarchs, and from formal treaties to correspondence about events on the Island of Monte Cristo (a UK national got into difficulties with the local authorities). It is not restricted to UK matters. If you can access it, browse and wonder.

LL.M. at McGill University (partly supporting himself by helping to build the foundations of Place Ville Marie in down-town Montreal) and followed up with a Ph.D. at Yale which resulted in an invitation to co-author the first major book on Space Law.[10] After teaching in Florida and Ottawa he joined the Faculty of Law at McGill in 1963 where I was a member of his first class in Space Law. At first I found him a rather forbidding figure, but soon a robust but kind sense of humour manifested itself. This was occasionally directed at myself, the baby of the class, often addressed as 'the Scot', or as a pre-Star Trek 'Scotty'. As part of the curriculum we had to write two term papers and I proposed as one of mine 'Who owns the Moon?'. Ivan's response was a growl. 'There's more interesting things.' Then a smile. 'Have you looked at radio frequencies?' I did, and was intrigued. So began my interest in such matters. I remain grateful to him for that suggestion back in 1963.

I am also grateful for his reference when I applied for the Chair of Public Law at Aberdeen in 1973. It was generous (such things can sometimes leak) and living up to it was a stimulus over the years, especially when meetings and other administrative tasks proliferated and scholarly activity could have been sidelined. We last met at the UN Fiftieth Birthday celebrations in New York in 1995. He was in good form, as ever. I deeply regret he will not read these words.

Francis Lyall, May 2011

10 M.S. McDougal, H.D. Lasswell and I.A. Vlasic, *Law and Public Order in Space* (New Haven: Yale UP, 1963).

Abbreviations and Acronyms

(Excluding obvious abbreviated references)

AASL	Annals of Air and Space Law, McGill University.
AJIL	American Journal of International Law, 1906-present.
Art. RC	An Article of the UPU Letter Post Regulations.
Art. RL	An Article of the UPU Parcel Post Regulations.
ATS	Australian Treaty Series.
BDT	Telecommunication Development Bureau.
Bevans	C.I. Bevans, *Treaties and Other International Agreements of the United States of America*, 13 vols. (Washington DC: Department of State, 1968-1978).
CCPS	Consultative Committee on the Postal Service (UPU) 1957-1969; Consultative Council on the Postal Service, 1969-1994.
CFR	Code of Federal Regulations (US).
Codding I	G.A. Codding, Jr., *The International Telecommunication Union: An Experiment in International Cooperation* (Leiden: Brill, 1952; New York: Arno Press, 1972).
Codding II	G.A. Codding, Jr. and A.M. Rutkowski, *The International Telecommunication Union in a changing world* (Dedham, MA: Artech House, 1982).
Codding III	G.A. Codding, Jr., *The Universal Postal Union* (New York: New York U.P., 1964).
Collection	*Collection of the basic texts of the International Telecommunication Union adopted by the Plenipotentiary Conference*, 3d Ed. 2007 (Geneva: ITU, 2007) (new ed. taking account of the Final Acts of the Guadalajara Plenipotentiary Conference held in October 2010, electronically available, Geneva: ITU, 2011).
Const.	Universal Postal Union, Constitution.
Conv.	Convention, *or* Universal Postal Union, Convention.
CS	International Telecommunication Union, Constitution. Immediate reference is to CS articles. Additional numbers in brackets refer to the now customary paragraph numbering.
CTS	C. Parry, ed. *The Consolidated Treaty Series* (Dobbs Ferry, NY: Oceana).
CV	International Telecommunication Union, Convention. Immediate reference is to CV articles. Additional numbers in brackets refer to the now customary paragraph numbering.
Decl.	Declarations and Reservations.

DR	Detailed Regulations of the Universal Postal Union.
ELC	UPU Executive and Liaison Committee, 1947-2004 (now the Council on Administration: CA).
GR	ITU General Rules of Conferences, Assemblies and Meetings of the Union, available in *Collection of the basic texts of the International Telecommunication Union adopted by the Plenipotentiary Conference*, 3d Ed. 2007 (Geneva: ITU, 2007) (new ed. pending to take account of the Final Acts of the Guadalajara Plenipotentiary Conference held in October 2010). *or*
GR	UPU General Regulations of the Universal Postal Union.
Hague Recueil	Hague Academy of International Law, Recueil des Cours, cited by vol. no, and year/vol.
Hudson	M.O. Hudson, *International Legislation*, 9 vols. (Washington DC: Carnegie Endowment for International Peace, 1931-1950).
IB	UPU, International Bureau, 1874-present.
ICJ	International Court of Justice, Reports, 1946-present.
ILM	*International Legal Materials*, American Society of International Law, 1961-present.
ITR	International Telecommunication Regulations, cited by Article and para number.
ITU	International Telecommunication Union: http://www.itu.int.
ITU-D	ITU Development Sector.
ITU-R	ITU Radiocommunication Sector.
ITU-T	ITU Standardisation Sector.
Leive	D. M. Leive, *International Telecommunications and International Law: The Regulation of the Radio Spectrum* (Leiden: Sijthoff; Dobbs Ferry, NY: Oceana, 1970).
Lyall	F. Lyall, *Law and Space Telecommunications* (Aldershot UK: Dartmouth; Brookfield VT: Gower, 1989).
Lyall/Larsen	F. Lyall and P.B. Larsen, *Space Law: A Treatise* (Farnham, UK and Burlington, VT: Ashgate Publishing, 2009).
Malloy	W.M. Malloy, *Treaties, Conventions, International Acts, Protocols, and Agreements between the United States of America and Other Powers*, 4 vols (Washington DC: US GPO, 1910-1938).
MIFR	ITU Master International Frequency Register, maintained by ITU-R.
PCIJ	Permanent Court of International Justice, 1922-1946.
POC	UPU Postal Operations Council, 1994-present.
PP	ITU Plenipotentiary Conference.
RA	ITU Radiocommunication Assembly.
RAG	ITU Radiocommunication Advisory Group (in ITU-R).
RC	UPU Parcel Post Regulations (cited Art. RC xx).
Reg.	Regulation.

Resn.	Declarations and Reservations.
RIAA	Reports of International Arbitral Awards, UN: Geneva, 1949-present.
RL	UPU Letter Post Regulations (cited Art. RL xx).
RR	Radio Regulations (Geneva: ITU). RR are normally cited numerically without inclusion of 'Art.'
RRB	ITU Radio Regulations Board, 1996-present.
RRC	ITU Regional Radio Conference.
Rules	Rules of Procedure of indicated UPU bodies.
TDAG	ITU Telecommunication Development Advisory Group (in ITU-D).
TDC	ITU Telecommunication Development Conference.
Tomlinson	J.D. Tomlinson, *The International Control of Telecommunications* (Thesis 41, 1938, University of Geneva; Rep. New York: Kraus Reprint, 1972).
TSAG	ITU Telecommunication Standardisation Advisory Group (in ITU-T).
UPU	Universal Postal Union: http://www.upu.int.
WRC	ITU World Radiocommunication Conference.
WTDC	ITU World Telecommunication Development Conference.
WTPF	ITU World Telecommunication Policy Forum.
WTSA	ITU World Telecommunication Standardisation Assembly.
YBILC	Yearbook of the International Law Commission

Chapter 1
Introduction: A General Survey

Communications have undergone massive change in the last two hundred years. Old roads were improved and new road systems built. The railway came on the scene. Shipping was transformed as engines replaced sails. Aviation was developed. These all facilitated the carriage of mail. Inventors produced the telegraph, and the railway helped the laying of electrical communications networks. Further experiment led to wireless communication. Computers and the Internet, using both cable and radio, have come on the scene. Technology has improved and the pace of innovation has increased. Of course it is arguable whether technical development and rapidity of communication has been an entirely good thing – that is material for a separate book.[1] But our modern communications infrastructures are there. The 'post' distributes physical objects – letters and parcels. All modes of electrical communications carry data, documents, photographs and movies, news and trivia. We have to learn to live with these facilities.[2] And, as we live with them, most either ignore, or are ignorant of, the substantial body of international law and less formal agreements that underlie modern international communications.

This book attempts a discussion of the two major international institutions through which international communications have been developed and are facilitated, the International Telecommunication Union (the ITU) and the Universal Postal Union (the UPU). With the arguable exception of the Rhine Commission,[3] traced from their respective roots these two are the oldest international institutions that still operate in our modern world. Their histories are complex and considerable.

1 The 'twenty-four hour news' environment may not be conducive to good decision-making by politicians, by businesses or by individuals. It fosters re-action rather than deliberation before action. The automatic instruction by computer programs without human intervention of the sale or purchase of stocks and shares depending on pre-identified market movements can cause major problems in the stock market, in international finance and in currency trading. High frequency trading (not to say churning) is a menace.

2 Cf. F. Cairncross, *The Death of Distance 2.0: How the Communications Revolution Will Change Our Lives* (London and New York: Texere, 2001).

3 The Central Commission for Navigation on the Rhine originates out of agreements at the Congress of Vienna in 1815 following the end of the Napoleonic Wars. In 1831 a formal Convention was agreed at Mainz, Germany, which was replaced in 1868. The new Convention signed at Mannheim contained provisions which are still in force. On the Rhine Commission, its current text Convention and Protocols see http://www.ccr-zkr.org. Technically the Rhine Commission antedates both the ITU and UPU as an extant international organisation. On the other hand its area of responsibility is significantly less than that of either of these bodies.

In general I therefore omit the internal or municipal arrangements through which individual states organise their communications.

How to organise the world is a matter of continuing debate.[4] But many may take issue with the preceding sentence. Its formulation implicitly suggests an overarching authority which will dictate on a global basis and reduce the separate and individual powers of the state – a view that is incompatible with the hallowed doctrine of state sovereignty.[5] The question may be better expressed as how the world should be organised, leaving the means obscure. The notion that 'sovereignty' might have to be infringed in order properly to 'organise' is thereby avoided.[6] Modern discussions have therefore chamfered the language of discourse preferring to discuss 'global governance'.[7] The fact to be faced is that there is now a considerable number of international organisations and associations through which are regulated (or, more congruent with reality, which regulate) international intercourse of many kinds and which, as a result, can affect matters traditionally the exclusive province of the 'sovereign right' of a state.[8]

Reliable communications are essential for the existence of modern civilised society. The internal functioning of individual states requires good communications.

---

4 I side-step the debate as to whether states obey law, or that international law is complied with only when national interests are served. Cf. M. McDougal, H.Lasswell and J. Miller, *The Interpretation of Agreements and World Public Order* (New Haven, Conn.: Yale UP, 1967); O. Schachter, 'Towards a Theory of International Obligation' (1968) 8 *Va. J. Int. L.* 300; T.M. Franck, 'The Power of Legitimacy and the Legitimacy of Power: International Law in an Age of Power Disequilibrium' (2006) 100 AJIL 88; M.J. Glennon, 'The New Interventionism: The Search for a Just International Law' (1999) 78 *For. Aff.*, 2, 2; G. Simpson, *Great Powers and Outlaw States: Unequal Sovereigns in the International Legal Order* (Cambridge: Cambridge UP, 2004).

5 The usual referent is the Convention on the Rights and Duties of States, Montevideo, 26 December 1933, (1936) 165 LNTS 19; 49 Stat. 3097; UST 881; (1934) 28 AJIL Supp. 75, Art. 1 of which states: 'States are juridically equal, enjoy the same rights, and have equal capacity in their exercise. The rights of each one do not depend upon the power which it possesses to assure its exercise, but upon the simple fact of its existence as a person under international law.'

6 At its most absolute the concept of 'sovereign' has some roots in theology. In UK history it was developed by A.V. Dicey, particularly in relation to the 'sovereignty of the (Westminster) Parliament': *Introduction to the study of the law of the Constitution* (London: Macmillan, 1885: 10th ed., 1962).

7 M.P. Karns, *International Organizations: the politics and processes of global governance* (Boulder, CO: Rienner, 2010); C. Joerges, I-J. Sand and G. Teubner (eds), *Transnational Governance and Constitutionalism* (Oxford: Hart, 2004); D. Sarooshi, *International Organizations and their Exercise of Sovereign Powers* (Oxford: OUP, 2005).

8 E. Stein, 'International Integration and Democracy: No Love at First Sight' (2001) 95 AJIL 489. G. Clarke and L.B. Sohn, *World Peace through World Law: Two Alternative Plans* (Cambridge Mass.: Harvard UP, 1958) was over-optimistic, though influential when I was a student. Cf. C. Tietje and A. Brouder, *Handbook of Transnational Economic Governance Regimes* (Leiden: Nijhoff, 2009).

Internationally, communications between the ruling authorities of sovereign states are important, but in many ways it is the communication between companies, financial institutions and other commercial entities, that mould our lives. These cannot conduct their business without internal messaging between branches and between the enterprise, its suppliers and its market. There is also a demand for personal communication between individuals, family and friends. Email and the holiday postcard, the telephone and birthday cards, the news media, journals and book publication, all need communication services. Trustworthy communication systems, whether international or domestic, make sense in modern societies, and many now consider access to such systems to be a human right that should be available to all.[9]

Under the traditional rules of 'state sovereignty' it is for each state to determine how communications are organised within its territory. In the past many states fused their postal and electrical communications services into a single agency, usually classified for historical reasons as a PTT (a Postal, Telegraph and Telephone agency or service), albeit that the term clearly antedates the prevalence of radio services. Some have therefore come to consider communications as a public service to be provided by the state. On the other hand there has been a recent significant ingress of private enterprise communications providers, a development often accompanied by other 'privatisation' of state services. Nonetheless, without exception all states impose a measure of control on their internal communications for reasons of military and state security. Some also do so (or wish so to do) in respect of the content of communications entering or leaving their territories.[10]

---

9 American Declaration of the Rights and Duties of Man, (1948, OAS Res. XXX) Art. X, http://www1.umn.edu/humanrts/oasinstr/zoas2dec.htm; Arts. 11 and 13 of the American Convention on Human Rights: Pact of San Jose, Costa Rica, 1978, 1144 UNTS 143; Universal Declaration of Human Rights (UNGA Res. 217 (III)), 8 December 1948, Arts. 12 and 19, http://www.un.org/Overviews/rights.html; European Convention on Human Rights, Rome, 1950, Arts. 8 and 10, http://www.hri.org/docs/ECHR50.html. Cf. provisions in the constitutions of many states. The ITU Constitution (Art. 33 (179)) speaks of Members recognising the right of the public to use the international telecommunication services. The UPU Conv. Art. 3.1 requires that all members 'shall ensure that all users/customers enjoy the right to a universal postal service involving the permanent provision of quality basic postal services at all points in their territory, at affordable prices'.

10 Cf. the 1970-80s UNESCO debates. Some states sought control over incoming and outgoing communications as necessary both in recognition of sovereignty and for the preservation of political, economic and cultural identity. A Commission, chaired by S. MacBride, called for a 'New International Communication Order' (a.k.a. the 'New Information Order' (NIO), the 'New World Information Order' (NWIO) or the 'New World Information and Communication Order' (NWICO)) in a 1980 report *Many Voices, One World: Towards a New, More Just, and More Efficient World Information and Communication Order*. The US in 1994 and the UK in 1995 withdrew from UNESCO over the questions of 'freedom of information' and the 'freedom of the press', respectively returning in 2005 and 1997. Cf. (1984) 23 ILM 220-30 and (1985) 24 ILM 489-9; 'United

So much for the organisation and control of communications within a state, entering it or emanating from it. However, although considerations as to content remain, for practical purposes international communications require a modification of the internal powers of states. For there to be international communications connections it is both sensible and desirable that systems and procedures are agreed between the states concerned and that they are complied with. Common usages and practices develop to cope with international traffic. Once that happens there is little point in the internal communication systems of a state differing unnecessarily from the relevant agreed international system. Effectively the internal variant would be redundant. The result is that internationally agreed arrangements are considerably determinant of national systems at least in their technical aspects.[11] Thus the ITU Radio Regulations determine within each state the signal characteristics of radio stations that are capable of interfering with the use of similar stations in a neighbouring state. More anciently, through the UPU an envelope is delivered in a state other than that of its origin because it bears an address front and middle, and at top right a 'frank', usually a 'stamp' affixed in its state of origin,[12] that has been cancelled at the time of its receipt into the postal

---

States' Return to UNESCO', Contemporary Practice of the United States (2003) 97 AJIL 977; M.J. Farley, 'Conflicts over Government Control of Information – the United States and UNESCO' (1985) 59 *Tul. L. Rev.* 1071; P.A. Hoffer, 'Upheaval in the United Nations System – United States' Withdrawal from UNESCO' (1986) 12 *Brook. J. Int. L.* 161; C.C. Joyner and S.A. Lawson, 'The United States and UNESCO: Rethinking the Decision to Withdraw' (1985-1986) 41 *Int. J.* 37; Lyall/Larsen 258-69.

The UNESCO Constitution of 1945: 4 UNTS 275; 1946 UKTS 50, Cmd. 6963; 61 Stat. 2495, TIAS 1580; 9 Hudson 786; 3 Bevans 1311; (1947) AJIL Supp. 1. Current text at http://unesdoc.unesco.org/images/0013/001337/1337e.pdf#page=7.

For cultural questions, cf. the UNESCO 'Convention for the Safeguarding of the Intangible Heritage' 2003: http://www.unesco.org/culture/ich/index.php?lg=en&pg=00022; E.K. Slattery, 'Preserving the United States' Intangible Cultural Heritage: An Evaluation of the 2003 UNESCO for the Safeguarding of the Intangible Cultural Heritage as a Means to Overcome the Problems posed by Intellectual Property Law' (2006) 16 *DePaul J. Art. & Int. L.* 201; M. Braun and L. Parker, 'Trade in Culture: Consumable Product or Cherished Articulation of a Nation's Soul' (1993) 22 *Denv. J. Int. L. & Pol.* 155; F. Francioni, 'Beyond State Sovereignty: The Protection of Cultural Heritage as a Shared Interest of Humanity' (2004) 25 *Mich. J. Int. L.* 1209.

11 For early and prescient articles see P.S. Reinsch, 1. 'International Unions and their Administration' (1907) 1 AJIL 579, and 2. 'International Administrative Law and National Sovereignty' (1909) 3 AJIL 1. Art. 24 of the UPU Constitution preserves the freedom of a state to make its own internal postal arrangements, but the result of Arts. 6 (37-8) and 48 (202-4) of the ITU CS is to allow such freedom only in relation to military services or radio services that are without international effect.

12 Depending on local rules a 'stamp' may be a separate specially designed indicator affixed by an adhesive, impressed on the relevant envelope or printed on to the material itself. In the US the signatures of designated persons, including members of Congress, the

system of the dispatching state both to signify that postal charges have been paid and to prevent its later re-use.

Curiously, the importance of the ITU and UPU now remains largely unacknowledged although without them (or something very like them) international communications would not exist. In general the two work well, and, working well, they are taken for granted.[13] As the following pages demonstrate they are, however, the outcome of much discussion, negotiation, compromise and occasional conflict. Both have had documentary histories of almost a century and a half.

* * *

The evolution of the ITU and UPU to their present state has been complex. During the process they have had to meet various challenges and solve numerous problems. Of these certain may be summarised.

Constitutional Revision

Any international organisation must remain efficient and relevant. This requires the occasional revision of the constitution. The evolution of the constitutions of the ITU and UPU illustrate an insightful recommendation of C.W. Jenks.[14] Surveying a vast number of institutions, in 1945 Jenks warned against inflexibility, undue flexibility, undue speed, or the overriding of a large and powerful minority in the modification of the constitutional instrument(s) of any international organisation.[15] The passage of time produces the need to modify, particularly when

---

President and former Presidents and their wives, are printed on envelopes and function as 'stamps' for postal purposes. See Chapter 8, 'Postage Stamps', *infra* p. 300.

13 To repeat a quotation from the Preface in case you have not read that part of this book: 'No-one notices something that works too well,' *per* Lu-Tze in T. Pratchett, *Thief of Time* (London: Doubleday, 2001) 115. Cf. F.H. Williamson, 'The International Postal Service and the Universal Postal Union' (1930) 9 *J. Royal Inst. Int. Aff.*, 68 at 68: 'The International Postal Service can claim to be one of the mainsprings of modern civilisation; but it works with such smoothness and on so extensive a scale that probably few of those who habitually use it have ever given a thought to the extremely complicated machinery and the comprehensive and detailed organisation which is necessary to ensure this desirable result. It is not unfair to say that the International Postal Service works in an obscurity which is the direct result of its efficiency.'

14 C.W. Jenks was important both as an international administrator in the International Labour Office (latterly as its Director-General), and as an influential writer on international law. See 'Clarence Wilfred Jenks', (1972-1973) 46 BYIL xi-xv by the Editors, H. Waldock and R.Y. Jennings, and 'Wilfred Jenks in the I.L.O.' at xvi-xxx by F. Morgenstern.

15 C.W. Jenks, 'Some Constitutional Problems of International Organizations' (1945) 22 BYIL 11 at 68: 'It would seem desirable to include in all future international constitutional instruments provisions laying down an appropriate procedure for their

an organisation deals with technical matters. What was sensible or desirable at one period of its existence may become outmoded, irrelevant or even deleterious. New developments have to be recognised and integrated into its working. In the Nineteenth century the normal method by which this was done was the holding of successive conferences, usually of plenipotentiaries, at which a new constitution was adopted. In the early ITU and UPU agreements this led to a problem. Each new Convention had to be ratified, but ratifications were not always speedily or timeously forthcoming. Different members might therefore be bound by different versions of the organisation's documents. The UPU showed one possible solution. In its second Convention, that of Paris, 1878,[16] Art. 23 1 provided: 'After the date on which the present Convention takes effect, all the stipulations of the treaties, conventions, arrangements, or other acts previously concluded between the various countries or administrations, in so far as those stipulations are not in accordance with the terms of the present convention, are abrogated, without prejudice to the rights reserved by Article 15 above'.[17] A similar provision appeared in successive UPU Conventions for nearly ninety years.[18] The current UPU Convention, that of 1964 as amended,[19] provides that whether a country does not ratify it or does not approve other UPU Acts, they remain valid for the other members (Art. 25 4). Otherwise the UPU Convention, General Regulations and other Agreements enter into force simultaneously, and from that date the corresponding Acts of the previous Congress are abrogated (Art. 31 2). In other words a UPU member

modification; such provisions should relax the requirements to be fulfilled for the coming into force of an amendment sufficiently to avoid the danger of undue rigidity; but while the amendment of an international organisation should not be impossibly difficult, it is equally undesirable that such a constitution should be subject to amendment by a snap vote, that an important amendment should come into force against the opposition of a large and powerful minority or that an international organisation should get into the habit of amending its constitution lightheartedly. These conflicting considerations must all be weighed in endeavouring to strike the balance between undue rigidity and excessive flexibility most appropriate to the requirements of the individual case.' Cf. E. Schwelb, 'The Amending Procedures of Constitutions of International Organisations' (1954) 31 BYIL 49; L.H. Phillips, 'Constitutional Revision in the Specialized Agencies' (1968) 62 AJIL 654; D.W. Bowett, *The Law of International Institutions*, 4th ed. (London: Stevens, 1982) and P. Sands, *Bowett's Law of International Institutions*, 6th ed. (London: Sweet and Maxwell, 2009).

16 Universal Postal Union, Paris, 1 June 1878, in force 1 April 1879; 152 CTS 235; 69 BFSP 210; 20 Stat. 734; 1 Bevans 51.

17 Article 15 preserved the right of members to make other treaties, including to establish more restricted Unions in order to improve postal relations usually in a region.

18 Cf. Art. 15 4 of the Universal Postal Union Convention: Paris, 5 July 1947; in force 1 July 1948; 62 Stat. 3157, TIAS 1850; 1949 UKTS 57, Cmd. 7794; 148 BFSP 521; 4 Bevans 482; 1948 25 BYIL 465, and Art. 23 3 of the Brussels Convention of 1952.

19 Universal Postal Union: Constitution and General Regulations, Vienna, 10 July 1964, 611 UNTS 7; 1966 UKTS 70, Cmnd. 3141; 16 UST 1291, TIAS 5881; 1964 UN Jur. YB 195.

can either ratify, or, at least technically, cease to be a member, its relationships with those members that ratify the new order having been cancelled as the old order has passed away.[20] In the case of the ITU the early agreements as to wire communications did not require such measures. The wire service connections either existed, or they did not. Residual arrangements could be tolerated. It was only with the Madrid Telecommunication Convention of 1932 that its Art. 1 1 specifically provided that the new ITU replaced the old Telegraph Union, and its Art. 8 that all the previous Telegraph and Radio Conventions and their Regulations were abrogated and replaced.[21] Similar provision was made by Art. 23 of the 1947 Atlantic City and later ITU Conventions. Now Art. 58 2 (239) of the ITU Constitution of Geneva, 1992, provides that the Nairobi Convention was abrogated and replaced as between the parties that had ratified the Geneva documents.[22] The sanction for non-ratification is that by CS Art. 52 2.2 (210) a party loses its right to vote if it has not ratified the relevant documents within two years of their coming into force. However, the possibility of different members being bound by different versions of basic documents remains.

So says a strict interpretation of the texts. However, in any event as a matter of practice the ITU applies new provisions once they are in force, whether or not a particular state has ratified them. The UPU does similarly. In short, the complexity of the international communications networks for postal and electrical communications requires there to be uniformity so far as possible in such matters, and in practice that uniformity is applied irrespective of the technicalities of 'hard law'. However, the slowness or failure of states to ratify is disappointing. Both institutions are considering moves towards a more stable constitution where the need for regular ratification is diminished.

Constitution, Convention and Regulations

In 1857 the Austro-German Telegraph Union (a major forerunner/antecedent of the ITU) pioneered the division of its constituent documents into a basic agreement and supplementary documents ('Regulations', 'Instructions' and the like) which, while of the same legal status as the 'basic law' documents, were likely to be regularly

20 See C.W. Jenks, 'The Conflict of Law-Making Treaties' (1953) 30 BYIL 401 at 418; E. Schwelb, 'The Amending Procedure of Constitutions of International Organisations' (1954) 31 BYIL 49 at 51.

21 Telecommunication Convention, Madrid, 9 December 1932; 151 LNTS 4; 49 Stat. 2393, TS 867; 6 Hudson 109; 3 Bevans 65. Since formally speaking there never was a Radio Union, its informal existence did not have to be mentioned, the abrogation of the Radio Convention and Regulations sufficing.

22 Constitution and Convention of the International Telecommunication Union: Final Acts of the Additional Plenipotentiary Conference, Geneva, 22 December 1992 (Geneva: ITU, 1993), 1825 UNTS 1; 1996 UKTS 24, Cm. 3145; US Tr. Doc. 104-35.

altered to cope with new problems and situations. This device is now found in both the ITU and the UPU. The model has been adopted in other international agreements that deal with technicalities additional to their general obligations and structural provisions.[23] The division between constitutional and regulatory instruments can to an extent avoid the ratification problem outlined above.

Experts

Experts are needed both for the negotiation of agreements that regulate technical matters, and for the operation of those agreements in practice. We deal with these in that order.

A potential problem in the creation of international law by treaty is the competence of those who negotiate. While one aspect of 'competence' is negotiating skill, another is the extent to which a negotiator understands the nature of the subject that the negotiations are about. Diplomats, who are the officers through which a state normally negotiates, may not possess that competence when technical or practical matters are under consideration. In such a case it is therefore to be hoped either that diplomats comprehend the degree of their ignorance and seek advice or, perhaps better, that the state entrusts the negotiation to knowledgeable non-diplomats – in short to experts.

A feature of both the ITU and UPU is the role that experts play. 'Experts' were not unknown in the negotiation of early postal agreements when agreement between Post Offices depended on a thorough knowledge of the problems and the practicalities of the physicalities. Sometimes the expert was part of the diplomatic representation and sometimes merely an adviser. Nowadays in both Unions it is the experts, suitably authorised by their home states but without formal diplomatic status, who effectively hammer out the practical arrangements concerned. It must be acknowledged that when the practice began in the nascent ITU and UPU the presence of experts in international delegations was not novel. International conferences were considering and making recommendations on a variety of matters of common concern to states.[24] However, until the 1860s such conferences did not

23 Thus both the 1919 Paris Convention for the Regulation of Aerial Navigation, 1919, 11 LNTS 173; 1922 UKTS 2, Cmd. 1609; 1 Hudson 359; 13 Martens (3d) 61; (1923) 17 AJIL Supp. 195, and the Chicago Convention on Civil Aviation, 1944, 15 UNTS 295; 61 Stat. 1180, TIAS 1591; (1953) UKTS 8, Cmd. 8742; 9 Hudson 168; 3 Bevans 944; (1945) 39 AJIL Supp. 111, adopted the 'basic convention plus rules' model.

24 A physician and a diplomat from each state were the delegates to the International Sanitary Conference of 1851-2, and each voted separately: Charnovitz, *infra,* n. 31, at 198. The result was the International Sanitary Convention between France, Portugal, Sardinia and Turkey on 3 February 1852, 107 CTS 345. On the growth of international Unions created to deal with matters of common interest see A.S. Hershey, 'History of International Law since the Peace of Westphalia' (1912) 6 AJIL 30 at 53-5.

usually result in a treaty. Their function was the exploration of a particular problem not the adoption of rules for its solution. Law-making thereanent was a separate diplomatic function. In the 1860s the creation of international organisations to cope with international communications merged the functions of discussion and law-making.

How to marry the input of technical experts and the diplomatic duty to preserve the interests and rights of the national home state can be difficult. Sometimes professional diplomats do a better job than politicians. Sometimes experts do a better job than professional diplomats. What might make the best technical sense to experts might involve a state in concessions which for a variety of reasons it is unwilling to make. Balance between the technical ideal and practical politics can usually be achieved only in a delegation of mixed competences. That said, the presence of experts within a delegation recognises that in the regulation of technical matters those who understand the technology should play a major (though not necessarily an overriding) role. The 1862 suggestion by Montgomery Blair, then US Postmaster General, that an international conference be called to discuss international postal problems included the point that since the matter was one of technicalities the usual form of diplomatic conference should not be used. 'The practical knowledge of details necessary and the special character of the interests involved indicate the propriety of a conference between postal representatives to arrange the propositions of improvement, rather than to submit them to the usual dilatory course of diplomacy ...'[25] That suggestion was followed in the resultant conference of 1862, and postal personnel formed many of the delegations at the eventual 1874 congress which set up the UPU.[26] However, this was not new. As will be seen in the initial pages of Chapter 7, many bilateral postal agreements were in reality agreements between post office officials.

Negotiation of the 'original' telecommunication arrangements also used experts. Before the general ITU was formed the deliberations that led to both the Eastern and Western Telegraph Unions were largely conducted by persons who were in fact officials of the relevant telegraph agencies. This carried over to the general institution.[27] The 1865 International Telegraph Conference was convened in Paris in order to establish an institution that would bring together the major telegraph networks of Europe. Formally speaking the conference negotiations were conducted by the Paris-based diplomatic agents of the twenty states that were represented.[28] Each agent was, however, accompanied by one or more experts in telegraphy and in the operation and regulation of the existing telegraph networks.

25 Codding III, 20-1; J.F. Sly, 'The Genesis of the Universal Postal Union: A Study in the Beginnings of International Organization' (1926-7) No. 233, 11 *Int. Conc.* 391 at 397; M.A.K. Menon, 'Universal Postal Union' (1964-5) No. 552, 35 *Int. Conc.* 1 at 1.

26 See Chapter 7, following n. 63 and after n. 73.

27 See Chapter 2.

28 International Telegraph Convention, Paris, 17 May 1865, 130 CTS 198; 56 BFSP 295. Present were representatives of Austria, Baden, Bavaria, Belgium, Denmark, France,

These were included in the delegations to ensure that the outcome of the conference was practicable and technically acceptable. The experts advised on many technical elements of the Convention itself and themselves drafted and agreed the Service Regulations that 'complete' the 'dispositions' made by the Convention – the bits that actually made the new system work.[29]

The presence of 'experts' with or without formal powers of negotiating makes sense when what is involved is a matter of administration, of establishing a structure and/or procedures for the regulation of a technical matter. But that can go beyond 'officials'. In the telecommunication sphere manufacturers and operators were also obvious sources of informed opinion that could usefully contribute to international discussion of common problems and to formal decision making thereanent. It is therefore interesting that, after a degree of internal debate, not to say dissension, private companies were invited to take part in the discussions of the telegraph conference held in Rome from December 1871 to January 1872. In short, within six years of the creation of the International Telegraph Union the range of participants in its discussions was extended beyond 'official' representatives of its state members, through experts nominated by the states, and on to include affected private enterprise operators and the manufacturers of the equipment used in providing the service.[30] This has continued. Nowadays the category 'Associate Member' is a major component of the ITU Study and Working Groups which draft much of the detailed regulation and recommendations on which modern telecommunications depend.

The developing involvement of experts in international administration (not only in post and telecommunications) was, therefore, important of itself. It was important also in that it provided a model or excuse for giving informal groups access to formal international debate and decision. The Nineteenth century saw the emergence of a number of what we now call 'non-governmental organisations' (NGOs). These associations of persons of like mind sought and seek to influence governmental action or decision on particular matters. The precedent of the involvement of technical experts as part of formal negotiations in communications was to facilitate the interaction between governments, international organisations and NGOs when those beasts became more prevalent.[31]

The other area where experts are required is in the operation of the agreements that regulate technical matters. Most obviously in the ITU many important positions are held by persons having technical qualifications. The members of the former International Frequency Registration Board (IFRB) were to be technically

Greece, Hamburg, Hanover, Italy, The Netherlands, Portugal, Prussia, Russia, Saxony, Spain, Sweden-Norway, Switzerland, Turkey and Württemberg.

29 Reinsch 1, *supra*, n. 11, at 583.

30 Codding I, 25-6; D.P. Myers, 'Representation in Public International Bodies' (1914) 8 AJIL 81 at 102.

31 S. Charnovitz, 'Two Centuries of Participation: NGOs and International Governance' (1997) 18 *Mich. J. Int. L.* 183.

qualified: their successors in the Radio Regulations Board are required to be 'thoroughly qualified in the field of radiocommunications' and possess 'practical experience in the assignment and utilisation of frequencies'.[32] In the UPU it is required that the representatives of the elected members of the Council of Administration 'shall be competent in postal matters'.[33]

An International Bureau

Concomitant with the reliance on experts rather than on diplomats for the technical elements of specialised international agreements is the necessity of providing a trusted central source for the collection and distribution of relevant and reliable information. It can also be used to conduct studies. In the case of the telegraph such an organ was considered at the first general international telegraph conference in 1865 and constituted by Art. 61 of the Vienna Convention of 1868 as the 'International Bureau of Telegraphic Administrations' (the 'Bureau Internationale des Administrations Télégraphiques').[34] Theoretically peripatetic, the International Bureau was established in Geneva, Switzerland, where its successor remains. Its functions included helping to organise conferences, the execution and application of the Convention and collecting data, statistics and information as to tariffs and practices, disseminating them as necessary. This latter function included publishing a regular journal (in French) on telecommunications. The International Bureau was also to conduct such special studies as the regular telegraph conferences might direct. It did its job so well that, when radio came on the scene, states were content that the Bureau of the Telegraph Union should act in radio matters as well. Similarly, when the UPU was instituted in 1874 the need for a central office to collect, coordinate and disseminate was recognised as necessary. These bodies therefore provided models for the bureaux and secretariats of later international organisations.

Finance

The financing of every international organisation has proved a bone of contention over the years. Now most of the UN family of agencies draw their funding from their state members, each 'fee' being set with regard to Gross National Product.

---

32 ITU Constitution, Art. 14.1 (93). See Chapter 5, 'Radio Regulations Board'.

33 UPU GR, Art. 102.4 and CA Rules of Procedure, Art. 2.2. Representative of members elected to the Postal Operations Council are to 'have responsibilities for delivering [postal] services' (GR Art. 204.3; POC Rules of Proc. Art. 2.2).

34 International Telegraph Convention, Vienna, 21 July 1868, 136 CTS 122 and 292: 59 BFSP 322; 10 De Clercq 121.

Both the ITU and UPU were, however, in existence long before the UN system came into being, and, indeed, before the League of Nations.

A standing international body such as an International Bureau has to be paid for. Both the Telegraph Union and the UPU adopted early a solution for their requirements, albeit not one which has found favour in the constitutions of later international organisations. Both organisations capped the budget for the central office, a feature which others have copied. However, for ingathering the needed funding both adopted a system which only they now use. Both operate a system of 'contributory units', each member being able (within limits) to select its category or class of contribution. ITU and UPU members therefore choose their level of contribution to central funds through voluntarily taking up a particular unit of contribution. This has advantages. It reflects the interest of the contributing state in the organisation. No contributor could (should?) feel that its contribution dwarfs the benefit it gains from membership of the organisation. The withdrawal of the contribution of any particular member, or even of a number, is not such as will cripple the organisation. However, as noted, the rest of the UN family of specialised agencies has elected to set membership fees by Gross National Product, on the argument that international organisations should be financed by objective reference to the financial means of a member. Although all modern international organisations operate a cap for the higher 'payers', support for the poorer members of the international community is accepted by most as a significant motivating justification for contribution by GNP. Both the ITU and UPU have other routes to that end.

However, whether voting weight should reflect financial contribution, at least to some extent, in technical organisations such as the two Unions is an argument to which we will return. It certainly has traction in relation to the ITU.

Decision-Making: Voting

Equality between states in voting in an international organisation is now the norm. It stems from the basic assumption that all states have full international personality and therefore an equal voice in international decisions.[35] However, although that is the current general position it was not always thus. The histories of the 'International Radio Union' and the UPU contain a number of occasions when the voting 'weight' of a participant became a matter of debate, not to say dispute. In general these debates related to the 'weight' formally or impliedly to be exercised through the designation of separate elements of an empire.[36] Both the

35 For this it is usual to cite the Convention on the Rights and Duties of States, Montevideo, 1933, *supra*, n. 5.

36 This was the era of the British, French, Belgian, Dutch and German Empires, although, particularly in the case of the UK (notably with regard to Australia, Canada and New Zealand), major elements of the Empires were beginning to ask for special recognition

ITU and UPU have now avoided such questions, their members each having one vote. However, as indicated at the end of the previous section, whether this should remain the case is a matter to which we will return.

* * *

Although both are concerned with the working of international communications the UPU and ITU do different jobs. The UPU is concerned with the quality of an international service. Much of the ITU deals with the quality of international facilities. These qualities are correlative, but by no means identical.

The UPU deals with international services that require the physical transportation and delivery of letters, packets and packages. It is the major international institution that underpins and facilitates that ancient form of international communication. It organises the cooperation which undergirds these services. Through it postal rates are set, and members compensated for carrying mail in transit through their territories, and for delivering mail that has been paid for in a foreign land. Historically speaking, of course, postal arrangements and services are old – ancient indeed. Letters have been carried for millennia, and bilateral arrangements go a long way back.[37] Curiously, however, as a formal general international organisation it post-dates that of electrical telecommunications. Although it has strayed into the realm of electronics,[38] the UPU remains separate and distinct from the ITU and there is no reason why the two should not remain independent of each other.

The ITU deals with electrical communications, whether by wire or by radio, and, curiously to the modern mind, with optical communication systems. First formally defined for international purposes in 1932, 'telecommunication' is: 'Any telegraph or telephone communication of signs, signals, writings, images, and sounds of any nature, by wire, radio, or other systems or processes of electric or visual [semaphore] signalling.'[39] The ITU remit is the international regulation of the use of technology to transmit data by electro-magnetic means whether by wire (telephone and telegraphy) or wirelessly (radio). Unlike all other international

of their separate interests. See Myers, *supra*, n. 30, and materials there cited (Myers discusses the radio conference experience of this problem, and the UPU, at 103-104); R. Lansing, 'Notes on Sovereignty in a State' (1906) 1 AJIL 105-28 and 297-320; Reinsch, 1 and 2, *supra*, n. 11. Cf. W.J. Aceves, 'Critical Jurisprudence and International Legal Scholarship: A Study on Equitable Distribution' (2001) 39 *Col. J. Transnat. L.* 299-394.

37 Cf. the many bilateral postal agreements in the Consolidated Treaty Series. See Volume 2 of the Index-Guide to the Consolidated Treaty Series.

38 In addition to its 'normal' activities the UPU also facilitates the transfer of monies through its arrangements. This facility is provided in part by telecommunications. Some tracking of postal items is carried out by Internet connections.

39 Annex: Definition of Terms Used in the International Telecommunication Convention, Telecommunication Convention, Madrid, 9 December 1932; 151 LNTS 4; 49 Stat. 2391, TS 867; 6 Hudson 109 at 132; 3 Bevans 65 at 82. Radio communication is defined as '[A]ny telecommunication by means of Hertzian waves'.

organisations, the ITU has one major advantage compelling its members to negotiate, to compromise interests and to reach mutual agreement. The UPU operates as a matter of convenience. The ITU operates as a necessary organisation since behind it stands the Law (or Laws?) of Physics. Physics cannot be avoided, altered or repealed by international agreement even were that agreement to be forged by the most high and significant plenipotentiaries. As the rumoured attempts legislatively to alter the value of 'Pi' have shown, Physics can not be varied, amended or altered by human law.[40] Accordingly, variant state interests have to be compromised internationally to ensure that international electrical communications systems do not impede or render impossible the transmission of the messages they are intended to convey.

Both organisations intrigue. To summarise: their financial arrangements remain distinctive, the normal UN system not having been adopted despite pressure. Both early devised methods of work and divisions of responsibilities that remain identifiable though transmuted over time. Both have systems under which proposals for the work of regular conferences are circulated to all parties in advance, and on occasion measures can be agreed informally and adopted without the need for major debate. Both early grappled with the problem of balancing the standard doctrine of 'one state, one vote' with the need somehow to reflect the widely divergent responsibilities and importance of each state. In the later Nineteenth century some states were sovereign over or otherwise in charge of the international affairs of vast areas of the globe while others were tiny in territorial terms as well as in financial clout. Again the Unions recognised that private entities and even individuals might through their technical expertise and understanding be best able to develop suitable rules, practices, regulations and in addition what we now call 'soft law' that would facilitate the equitable availability and operation of the new media.[41]

---

40 'Pi' is the mathematical constant that represents the relationship between the circumference of a circle and its diameter, or the ratio of its area to the square of its radius as determined in Euclidean space. It is a non-repeating irrational number that starts 3.1415926535... . Scuttlebutt indicates a variety of attempts legislatively to tidy up the value of 'pi', including by Kansas, Oklahoma and Tennessee in the US. Scuttlebutt is, however, as often, erroneous. The sole attempt at actual legislation appears to be Bill No. 246 introduced by one Dr Record to the Indiana (US) legislature in 1897 at the request of his friend Dr Edwin Goodwin. The Bill did not proceed. See Ars Hermeneutica: Scienticity: http://scienticity.net/wiki/Legislating_the_Value_of_Pi. See also http://tafkac.org/legal/indiana_pi_bill.html, and 'Cecil's Storehouse of Human Knowledge' at http://www.straightdope.com/columns/read/805/did-a-state-legislature-once-pass-a-law-saying-pi-equals-3.

41 On 'Soft Law' cf. O. Schachter, 'The Twilight Existence of Nonbinding International Agreements' (1977) 71 AJIL 296-304; M. Ferrazzani, 'Soft Law in Space Activities', in G. Lafferanderie, ed., *Outlook on Space Law over the Next Thirty Years* (The Hague: Kluwer, 1997) 429-447; G. Danilenko, *Lawmaking in the International Community* (Dordrecht: Martinus Nijhoff, 1993) 203-10: A. Boyle and C. Chinkin,

International law governs relations between states. Technically speaking its content is determined by states either through the development and subsequent compliance with customary international law,[42] or through formal agreement expressed in treaty form. The latter is suitable for the regulation of practicalities in a way that custom is not. The matériel with which the ITU and UPU deal is severely practical, and they were amongst the first to seek to cope with it. They were therefore early considered as affording examples of features that might have a place in the structures of the future governance of the world.[43] Indeed, to a degree this came to pass. They grappled with practical and technical questions, inventing procedures and coping with practicalities with results that do not always comply with hard-line theories of international law.[44] They were innovators. Now, various of their features have reappeared in the various agencies that now comprise the UN family.[45] Finally, although the Reservations and Declarations made to various sets of Final Acts in both Unions contain clear political statements (for example as to territorial claims, objection on occasion to the very existence of others, and rejecting the possible financial and other consequences of a failure by others to play their part), both Unions work. Compromise and mutual accommodation produces workable arrangements from which we all benefit. That can be learned from.

The Making of International Law (Oxford: Oxford UP, 2007) 'Soft Law' 211-29; C. Chinkin, 'The Challenge of Soft Law: Development and Change in International Law' (1989) 8 ICLQ 850; Lyall/Larsen, 50-2.

42 Customary international law is formed by state practice entered into or complied with in the belief that the practice is required as a matter of law, not by simple convenience or mutual comity. See any standard international law text-book.

43 S.E. Baldwin, 'The International Congresses and Conferences of the Last Century as Forces Working Toward the Solidarity of the World' (1907) 1 AJIL 565, with 'Appendix' listing such congresses but 'excluding those mainly concerned with the results of a particular war' at 898; Reinsch 1 and 2 *supra*, n. 11; H. La Fontaine, 'The Existing Elements of a Constitution of the United States of the World' (1907-1911) 1 *Int. Conc.* 3 (Doc. No. 47); H.S. Amos, 'History of International Law since the Peace of Westphalia' (1912) 6 AJIL 30; M.O. Hudson, 'Aviation and International Law' (1930) 24 AJIL 228 and (1930) *Air L.R.* 183; F.C. De Wolf, 'Telecommunications in the New World' (1945) 55 *Yale L.J.* 1281; cf. P.E. Corbett, 'What is the League of Nations?' (1924) 5 BYIL 119 at 147 suggesting that the more limited remit given to the problem-specific Unions (e.g. the International Telegraph Union) is qualitatively different from that of the League of Nations. For later cf. 'Documents on the Development and Codification of International Law' (1947) 41 AJIL Supp. 29 (particularly Part I), comprising UN Memoranda in the series A/AC.10.

44 Cf. B. Akzin, 'Membership in the Universal Postal Union' (1933) 27 AJIL 649.

45 See O. Schachter and C.G. Joyner (eds), *United Nations Legal Order*, 2 vols. (Am. Soc. Int. Law/ Grotius Publications, Cambridge UP., 1995).

Chapter 2
The International Telegraph Union

The strict etymology of 'tele-graph' indicates it is writing at a distance: 'tele' = distance; 'graph' = writing.

The simple explanation of the electric telegraph is that an electric current passing down a wire can be coded and used to pass a message from one end of the wire to the other. The technology progressed from the simple interruption of a current, or its sporadic emission, to its modulation.

Many advantages of the telegraph were identified. On the railway the telegraph allowed information as to the departure and arrival of trains to be sent along the network.[1] A corollary was that rail track routes provided corridors down which telegraph cables could be laid without the need to negotiate a succession of way-leaves. Both sides benefitted. Then, because the telegraph was required to pass only relatively brief messages for the running of the railway, there was spare messaging capacity. Businessmen therefore sought to use telegraphs to pass commercial and other data. A further, less stated but obvious, factor was governmental interest in the use of swift, accurate communications. For economic and security reasons governments always want to know what is going on. The military also has a particular interest in security and accurate information. Telegraphy – a swift and secure messaging system – was a welcome development for both business and the state.[2]

The first telegraph apparatuses were idiosyncratic, employing different electrical frequencies and signal strengths as well as using divergent operational

---

1 A by-product of the development of rail networks was that the larger states, or large areas within states, adopted a common standard time. Before the railway, cities and towns ran on time based on the zenith of the sun with the bells of local clocks on church steeples indicating the hours and sometimes the quarters. National uniformity was required to allow timetabling so that when a train left, say, London, it would arrive at a known hour at, say, Birmingham. The telegraph also made it possible down-line to know when it passed points en route. The clock at Bristol Temple Meads station still shows both Bristol and London time.

2 A criminal case in 1845 brought the advantages of the telegraph to public attention in the UK. John Tawell was convicted and hanged for murder, having been arrested on his arrival by train in London. He had been seen leaving a house in Slough where a murdered woman had soon after been found. A message was sent to Paddington Station by the local police at Slough who had been told Tawell had boarded a slow train to London. Tawell was identified on his arrival through his wearing a long 'Quaker-style' coat. See 'John Tawell: The Man Hanged by the Electric Telegraph': http://www.cntr.salford.ac.uk/comms/johntawell.php, and the Wikipedia entry for 'John Tawell'.

protocols.[3] Cable diameters might vary, affecting the efficiency of the system. Interconnection was therefore not readily available and for many years long-distance messages had to be manually transcribed at state borders and then keyed in to the next cable in a sequence. Progress towards standardisation came first from the German principalities.[4] Most German states were small and it was sensible for neighbours to work to a common system rather than to confine their telegraph each to their own individual territory.

The Eastern (Austro-Prussian) Telegraph Union

The first truly international accord between major states came on 3 October 1849 when Austria and Prussia agreed to establish a telegraph link between Vienna and Berlin along the railway route between the two capitals, although the two telegraph systems were not physically connected.[5] As Codding narrates its provisions, the common junction point between the systems of the two states was at Öderburg in Austria. Priority was to be given in order, first to government messages, second to messages anent the functioning of the railway, and then to public correspondence. On 'even' days messages from Austria were given priority down the line, with Prussian messages having priority on 'odd' days. Senders paid a charge which was the cumulation of the rates for the distance their message travelled in the two states.[6] Similar agreements soon followed, between Prussia and Saxony on 17 October 1849 and between Austria and Bavaria on 21 January 1850. It therefore made sense that on 25 July 1850 the four states, already bilaterally linked, signed a Convention at Dresden creating an Austro-German Telegraph Union.[7] The Dresden Convention provided for tariff zones and for the cost of international transmissions to be based on distance. The contracting states agreed to introduce uniform national legislation as to the operation of telegraph services and undertook to meet regularly to deal with matters of common concern. These

3 See *infra* as to the adoption of the Morse system (n. 39) and the Hughes system (n. 48). See also Appendix I.

4 Modern Germany did not exist as a state until after the Franco-Prussian War of 1871 when Wilhelm I of Prussia was proclaimed as the Emperor of the German Empire at Versailles following the defeat of France. From the collapse of the Holy Roman Empire (which was never a unified state) in 1806 under the assaults of France (Napoleon), 'Germany' had consisted of many differently sized principalities. Among them Prussia had become increasingly prominent, particularly under the stewardship of Graf von Bismarck (1815-1898).

5 Telegraph Convention between Austria and Prussia, Berlin, 3 October 1849, 103 CTS 291; (1843-52) 14 Martens 591.

6 Codding I, 13.

7 Treaty on the Establishment of the German Telegraph Union [Austria, Bavaria, Prussia and Saxony], Dresden, 25 July 1850, 104 CTS 165.

conferences were held in Vienna in 1851,[8] Berlin in 1853,[9] and Munich in 1855.[10] Of these the Vienna meeting was of particular significance because it called for the physical connection of the cables of the networks involved. This meant that the former practice of transcribing a message at the end of the national system and re-keying it into the system and coding of the next state would be unnecessary.[11] However, it also meant that the new cabling connections had to have their technical characteristics and coding agreed before construction, let alone before operation. The arrangements for payment were also reconsidered, tariffs being set for zones, payment being made on the basis of a straight-line computation of the distance between zones. Payment for international traffic was set aside as 'common revenue' and was annually divided among the parties proportionate to the actual mileage (kilometridge(?)) of the telegraph lines within each state.

By 1857 the provisions governing the Austro-German Telegraph Union were therefore contained inconveniently in four separate documents, the agreements of Dresden (1850), Vienna (1851), Berlin (1853) and Munich (1855). Accordingly at Stuttgart in November 1857 new arrangements were adopted to replace these four.[12] At this point in history, what has become a major feature of international telecommunications agreements appeared. Matters considered unlikely to be modified were put in the Convention, and two additional separate documents were adopted to contain other more mutable provisions. 'Regulations' dealt with a variety of matters including the relationship between the Union and the general public, while 'Service Instructions' contained technical prescriptions for the actual telegraph systems that were subject to the agreements of the Union and its operation. In effect, of course, the 'Service Instructions' governed the entire national systems as well, since it made no sense to have one set of 'instructions' for internal and another for international services.

8 First Supplementary Convention of the Austro-German Telegraph Union [Austria, Bavaria, Prussia Saxony and Württemberg] Vienna, 14 October, 1851, 106 CTS 371.

9 Telegraph Convention between Sardinia and Austria (in the name of the Austro-German Telegraph Union), 28 September 1853, 111 CTS 125 and 148. The convention was replaced by the Telegraph Convention between the same parties, 3 October, 1856, 115 CTS 478. (At the time the Kingdom of Sardinia ruled much of north Italy. See *infra*, n. 16.)

10 Codding I, 14, notes that over this period Württemberg (1851), Hanover (1852), The Netherlands (1853), Baden and Mecklenburg-Schwerin (both 1854) adhered to the Dresden Convention.

11 On occasion a transcribed message had to be physically carried some distance to the proximate message station of the next system on which it was to pass. In other instances it was re-keyed within the same building.

12 Revised Convention of the Austro-German Telegraph Union, Stuttgart, 3 October 1857, 118 CTS 5.

The Western Telegraph Union

The German sphere was not the only area taking steps towards wider cooperation.[13] In the west France led, entering into bilateral agreements with Belgium in 1851,[14] Switzerland in 1852,[15] Sardinia in 1853[16] and Spain in 1854.[17] Mimicking the Austro-German developments of 1850, these five came together in Paris in 1855 to form a West European Telegraph Union.[18] That Union was agreed to exist for four years in the first instance, but was to carry on by tacit relocation thereafter.[19] In many ways the Paris agreement drew on the provisions of the 1850 Dresden Convention, including the concept of tariff zones and of rates dependent on distance from zone to zone. However, as Codding notes, the 'west' rates were considerably lower than those exigible within the eastern Telegraph Union. The languages acceptable for use on the inter-related western systems were specified as French, German, Italian and Spanish with, in addition, English, although the UK was not a member of the western Union.[20] In 1856 The Netherlands and Portugal adhered to the West European Telegraph Union, and their languages were added to the authorised list in a revision of the 1855 Paris Convention at Berne in 1858.[21] Also in 1858 two other groups agreed to be bound by the rules of the western Union. These were 'Les Iles de la Méditerranée' and 'Les Iles Britanniques'.[22] In 1860 the Vatican and the Kingdom of the Two Sicilies adhered to the Berne version of the Western European

13 Codding I, 16.

14 Provisional Telegraph Convention [France-Belgium] 105 CTS 365.

15 Telegraph Convention [France-Switzerland] 23 December, 1852, 109 CTS 195.

16 Telegraph Convention [France-Sardinia] 18 March, 1853, 109 CTS 483. Sardinia was a separate kingdom until the 'Unification of Italy', a process which basically ran from the Congress of Vienna in 1815 until 1871. The Kingdom of Sardinia had a turbulent history, *inter alia* being part of the Piedmont monarchy based in Turin. When it became part of the Kingdom of Italy in 1861 it was conjoined with Parma, Tuscany, Modena and the Romagna, Sardinia/Piedmont being in fact the foundational element of the new Kingdom of Italy and its King becoming the monarch of the new state.

17 Telegraph Convention [France-Spain] 24 November 1854, 112 CTS 281.

18 Telegraph Convention [France, Belgium, Sardinia, Spain, Two Sicilies], 29 December 1855, Paris, 1855, 114 CTS 139.

19 'Tacit relocation' is a term of Scots law, meaning that an arrangement may continue without formal agreement thereto by the unexpressed but mutual consent of its parties. Further conferences were held in Turin in 1857 and Berne in 1858.

20 For reasons unknown Spain was allowed to reject messages in German (Codding I, 16).

21 Telegraph Convention [Belgium, France, Netherlands, Sardinia, Switzerland], 1 September 1858, Berne, 119 CTS 461; 56 BFSP 377.

22 Codding I, 16. In n. 69 Codding cites a discussion of the Berne Conference in (1924) 48 *Journal télégraphique* 223-5; which suggested that, since at the time UK telegraphs were operated by private companies, the UK itself could not be a formal member of the Union. However, it was possible for the UK companies to signify their intention to 'play by the rules'. The UK telegraph companies were bought over by the state under the

Telegraph Union. The Berne Conference was therefore important, establishing a wide-ranging Convention between a significant group in Europe not based on a common Germanic root, and with connection to the UK. Things might have progressed significantly further had the Austro-German Telegraph Union taken up an invitation to take part in the Berne meeting, but it was to take another eight years before a general European agreement was arrived at.

East-West Interconnection

As Codding (I, 16ff) points out, it would be wrong to think that the two Unions, the Austro-German and the West European Telegraph Union, were mutually exclusive and self-contained. Bilateral agreements between individual members of each were frequent, and in fact The Netherlands had joined the Austro-German Telegraph Union in 1853 prior to its entry to the western Union.[23] At Paris on 4 October 1852 Belgium, France and Prussia concluded a Convention, the Prussian representative acting both for his home state and for the Austro-German Union.[24] This largely adopted the rules of the Austro-German Convention of 1857, but had also features then unusual. Notably a telegraph system was to be established exclusively for international traffic and to be of a capacity sufficient to cope with the expected service demand. The cable system was to cross borders, eliminating the need to re-key between different segments of the network. There was to be a right of public correspondence subject only to the payment of appropriate charges at the point of initiation of a message.[25] The secrecy of public correspondence was to be assured. Messages might be in English,[26] French or German, and only government messages might be in cypher.

The Paris Convention was revised at Berlin in 1855 by the same parties.[27] The responsibilities of the operating governments were truncated and they were given the right both to suspend and to police the use made of the international system. In addition the liabilities of the governments for the system were vastly diminished. Further, telegrams from different users were prioritised. As in the Austro-Prussian agreement of 1849, the order of priority was first, government messages, second,

---

Telegraph Acts 1868 and 1869. Thereafter the UK telegraph network was operated by the Post Office.

23 See *supra*, n. 10.

24 Telegraph Convention [Belgium, France and Prussia], Paris, 4 October 1852, 109 CTS 27. (An additional Article of 22 September 1854 is annexed to the CTS version.)

25 Charges were refunded if the message was lost, or unduly delayed.

26 The UK government was not involved in continental negotiations at this time since its telegraphs were in private hands. Notwithstanding, the inclusion of English as an authorised language clearly reflects the communications requirements of UK/Continental business. See also *supra*, n. 22.

27 Telegraph Convention [France, Belgium and the Austro-German Telegraph Union represented by Prussia], Berlin, 30 June 1855, 113 CTS 205.

service messages anent the functioning of the system itself, and only third were messages of public correspondence transmitted. Revenues were divided quarterly between the parties on the basis of the distance the telegram travelled within each party. The acceptable languages were increased, but on the basis that only some transmitting stations would accept messages outwith the English, French and German of the 1852 agreement.

The Telegraph Convention, Brussels, 1858

The 1855 Berlin Convention was to remain in force for two years with a further conference to be held in 1858 for its revision in which the reduction of tariffs would also be considered. That conference was duly held, a Convention being signed in Brussels on 30 June, 1858, along with an annexed 'Instruction' containing 'Service Regulations'.[28] Tariffs were reduced as had been intended. However, other curious changes were made. Only telegrams in French or German were acceptable at all stations in the international system governed by the Brussels agreement: English as universally acceptable was dropped. Numbers were permitted in messages provided they were part of a commercial business message, though any government telegrams could also use that facility. A maximum of seven syllables was set as normal for any word in a message, a provision which foreshadowed later argument over coded messaging.

The Brussels Convention was successful. In addition to the formal parties of 1858 it was soon adhered to by Switzerland, Spain, Sardinia, Portugal and Turkey (all 1859), Denmark, Sweden and Norway (at the time united), the Vatican, Russia, and the Two Sicilies (all 1860) and Luxemburg (1861). Further, the submarine cable companies of Algeria, Malta and Corfu agreed to abide by its rules. The eventual parties to the Brussels Convention therefore were more than that of the combined membership of the western Telegraph Union together with Prussia and the Austro-German Union. But clearly a problem was emerging. As Codding I, 19, notes, dependent on its routing a particular telegram might be subject separately or successively to the regimes of the 1857 Stuttgart Convention of the Austro-German Telegraph Union, to the 1858 Berne Convention of the Western European Telegraph Union and to the 1858 Brussels Convention, regimes which were not uniform in their provisions. Some attempts were made to resolve these differences but only by bilateral discussions, not in a general conference of the parties to the relevant conventions. Thus a conference was held in Friedrichshaven in October 1858 between Switzerland, Austria, Baden and Württemberg, the latter three representing the Austro-German Telegraph Union. The resulting Convention[29] was

28 Telegraph Convention, Brussels, 1858, 119 CTS 219.

29 Telegraph Convention [Switzerland and the Austro-German Telegraph Union], Friedrichshaven, 26 October, 1858, 120 CTS 29.

further amended with the addition of Bavaria at a further conference between the parties which was held in Bregenz in November 1863.[30]

Throughout the period 1850-1860 there was also a plethora of bilateral telegraph agreements which are not here cited.[31] It was time for a more general agreement.[32] As Codding I, 20, notes, the outcome of the limited conferences of 1858 and 1863 was a document that more closely resembled the 1858 Berne Convention of the West European Telegraph Union rather than the then ruling 1857 Stuttgart Convention of the Austro-German Telegraph Union. A common underlying geology that was to form the basis for wider agreement in 1865 was being laid.

The International Telegraph Convention and Regulations, Paris, 1865

In 1865 France convened a conference which was attended by Austria, Baden, Bavaria, Belgium, Denmark, France, Greece, Hamburg, Hanover, Italy, The Netherlands, Portugal, Prussia, Russia, Saxony, Spain, Sweden-Norway, Switzerland, Turkey and Württemberg. The jurisdiction of these states extended to a significant portion of the land territory of Europe, but did not consist of the totality of the parties to the Berne or Stuttgart Conventions.[33] The participants in the conference were diplomatic agents of the several states, but each was accompanied by one or more technical experts skilled in the telegraph. The latter were largely responsible for the formulation of the 'Service Regulations' annexed to the eventual Convention and these were signed for each state by these expert delegates – another example of the incorporation of technical expertise in the international inter-state process.[34] It should also be noted that the German delegation contained Heinrich von Stephan, who had been a major force in the creation of the German-Austrian Postal Union, and was urging the creation of a

30 Supplementary Telegraph Convention [Switzerland and the Austro-German Telegraph Union], Bregenz, 1 November 1863, 127 CTS 42, 142.

31 See Volume 2 of the Index-Guide to the Consolidated Treaty Series for an exhausting list of the telegraph treaties and agreements collected in that Series.

32 A map of the 'Telegraphs of Europe' published by the (UK) Electric and International Telegraph Company in 1860 is available at http://distantwriting.co.uk/telegraphmap.aspx. It clearly shows the complexity of the telegraph networks of the time. 'Distantwriting.co.uk' provides a very useful history of the UK telegraph and the various UK providers down to their nationalisation by the Telegraph Acts 1868 and 1869, the takeover being finally completed in 1870.

33 As in the case of the West European Telegraph Union conferences, the UK was not invited since its telegraph networks were at this stage still in the hands of private companies. See *supra*, n. 22.

34 P.S. Reinsch, 'International Unions and their Administration' (1907) 1 AJIL 579 at 583. See also Chapter 1, 'Experts'. Cf. the use of Post Office officials to negotiate and agree postal agreements: see Chapter 7, nn. 39 and 65.

world postal agreement simultaneously with his telecommunications involvement at Paris.[35]

At Paris what was hoped for was a uniformity in tariffs, codes, routing and operational matters through generally agreed regulations which would bring together the European networks at least in their international traffic, even were quirks to remain in internal national systems. The result was the Convention of 1865 which, for the parties that had ratified it by then, came into force on 1 January 1866.[36] The remainder soon also ratified and a number of other states which had not been at the conference also adhered.[37] In broad the Convention mirrored the West European Telegraph Convention of Berne of 1858. Obviously its provisions would bind the parties to it in their operation of state-run networks. However, in the interests of commonality or uniformity the parties formally agreed so far as possible to impose its provisions and requirements on companies operating under concessionary agreements either in their territories or through operating submarine cables (Art. 61). Again, so far as possible the contracting states were to negotiate the reduction of traffic rates charged by independent companies to the levels of those established in the Convention (Art. 61). However the parties also agreed that each could still enter into arrangements that did not affect the generality of the international service. Such could include agreement as to equipment, special vocabulary, local taxes and service messages as to meteorology and other matters of general public interest (Art. 59).

Oddly, to the modern eye, the 'Purpose' of the Union is not stated, but rather was assumed by the 1865 Convention.[38] Article 1 simply called for the creation of an international network of dedicated cable connections to be built to the best available practical conditions and in number sufficient to provide a rapid transmission of messages. By Art. 2.1 the service between important cities and towns of the contracting states was to be permanently maintained, day and night, without interruption. From April to September major telegraph stations were to be open to the public between seven in the morning to nine at night, opening time moving to eight in the morning for the other months of the year (Art. 2.2). The opening hours of stations providing limited service were at the discretion of the relevant state (Art. 2.3). However, a 'limited service' station could not close down

35 See Chapter 7 at n. 69.

36 International Telegraph Convention, Paris, 17 May 1865, 130 CTS 198; 56 BFSP 295; available via link at http://www.itu.int/en/history/plenipotentiaryconferences/Pages/1865Paris.aspx. Reading the text of the Convention takes one back to a vanished era, the first four pages of the CTS version consisting of the rehearsal of the identities, dignities and honours of those representing their respective states.

37 By Art. 60 of the Paris Convention adherence was possible without the requirement of the consent of the existing parties. However, adhering states had to accept the totality of the Paris provisions: reservations were not permitted (Art. 60.3).

38 A statement of 'Purpose' did not come until the International Telecommunication Union Convention of Madrid in 1932 united the wired and wireless Unions. See Chapter 4.

before it had passed on to one of the permanently operational telegraph stations all the international messages which it had received prior to shutting its doors (Art. 12). Finally, reflecting the fact that in 1865 there was no 'common time' within Europe or even within some of its component states, Art. 2.5 provided that the 'time' of each telegraph station within a state would be that of the capital of that state. Article 4 provided for a public right of correspondence by telegraph, and Art. 5 for the secrecy of communications and the speedy transmission of messages. However, the contracting states disavowed any responsibility for the telegraph service (Art. 6). The Morse system was provisionally adopted as the acceptable apparatus for the international network (Art. 3).[39] As in previous Conventions, priority of service was accorded first to state telegrams, second to network-service telegrams and third to private communications (Arts. 7 and 11).[40] Article 10 dealt with the form in which a message had to be presented, providing for its legibility, for the address and signature of its sender, and for a sufficient identification and address of its intended recipient. Subject to requirements as to their secrecy the originals were to be archived at the initial receiving station for a minimum of twelve months (Art. 21). The language of telegrams might be those of any of the contracting states, although a state might choose which of its languages was or were to be used if there was more than one in use in its territory (Art. 9). Coded messages and messages containing numbers were allowed in the case of state messages and the same was possible for private messages sent internationally provided that the state of initial transmission and the state of reception so permitted (Art. 9). Presumably this meant that, notwithstanding Art. 5 on secrecy, a state could prohibit encryption and intercept and read suspect messages. Anarchism and revolutionary movements may have been feared: 1848, the 'Year of Revolutions', was still of recent memory. In any event Art. 19 allowed the stopping of private messages which might threaten state security, or of messages that might be contrary to local law or good morals, and this power was exercisable by stations on the network without recourse to a central authority. Further, by Art. 20 each government reserved the right to interrupt service in whole or in part on its telegraph systems for such period as it might determine. Where there was an interruption it was up to each government to decide how to clear any back-log of messages, and this might include the use of the postal service (Art. 14).

Other parts of the 1865 Convention covered important technicalities, some very specific. As indicated the draft telegram had to be appropriately certified with address of sender and recipient (Art. 10). However, 'post restante' or 'bureau télégraphique restant' were also acceptable destinations (Art. 16). Although priorities as between state, service and private messages were set (Art. 11), once started the transmission of a message was not to be interrupted even to send a message of higher ranking priority except in cases of absolute urgency. Messages

39 Reference point n. 3, *supra*.

40 Art. 7 defined the categories; Art. 11 set the order of priorities. Art. 8 provided for the certification of state and private telegrams.

within each category were to be transmitted in the order of their receipt at the transmitting station (Art. 11). Where two stations in the network were in direct communication they were to alternate in sending and receipt, although this rule could be departed from in the interest of speeding the service and within each state its government could determine such questions (Arts. 11 and 13). On reception at a telegraph station a message for an address close to the receiving bureau was to be taken to the relevant address.[41] Messages furth of the locality of a receiving station (defined by the relevant state) were either to be put into the local postal system or conveyed by some other swift service at the option of the telegraph administration (Art. 16). Telegrams could be accepted or received not only by the addressee but also by adult members of the family, by employees, or by a host (if the addressee was resident) (Art. 18.1). Failing these, a note of the failure to deliver was to be left at the destination address (Art. 18.3). Undelivered messages so notified could be collected at the telegraph office within six weeks (Art. 18.4). Similar arrangements were set for messages to a 'bureau restant'(Art. 18.5).

Telecommunication incurs a cost which is recouped through charges. Indeed the charges and taxes exigible formed a major element of most of the telegraph conventions, both multi- and bi-lateral, of the time. The 1865 Convention therefore contained a number of provisions for that purpose.[42] A comparability had to be set between the currencies concerned. By Art. 30.3 the French gold franc was set as the unit in which international tariffs were to be calculated. Further, Art. 30.5 established the exchange rate at which the international tariff was expressed in local currency. A standard minimum charge applied to messages of up to twenty words, with an additional charge for every ten words over that limit, the first word of each new decile incurring the additional impost (Art. 30.3). That, naturally, led

---

41 In the UK the 'Telegraph Boy' with his red uniform and pill-box hat on his red bicycle with its flat pannier in front to carry his message bag was a well-known figure, particularly in cartoons.

42 By Art. 59 the original parties to the Convention could make a reservation on such matters and make separate arrangements between themselves reflecting existing arrangements (e.g. Austria, Prussia and Russia came to agreement perhaps during the gathering for the major convention, on 15 April 1865 in Paris, 130 CTS 103). Only Belgium, Luxemburg and Switzerland made that reservation at first. Parties later acceding to the Convention could not make any reservation (Art. 60.3). However, in later years various parties did make separate agreements between themselves as to rates, particularly on the question of transit rates where the destination of the message was outside their territories. See the Convention regarding a direct telegraph link between Austro-Hungary, France, Serbia, Switzerland and Turkey signed at Vienna, 22 July 1868, 10 De Clercq 156; and the Telegraph Conventions between France, Portugal and Spain, Paris, 14 March 1880, 155 CTS 487; between France, Belgium and the Netherlands, Paris, 30 March 1880, 156 CTS 26; between the UK, The Netherlands, Belgium and Germany, London, 31 May 1880, 156 CTS 42; between the UK and Spain as to rates from France to Gibraltar, London, 21 March 1881, 157 CTS 316, 72 BFSP 5; and between Belgium, Germany and The Netherlands, Berlin, 4 May 1889, 171 CTS 402 (which lasted until 1926 – see 54 LNTS 435).

to debate as to what was a 'word'. This was dealt with by the various provisions of Art. 33. A word might have up to seven syllables, any excess being counted as a separate chargeable word. Words separated by an apostrophe were counted as separate words. The proper names of towns, people, places, streets etc., titles, first names, particulars and qualifications were computed according to the number of words required to formulate them. Numbers expressed in Arabic figures were counted as if written in words up to five in number with an additional word counted for any excess. Single letters counted as one word, but punctuation marks were ignored. Article 34 took account of the possibility that messages might be sent in code or by the use of numbers to indicate words. In that case the content of the message for charging purposes was to be calculated by totalling the number of the elements of the message and dividing it by five then adding the elements of the address and destination. The name of the originating office together with the date, hour and minute of the receipt of the message were also to be transmitted to the receiving office (Art. 35). All such requirements contributed towards the rate to which a particular transmission might be subjected (Arts. 36 and 37). Further provisions as to charging agreed in Arts. 38-43 allowed for other charges to be made (payable by the sender) in particular circumstances. Of these, Art. 43 is probably the most intriguing to the modern eye. It provides for the 1865 Convention to govern the charge for messages exchanged with ships at sea where a portion of the route involved the use of semaphore, unless the states involved had a separate rule for such messages.

Using language still to be found in the ITU documents, Art. 54 of the 1865 Convention provided that the Convention was 'completed' as to international services by detailed rules set out in annexed Service Regulations. These were to come into force simultaneous with the Convention itself, be complied with by all telegraph administrations, and to remain in effect throughout the currency of the Convention.[43] However the Regulations might be altered by the common consent of the Convention parties at any time.

The measures required for the administration of the 1865 Convention were left as the immediate responsibility of France, the state which had convened the conference (Art. 55).[44] These included the drafting of amendments to existing rules to reflect the new requirements. It also included acting as the secretary to the new Union through receiving suggestions for alterations to the arrangements,

43 Note that by Conv. Art. 61 the Service Regulations were applied to private operators as well as to state networks.

44 Referring to the documents of the Paris conference, Codding I, 22 states that during the conference France had pressed for the establishment of a permanent commission to map the international networks and study matters relevant to the telegraph service. The commission would have had one delegate from each member of the Union and would sit successively at the capital hosting the immediately previous Union conference. In fact the commission did not come into being. The duties left with France, though less than the French proposals, were more than Codding indicates. See following text.

consulting the parties, notifying all parties when there was unanimous consent to any particular alteration, and the date of coming into effect of modifications. However, this responsibility was not to remain that of France but was to pass successively to the state hosting a conference for the revision of the Paris agreements (Art. 54). To facilitate the new European international networking all parties agreed regularly to inform each other of the internal administration of their networks, of intended alterations and modifications, of new lines and of the closing of old ones, of service breaks, and of private networks that might allow service breaks to be circumvented (Art. 57). In addition annual reports of statistics of use, network circulars and instructions were to be made available (Art. 57). Finally, as part of its administrative duties the French telegraph administration was to prepare, maintain and publish a map of the telegraph system of the Union (Art. 58).

In common with the previous telegraph conventions and agreements, Art. 56 of the 1865 Convention provided for its periodic revision, with conferences to be held successively in the capitals of the member states. To that end Vienna in 1868 was set for the next meeting of the Union.

The International Telegraph Convention and Regulations, Vienna, 1868

The 1868 Vienna conference had a lot to do. Once the 1865 Convention had come into force, the administration of the new arrangements, particularly the mutual exchange of information, proved to be complex. Membership of the Union was increasing.[45] So was the volume of international telegraphic traffic.[46] The Vienna agreements considerably repeated the provisions of the 1865 Convention, extended some of its detail, and made important innovations.[47] As before, the parties undertook to construct and maintain the international telegraph system to the highest standards (Art. 1.1-2). However, this time a minimum cable diameter of 5 mm was set for the direct lines to be established between the principal towns of the participant Administrations, and on which service would remain separate from that of traffic between intermediate telegraph stations (Art. 1.3). Opening times for major and minor bureaux were agreed, as was public access to them (Art. 2). The right of public correspondence was recognised (Art. 4), as was the

45 Newcomers were Great Britain (on behalf of India), Greece, the Holy See, Luxemburg, Persia, Serbia, Switzerland and the United Principalities of Moldavia and Wallachia.

46 This was a time of vast increases in international business as light and heavy-duty manufacturing and related exporting burgeoned. Cf. the 'Great Exhibition', London 1851.

47 International Telegraph Convention, Vienna, 21 July 1868, 136 CTS 122 and 292: 59 BFSP 322; 10 De Clercq 121; available via link at http://www.itu.int/en/history/plenipotentiaryconferences/Pages/1868Vienna.aspx. British India (not Great Britain) and North Germany were signatories.

secrecy and swift transmission of correspondence (Art. 5). Intriguingly, while Art. 3 of the 1865 Convention had provisionally identified the Morse system as the one to be used, Art. 3 of the 1868 Convention made the Morse and the alternative US Hughes apparatus concurrently usable until there was common consent on a single standard, and the Service Regulations were amended accordingly.[48] Of obvious importance to the parties was the revenue generated by the telegraph system. Charges and taxes were again dealt with, the French gold franc being retained as the international unit of account and of tariff comparability (Arts. 33.1 and 54.2), Art 33.2 re-calibrating its exchange rate for use in local currencies.

Several aspects of the 1868 Convention may particularly be noted. First there is the extent of its range. Technically an international treaty is an agreement between states laying down for them rights and obligations. Article 61 of the 1865 Convention had bound its parties to impose its general terms on all telegraph operators of terrestrial or submarine services under their several jurisdictions whether operators by the state or private enterprise, and in particular to seek the reciprocal reduction of rates to a common base. Article 66.1 of the 1868 agreement made similar provision. However, to offset that imposition upon them the second paragraph of Art. 66 offered an inducement to the private telegraph companies. Private companies having the consent of their relevant national administration were given the right to accede to the Convention and Regulations, thereby giving them access to advantages under the Convention (Art. 66.2). These advantages were not specified in the text, and they were not to be given a vote, but herein we can perceive an advance on the presence of 'experts within a delegation at a telegraph conference' as pioneered in the 1865 Paris Conference.[49] Second, by Art. 65.3 and Art. 66.3 further pressure was applied on all operators towards the reduction of rates and charges. The contracting parties could refuse to accord to newcomers to the Convention (including companies accepting the Convention in terms of Art. 66.2) the benefits of the tariff reduction provisions unless the newcomers themselves applied those reductions (Art. 66.3).[50] Third, messages to and from non-contracting states or to and from private telegraph operators not bound by their adherence to the Convention under Art. 66.2, were to be treated in the same way as messages between formal state parties, charges being multiples of the existing inter-party tariffs.

Of crucial importance for the future organisation of world telecommunications were the administrative developments adopted at Vienna. First, procedures were set in place for the determination of differences as to the interpretation of the

48 The Hughes was quite widely used, and was the operating system for the (US) Western Union Telegraph Company. It was also used in Europe as an alternative to the Morse apparatus and remained recognised by successive versions of the Service Regulations. The Cooke/Wheatstone system was not widely used except by the UK. See Appendix I.

49 See *supra* at n. 36.

50 The telegraph systems of railway companies were exempted from the penalties of Art. 66.3 by Art. 66.4.

Convention and/or Regulations. On the request of one or more administrations the telegraph administration of the state where the last telegraph conference had been held was to convene a Special Commission of all parties.[51] The decision of the Commission bound all administrations whether or not they took part in its deliberations and determination.[52] In short, we see here a binding procedure for dispute resolution in the regulation of international telecommunications.

The second major development of Vienna, 1868, was the creation of a permanent international organ to administer the practicalities of the International Telegraph Union. By Art. 61 an 'International Bureau of Telegraphic Administrations' (the 'Bureau Internationale des Administrations Télégraphiques') was set up. It may be recalled that at the 1865 conference France had suggested that a permanent commission should be established to administer the new arrangements.[53] However, while the 1865 Convention had called for a considerable amount of administrative activity, exactly how that would be organised had been left vague. The French proposal had called for a commission to follow in the wake of the seat of successive conferences, a procedure which would have been unwieldy. At Vienna Switzerland proposed that the administrative organ should be permanent, and, while the idea of a peripatetic Bureau was retained for the ensuing discussion, it seemed good to the Conference that such a Bureau be established in Switzerland. A Bureau charged with the execution and application of the Convention was considered to be in the interest of all (Art. 61.1). It was to provide the centralised administration of data, statistics and information as to tariffs and practices, disseminating them as necessary. It was to publish a regular journal (in French) on telecommunications. In addition it was to conduct such special studies as it might be directed (Art. 61.2). It was also to gather proposals for changes to the Convention and Regulations, and, when there was unanimity on such, to inform all members of modifications so agreed (Art. 61.4). A budget of 40,000 Swiss francs was set for the Bureau but that might be increased by common consent of the members of the Union.[54] This sum was to be contributed voluntarily by the parties, each selecting from a list a class of units for its contribution. There were six classes: Class 1, 25 units; Class 2, 20 units; Class 3, 15 units; Class 4, 10 units; Class 5, 5 units and Class 6, 3 units.[55] The value of a single unit was calculated when the total of the units subscribed was known. That total was divided into the budget figure to give the value of an individual unit. So was set a pattern of financing that has persisted.

51 1868 Conv. Art. 60, and Service Regulations, Art. 30.

52 1868 Conv. Art. 60.2, and Service Regulations, Art. 30.2.

53 See *supra*, n. 44.

54 Service Regulations, Vienna, 1868, Arts. 31-3.

55 Service Regulations, Vienna, 1868, Art. 61.

The International Telegraph Convention and Regulations, Rome, 1872

As with the 1865 Convention, Art. 62.1 of the 1868 Convention provided for its revision, Art. 62.3 specifying Florence in 1871 for the next meeting of the parties since that was then the capital of the new Kingdom of Italy. As it happened, however, the conference took place in Rome. The Papal States having been conquered by the forces of Italian Unification ('Il Risorgimento') Rome was taken in September 1870,[56] and the capital of Italy relocated. The revision conference therefore took place there, convening on 4 December 1871 and ending on 14 January 1872. Important new members of the Union were Persia and the UK (which had nationalised its telegraph networks under the Telegraph Acts 1868 and 1869, the takeover having been finally completed in 1870). Intriguingly, and adumbrating the eventual world organisation, Japan sent an observer.[57] The acting director of the new International Bureau, supported by an official seconded from the Italian telegraph administration, supervised the conference secretariat – another precursor of the structures of the eventual international agency.

In broad the Rome Telegraph Convention repeated the provisions of 1865 and 1868.[58] For our purposes one significant advance lies with the extended participation of 'experts' in the discussions. As recounted by Codding who cites the relevant conference documents (I, 25-6), the question of the potential role of non-state entities was raised by the host, Italy.[59] A number of countries operated national networks, some had nationalised their telegraph systems, but a number had private networks within their territories. Although both the 1865 Convention by its Art. 61 and the 1868 Convention by its Art. 66.1 had obliged the signatories to impose the terms of the Convention and Regulations on private companies under their jurisdiction, and although the 1868 Convention had allowed the private companies to accede to the Convention and Regulations (Art. 66.2), the benefits of doing so had not been apparent to entrepreneurs. At Rome many realised that it would be sensible to allow private operators as well as state operators to advise on the terms of the Service Regulations as they had in effect done in the past. The question, however, was the extent to which private operators should be allowed to participate in the work of the conference as opposed to merely providing advice. The matter was decided by a narrow majority, but ten private

56 The Papal States had effectively been run by Napoleon III, but he had withdrawn his troops during the Franco-Prussian War of 1870-1.

57 The provisions of the Rome Regulations were applied to all telegrams between Europe and Japan from 1874: Codding I, 27.

58 International Telegraph Convention and Regulations, Rome, 14 January 1872, 143 CTS 411; 66 BFSP 975; available via link at http://www.itu.int/en/history/plenipotentiaryconferences/Pages/1871Rome.aspx.

59 Codding I, 26. Italian telegraphs were both state and privately operated. In calling the conference Italy suggested that the operators of either kind could contribute to the discussions. This was discussed when the delegates arrived, and agreed.

companies, selected and nominated by the conference chairman, were eventually allowed to be present at all meetings and take part in discussions, albeit without the right to vote.[60] The work of the International Bureau to date was reviewed and its budget was increased. The Bureau was also entrusted with the duty of proposing revisals of the Telegraph Convention and Service Regulations. Matters of permanent general interest were to be contained within the Convention. The Service Regulations should include the detailed rules, which, *ex hypothesi*, might well be subject to frequent and necessary change as technology developed.[61] The draft new Convention and Service Regulations were to be presented to the next revision conference to be held in St Petersburg in 1872 (Art. 61). In fact the St Petersburg conference met during June and July 1875, the delay being in part because of the Franco-Prussian War of 1870-71.

The International Telegraph Convention, St Petersburg, 1875

The St Petersburg Conference must be judged as a significant success. Complying with the instructions given it at Rome, the International Bureau duly presented its proposals and these grounded the discussions and decisions. The new International Telegraph Convention adopted on 22 July 1875 was to remain in effect without further revision throughout the existence of the International Telegraph Union.[62] The Service Regulations annexed to it were, however, to be revised at intervals just as the Rome Conference had contemplated.[63]

---

60 Codding I, 26, n. 177, lists the Falmouth, Gibraltar and Malta Telegraph Company; the Marseilles, Algiers and Malta Telegraph company; the Anglo-Mediterranean Telegraph Company; the British Indian Submarine Telegraph Company; the British Indian Extension Telegraph Company; the British Australian Telegraph Company; the China Submarine Telegraph Company; the Telegraph Construction and Maintenance Company; the Indo-European Telegraph Company; the Great Northern Telegraph Company; the Great Northern China and Japan Extension Telegraph Company; the Anglo-American Telegraph Company and the Société du Câble transatlantique français. The spread of their interests should be noted.

61 Codding I, 26, citing the documents of the Rome Convention and attributing these suggestions to Belgium. The notion of a division between permanent and mutable documentation was to re-emerge in the reconstruction of the ITU in the 1990s: see Chapter 5, *ad fin*.

62 International Telegraph Convention, with annexed regulations and schedule of rates, St Petersburg, 22 July 1875, 148 CTS 416; 66 BFSP 19; 3 Martens (2d) 614; 57 LNTS 201; (1913) AJIL Supp. 276 (Conv. Arts. 1-3, 5-8, 11-12 and 17 only); available via link at http://www.itu.int/en/history/plenipotentiaryconferences/Pages/1875StPetersburg.aspx.

63 Revisions by formal telegraph conferences were to come in 1879, 1885, 1890, 1896, 1903, 1908, 1925 and 1926. See list and availability at http://www.itu.int/en/history/administrativeconferences/Pages/CompleteListAdminConferences.aspx. Other developments occurred through the spread of a limited practice among members.

In contrast to its predecessors the St Petersburg Convention is short, consisting of twenty-one Articles, the operative text taking up only two half pages and two full pages of the version in the Consolidated Treaty Series. Its arrangement intrigues as it indicates the 'permanent' elements which were thought necessary in the international arrangements dealing, as Codding notes, with, first, the relationship of the states to the users of the international system, second, with the relations of the contracting states *inter se*, third, with the composition of the Union itself, and last, with the technicalities of the application of the Convention and Service Regulations. Adherence to the Convention and Service Regulations was competent provided only that adhering states had to accept the totality of their provision without reservation (Art. 13). Messaging to and from non-party states or from those having private companies under their jurisdiction were to be ruled by the Convention (Art. 19).

The Convention itself cherry-picked from its predecessors those elements which first, the International Bureau, and second, the conference participants at St Petersburg, considered as 'permanent' and therefore in a sense 'fundamental'. It begins with the recognition of a public right of access to the telegraph system (Art. 1), of the right to have correspondence sent as swiftly as possible, and of the secrecy of telegraph communications (Art. 2 and Service Reg. 2). While the contracting states disavowed responsibility for the international telegraph service (Art. 3), and any modification to it (Art. 19), they undertook to ensure the provision of dedicated cables constructed to the best known standards in sufficient numbers to provide a swift service (Art. 4.1-2). As before messages were classified into state, service and private telegrams, though this time state telegrams were accorded priority and no priority was indicated of service over private messages (Art. 5). State telegrams could be encrypted, but private messages only if the sending and receiving state permitted 'secret language' (Art. 6.1-2). However, states that did not permit 'secret language' were to allow such messages to pass through their systems unless the system itself had suspended service (Art. 6.3). Private messages could be stopped on grounds of state security, for illegality, or as being contrary to public morals (Art. 7). The suspension of service in whole or in part within a state was competent for a determinate or indeterminate period subject only to the suspending state informing all other parties to the Convention. However, the suspending state was not required to justify its action or indeed to give reasons (Art. 8). Rates were to be publicised and profit margins systematised (Art. 9). For international services taxes were to be harmonised, the French gold franc remaining the unit of computation (Art. 10). Service messages were to pass without charge (Art. 11), and accounting was to take place between parties (Art. 12).

The Convention then passed to administrative questions. By Art. 13 it was agreed that the Convention was 'completed' by the annexed Regulations, and that the Convention might be amended by common accord between the contracting states. However, unlike its predecessors its currency was set to begin on 1 January

1876 (new style[64]) but this time for an indefinite period (Art. 20). Neither a date nor place were specified for the purpose of revision or attaining a common accord. Although not named as the 'International Bureau', Art. 14 provided for the existence of a 'central organ', subject to the authority of a designated contracting party and funded by the telegraph administrations (Art. 14.2), to be charged with gathering, coordinating and publishing material relevant to the international telegraph. It was to gather suggestions for changes in tariffs and to the Service Regulations and was also to conduct studies as required.

In accordance with the Rome instructions tariffs and taxes and various other matters of detail which had previously taken up space in the Convention were relegated to the Service Regulations. These, annexed to the Convention, were declared to be of legal status equal to that of the Convention itself and were to take effect simultaneously with it (Art. 15.1). Revision of the Service Regulations was competent, but by a process different from that of the Convention itself. The Convention could be revised by a diplomatic conference of the contracting states (Art. 13). The Service Regulations were to be revised by periodic administrative conference (i.e. not full 'diplomatic conferences') of the Telegraph Administrations of the contracting states (Art. 16.1), each such conference setting the time and place for the next (Art. 15.3). At administrative conferences each Administration present was to have one vote, but, taking account of the various 'empires' of the time, it was competent for a contracting state to authorise the presence of more than one telegraph administration should there be more than one under its jurisdiction (Art. 16.2). That said, although the 'voting rights' therefore favoured major states, any revision of the Service Regulations could go into effect only after having been approved by all the contracting states (Art. 16.3). In this way some balance between voting weight and outcome was achieved. Compromise between the large states responsible for many administrations and the states responsible for only one administration was thereby encouraged. It seems to have worked.

The new Service Regulations reflected the content of the Convention, elaborating the detail on many matters. Usefully, in appropriate places the text of the relevant Convention Article is given ahead of the Article of the Service Regulation that explicates or otherwise implements its principle. Thus Section 15 of the Regulations, headed 'Bureau International : Communications Réciproques', begins by reprinting Convention Art. 14 which, as noted above, provided for the existence of an unnamed 'central organ' for the administrative purposes of the Union. Articles 77-80 of the Regulations then fill in the detail. Article 77.1 gave the 'central organ' its title – the International Bureau of Telegraph Administrations ('Le Bureau International des Administrations Télégraphiques'), then Art. 77.2 designated the Swiss government as the Convention party to be responsible for

64 'New style' refers to the alteration of the dating of calendar years to 1 January and the use of the Gregorian calendar accepted by most states, but not by all, at the time of the St Petersburg conference. Article 20 therefore imposed a common start for the Convention for all parties.

organising the International Bureau in accordance with Arts. 78-80. Article 78 dealt with the financing of the Bureau. By Art. 78.1 the budget was set at 60,000 francs, but this was not to include the costs of international conferences and could be altered by the common consent of Administrations. Switzerland was to supervise financial transactions, make any necessary advances, and provide an annual accounting (Art. 78.2). As previously, the expenses of the Bureau were to be met by the contracting states. The selection of unit classes continued, as did the six available classes of unit – Class I, 25 units; Class II, 20 units; Class III, 15 units; Class IV, 10 units; Class V, 5 units and Class VI, 3 units (Art. 78.3). Again, when the total number of units taken up was known that figure was used to establish the value of a single unit by dividing that number into the budget figure (Art. 78.4).[65]

Article 79 specified the duties of the various administrations vis-à-vis the International Bureau, Art. 79.1 requiring the provision of various documentation, in general to be dealt with by the International Bureau (Art. 79.2). Postal and other means were to be used to transmit data on tariffs, new and closing links, hours of operation and similar matters, as well as suggestions for alteration to the agreed rules (Art. 79.3). Of particular importance was the notification by telegraph of interruptions to service and its reestablishment (Art. 79.4). It was also the responsibility of the International Bureau to compile annual statistics including of usage, the condition of telegraph lines, the number of telegraph bureaux and of their apparatuses (Art. 79.5). The International Bureau was also to receive two copies of materials published by each Administration (Art. 79.6). The Bureau was also to receive communications by other means as to how the international system was in fact operating (Art. 79.7). Finally, Art. 80 spelled out the duties and responsibilities of the Bureau itself. These included the speedy communication to Administrations of data, particularly that required by Art. 78.3-4 (Art. 80.1), the preparation of statistics (Art. 80.2), the publication of a journal in French dealing with telegraph matters (Art. 80.3), the preparation, publication and regular revision of a map of the telegraph system (Art. 80.4), and being available at all times to provide advice to Administrations (Art. 80.5). Documents published by the International Bureau were to be distributed to Administrations in quantities proportionate to the unit contribution of each (Art. 79.6). Demands placed on the Bureau had to give it time to respond (Art. 80.7). The Bureau was to receive proposals for changes to the Regulations and, if agreeable to all parties,[66] the change was to be notified to all

65 Art. 78.5 lists the actual unit classes as taken up at St Petersburg: Class I – Austro-Hungary, Britannic India, France, Germany, Italy, Russia, Turkey and the UK; Class II – Spain; Class III – Belgium, The Netherlands, The Netherlands Islands [i.e. the Dutch Far East possessions], Romania and Sweden; Class IV – Denmark, Egypt, Norway and Switzerland; Class V – Greece, Portugal and Serbia; Class VI – Luxemburg and Persia. The value of the 'unit' was therefore rounded to 160 francs.

66 Parties had four months to respond. Silence beyond that period was deemed consent to the proposal (Art. 80.9).

by the Bureau, but such changes could not come into force until two months after that notification (Art. 80.8).

The last sections of Art. 80 dealt with international conferences. It was the responsibility of the Bureau to prepare for and act as secretariat for telegraph conferences whether diplomatic (dealing with the Convention) or administrative (reviewing the Service Regulations) (Art. 80.10). The Director of the International Bureau was to participate in conference discussions, but without a vote (Art. 80.11). Finally, an annual report of the work of the Bureau was to be prepared and circulated to all Administrations (Art. 80.12), including the results of any conferences that had been held (Art. 80.13).

The Service Regulations were considered by administrative conferences at intervals over the next thirty years, in London in 1879,[67] Berlin in 1885,[68] Paris in 1890,[69] Budapest in 1896,[70] London in 1903,[71] and Lisbon in 1908.[72] Thereafter, thanks to the political circumstances of the time, no general administrative telegraph conference was held until Paris in 1925.[73] After that a conference was held in Brussels in 1926, and another there in 1928.[74] In the meantime membership of the International Telegraph Union increased, particularly after the First World War.

67 Regulations in execution of the international telegraph convention of July 22, 1875, London, 28 July, 1879, 154 CTS 255; 70 BFSP 62; 8 Martens (2d) 51; 12 De Clercq 442. See http://www.itu.int/en/history/administrativeconferences/Pages/1879London.aspx.

68 Regulations in execution of the international telegraph convention of July 22, Berlin, 17 September, 1885, 165 CTS 212; 76 BFSP 597; 12 Martens (2d) 205; 15 De Clercq 816. See http://www.itu.int/en/history/administrativeconferences/Pages/1885Berlin.aspx.

69 Revised telegraph regulations annexed to the International Telegraph Convention of July 22, 1875, Paris, 21 June, 1890, 172 CTS 378; 82 BFSP 869; 17 Martens (2d) 294; 18 De Clercq 420. See http://www.itu.int/en/history/administrativeconferences/Pages/1890Paris.aspx.

70 Revision of the international service regulations annexed to the International Telegraph Convention of July 22, 1875, Budapest, 22 July, 1896, 183 CTS 159; 88 BFSP 1120; De Clercq 433. See http://www.itu.int/en/history/administrativeconferences/Pages/1896Budapest.aspx.

71 Regulations annexed to the Revised International Telegraph Convention, London, 10 July, 1903, 193 CTS 327; 97 BFSP 736; 22 De Clercq 296. See http://www.itu.int/en/history/administrativeconferences/Pages/1903London.aspx.

72 Regulations in execution of the international telegraph convention of July 22, 1875, Lisbon, 11 June 1908; 207 CTS 89; 102 BFSP 214; 5 Martens (3d) 208. See http://www.itu.int/en/history/administrativeconferences/Pages/1908Lisbon.aspx.

73 International Service Regulations annexed to the International Telegraph Convention of July 22, 1875, Paris, 29 October, 1925; 57 LNTS 201; 3 Hudson 1695. See http://www.itu.int/en/history/administrativeconferences/Pages/1908Lisbon.aspx.

74 Protocol regarding certain additions and modifications to the International Service Regulations, Brussels, 22 September 1928, 88 LNTS 347, 3 Hudson 1756. See http://www.itu.int/en/history/administrativeconferences/Pages/1928Brussels.aspx.

Over time the Service Regulations became more complex, but retained their basic form. Since the Regulations were always adopted 'in execution of' the 1875 Convention, their pattern was prescribed by the arrangement of the St Petersburg Convention itself, and the Regulations, although numbered consecutively, were divided into sections accordingly. As always the Regulations laid down detailed rules for the setting up and operation of the international system. This included duties as to the creation and maintenance of the system as well as its operation. Priorities were set as before. Rules were set as to the acceptance and delivery of messages. Tariffs were agreed for the duration of each set of Regulations. Particular attention was always given to the calculation of the charges to be levied for the service. What constituted a 'word' was established. Short 'codes' were set out for particular service purposes, and on occasion separate provision was made depending on whether a Morse or Hughes apparatus was being employed.[75] Throughout the Regulations the financing of the International Bureau remained to be met by the voluntary contribution of a sum based on a choice of units by each Administration. The classes of units, originally set in Vienna in 1868, were to remain six in number (25, 20, 15, 10, 5 and 3 units) throughout the period in which the Telegraph Union was a separate entity, the totality of the units being used to determine the value of each unit in relation to the budget.[76] Naturally, however, the budget itself increased over time.[77]

Without going through the successive sets of Regulations individually, certain innovations and major alterations may be noted.

75 See *supra*, n. 48.

76 Cf. Art. 84.3 of the Paris Regulations of 1925, *supra*, n. 73. Art. 84.5 of the Paris Regulations lists the then contributors and their class selection as: Class I – Argentina, Australia, Brazil, Chile, China, France, Germany, India, Italy, Japan, Russia (USSR), South Africa, Turkey and the UK; Class II – Poland and Spain; Class III – Belgium, Czechoslovakia, Finland, Greece, Irish Free State, The Netherlands, The Netherlands Indies, Norway, Romania, the Kingdom of Serbia, Croatia and Slovenia, and Switzerland; Class IV – Austria, Bolivia, Denmark, Egypt, French Indo-China, Hungary, Morocco, New Zealand, Switzerland and Uruguay; Class V – Albania, Bulgaria, Estonia, Lettonia [Latvia], Lithuania, Madagascar, Portugal, Senegal, Siam, Tunisia and Venezuela; Class VI – Angola, Belgian Congo, Ceylon, Cyrenaica, Danzig, the French Coast of Somalia, Iceland, Italian Somalia, Luxemburg, Mozambique, Persia, Portuguese African Colonies (except Angola and Mozambique), Portuguese Colonies in Asia and Oceania, the Saarland, Syria, and Tripolitania.

77 Paris Regulations, 1925, *supra*, n. 73, Art. 84.1.1 set the budget at 200,000 francs.

Telephony

The 1885 Berlin Telegraph Conference brought the new-fangled telephone mechanism within the competence of the Union and made more detailed provision for the functioning of the International Bureau.[78]

As far as the telephone was concerned a new Section 11 of the 1885 Berlin Telegraph Regulations contained a single Article, Art. 67.[79] It provided that states might set up international telephone services by either using existing lines or by installing new connections (Art. 67.1). Unless in the case of special arrangements between individual Administrations,[80] the international telephone lines were to pass through a central exchange in each state and might be connected from there with public telephone boxes, or to private houses and properties (Art. 67.2). While Administrations retained choice as to the telephone systems to be used and the service provided, they were to agree the appropriate tariff for the use of each link whatever the system or service (Art. 67.3). Five minutes was set as the unit of charge for conversations (Art. 67.4).[81] A telephone link was to be used in the order in which its use was applied for. Not more than two consecutive conversations might be conducted by the same parties, each lasting no more than the five minute unit, unless no other demand for service was received either before or during these conversations (Art. 67.5). Similar provisions are to be found in the 1903 Telegraph Regulations,[82] those of 1908[83] and of 1925.[84]

Radio Telegrams

The early 1900s saw the emergence of the new medium, radiotelegraphy. For reasons to be considered in Chapter 3, the International Telegraph Union remained

78 Regulations in execution of the International Telegraph Convention of 22 July, 1875, Berlin, 17 September 1885, 165 CTS 212, 76 BFSP 597; 12 Martens (2d) 205; 15 De Clercq 816. See http://www.itu.int/en/history/administrativeconferences/Pages/1885 Berlin.aspx.

79 The part of the Telegraph Regulations dealing with telephony remained a single article right through to the Paris revision of 1925, where it is Art. 71, its Sections A-T occupying 12 columns of the Hudson version.

80 This exception allowed a sensible establishing of telephone services across borders, but only between proximate cities and towns.

81 This was later reduced to three minutes, which remained the charging unit for UK public telephone boxes into the 1990s.

82 Part 15, Art. 68, Section A-O, London Telegraph Regulations, 1903, 193 CTS 327; 97 BFSP 736; 22 De Clercq 296. *Supra*, n. 71.

83 Part 15, Art. 68, Sections A-P, Lisbon Telegraph Regulations, 1908, 207 CTS 89; 102 BFSP 214; 5 Martens (3d) 208. *Supra*, n. 72.

84 Part 24, Art. 71, Sections A-T, Paris Telegraph Regulations, 1925, 57 LNTS 201; 3 Hudson 1695. *Supra*, n. 73.

separate from the International Radio Union until the Madrid Conference of 1932. However, telegraph messages carried by radio were fed into the general telegraph system. At first the main radio market was the ship-to-shore and ship-to-ship service. The Telegraph Regulations already had made provision for the passing of messages to ships by semaphore.[85] However, while the technicalities of frequencies and the like could be left to the Radio Union, radiotelegraphy required rules for charging and routing. Provision began with the first revision of the Telegraph Regulations held after the Berlin Radiotelegraphic Conference of 1906, that of Lisbon, 1908,[86] and was to be further elaborated over the ensuing years.

Code Language

One matter that rumbled for many years through the Telegraph Union was the use of 'code language'. That the calculation of the cost of sending a telegram was based on the number of words it contained was open to an obvious stratagem – code language.[87] It is always possible for individuals to agree that a particular word, or short series of letters, can transmit a complex message. At first the various telegraph conventions set out which languages would be acceptable on their routes, but then interconnection meant that any language approved by a state could pass along the networks. The 1865 Convention relegated approvals to the Service Regulations, and over the years this list extended.[88] Underlying questions were what constituted a 'word' for the purpose of charging, and the potential use of codes to avoid restrictions on messages contrary to law, to morals or to state security.[89] The major first steps to deal with code language were taken at

85 Cf. Arts. 60 and 61 of the London Telegraph Regulations, 1903, 193 CTS 327.

86 See Arts. 61 and 62 of the Lisbon Telegraph Regulations, 1908, 207 CTS 89.

87 In the UK a famous example is the transmission by General Charles Napier of the single word 'Peccavi' to the Governor General of India in 1843. Napier had been instructed to conquer the North-West India region, known as 'The Sindh'. In Latin 'peccavi' means 'I have sinned'. The punning use of one single word gave news of Napier's success, and at minimum cost.

88 Codding I, 66, n. 294, states that by the time the London Regulations of 1908 came into force in 1909 the following languages had been recognised for use on the international telegraph system: Albanian, Ammonitish [Palestine], Annamese [Vietnamese], Arabic, Aramaic, Armenian, Bohemian, Bulgarian, Chinese, Croatian, Danish, Dutch (Netherlands), English, Finnish, Flemish, French, German, Greek, Hebrew, Hungarian, Icelandic, Illyrian, Italian, Japanese, Kiswahili, Lao, Latin, Little-Russian, Lugandan [Uganda], Luxemburgian, Malay, Norwegian, Persian, Polish, Portuguese, Romanian, Russia, Ruthenian [Eastern Slavic], Serbian, Siamese, Slavonian, Slovak, Slovenian, Spanish (Castilian), Swedish, Turkish, and Wolof [Senegal, The Gambia and Mauretania].

89 Cf. Article 9.3 of the Telegraph Convention, Paris, 1865 (*supra*, n. 36) and Art. 6 of the Service Regulations of St Petersburg, 1875, *supra*, n. 62.

St Petersburg in 1875,[90] Art. 21 of the Regulations setting the maximum length of words within Europe at fifteen characters, and at ten for outside Europe. In 1885 at Berlin, Reg. Art. 8.1 defined code language as the use of words which each have an intrinsic meaning but do not form expressions intelligible to the service operators. By Reg. Arts. 8.2-3 the code had to use an approved vocabulary for codes, and consist of normal words in German, English, Spanish, French, Italian, Dutch, Portuguese or Latin, but it was competent to use words from any of these. The words selected had an individual maximum length of nine characters (Reg. Art. 8.3). Proper names could not be used as the message (Reg. Art. 8.4) and the receiving office could demand to know what vocabulary was being used in order to control any abuse of the message system (sc. the ability to refuse messages contrary to local law, morals on state security). Later, given the availability of many languages for messages,[91] an Official Vocabulary was drafted by the international Bureau, but this did not gain acceptance. The matter became more complex during and after the First World War, although the pre-War system was retained in the Paris Regulations of 1925.[92] A major consultation was held during the 1925 Paris conference and a special working-party considered the matter at Cortina d'Ampezza, Italy, in 1926. The result was reported to a Brussels conference of 1928.[93] The majority view was to move to a new classification of words and code language, while the UK alone argued for the retention of the arrangements of the Paris Regulations of 1925 which worked with a ten-letter code system.[94] The resultant amendment to the Telegraph Regulations involved a new Art. 9 which split telegrams in two categories. While it retained the definition of Art. 8.1 of the Berlin 1885 Regulations, Category A messages comprised texts of code words not exceeding ten letters but with each word including one vowel if up to five letters long, including two vowels in words of six to eight letters and at least three vowels if of nine or ten letters. There were also rules as to whether the vowels were placed in the code word. Category B messages were messages of words of no more than five letters. These categories were differently rated.[95]

90 St Petersburg Convention and Regulations, 1875, *supra*, n. 62.

91 See *supra*, n. 76 for countries and n. 88 for languages.

92 International Service Regulations annexed to the International Telegraph Convention of July 22, 1875, Paris, 29 October 1925; 57 LNTS 201; 3 Hudson 1695. *Supra*, n. 73.

93 Protocol regarding certain additions and modifications to the International Service Regulations, Brussels, 22 September 1928, 88 LNTS 347, 3 Hudson 1756. *Supra*, n. 74.

94 *Supra*, n. 73.

95 I. Stewart, 'The International Telegraph Convention of 1927 and the Problem of Code Language' (1929) 23 AJIL 292; H.S. Le Roy, 'Wrestling with the International Telegraph Code' (1929) 15 *Am. Bar Assoc. J.* 445. The matter was also considered at the Conference of the International Radio Union of 1927, but it was decided that this matter lay within the competence of the Telegraph Union rather than the Radio Union: see H.S. Le Roy, 'International Radiotelegraphic Conference' (1928) 14 *Am. Bar Assoc. J.* 86; I. Stewart, 'International Radiotelegraphic Conference of Washington' (1928) 22 AJIL 28;

Consultative Committees

As we have seen, another matter that developed through the conferences of the International Telegraph Union was the use of experts and delegates from private enterprise – whether they should be there, and what voting weight if any they might have. After the First World War more formal steps were taken to incorporate advice from such bodies. First a group from within the membership of the Union gathered in Paris in 1924 to consider long-distance telephony and discuss its particular common problems and their solution.[96] The group proceeded to form a Consultative Committee on Long-Distance Telephony[97] and this was brought into the structure of the Union the very next year at the Paris administrative conference of 1925 as the International Consulting Committee on the Telephone (CCIF).[98] Further at that Paris meeting (and virtually on the floor of the Conference) the example of the telephone initiative produced a parallel Consultative Committee on the International Telegraph (CCIT).[99] These bodies were to do significant work, and were to be easily carried over into the union of the Unions. It may be noted, however, that these new bodies were created within the relevant Service Regulations. The International Telegraph Convention itself was not amended to include or acknowledge their existence.

Cable Protection

It should not be thought that international agreements were restricted to bilateral and 'Telegraph Union' concerns. Long-distance undersea cable technology made major advances and this was subject to agreements for the laying and protection of undersea cables separate from mechanisms of the Telegraph Union *per se*. Initial agreement was reached in 1864 (one year prior to the creation of the International Telegraph Union) as to the laying of a cable between Europe and South America.[100] However, the first trans-Atlantic cable was actually laid in 1866 on the shorter route between south-west Ireland and Newfoundland

M. Davis, 'International Radiotelegraphic Conventions and Traffic Arrangements' (1930) 1 *Air L. Rev.* 349.

96 Members of the group were all from Europe, i.e. states which were telephonically connected: Austria, Belgium, Czechoslovakia, Denmark, Finland, France, Germany, Hungary, Italy, Serbia, Croatia and Slovenia, Latvia, Luxembourg, The Netherlands, Norway, Poland, Spain, Sweden, Switzerland and the UK.

97 The 'Comité consultatif international des communications téléphoniques à grande distance' (CCI).

98 Art. 72, Section S, of the Telegraph Regulations, Paris, 1925. *Supra*, n. 73.

99 Art. 87 of the Telegraph Regulations, Paris, 1925. *Supra*, n. 73.

100 Telegraph Convention for the Establishment of a Telegraph Line between Europe and South America, Paris, 16 May 1864, 128 CTS 377; Protocol regarding the interpretation of the treaty, Paris, 31 August 1869, 139 CTS 1; abrogated 20 April 1872, 144 CTS 24.

(not then part of Canada). Soon the UK and other colonial powers were busy establishing networks linking the elements of their Empire using both land and sea connections. Of course the protection of these connections was a matter of concern and gave rise to calls for a general agreement on the matter. However it was not until 1884 that a general treaty was adopted for the protection of undersea cables.[101] That said, the protection of cables was not something which required regular consideration. Suffice it to say that there is still a relevant body of law but this lies outwith the scope of the administration of the telegraph network and its later improvements.[102]

War

The protection of cable networks from damage brings up the question of the disruption of cable systems as a tactic of war, and that raises the related question of the use of cable networks in time of war. The British interception and decryption of the Zimmermann Telegram of January 1917, in which the German Ambassador to Mexico was instructed to ask Mexico to declare war on the US to prevent US entry to the European war, helped change history. Its disclosure to the US and later publication, together with the German resumption of unrestricted submarine warfare, helped bring the US into the War.[103] In fact the international telegraph agreements skated round such questions. Article 7 of the St Petersburg Convention of 1875 provided simply that the parties reserved the power to halt the transmission of all private telegrams which appeared to

101 Convention for the Protection of Submarine Cables, Paris, 14 March 1884, 163 CTS 391; (1884-5) 85 UK Parl. Papers 797 C. 5910; 75 BFSP 356; 24 Stat. 989, 25 Stat. 1424, USTS 380, 380-1, 380-2, 380-3; 11Martens (2d) 281; 2 Malloy 1949; 1 Bevans 89. See also the Declaration as to the interpretation of Arts. 2 and 4, 1 December 1886, 168 CTS 337, 77 BFSP 1140; 15 Martens (2d) 69; 2 Malloy 1856; 1 Bevans 112. The initial parties were Argentina, Austro-Hungary, Belgium, Brazil, Costa Rica, Denmark, Dominica, France, Germany, Greece, Guatemala, Italy, The Netherlands, Portugal, Romania, Russia, Salvador, Serbia, Spain, Sweden-Norway, Turkey, UK, USA and Uruguay. In addition the Convention was soon acceded to by Japan (1884), South Australia and Victoria (both 1885), Queensland (1886), Canada, Newfoundland, Cape Colony, Natal, New South Wales, Tasmania, Western Australia, New Zealand (all 1888), Tunis (1889), Czechoslovakia (1925), Danzig (1926), Poland (1935), French Morocco (1936). Among that list it is interesting to see components of the British Empire acceding individually. The (UK) Submarine Telegraph Act 1885, c. 49, which incorporates the provisions of the 1884 Convention into UK law, though partially amended over the years, is still in force.

102 See now particularly Arts. 51, 79, and 112-115 of the UN Law of the Sea Convention, Montego Bay, 10 December 1982, 1833 UNTS 3; 1999 UKTS 82, Cm. 4524; US Tr. Doc. 103–39; (1982) 21 ILM 1261.

103 B. Tuchman, *The Zimmermann Telegram* (London: Constable, 1959).

endanger state security or which might be contrary to local law, to public order or good morals. This was considered by some to allow enemy correspondence to be blocked, although it specifically referred to 'private communications', Art. 5 of the Convention having defined that term as something different from 'state communications', also there defined. Suffice it here to say that though the matter was discussed here and there by military and other authorities,[104] when war was declared the participants cut communication ties with each other, and sought to prevent the transmission of messages by the other side through the networks of neutral states.[105] Accordingly during the First World War the International Bureau had little to do. Of course there are some provisions in treaties respecting the conduct of war, but when it came down to it these were not really effective.[106]

After the First World War there was a scramble to reestablish communications links in general and in particular with and through Europe. The bulk of this work was done not through either the International Telegraph Union or its radio counterpart. Conferences were held for European concerns in Paris in 1920 and 1921.[107] Separately, a Washington conference in 1920 dealt with the broader picture, the future of international communications.[108] It was not until 1923/4 that the International Telegraph Union resumed its activities.

Finally, the Thirteenth International Telegraph Conference was convened at Madrid in 1932. This was the first diplomatic conference of the state parties to

104 Cf. Naval War College, 'International Law Situations with Solutions and Notes, (Washington USGPO, 1905) Situation VI, 'Use by Belligerents of Neutral Telegraphs' (1904) *Int. L. Stud. US Naval War Coll.* 94 and Situation VII, 'Newspaper Correspondents and Wireless Telegrams' at 105; 'Censorship of Telegrams Transmitted by Cable and Wireless', in 'Correspondence between the US and Belligerent Governments Relating to Neutral Rights and Commerce', (1915) 9 AJIL Spec. Supp., 270-313; C. Bright, 'Telegraphic Communication During War', (1918) 18 *J. Comp. Legis. & Int. L.* (n.s.) 210.

105 The UK sought to keep its interception of the Zimmerman telegram secret since it was obtained from a neutral cable, not, as I had previously thought, by a radio intercept. Disclosure of the interception would have alerted Germany to the insecurity of its international communications.

106 Cf. from a later date the Declaration for the Purpose of Establishing Similar Rules of Neutrality, Stockholm, 27 May 1938, 8 Hudson 55 (with bibliography). Denmark, Finland, Sweden and Norway had long sought neutral status. Art. 12 of the Annex prohibited to belligerents the use of wireless for war purposes while in Danish territory, distress messages and communications with Danish authorities excepted. Similar declarations were made for other parts of the Baltic region: cf. Protocol concerning a Uniform Neutrality Law, Riga, 18 November 1938, 8 Hudson 202. In retrospect it all seems rather futile.

107 Codding I, 33-4. The conferences were: the International Conference on Postal, Railway, Telegraphic, Telephonic and Radiotelegraphic Communications, Paris, 1920, attended by twenty-one European nations, and the International Telegraphic Conference, Paris, 1921, attended by eight Eastern-European states.

108 The Preliminary Conference of the International Communications Conference, Washington DC, 1920: Codding I, 111-2. See also Chapter 3, at n. 68.

the Telegraph Union since that of St Petersburg in 1865, two-thirds of a century earlier. At the same time the Radio-telegraph Union held its plenipotentiary Conference. Both Unions carried out their respective revisions of their Service Regulations, but overshadowing that was the understanding that the two Unions were going to be brought together. This duly happened. The outcome was the International Telecommunication Union.[109]

109 Telecommunication Convention, General Radio Regulations, Additional Radio Regulations, Additional Protocol (European), Telegraph Regulations and Telephone Regulations, Madrid, 9 December 1932; 151 LNTS 4; 49 Stat. 2391, TS 867; 6 Hudson 109; 3 Bevans 65. See http://www.itu.int/en/history/plenipotentiaryconferences/Pages/1932 Madrid.aspx.

Chapter 3
The International Radio Union

The invention of wire-less communication through the use of the 'radio' portion of the electromagnetic spectrum came late in the nineteenth century. In its various manifestations radio has transformed society through general broadcasting services, the telecommunication of messages between individual receivers, and through other forms of data transfer. Wire or cable – particularly now, optical cabling – remain major telecommunication carriers, but the advantage of the new technology was and is that it avoids the problems of the cable. However it had its own problems. Many developed their own systems, and the scene was set for much dispute both legal and practical.

When wireless telecommunication came on the scene those who had invested considerable sums in 'wired' systems were less than pleased, and did not welcome a competitor. As a result 'wireless' communications companies found the main initial niche for their services in the one environment in which wired service could not be provided, ship-to-ship and ship-to-shore communications. The naval military interest was, naturally, significant, although not exclusive of the civilian.[1] The Marconi system proved to be the most successful of all at least in European waters, although other manufacturers and systems also provided facilities.[2]

The Marconi Company was incorporated in the UK as the Marconi Wireless Telegraph Company in 1897.[3] In a short time the Company established a near-monopoly in inter-ship and ship-to-shore communications, placing land stations along major shipping arteries. In an attempt to consolidate that monopoly the Marconi Company generally refused to communicate or receive from radio stations operating other systems. This inhibited the commercial development of the other radio systems which, thus restricted in their potential, were rendered less obvious as a choice for adoption by shipping companies. The Marconi 'rule' also had effects on the more important question of 'safety of life at sea'.

---

1 H.E. Hancock, *Wireless at Sea: The First Fifty Years* (Chelmsford UK: Marconi Co., 1950); T.H. White, 'Period Overview', *United States Early Radio History*: http://earlyradiohistory.us/sec001.htm; 'Radio at Sea (1891-1916)', http://earlyradiohistory.us/sec005.htm.

2 Marconi also had a foothold in Italy, leading to that country having to defer the application of certain parts of the first Radiotelegraphic Convention (*infra* n. 16) until it had regularised its contractual relations with the Marconi Company. See Art. XI of the Final Protocol.

3 W.J. Baker, *A History of the Marconi Company* (London: Methuen, 1970); F. Donaldson, *The Marconi Scandal* (London: Hart Davies, 1962).

Complaints proliferated. France complained that the Marconi system stations had rendered some of the radio stations on its north coast partially ineffective by its unwillingness to communicate with them, and the US complained that a Marconi-equipped ship had refused to answer radioed queries as to the position of a derelict in the shipping lanes.[4] However it was the mundane refusal of a Marconi station to accept a message that produced the first real steps towards the international regulation of radio. A Prince took umbrage.

The Preliminary Conference on Wireless Telegraphy, Berlin, 1903

It is said that the final trigger for the creation of the International Radio Union[5] was offence given to (or taken by) Heinrich, the then Crown Prince of Germany and brother to Kaiser Wilhelm in March 1902.[6] Heinrich had been entertained 'royally' in the US by President (Teddy) Roosevelt and others and journeyed home on the German registered S.S. *Deutschland.* As the ship travelled along the English Channel it came within range of the English coastal Marconi radio stations. Heinrich decided he wanted to send various telegrams. Some were intended for his *quondam* hosts thanking them for their hospitality, and others forward to his destination. The messages were received by the Marconi land stations and could have been channelled into the relevant wire services.[7] However, the Marconi stations refused to process them because they originated from a rival radio system.[8] The *Deutschland* operated the 'Slaby-d'Arco' (Telefunken) apparatus marketed by the German 'Algemeine Electricitäts Gesellschaft'. Apart from its general rule as to non-correspondence with other systems, it seems that this incident may also have been aggravated by the fact that the Marconi Company considered that the Slaby-d'Arco system was based without appropriate permission on Marconi intellectual property.[9]

4 Tomlinson, 22.

5 Technically the name 'International Radio Union' is incorrect since the 'Union' never formally existed, but it is convenient to use the term. See also *infra* n. 17.

6 The following narrative differs slightly from that in my *Law and Space Telecommunications* (Aldershot, UK: Dartmouth, 1989). I have found out more.

7 The Marconi land stations would accept emergency communications, but refused ordinary correspondence sent from rival systems.

8 The '*Deutschland* Incident, 1902'. See W. Blades, 'Mr Marconi and His Critics', *Electrical World and Engineer*, 12 April 1902, 656-658: http://earlyradiohistory.us/1902ew.htm. There is a later 'Deutschland Incident' of 1937 during the Spanish Civil War when a German pocket battleship of that name was bombed by planes of the Republican Air Force while in Ibiza.

9 Adolph Slaby, a Professor at the Technical University in Berlin, together with his then assistant, Georg von Arco, had taken part in Marconi experiments at the English Channel in the 1890s. Back in Germany they continued to experiment and developed their

The German government decided that such difficulties had to be sorted out and therefore called a Preliminary Conference to identify the principal problems of radio and the possible international regulation of the new facility with a view to a later binding international instrument. The Conference met in Berlin in 1903.[10] Nine countries attended.[11] The result was a Final Protocol.[12] This identified a variety of matters requiring international attention, decisions on which should form the basis of a convention to regulate radio communication. Many of these elements remain basic to the current regulations. Thus all radio stations engaged in communication (as opposed to broadcasting) should accept messages from all other stations irrespective of the equipment used, and tariffs should be internationally agreed. The most important of the Conference recommendations was identified on the initiative of M. Bonomo, the Italian delegate – the question of interference. Bonomo argued the need for all countries to join in an international plan to ensure that there would be no overlapping of frequency use, either because of the utilisation of similar or overlapping wavelengths, or through the employment of excessive power by one radio station which would thus monopolise the frequency on which it was operating.[13] The Conference was persuaded, and Art. V of the Final Protocol stated:

> The service of operating wireless telegraph stations should be organised as far as possible in a manner not to interfere with the service of other stations.

In these few words, and the insights of M. Bonomo, are the justification of the fundamental ITU procedures that still regulate the use of the radio spectrum at the international level.

---

own system. The Slaby-d'Arco system used inductive antennae rather than the spark-gap antennae employed by Marconi.

10 M. Davis, 'International Radiotelegraph Conventions and Traffic Arrangements' (1930) 1 *Air L. Rev.* 349. One month prior to the Berlin Conference the Institute of International Law had met at Ghent, but their draft 'project', though sensible with regard to aviation, did not advance radio law: see 'Project drafted by the Institute of International Law for the Regulation of Aerostats and wireless telegraphy' (1906) *Ann. de l'Inst. de Dr. Int.*, 327, translated (1913) 7 AJIL Supp. 147.

11 Austro-Hungary, France, Germany, Italy, Spain, Russia, the UK and the US. A photograph of the participants in the 1903 Conference in the ITU archives is available at http://www.itu.int/ITU-R/information/promotion/100-years/almanac/1903-2.html.

12 Preliminary Conference at Berlin on Wireless Telegraphy, Procés Verbaux and Protocole Finale (UK) (1903) Cd. 1832, (1904) UK State Papers, vol. CXX; 97 BFSP 467; 194 CTS 46; 33 Martens (2d) 471. The Final Protocol is also available at http://earlyradiohistory.us/1903conv.htm.

13 See 'Memoir', Procés Verbaux, *supra*, n. 12, at 54. Cf. *infra* at n. 32.

The International Radio Telegraph Convention, Berlin, 1906

Three years later and again in Berlin, the results of the 1903 Preliminary Conference were considered by a much enlarged group.[14] Twenty-seven states were represented including from the Americas additional to the US, as well as Japan from the Far East, demonstrating the world-wide interest that had been aroused.[15] The resultant International Radiotelegraph Convention, together with its Supplementary Agreement, Final Protocol and Service Regulations, contain principles which remain basic to the regulation of the use of radio.[16] The setting aside of frequencies identified for particular purposes (allocation to services), the minimising of interference through the use of the minimum power needed to pass a message to an intended recipient, and that the best available technology should be employed as soon as possible, are all found in the Berlin arrangements of 1906. From the Telegraph the conference took over into the world of wireless various standardisation measures – standardisation being an important aspect of the responsibilities of the modern ITU. Such measures are lineally and intellectually the direct ascendants of principles and mechanisms still operated by the ITU in its radio responsibilities. Again the distinction made between the Convention and the Service Regulations, which are stated to be supplementary but are of the same force as the Convention (Art. 11.1), copied the method of the International Telegraph Union and is a device still found in modern ITU documentation. Less importantly,

14 Davis, *supra*, n. 10, 351-6; Tomlinson, 17-27. The 1903 Preliminary Conference had scheduled its successor for 1904, but the outbreak of the Russo-Japanese War of 1904-5 caused a delay. Both Russia and Japan were interested parties in the Berlin process. See Tomlinson, 17.

15 Germany, Argentina, Austria, Hungary, Belgium, Brazil, Bulgaria, Chile, Denmark, France, Greece, Italy, Japan, Mexico, Monaco, The Netherlands, Norway, Persia, Portugal, Romania, Russia, Spain, Sweden, Turkey, Uruguay, the UK and the US.

16 Radio-telegraphic Convention, Final Protocol and Regulations, signed at Berlin, 3 November 1906, 1909 UKTS 8, Cd. 4559; 99 BFSP 321 and 333; (1906) UK Parl. Papers, HC 368, (1906) UK State Papers, vol. CXXXVIX; and http://earlyradiohistory.us/1906conv.htm. The Convention and Final Protocol (but not the Service Regulations) are at 203 CTS 101; 99 BFSP 321; (US) 37 Stat. 15665, TS 568; (1906) 3 AJIL Supp. 330-40; (1923) 3 Malloy 2889; 1 Bevans 556. A version of the 1906 Convention and the Service Regulations together with 'Propositions for the [subsequent] International Radio Telegraph Conference of London' [held in 1912] intercalated with the text is in the ITU archives at http://www.itu.int/ITU-R/information/promotion/100-years/documents/1906-Berlin-E.pdf, and in a US Navy document of 1912, USGPO 1912, available at http://ia341019.us.archive.org/0/items/internationalrad00interich/internationalrad00interich.pdf. The US did not proclaim (apply) the 1906 arrangements until May 1912. The US version of the 1906 Radio Regulations published by the US Department of Commerce is *Regulations Governing Radio Communication* (US GPO, 1912) at http://earlyradiohistory.us/1912reg.htm.

from the Berlin documents may be traced the present common nomenclature for the facility – 'radio' as opposed to 'wireless'.[17]

As in the Telegraph Conferences, the voting weight of participants at the Berlin conference proved a difficulty, but the example of the telegraph was followed *ad interim*, with real decisions postponed to the negotiated text.

The 1906 Convention established mechanisms through which radio matters might be arranged internationally, but did not formally constitute an official body for the purpose. Although it has become customary to refer to the 'International Radio Union', technically that is an error because a formal body was not constituted for the purpose, but *communis error facit ius* (sc. 'a generally accepted error becomes law'). Instead Art. 11.2 simply provided that the Convention and the annexed Service Regulations:

> may at any time be modified by the High Contracting Parties by common consent. Conferences of plenipotentiaries or simple administrative conferences, according as the Convention or Service Regulations are affected, shall take place from time to time; each conference shall fix the time and place of the next meeting.

This mirrored the usage of the International Telegraph Union, but was not to persist.

Two things may be noted about the radio process. First, in 1906 a distinction was made between the revision of the Convention and of the Service Regulations, administrative conferences being used for the latter (Art. 11.1). The distinction between formal plenipotentiary conferences to revise the Convention (and now the Constitution as well) and administrative conferences for other purposes is preserved in the modern arrangements. However, all conferences of the Radio Union were plenipotentiary in character and indeed the option of administrative conferences amending the Regulations was to be dropped in 1912. Radio required plenipotentiaries to meet. Second, although Art. 11.2 provided for revision conferences to set the date and place of their successors, the Berlin conference did not designate its successor. In fact no regular schedule was ever created for the calling of revising conferences and no practice developed by which one conference would set a date and place (or host) for its successor to be convened. This led to the intervals between radio conferences becoming very variable and occasionally long, albeit the effects of war have to be considered. Indeed, it was not until the

17 The title of the French (official) text of the Convention is 'Convention Radiotélégraphique Internationale' – giving rise to 'radio'. 'Télégraphie sans fil' (without wire) would have translated as 'wireless telegraphy'. The unofficial English text is entitled the 'International Wireless Telegraph Convention'. 'Radio' appears *simpliciter* in the text of Arts 2, 7, 8 and 9. 'Wireless' has remained an alternative to 'radio' in English speaking countries. Its use is fading although 'wifi' (a wireless radio system providing a local area network) preserves its linguistic root.

revisions of 1992/4 that a regular four-year rolling programme was instituted for ITU plenipotentiary conferences, with regular administrative conferences and other meetings being fitted into that cycle.

While no formal institution was set up for radio it was recognised that some sort of central office was needed through which much necessary documentation could be accumulated, processed and circulated. Accordingly Conv. Art. 13 and Service Regulations XXXVII-XXXVIII provided for an International Bureau to be charged with such duties, some of the data it was expected to amass and circulate being specified in Regulation IV.[18] The expenses of running the Bureau were to be shared between the contracting states (Art. 13.2). However the 'International Radio Union' never did establish its own 'International Bureau' and instead made use of the existing International Bureau of the International Telegraph Union (Art. 13.1; Reg. XXXVII.1).[19] The expenses to be incurred by the Bureau additional to its 'telegraph' duties were capped at 40,000 francs per year (Reg. XXXVII.2). This sum was the responsibility of the governments contracting as to radio, each contributing in the same proportions as their respective contributions under the Regulations of the International Telegraph Union (Reg. XXXVII.3). Mimicking the telegraph arrangements, prior to later conferences each party was to inform the Bureau of the class of contribution it was intending to make (Reg. XXXVII.3).[20]

Reflecting the original circumstances and the discussions that had led up to it, the Berlin Radio Convention was mainly concerned with maritime communications, whether ship-to-ship or ship-to-shore. The new medium was being used for purposes ranging from navigation information and indications of the expected time of arrival of cargo, to ordinary correspondence. The fundamental was that what was offered was a communication service whose providers (if commercial entities) sought to run their businesses at a profit, and (if governmental agencies) sought to recoup their costs. Accordingly, Conv. Art. 10 provided for a system of charges and rates, while Regulations XII-XIV set out those rates and how they were to be collected. By this time, of course, wired telegraphy had an extensive set of rules for the calculation of charges for communications through the cable network. For radiotelegraphy Berlin Art. 10 therefore provided that the 'sea' section of a communication was to be charged a fee for the coast station plus a fee for the ship station involved, the relevant government setting each. Any 'land'

18 The data included that provided by states in terms of Conv. Art. 6: see *infra* n. 27.

19 See Chapter 2, at n.53. The consent of the Swiss government which was supervisor of the International Bureau of the Telegraph Union and that of that Telegraph Union itself were required for this arrangement. Given the commonality of membership between both Unions, that permission was easily obtained.

20 In the International Telegraph Union contributions were made by the selection of a class of contribution units. These classes were: Class 1, 25 units; Class 2, 20 units; Class 3, 15 units; Class 4, 10 units, Class 5, 5 units and Class 6, 3 units. The value of each unit was calculated by dividing the total number of units subscribed into the budget figure. See Chapter 2 at n. 55.

section was charged as for wired telegraphy. Charges were based on a word-count, and were to provide an equitable return for the service. However, they were not to exceed a maximum agreed between the parties.[21] Thereafter the usual rules for the use of the particular wired connection applied. In the case of inter-country transmissions parties were to charge the same as for telegraphic communications by land lines. Berlin Regulation XXXV dealt with rebates and refunds and Reg. XXXVI covered accounts and their settlement.[22] By Reg. XLI, in the absence of special agreement between the relevant governments the rate-setting, accounting and other provisions of the Convention and Regulations were applicable to ship-to-ship communications.

It was, of course, necessary to define which radio stations were covered by the new provisions. Stations not close to the sea were not at this time of interest since their transmitting power was low and broadcasting was not an active possibility since reception sets were bulky and expensive. Convention Art. 2 appropriately defined 'coastal stations' and 'stations on ship-board', while Art. 1 bound the High Contracting Parties themselves to apply the provisions to their own coastal and ship-board stations and to impose its requirements on any relevant private enterprises which they might authorise.[23] With a limited exception,[24] coastal and ship stations were required to exchange messages without distinction as to the radio system used (Art. 3)[25] and the Parties bound themselves either to connect their coastal stations with the land-based telegraph network or 'at least' to take suitable measures to secure a rapid exchange between a coastal station and the telegraph network (Art. 5). However, a clear duty as to the exchange of messages between ships (as opposed to ship/shore communications) was reserved to a Supplementary Agreement, an agreement to which at that stage not all Parties were willing to subscribe.[26] Parties were to inform each other of the names of their coastal and ship-board stations and to provide the data needed to facilitate

21 A higher charge could be made for transmissions in excess of 800 km.

22 Under Reg. XXXVI it remained competent for governments to agree their own arrangements on such questions *inter se*.

23 Article 19 bound the parties 'to take or propose to their respective legislatures' the measures needed to give effect to the Convention and Regulations – an intriguing formulation of the duty. However, not all parties were willing to extend Art. 1 to their ships. See *infra* n. 26.

24 By Art. 4 a station might be 'reserved for a limited public service determined by the object of the correspondence or by other circumstances' but this was to be independent of the radio system being used.

25 This had been a proposal of the 1903 Conference: see *supra*, following n. 12. In anticipation of international agreement the UK took powers by the Wireless Telegraphy Act 1904 to enforce this obligation both territorially and for UK ships beyond its territorial waters. 'Intercommunication' is now required by Art. 11 (501-503) of the ITU Convention.

26 An 'Additional Engagement' annexed to the Convention provided for a duty that Art. 1 be applied to all stations of a state including ships (Art. I) and for other states later to be allowed to adhere to the Convention on demand. Great Britain, Italy, Japan, Mexico,

the exchange of messages (Art. 6).[27] Notwithstanding, in the case of stations for 'special radio communication' (presumably military and state) only the name was required to be published (Art. 7).[28] That maritime communications were in mind was made clear through a duty to give 'absolute priority' to messages of distress and to take any necessary action (Art. 9), a duty repeated in Reg. XVI of the Service Regulations.[29] The well-known 'SOS' signal in Morse Code (··· - - - ···) was set as the distress signal by Reg. XVI, supplanting the Marconi 'CQD' which had been adopted only two years earlier.[30]

While the initial thrust of the 1906 Convention was directed towards the operation of coastal radio stations, it was obvious from an early stage that the principles it adopted could be of general application irrespective of the site of the station. What was and is important is the range of the transmissions of a radio station and the possibility/probability of its signals interfering with those of others. Such matters are clearly dealt with in various parts of the agreed texts.

Article 8 of the Convention repeated Art. V of the recommendations of the 1903 Conference, but converted that recommendation into a duty:

> The service of operating wireless telegraph stations shall be organised, as far as possible, in such a manner not to interfere with the service of other stations.

Persia and Portugal did not sign this Additional Engagement (99 BFSP 327). The UK signed and ratified in 1912.

27 Regs. IV, XXXVIII and its Supplement required the notification in respect of each coastal station of its name, nationality, geographic location, call letters, normal range, radio system, the class of receiving apparatus, wave lengths employed with the main one indicated, the nature of the service provided, hours of opening, and the rate for its use including the minimum rate for messages. For ship-board stations the requirements were for name, nationality, distinguishing signal of the international code of signals, home port, call letters, normal range (distinguishing between war and merchant vessels), the radio system, the receiving apparatus, wavelengths utilised, nature of service provided, hours of operation, and shipboard rate, including the minimum rate for messages. In addition for both coastal and ship stations additional remarks might be given. The 'International Bureau' was to gather and publicise this information.

28 Cf. the exempt status still afforded to military communications in the current ITU agreements. See *infra* Chapter 5 at n.22. A military station engaged in public correspondence was required to comply with the general rules as to transmissions and rates (Art. 21.2).

29 Art. 21.1 of the Convention required military stations to comply with this duty. That priority should be given to distress messages unless practically impossible was stated by Art. IV of the 1903 Berlin Preliminary Conference (*supra*, n. 11).

30 The Morse International Code was adopted as standard by Reg. XV. See also *infra* n. 35. It is said that Marconi operators continued to use 'CQD' for a number of years thereafter. See also N. McEwen, '"SOS", "CQD" and the History of Maritime Distress Calls' (1997/9) 2 *The Telegraph Office Magazine*, at http://www.telegraph-office.com/pages/arc2-2.html.

Building upon that general principle (which also applied to military radio stations (Art. 21)), the Berlin arrangements laid down rules and procedures to regulate specific problem areas. Service Reg. VI.1 provided for each ship-board station to be licensed by its national government, which, as we have seen, was required to ensure that the international rules were complied with by Convention Art. 1.

The notion that specific wave-bands should be set aside for specified services (allocation to services) is clear in the Regulations. Regulation II designated the 300 metre (1000 Kc/s) and 600 metre (500 Kc/s) wavelengths for use in general public correspondence, and long distance communication and coastal stations were required to use them.[31] However, governments might authorise coastal stations to use other wave-bands for long distance service or any service other than general public correspondence provided that the wavelengths employed were either under 600 metres (500 Kc/s) or above 1600 metres (below 185 Kc/s). Regulation III.1 allocated the 300 metre (1000 Kc/s) wavelength to all ships carrying equipment capable of transmitting on that wave-band. Ships might use other wavelengths, but these might not exceed 600 metres. The equipment required was, however, in those days bulky. Accordingly Reg. III.2 allowed ships too small to carry such equipment to use wavelengths lower than 300 metres (1000 Kc/s) but nothing higher than that. Special services other than general correspondence were available only to coastal radio stations and these had to be transmitted at under 300 or over 600 metres thus avoiding interference with the signals carried on those wave-bands.

Interference might, of course, still occur, and special provision was made to reduce, avoid or to stop such.[32] Regulation V prohibited the emission of superfluous signals and allowed equipment trials and operator practice only in so far as no interference was caused to stations in normal use. Ship stations were to transmit at not more than 1 kilowatt power unless the intended recipient was more than 300 km away or there were particular obstructions to be overcome. In any event Reg. XXVIII required radio stations to exchange signal traffic with the minimum power needed for effective communication. Regulation XIX dealt with interference being caused to transmissions already in progress. The general rule was that it was for the ship to call the shore and a ship station had to adjust its receiver to its highest degree of sensitivity before transmitting, and, prior to transmission, make sure that the coastal station was not already communicating with another receiver. If it were, the 'new' ship station had to wait for a pause, thus again ensuring that interference was minimised. If, despite all this, interference occurred then the coast station could require the newcomer to cease transmission

31 Metres refers to the distance between the peaks in the radio wave. Kilohertz (Kc/s) refers to the number of cycles per second with which the wave is propagated. The shorter frequencies are denominated in megahertz (MHz) and gigahertz (GHz). See Appendix I.

32 Reference point *supra*, n. 13.

while indicating how long the newcomer on the frequency should wait before renewing its call.[33]

As far as technology was concerned, Reg. I allowed coastal and ship stations a free choice of system so long as it was syntonised (Reg. VI.2).[34] Regulation I further required systems to 'keep pace with scientific and technical progress' so far as possible, a provision which advances in technology have made of continuing importance down through the years. Additional to the apparatus, the abilities of the radio operator were also relevant. Regulation VI.3 required operators to be licensed by the national state of the ship, and to be competent in adjusting the apparatus. Station operators had to be able to handle at least 20 words (not exceeding 5 letters) a minute, contributing to the minimisation of the use of the frequency employed. Call-up, acknowledgment and termination protocols were set out in the Service Regulations, notably Regs. XVII-XXIX, and the operators had to have a thorough knowledge of all such matters (Reg. VI.3.c). Correlatively, the Morse International Code was adopted as the general mode of communication of radiotelegraphy under the Convention (Reg. XV).[35]

The 1906 Convention and Regulations therefore dealt with the allocation of particular frequencies to identified services, took account of interference, required the minimising of signal power, and established protocols for communication procedures. Albeit these were at this stage only for maritime communications – ship-to-ship or ship-to-shore – these basic principles remain among those fundamental to the operation of the ITU system as to the operation of radio today.[36]

In other matters the arrangements for the wired telegraph provided more than a model. By Berlin Convention Art. 17 a number of Articles of the 1875 St Petersburg Telegraph Convention were declared directly applicable to 'international radio telegraphy',[37] and Reg. XLII made the International Telegraph Regulations

---

33 If there were a number of incoming calls it was for the coastal station to determine the order in which they were dealt with (Reg. XXIII). The main criterion was the facilitating of the maximum number of messages, so garrulity was prevented from monopolising a frequency.

34 Sc. capable of allowing two circuits to operate on the same frequency.

35 Reference point *supra*, n. 30.

36 See generally *infra* 'Radiocommunication'.

37 *Seriatim* the tenor of the Articles incorporated from the St Petersburg Convention comprised the following: the right of all persons to correspond by international telegraph (Art. 1); the secrecy and safe transmission of messages (Art. 2); the Convention parties did not accept responsibility for the international service (Art. 3); the categorisation of telegrams into state, service and private telegrams, state telegrams having precedence (Art. 5); secret language might be used, and countries that prohibited secret language or encryption within their territories nonetheless had to allow the transit of such coded messages (Art. 6); the right of a state to stop messages dangerous to its safety, otherwise unlawful, or in breach of public order or good morals (Art. 7); the right of a state to suspend transmission services wholly or partially, permanently or for a period, should it deem such suspension necessary (Art. 8), except for the duty to transmit service telegrams originating

'analogously' applicable 'in so far as they [were] not contrary to the provisions of' the new wireless regulations.[38] Of the rules thus incorporated, of particular importance to all telegraphic communications of the time was the duty under St Petersburg Art. 2 relating to the secrecy of correspondence. The St Petersburg rule existed because the transmission of a telegraph message then required the intervention of human operators. That they should not reveal the contents of the messages they passed between them was essential for the wired services of 1875, and was relatively easily secured.[39] However, the radio signals used by the new communications could be intercepted by anyone. Secrecy was therefore highly important for the radiotelegraph services. Indeed secrecy remains provided for under current ITU rules.[40]

Of course it had to be recognised that the application of the various rules, regulations and procedures might lead to dispute and allegations of contravention. By Reg. VII it was for the management of the telegraph service of a country to take action as to infractions committed by any station over which it had jurisdiction, including, in the case of repeated contraventions, the withdrawal of an operating licence. Beyond such 'internal' action it was in the first instance for the administrations of two countries to resolve a dispute, which failing, at the request of either, Art. 18 of the Convention provided an arbitral process. This was also the final mode of settlement of disputes between countries as to the interpretation or execution of the Convention or Regulations.[41] The parties otherwise preserved

---

from all parties (Art. 11); the duty to render accounts between parties (Art. 12); and the reservation of the ability of states to enter into separate agreements *inter se* in relation to service matters that did not affect parties generally (Art. 17).

38 The provision as to the applicability of the Telegraph Regulations did not specify which version was to be used, with the implication that revised versions of those regulations became applicable to radio when they came into force for the wired service.

39 Secrecy was a principle of the wired services. See Art 5 of the International Telegraph Convention, Paris, 17 May 1865, 130 CTS 198; 56 BFSP 295, repeated in Art. V of the International Telegraph Convention and Regulations, Rome, 14 January 1872, 143 CTS 411; 66 BFSP 975; and in Art. 2 and Reg. 2 of the related Regulations of the then ruling International Telegraph Convention, St Petersburg, 22 July 1875, 148 CTS 416; 66 BFSP 19; 3 Martens (2d) 614; 57 LNTS 201; (1913) AJIL Supp. 276.

40 Cf. Art. 17 of the 1912 Convention, *infra* n. 45, mirroring 1906 Art. 17; Art. 5 1927 Convention, *infra* n. 70, where the duty is expressed as it is in Art. 24, Madrid Convention, 1932, *infra* n. 93, in Art. 32 of the post-war International Convention on Telecommunications, Atlantic City, 1947; 193 UNTS 191; 1950 UKTS 76, Cmd. 8124; 148 BFSP 684; 63 Stat. 1399, TIAS 1901, and Art. 37 (184-5) of the current ITU Constitution.

41 Each country involved could choose as an arbiter a country not involved in the dispute. In the event of a tied vote of arbiters they might agree on yet another disinterested country to settle the matter, failing which each would nominate such a country and the determination of which was to serve was made by lot, chosen by the country where the International Bureau was situated (i.e. Switzerland). It is not clear from the documents whether the disputants, whether a service manager or a state, could actually select an individual to act as arbiter, or only a country to supply an arbiter.

'their entire liberty as' to 'wireless telegraph installations other than provided for in Art. 1, especially naval and military installations'. These were subject only to the obligations in Art. 8 in respect of non-interference, and Art. 9 as to distress calls from ships. However, when engaged in 'general service' military radio stations were to comply with the Berlin Regulations in respect of their modes of transmission and rates charged (Art. 21).

As indicated, Art. 11 provided that the Convention and Regulations might be amended by common consent of the parties. However, that article also allowed for conferences of plenipotentiaries or simple administrative conference respectively to amend the Convention or Regulations.[42] In such conferences each country had one vote (Art. 12.2). Mimicking the equivalent provisions of the Telegraph Union, if a country adhered to the Convention in respect of its colonies, possessions and/or protectorates, later conferences might consider such to be separate entities and allow it additional votes, up to a maximum of six (Art. 12.3).[43]

Article 22 provided that the Convention and the Regulations would go into effect simultaneously as between their ratifiers, and it and Reg. XLII set that date as 1 July 1908. Both Convention and Regulations were to remain in force indefinitely but a party might withdraw on one year's notice, such a withdrawal, however, not affecting the other Contracting powers (Art. 22.2). Other states might accede to the Convention on demand but were as far as possible to accept all the provisions of the Convention to the fullest extent (Art. 16).

In the immediate future agreements reached in other international bodies were to have something to say about radio – mainly as to its use in war – but these are not relevant for this book and need not detain us.[44]

---

42 As indicated earlier, notwithstanding this provision, all conferences of the Radio Union were plenipotentiary conferences.

43 The question of whether and if so what weight should be given in international deliberations to the voting power of colonial powers in respect of their 'territories' was increasingly debated in the early 1900s. See D.P. Myers, 'Representation in Public International Bodies' (1914) 8 AJIL 81 and materials there cited (Art. 12 of the 1906 Convention is one example noted). See also R. Lansing, 'Notes on Sovereignty in a State' (1906) 1 AJIL 105-28 and 297-320; P.S. Reinsch, 'International Unions and their Administration (1907) 1 AJIL 579-623 (in which the Telegraph and Radio Unions as well as the UPU are discussed in the section 'Communications' at 582-9); and his 'International Administrative Law and National Sovereignty' (1909) 3 AJIL 1; B. Azkin, 'Membership in the Universal Postal Union' 1933 27 AJIL 651. Cf. W.J. Aceves, 'Critical Jurisprudence and International Legal Scholarship: A Study on Equitable Distribution' (2001) 39 *Col. J. Transnat. L.* 299-394.

44 Stewart, *infra* n. 70, at n. 5 lists among these: the Convention respecting the Rights and Duties of Neutral Powers and Persons in War on Land (1907); the Convention for the Adaption to Naval War of the Principles of the Geneva Convention (1907), http://www.history.navy.mil/library/online/law.appenda.htm; the Convention concerning the Rights and Duties of Neutral Powers in Naval War (1907): http://www.history.navy.mil/library/online/law.appendb.htm; and the (unratified) Declaration of London (1909). Cf. the 'Draft

The International Radiotelegraph Convention, London, 1912

The next international radio conference was held in London from 15 June to 5 July 1912.[45] Wisely the participants at the 1906 Berlin conference did not consider that they had said the final word on radio matters. Indeed, Berlin Convention Art. 11 had provided for its amendment 'at any time' by conferences to be held 'from time to time'. In the following five years radio developed, and its potential had become increasingly appreciated. That is evident from the number and the varied nature of the participants in the London Conference.[46] Two stories had made the general public aware of the potential of radio. First, there was the crucial role of radio in the arrest, trial and execution of Dr Hawley H. Crippen in 1910.[47] Second, the

---

International Convention on Aerial Navigation', Paris 1910, Appendix to the Report of the (UK) Civil Aerial Transport Committee, 1918, 1918 UKSP Vol. V, 17, Cd. 9218: http://www.bopcris.ac.uk/imgall/ref8301_1_1.html.

45 Codding I, 102-8; Tomlinson, 27-44.

46 The Preamble to the 1912 Convention lists as its parties: Germany and the German Protectorates, the United States of America and the Possessions of the United States of America, the Argentine Republic, Austria, Hungary, Bosnia-Herzegovina, Belgium, the Belgian Congo, Brazil, Bulgaria, Chile, Denmark, Egypt, Spain and the Spanish Colonies, France and Algeria, French West Africa, French Equatorial Africa, Indo-China, Madagascar, Tunis, Great Britain and the various British Colonies and Protectorates, the Union of South Africa, the Australian Federation, Canada, British India, New Zealand, Greece, Italy and the Italian Colonies, Japan and Chosen (sc. Korea), Formosa, Japanese Sakhalin and the leased territory of Kwantung, Morocco, Monaco, Norway, The Netherlands, the Dutch Indies and the Colony of Curacao, Persia, Portugal and the Portuguese Colonies, Romania, Russia and the Russian Possessions and Protectorates, The Republic of San Marino, Siam, Sweden, Turkey, and Uruguay. There is room for a study of these named participants in the light of contemporary and later history. Cf. the argument as to voting *infra* at n. 53, and at Washington in 1927, *infra* n. 72.

47 Hawley Harvey Crippen (1862-1910), wanted in London for the murder of his wife, was identified as being on board the SS *Montrose* en route from Antwerp to Canada. Police, warned by a radio message by the Captain of the *Montrose*, were able to cross the Atlantic from Liverpool on a faster ship, the SS *Laurentic*, and going on board with the local pilot as the *Montrose* was proceeding up the St Laurence arrested the fugitive and Ethel Le Neve, his former assistant. Crippen and Le Neve were returned to England. A trial found Crippen guilty but Le Neve not guilty of murder. He was hanged in November 1910. Had the fugitives made for the US rather than Canada (a British Dominion) they might have evaded capture and certainly international extradition proceedings would have been required. It seems that the *Montrose* was the first ship available to them. The case still evokes interest. Recently, some have sought to cast doubt on the validity of the guilty verdict but on 7 December 2009 the (English) Criminal Cases Review Commission (http://www.ccrc.gov.uk) refused the request of a distant US relative of Crippen to refer the case back to the Court of Appeal: http://news.bbc.co.uk/1/hi/uk/8400142.stm. However, in January 2011 DNA evidence indicated that the body found in the basement of Crippen's house was that of a male, and hence not that of his wife.

loss of the RMS *Titanic* in 1912 only two months before the London Conference convened underscored the potential role of radio in safety of life at sea.[48]

General 'broadcasting' services still lay in the future when the London Conference was agreed to be held. In 1912 radio was a convenient method of passing telegraph messages between points not physically linked by cable. International opinion still considered maritime communications to be the primary role for radio. Personnel from the US Navy formed most of the US delegation, and for their aid the Navy Department produced a fascinating document which intercalated the 1906 texts with the various proposals for their amendment and improvement together with 'reasons' where their proposers had given them. Published by the US Government Printing Office in 1912, this document runs to 114 pages.[49] By contrast the US GPO version of the 1906 Convention and Regulations which was published in 1907 runs to only 42 pages.[50] Notwithstanding, at London many proposals were made for the improvement of the regulation of radio and for controlling other possible future uses of the new medium.[51] The result was a Convention and Service Regulations which, with some innovation, in many ways mirrored their predecessors.[52] As before, the interdependence and

---

According to Wikipedia, E. Larsen *Thunderstruck* (New York: Doubleday, 2006) interweaves the stories of Crippen and Marconi. The memoirs of the arresting officer, Walter Dew, *I caught Crippen: Memoirs of ex-Chief Inspector Walter Dew, C.I.D., of Scotland Yard* (London: Blackie, 1938) show the arrest of Crippen as the high point of his career, and a marketing asset for his book.

48 *UK Shipping Casualties (Loss of the Steamship "Titanic"): Report of a Formal Investigation into the circumstances surrounding the foundering on 15th April 1912 of the British Steamship "Titanic" of Liverpool, after striking ice in or near Latitude 41º 46' N., Longitude 50º 14' W., North Atlantic Ocean, whereby loss of life ensued*, (191213) 76 BFSP, Cd. 6352. 1517 people, some two thirds of the passengers and crew on board, died. The survivors were rescued by the SS *Carpathia* which picked up a distress call by radio. There was much dispute whether the SS *Californian*, which was nearer to the *Titanic*, should have switched on its radio after rockets were seen. The *Californian* had by radio previously warned the *Titanic* of pack-ice, and had itself hove to to wait out the hours of darkness. There are many books on the subject. See W. Lord, *A Night to Remember* (1955, various eds), although the investigations of Ballard have shown some of its data as to the break-up of the ship to be erroneous.

49 As indicated (*supra*, n. 16) the 1906 Convention and the Service Regulations together with 'Propositions for the International Radio Telegraph Conference of London' intercalated with the 1906 texts is available in the ITU archives at http://www.itu.int/ITU-R/information/promotion/100-years/documents/1906-Berlin-E.pdf, and in the US Navy archive at http://ia341019.us.archive.org/0/items/internationalrad00interich/international rad00interich.pdf.

50 The 1907 US GPO version of the 1906 texts is at http://earlyradiohistory.us/1906conv.htm.

51 Davis, *supra*, n. 10, 356-9.

52 International Radio-telegraph Convention, Final Protocol and Service Regulations, London, 1912: 216 CTS 244; 1 LNTS 135; 191; 105 BFSP 219; (1912) UKTS 10, Cd. 6873;

potential for amendment of both the Convention and Regulations were stated, but this time amendment could be carried through by plenipotentiary conference only, and in fact all later radio conferences were held at the plenipotentiary level. In any amending process each country was to have one vote, but as the 1906 conference had foreseen (and mirroring the equivalent in the Telegraph Union) there was recognition that some states had extremely wide responsibilities, a point which the UPU also had recognised many years earlier.[53] Making use of the power first given by Art. 12 of the 1906 Convention, 1912 Art. 12 added a number of 'countries' to those eligible to participate in the future, though again providing that in no case should one Government exercise more than six votes.[54]

The proposals for London were many and various. Farsightedly the Belgian Congo proposed an amendment to Art. 1 which would have included 'stations designed for regular service between fixed points which are not necessarily

38 Stat. 1672, USTS 581; (1913) AJIL Supp. 229, Service Regulations at 245; 1 Bevans 883 (Convention only); (1923) 3 Malloy 3048 (Convention with station codes and short coding for ship messages). A version of the 1912 documents, adapted for use in the US and containing the related US legislative texts, is in the US Department of Commerce publication: *Radio Communication Laws of the United States, and the International Radiotelegraphic Convention: Regulations Governing Radio Operators and the Use of Radio Apparatus in Ships and on Land* (US GPO, 1914) available at http://earlyradiohistory.us/1914reg.htm#LondonConv.

53 See Chapter 7, 'Postal Conference, Berne, 1876' at n. 105, and the following 1878 UPU Congress.

54 The countries added by 1912 Art. 12 were: German East Africa, German Southwest Africa, Kamerun [Cameroon], Togo Land, German Protectorates in the Pacific, Alaska, Hawaii and the other American possessions in Polynesia, The Philippine Islands, Porto Rico and the American possessions in the Antilles, The Panama Canal Zone, The Belgian Congo, The Spanish Colony of the Gulf of Guinea, French East Africa, French Equatorial Africa, Indo-China, Madagascar, Tunis, The Union of South Africa, The Australian Federation, Canada, British India, New Zealand, Eritrea, Italian Somaliland, Chosen (sc. Korea), Formosa, Japanese Sakhalin and the leased territory of Kwantung, The Dutch Indies, The Colony of Curacao, Portuguese West Africa, Portuguese East Africa and the Portuguese possessions in Asia, Russian Central Asia (littoral of the Caspian Sea), Bokhara [sc. Uzbekistan], Khiva [also sc. Uzbekistan], Western Siberia (littoral of the Arctic Ocean), Eastern Siberia (littoral of the Pacific Ocean). [The arrangement of the list replicates the colonial or other interests of major colonial states.] From this, including the 'home state' at future conferences, Germany was to have 5+1 votes, the US 7 (6 +1), Belgium 2 (1+1), Spain 2 (1+1), France 6 (5+1), UK 6 (5+1), Italy 3 (2+1), Japan 5 (4+1), The Netherlands 3 (2+1), Portugal 4 (3+1) and Russia 6 (5+1). The 'cap' of 6 votes was not needed. These provisions were not required, the 1927 replacement of the 1912 Convention does not contain a similar provision. 1927 Art. 19.2 provided that adherence by a government was ineffective in respect of its colonies etc. unless it so certifies. However, also by Art. 19.2 it was possible for the local 'government' of such colonies etc. separately to adhere or withdraw from the arrangements.

separated by the sea'.[55] This, doubtless actuated by the possibility of using radio rather than cable for communications in difficult territory, foreshadows the modern use of satellites for that purpose. The Belgian Congo also recommended that 'stations of general interest sending telegrams or services of public utility' (the latter to include services such as 'time, meteorology, etc.'[56]) should be taken within the compass of international agreement. Both these suggestions show an appreciation that non-coastal radio stations would require regulation. While they were not adopted in the forms they were made, their import was partially met by a new Art. 15 which made the provisions of Arts. 8[57] and 9[58] applicable to all stations situated anywhere. However, the new duties imposed on non-maritime stations by Art. 15 were imprecise in their terms, the various allocations to services, the technological accuracy of transmission and power restrictions expressed elsewhere in the Convention and Regulations remaining obligatory only for the maritime stations.

From 1907 the International Bureau of the Telegraph Union (Radiotelegraphic Service) had been issuing what had become known collectively as the 'Berne List', the 'International List of Radio Stations of the World', and an 'International Alphabetical List of Call Letters'.[59] *De facto* these provided some notice of existing radio stations and the frequencies which they were using, thus allowing later commissioned stations to avoid their frequencies.

Suggestions for new services were made. Italy wanted Art. 1 amended to extend the Convention to encompass 'aerial radio stations' which were 'stations installed on dirigibles, balloons and aeroplanes.'[60] Canada and others had proposals as to the collection of and accounting for fees.[61] The bulk of the proposals, however, related to the Service Regulations and not to the Convention indicating that the latter had attained some permanent status. Many proposals for amendment to the Regulations related to the use of particular wavelengths. France, for example, wanted the wavelengths employed for navigational positioning signals not to

55 For the implementation of this suggestion fifteen years later see *infra* n. 75.

56 As to time signals: the US had begun to broadcast time signals for navigational purposes in 1904. Cf. Report of Paul Morton, Secretary of the US Navy, in *Annual Reports of the Navy Department for the Year 1904* at 17-8 in http://earlyradiohistory.us/navy1.htm. The e-citation is to a number of Annual Reports which, for example, indicate at 313-4 and 319-20 that US Navy vessels were already regularly providing reports of meteorological conditions to the US Weather Bureau. Other states may have made similar arrangements by 1912.

57 Art. 8 required the organisation of the operation of a radio station so that the service of other stations was not disturbed.

58 Art. 9 provided for an absolute priority for distress messages binding on all radio stations, not just on coastal or ship stations.

59 Tomlinson, 277. Reference point Chapter 4, n. 88, Chapter 5, n. 184.

60 For the taking up of this suggestion fifteen years later see *infra* n. 74.

61 Note that it was the 'Canadian government' which made the point, not the UK on behalf of its territory.

exceed 100 metres (2500 Kc/s), and those for time signals and meteorological telegrams to be transmitted at 2500 metres (100 Kc/s), in both cases so as to avoid interference. Other states made other proposals as to particular wave-bands most of which were not adopted, but allocations of frequencies were made for time signals, meteorological reporting and radio beacons.[62]

Alterations to the Regulations included the addition to Reg. II of 1800 metres (166.7 Kc/s) as usable by ship stations transmitting direct to their home countries and not to the nearest coast station as had been required by 1906 Reg. XXV (the French proposal). However, such direct transmission was permitted only provided that the ship was at least fifty nautical miles (c. 90 km) from the nearest coast station and that no interference was caused to nearer coast stations (Reg. XXXV). By Reg. III 600 metres (500 Kc/s) was set as the normal shipping frequency, but, while smaller vessels which could not carry appropriate equipment were allowed to transmit on 300 metres (1000 Kc/s) they had to receive at 600 metres (500 Kc/s). Another French proposal was partially accepted through the inclusion of meteorological messages and time signals being given recognition and a limited priority by Reg. XLV.

Interference was an increasing problem, and the Regulations took further steps towards its minimisation. Spark transmissions were discouraged, and permitted only in limited areas by Reg. VII. Further, while tacitly recognising a general right to use radio, an attempt was made to limit the power of transmissions, Reg. VIII setting the normal maximum as 1 kilowatt unless special circumstances required higher power to establish the communications link.

The *Titanic* had its effect in the 1912 agreements. In place of the generalised requirement that the state of registry of a ship should license its radio operator, much more detail was laid down requiring the competence of an operator to be tested by examination.[63] In addition, the Service Regulations sharpened the requirements in respect of specific maritime safety matters. Larger ships had to carry emergency equipment (Reg. XI) and categories were established under which different requirements were set for radio watches to be kept on board (Reg. XIII). On receipt of a distress signal all stations had to cease transmissions except those relating to the distress call and frequencies adjacent to the incoming message were to be cleared from use thus aiding the reception of weak or remote signals (Reg. XXI). Regulation XXXII required that when transmitting long messages a station should pause every fifteen minutes for three minutes, thus providing a period within which a distress message might be heard. Further the 'distress' transmitter was allowed to be adjusted so as to produce a 'broad interfering wave' causing maximum interference and to increase transmission power to allow it to

62 London, Service Regulations (*supra*, n. 52) Reg. XLV.

63 Cf. US Public Law 264, 1912, Part III, regs. 96-162 in *Radio Communication Laws of the United States, supra*, n. 52, or http://earlyradiohistory.us/1912act.htm#RA4-1.

cover a maximum range, thus drawing attention to its existence.[64] Such provisions were supplemented two years later by the International Convention on the Safety of Life at Sea, 1914, which also provided that ships of various classes should carry appropriate radio equipment.[65]

In most respects the 1912 Convention otherwise repeated the provisions of the 1906 Convention. Intercommunication of radio systems irrespective of the system operated was contained in Art. 3. The duty to connect shore stations with telegraph land lines for the onward carriage of telegrams was in Art. 5. The relevant St Petersburg Articles were incorporated once again by reference in Art. 17. One aspect of this was the reaffirmation of the doctrine of secrecy of communications.[66] As with the 1906 situation, while secrecy of wired communications could be enforced relatively easily, the secrecy of radiotelegraphy messages was more difficult: at the time radio signals were broadcast, and might be intercepted by any receiver within range of the transmitter. Finally, the International Bureau of the Telegraph Union was retained as the conduit for collecting, coordinating and publishing information and generally acting as the Secretariat for the 'Radio Union'. The date for the coming into force of the Convention and Regulations was set as 1 July 1913 (Art. 22) and they were to remain in force indefinitely or until denounced.

The Radio Telegraph Convention and General Regulations, Washington, 1927

The First World War interrupted the progress of the international regulation of the radio. However, it considerably stimulated development of the technology. Germany, having lost much of its access to the rest of the world through the cutting of its North Sea cables, vastly increased the power of its radio stations and the range of frequencies used. Parallel developments occurred elsewhere, private

---

64 Cf. US Public Law 264, Regulations 7 and 8. See http://earlyradiohistory.us/1912act.htm#RA4-1.

65 The International Convention on the Safety of Life at Sea, London, 1914, 219 CTS 177, 108 BFSP 283, required all ships capable of carrying more than fifty passengers to carry radio equipment with a range of at least 100 miles and made provision for its use (Arts. XXXI-XXXVIII). The outbreak of the First World War marred its general acceptance. It was eventually supplanted and its requirements varied and extended, albeit with optional restrictions, by a similarly named Convention of London, 1929, 136 LNTS 81; 132 BFSP 568; 1932 UKTS 34, Cmd. 4198; USTS 910, 2 Bevans 282, (1938) 4 Malloy 5234, of which Arts. 26-32 deal with radiotelegraphy. See now the International Convention on the Safety of Life at Sea (SOLAS), 1974, 1184 UNTS 2; (1980) UKTS 46, Cmnd. 7874; 32 UST 47, TIAS 9700; (1975) 14 ILM 963. The 1914 London conference also inaugurated the International Ice Patrol, still run by the US: London Safety of Life Convention, 1914 (this note, *supra*) Arts. IV-XIV.

66 See *supra*, n.39.

enterprise in the US in particular, uninvolved in the War until 1917, being free to experiment and introduce new services including broadcasting.[67]

At the end of the War the importance of radio was clear. The portion of the radio spectrum usable by the technology of the time had increased. Radiotelephony had joined radiotelegraphy, including a trans-Atlantic service in the short-wave bands (3,000-30,000 KHz (30-3,000 MHz)). Broadcasting for large audiences was feasible and manufacturers of radio receivers had been coining money. As indicated in Chapter 2, in 1920 an international conference was held in Washington to consider the future of international communications.[68] Five nations, the US, the UK, Italy, Japan and France, took part, the work being divided between five subcommittees on which each was represented. Discussions were held on questions relating to cable and wired services. Of longer range interest were proposals for increased efficiency of communications between the five and the possibility for the introduction of new services. Most important for the future ITU was the notion that a universal communications union which would have separate sections on the telegraph and radio might be established. The upshot was agreement that such a union should be established when possible.[69] Again in relation to radio it was agreed that a process for the international allocation of portions of the radio spectrum for specific services should be established and brought into operation. Further technical discussions took place in the next few years, but one result of disagreement at them was that the question of a single union was postponed. Another result of these technical discussions was that very detailed proposals were drafted for what became the radio conference of 1927.

The Washington Conference met from 4 October to 25 November 1927.[70] Its initial stages saw argument as to the conference language, French, the language

67 See Appendix I. A. Briggs, *The Birth of Broadcasting* (New York: OUP, 1961); E. Barnou, *A tower in Babel: a history of broadcasting in the United States, to 1933* (New York: OUP, 1966); his *The Golden Web: a history of broadcasting in the United States, 1933 to 1953* (New York: OUP, 1968); completed by *The image empire: a history of broadcasting in the United States, from 1953* (New York, OUP, 9170); S. Smulyan, *Selling radio: the commercialisation of American broadcasting, 1920-1934* (Washington DC: Smithsonian, 1994).

68 The Preliminary Conference of the International Communications Conference, Washington DC, 1920. See Chapter 2, n. 108; Codding I, 111-2; Stewart, *infra* n. 70, at 29; Le Roy *infra* n. 70, at 87.

69 Cf. the Convention creating the Inter-American Union of Electrical Communications, Mexico City, 21 July 1924, 2 Hudson 1292, which never came into force.

70 Radio Telegraph Convention and General Regulations, Washington DC, 25 November 1927; 84 LNTS 97; 126 BFSP 330; (US) 45 Stat. 2760, TS 767; 1 Hudson 2197; 2 Bevans 683; (1938) 4 Malloy 5031, 26 Martens (3d) 234; (1929) 23 AJIL Supp. 40 (Convention only) [Oddly the numbering of the articles in the 23 AJIL Supp. version begins with an Art. Zero (0) and includes an Art. 4 *bis* and a 4 *ter*. These are Arts 5 and 6 in other versions, with consequent renumbering.]; I. Stewart, 'The International Radiotelegraph

of diplomacy, having been that of the Berlin and London texts.[71] There was also argument as to the voting allowance for countries with colonies, protectorates and the like.[72] The US had two further difficulties. First, since telecommunication in the US was in private hands, its delegation represented government not operators. Other participants came from states where the operating agency and the regulatory authority was the state. These delegations could therefore adopt rules affecting both elements. Second, although the US had latterly sent informal delegations to conferences of the Telegraph Union, it had never become a party to the Telegraph agreements. Where the Washington conference sought to establish detailed rules for the operation of services the US had to abstain. These problems were solved by dividing such matters into General Regulations (Gen. Reg.), having the same force and effect as the Convention itself, and Supplementary Regulations (Supp. Regs.) to which states might or might not assent.

A new regulatory development is to be seen in the arrangement of the 1927 Convention. It starts with definitions.[73] However, despite its placing, Art. 1 was actually one of the last adopted at the Conference, being drafted by a special subcommittee on the basis of how terminology had been used during the debates of the committees and the plenary meetings of the Conference itself. The definitions of Art. I set out what is meant by 'radio communication' and 'radio communication station', or simply 'station', in obvious terms. A 'fixed station' is permanently located and communicates with stations that are similarly located. A 'mobile station' is capable of moving and ordinarily does so. A 'land station' is a station other than a mobile station and is used to communicate with mobile stations. A 'mobile service' is a service carried between mobile stations or mobile stations and land stations. An 'international service' is one between countries or between a land station and a mobile station outside its country, or between two or more mobile stations on or over the high seas. However, in addition, any internal or national station likely to cause interference with services outside the boundaries of its country is also classed as an international service for the purposes of interference. A 'general communication system' is all existing channels, whether wire or wireless, that are open to the public, excluding mobile services. A 'public service' is a service for the use of the general public. A 'limited (or restricted) service' is one to be used only by specified persons or for specific purposes.

Conference of Washington' (1928) 22 AJIL 28; H.S. Le Roy, 'International Radiotelegraph Conference' (1928) 14 *A.B.A.J.* 86; Davis, *supra*, n. 10, 359-67.

71 Stewart, *supra*, n. 70, at 32; Le Roy, *supra*, n. 70, at 87.

72 Stewart, *supra*, n. 70, at 36-7; Le Roy, *supra*, n. 70, at 89-90; H.S. LeRoy, 'Treaty Regulation of International Radio and Short-Wave Broadcasting' (1938) 32 AJIL 719 at 921-2. Germany was allowed six votes although Arts. 119-154 of the Versailles Treaty of 1919 (225 CTS 188; 1919 UKTS 4; 3 Malloy 3329; 2 Bevans 43) and related instruments had stripped it of the colonies that had previously justified its voting strength.

73 The definitions of Art. 1 were supplemented by additional definitions made for specific purposes in the General Regulations.

'Public correspondence' comprises all communications which a station, being one in the public service, must accept from the public and transmit. A 'private enterprise' is any person, company or corporation operating one or more radio stations. Finally a 'radio-telegram' is one originating in or destined to a mobile station that is transmitted by radio over all or part of its route.

While most of the terms of the definitions in Art. 1 need no comment, others do. The 1906 and 1912 Conventions dealt with communications to and from ships – that is involving radio stations that were *ex hypothesi* mobile. However, that term was not employed. Now 1927 provided a definition of a 'mobile station' that was not restricted to ship stations. The reference to a station being 'on or over the high seas' in the definition of 'international service' indicated that radio stations on aircraft were included. The use of radio by aircraft during the First World War and thereafter had shown the rightness of Italy's suggestion made as far back as the 1912 London Conference.[74] More importantly for the future ITU, however, was the extension of the definition of an 'international service' to any international or national station capable of causing interference beyond the boundaries of its home state.[75] Article 15 of the 1912 Convention had limited the proscription of interference to coastal stations. The new definition meant that it was the range of a transmitter that was important, not its location. The possibility of a transmitter causing international interference remains basic to the function of the modern ITU.

As far as the new Convention and Regulations were concerned, much remained of the 1906 and 1912 provisions. The independence of states with regard to the international organisation of radio telecommunication services was again present, but that freedom was hedged about by requirements to apply the Convention and General Regulations (Arts. 2 and 3). Intercommunication was preserved subject to observance of Convention and General Regulations (Art. 3), but the use of systems incapable of intercommunication was permitted in the interest of scientific advance, provided that the incapability was inherent in the technology and not adopted in order to prevent intercommunication (Art. 3.3). Secrecy was brought out from the interstices of the rules of the St Petersburg Convention and made explicit (Art. 5 and Gen. Reg. 2). The earlier reference to the 1875 Convention was dropped since the new arrangements were not only to regulate telegraphy but had application to all radio communication. While radio stations were to connect to land systems, that duty was applied generally to the 'international service for public correspondence', language encompassing radio telephony as well as telegraphy (Art. 7). Interference caused to other radio stations was now made a distinct category, Art. 10.2 requiring stations 'so far as practicable' to be 'established and operated so as not to interfere' with other stations. To that end also Art. 10.1 required stations 'so far as practicable' to operate 'under the best conditions known to the practice of the service' and to 'be maintained abreast of scientific and technical progress'. Further by Gen. Reg. 4 emissions were to

74 Reference point, *supra*, n. 60.

75 Reference point, *supra*, c. nn. 55-8.

be maintained on their authorised frequency 'as exactly as the state of the art' permitted and non-essential emissions were to be avoided. Governments were to set tolerance levels for frequency drift and span and these were progressively to be reduced with the bandwidth set to reasonable parameters consistent with the developments in engineering practice. On the other hand a previous rule that a station had to use only sufficient power to connect with the nearest land station was dispensed with. The range of transmitters had greatly increased since 1912, so Gen. Reg. 26 required only that certain types of powerful transmitters should observe the requirement not to overwhelm others.

Elaborating the generalities of Conv. Art. 10 as to interference, Gen. Reg. 5 was extensive and directed to the avoidance and/or minimisation of interference. Its Sections 1-7 established a Table of Allocation of Frequencies, identified various services and allocated specific frequency bands for them in the range 10 Kc/s to 60,000 Kc/s. It was then for each national administration to license the transmitters over which it had jurisdiction to provide services in accord with the allocated bands as it thought fit. An alternative strategy might have been to assign whole portions of the spectrum to individual states to use as they would. However, the imbalance of actual and projected usage by various states made this suggestion unfeasible. Such as the US, for example, would have required a much greater portion of the spectrum than smaller less advanced states to meet its needs, but the sovereign equality of states meant that such a proposal could not have been adopted.[76] As it was in the adopted solution, where different countries authorising services within the allocated bands found that mutual interference might or would be caused, they were to confer and apportion the allocated frequencies among themselves. The idea was not new.[77] It proved to be the model under which various later Broadcasting Plans and regional radio conferences deal with matters specific to only selected areas of the world,[78] and it was to a degree successful.[79] However, a new assignment or authorisation

76 Cf. comment by Davis on the North American Agreement of 1929, *infra*, n. 79.

77 Some European nations had already adopted a consultation process in their implementation of the 1912 rules, and in the operation of their post-War stations. Elsewhere an Inter-American Committee on Electrical Communications had met in Mexico City in 1924 and its discussions implicitly approved such a consultative process. A broadcasting service as well as navigation and other services had been considered. See the Convention creating the Inter-American Union of Electrical Communications, 1924, (1931) 2 Hudson, 1292. Art. 7 required parties to minimise mutual interference. Art. 26 called for agreement on Service Regulations to complete the Convention provisions and to have equal force with it. See I. Stewart, 'The Inter-American Committee on Electrical Communications' (1936) 7 *Air L. Rev.* 351. Only Mexico, Dominica, Panama and Paraguay ratified the Convention. No Regulations were in fact agreed, and the Convention is not registered in the LNTS. The projected Inter-American Union had not achieved significant progress before it was overtaken by other agreements.

78 See Chapter 5 at n. 195.

79 Thus in 1929 a conference of Canada, Newfoundland (then separate from Canada), Cuba and the US agreed an allocation of 639 channels for various services in North America,

was not ordinarily to be made if it upset already existing spectrum and power uses. So far as practicable when authorising a new station a state was to prevent the new station from causing interference to existing international service stations whose frequencies had already been notified to the International Bureau.[80] It may be noted, however, that this 'protection' was limited. An authorising or assigning state had to act only 'so far as practicable' and, in the event of dispute, arbitration was competent, which might require parties to alter their existing uses. Since it was the frequencies below 37.5 Kc/s that were most likely to cause international interference, states were required to notify the International Bureau at least four months before the construction of a station intended to use such frequencies in the hope that this early and prior notification would reduce the probability of its transmissions causing problems, or give an opportunity to others to raise questions (Gen. Reg. 5.17).[81] One other major attack on interference was in Gen. Regs. 5.8 and 16.1: while they did not immediately bar 'damped wave' transmissions, their application progressively diminished their use.[82]

---

and in fact distance between transmitters actually allowed the authorisation of a total of 704 channels. Mexico did not attend the conference: see Arrangement relative to the Assignment of High Frequencies to Radio Stations on the North American Continent, Ottawa, 1 March 1929, I Hudson 2676 (the North American Agreement, 1929). See also I. Stewart, 'Recent Radio Legislation' (1929) 23 *Am. Pol. Sc. Rev.* 421 at 422; Segal, *infra* n. 83, at 196-8. Davis, *supra*, n. 10, at 369-70, was of the view that the US having twelve times the population of Canada and more than twelve times its messaging volume, had not done well in the negotiations. 103 shared or exclusive channels were allocated to Canada, 146 to the US, 20 to Cuba and 24 retained for other North America states. Davis considered that Canada and Newfoundland had obtained 'a most liberal share' of the available frequencies. By inference he blamed the fact that the negotiations had been conducted for the US by government officials, and not by representatives of US communications organisations. See also *infra* n. 84.

Europe also made regional progress. In April 1929, a conference at Prague agreed a division of the long and medium wave spectrum for broadcasting use among 22 European states: Austria, Belgium, Czechoslovakia, Denmark, Finland, France, Germany, Hungary, Iceland, Ireland, Italy, Latvia, The Netherlands, Norway, Poland, Spain, Sweden, Switzerland, Turkey, the UK, USSR and Yugoslavia. Allowance was made for aviation uses and for a 'common wave' within the agreed allocations. Note the presence of the USSR, which had not been invited to the Washington conference of 1927. See the Radio Service Bulletin, Department of Commerce, Washington DC, No. 146, 31 May 1929: Bulletins available at http://www.fcc.gov/mb/audio/decdoc/radio_service_bulletins.html.

80 As noted above, by Art. 1 the category 'international service' included any internal station capable of causing interference beyond national boundaries.

81 From 1928 the Berne List included information on the wavelengths used by the radio stations whose data had been intimated to the International Bureau, and the date of that intimation. This was known as the Master Frequency List. However, at this stage there was no legal compulsion on a newcomer not to use the same frequencies.

82 A 'damped wave' (also known as a 'Class B emission') is a method by which a spark gap transmission can be modulated. Now banned, its transmitters were 'noisy' and the emissions occupied a wide bandwidth. See Wikipedia *sub nom.* 'damped wave'.

Private experimental radio stations were permitted by Gen. Reg. 6, but were subject to the requirements of the Convention if engaged in general public correspondence. However, the bulk of such stations were operated by the emergent flock of enthusiastic amateurs ('radio hams') and their activities had to be supervised and checked, for some states in the interests of 'national security', and for others for the protection of the commercial communications networks.[83] In particular Gen. Reg. 6 provided that amateur intercommunication was barred if one of the countries involved objected. Where permitted, messages between experimental stations had to be conducted in plain language and relate to the experiments involved.[84] Other messaging by such means was allowed only where the message was of major importance but of a private nature and such that the ordinary routes for public correspondence by radio were unsuitable.

A major innovation in the 1927 Convention was the establishment by Art. 17 of an International Technical Consulting Committee on Radio Communications (CCIR).[85] This development mirrored the Consultative Committees on the Telegraph and Telephone of the Telegraph Union that had been created in 1925, and was influenced by their already proven utility.[86] Known throughout its existence from the acronym of its French title, the CCIR was to study 'technical and related questions pertaining to' radiocommunication (Art. 17.1). This acknowledged the fact that radio was (and is) a technology of high technical and scientific complexity, and it was therefore unsuitable for an international conference to take untutored, not to say potentially ignorant, regulatory decisions about it. Technology was developing fast. Good advice was needed.

The composition, activities and operation of the CCIR were set out in Gen. Reg. 33. However, these provisions mask both the importance of the body and its then lack of power. As to its composition Gen. Reg. 33 called for each meeting of the CCIR to comprise experts sent by administrations (i.e. governments) and representatives of private enterprises who wished to take part in that meeting. In other words the intention was that discussions would be between the knowledgeable. However, there was intense discussion on the relationship of state and private

---

Cf. the Report of SubCommittee 6 on 'Interference Problems' in the (US) *Recommendations for Regulation of Radio Adopted by the Third National Radio Conference* (Department of Commerce: US GPO, 1924) – http://earlyradiohistory.us/1924conf.htm. See also ITU RR Appendix 1 – http://life.itu.int/radioclub/rr/ap01.htm.

83 On US 'radio hams' of the time see P.M. Segal, 'The Regulation of Amateur Radio Communication' (1931) 2 *Air L. Rev.* 153. The huge number of hams swamped the frequencies available for their use.

84 In 1928, 1929 and 1934 the US and Canada negotiated rules for the licensing of private experimental radio stations and amateur stations in their respective territories: http://www.lexum.umontreal.ca/ca_us/en/cts.1929.02.en.html; http://www.lexum.umontreal.ca/ca_us/en/cts.1934.05.en.html.

85 I. Stewart, 'The International Technical Consulting Committee on Radio Communication' (1931) 25 AJIL 684; Stewart, *supra*, n. 70, at 45-6.

86 See Chapter 2, nn. 97-9.

enterprise in the CCIR since in its deliberations each country represented was to have one vote. In most countries radio was a government function or responsibility so the attending expert would most likely be a state official. But, as before, in the US the development of radiocommunication was almost entirely in the hands of private companies. US experts attending the CCIR would therefore be drawn from private enterprise not government. The US successfully argued that, where a state was not represented at the CCIR by an official state delegation, one representative from the authorised private enterprises from that state would exercise a single vote on behalf of all the 'private' representatives from that state – the right that each state delegation possessed. Other states had been of the view that the inclusion of 'private' experts would diminish the authority of the CCIR if they had the same voting rights as states. For them it would suffice that private companies should be present in an advisory and consultative capacity only, with only state members having the right to vote on proposals. But, as the US argued, any inability to vote would at the minimum diminish the participation of its representatives and at worst make it ineffective. As it was the arrangements of Gen. Reg. 33 that were agreed meant that the expertise of the US private companies was made available to the world at large and able properly to influence the outcome of the discussions.

The CCIR was restricted in what it could discuss. It could deal with only matters referred to it by states or private enterprises and, at this stage in its being, it could only provide advice which was to be circulated by the International Bureau. There was to be no possibility that the CCIR might become over-mighty. The notion that CCIR advice might be binding was unacceptable.[87]

Otherwise most of the detail of the 1927 Convention and Regulations require no further comment. Suffice it to say that in various ways the existing rules were considerably both augmented and tightened. The qualification levels and technical capacities required of candidates for the certification and licensing of operators were increased (Gen. Reg. 8). Much detail was added for the operation of mobile radio stations (Gen. Regs. 9-12, 16-19 and 22-4) and working hours for land stations in the mobile services were set (Gen. Reg. 20). Call signs were standardised to begin with a letter designating the nationality of the station (Gen. Reg. 14). The detail required to be reported to the International Bureau was increased and the Bureau was required to publish it regularly and frequently (Gen. Reg. 13). Naturally as always there was much as to rates, payments and the settlement of accounts in services of public correspondence. All in all one has sympathy with the comment of Manton Davis: 'In reading all these the thought intrudes that when one is about to be lost in the rules and regulations to be complied with and the measures to be

87 Technically this remains the case for ITU Radiocommunication (ITU-R) and Standardisation (ITU-T) Study Groups. Their work programs are authorised by international conferences of the Sectors and their output is legally binding only after being adopted by states. However, as we will see, in the latter aspect practical inroads have been made.

taken are so complicated that it seems doubtful whether he will ever be able to manage it.'[88]

One matter that was raised but postponed at the 1927 Conference illustrated the undesirability of the continued separate existence of the two telecommunication unions. As indicated in Chapter 2 the use of code in telegraphy was then a matter of contention.[89] A short, apparently abstract group of letters could be used to communicate a great deal.[90] The problem had begun in the wire service, but it inexorably infected the radiotelegraphy service. As described in the previous chapter a conference held in Cortina, Italy, in 1926 at the behest of the Paris International Telegraph Conference of 1925, had made recommendations on code language and these had been approved at the Brussels International Telegraph Conference in 1928.[91] However, the US had never acceded to any of the Telegraph Conventions and not all the Washington participants had been involved in the 1925 decision. It was therefore considered inappropriate for the 1927 Radio Conference to take up such matters.[92] Progress had to await the union of the Unions in 1932 at Madrid.[93]

88 Davis, *supra*, n. 10, at 366-7.

89 See Chapter 2 at n. 87.

90 Cf. today's 'texting' language with its contractions and common usages.

91 I. Stewart, 'The International Telegraph Conference of Brussels and the Problem of Code Language' (1929) 23 AJIL 292; Stewart, *supra*, n. 70, at 38-40; Davis, *supra*, n. 10, at 367-9.

92 See Chapter 2, c. n. 87.

93 Telecommunication Convention, General Radio Regulations, Additional Radio Regulations, Additional Protocol (European), Telegraph Regulations and Telephone Regulations, Madrid, 9 December 1932; 151 LNTS 4; (US) 49 Stat. 2391, TS 867; 6 Hudson 109; 3 Bevans 65.

Chapter 4
The ITU – 1932-1992: Fusion, Reconstruction, Sclerosis

This chapter deals first with the creation of the single ITU at Madrid in 1932 through the fusion of the International Telegraph Union and the International Radio Union. It there goes into a fair amount of detail as to the first general ITU Convention, that of Madrid, 1932, and the various Regulations there adopted. The re-creation of 1947 at Atlantic City requires a similar level of treatment. Thereafter, however, the modifications of the basic structure can be noted more summarily. In the period the radio responsibilities of the ITU were to increase significantly. I leave the Radio Regulations themselves from 1947 to a separate treatment in Chapter 5.

* * *

It may seem curious that the bringing together of the regulation of the international electrical communications system by a single agency did not occur sooner than it did. When radio arrived there had been opposition to 'wireless' by those who had invested vast sums of money in the 'wired' networks. However, the wireless did carry telegraphic messages which could be fed into the wired system. It was therefore reasonable that the charging rules for the use of any form of 'telegram' should be approximately the same whatever the medium of transmission. 'Radio-telegram' use of the wired service was therefore taken account of by the Telegraph Regulations of 1908,[1] only two years after the first treaty on the 'wireless', Berlin, 1906.[2] However the technologies of the two media were very different. Cables ran point-to-point and therefore formed a known and distinct structure with technology which had been developed for half a century before radio appeared. In contrast radio scattered its signals 'broadcast' without regard to national boundaries so sovereign states had an immediate interest in international agreement to solve technical problems (including that of interference). These were fundamentally different from the wired technologies. There was one other major difference between the realm of the wired service and that of radio. At that time the wired services were by and large provided by publicly-owned networks, many of which were in fact departments of state. Radio began as the province of a few commercial

1 Arts. 61 and 62 of the Lisbon Telegraph Regulations, 1908, 207 CTS 89.

2 Radio Telegraphic Convention, Final Protocol and Regulations, Berlin, 3 November 1906, 1909 UKTS 8, Cd. 4559; 37 Stat. 15665, TS 568; 203 CTS 101; 99 BFSP 321; (1906) 3 AJIL Supp. 330-40; 3 Martens (3d) 147; 1 Bevans 556. See Chapter 3 at n. 16.

enterprises, including the Marconi Company and its competitors. There was a stark contrast between the civil-service mentality developed over decades by the wired service and that of enterprises for which broadcasting rather than the passing of individual messages from sender to recipient was a prime purpose. Finally, the international political tensions of the early Twentieth century discouraged thought of the labour of creating a single telecommunication union out of the disparate elements that had been developed to deal with the different technologies.

In the confusion immediately after the First World War international attention was largely devoted to matters other than communications. To a degree telecommunications were operating satisfactorily, and therefore straightening out an international regulatory system for telecommunications was not as urgent as other concerns. In any event the legal structures surrounding the two media were different, which meant that bringing them together would be a major task. Cable services were dealt with by fairly frequent alteration to service regulations by administrative conferences as authorised by the St Petersburg Convention of 1865.[3] In contrast radio had been dealt with only by two plenipotentiary Conferences, that of Berlin in 1906[4] and London in 1912.[5] And there was the further problem that, although it had emerged as a major power thanks to the War, the US still organised its communication services differently from most of the rest of the world. Notably as a result, it had never become a formal party to the general international telegraph and telephone arrangements.

Things changed in the 1920s. The two Unions had their separate meetings – in the case of the wired services in 1925 and 1928,[6] and the wireless in 1927[7] – and in both Unions the desirability of a single union for telecommunications was accepted. In 1932 the step was taken and the International Telecommunication Union was formed. However, comparatively shortly after its creation another World War intervened. In 1947 as part of the reconstruction of the world order after the Second World War the 1932 arrangements were revisited and a structure consistent with the models of the newly emergent United Nations 'family' of international organisations was adopted. This new structure was to remain with little change for sixty years – an astonishing period given the rapid expansion and metamorphosis of electrical telecommunications over the period. The 1947 ITU

3 International Telegraph Convention, with annexed regulations and schedule of rates, St Petersburg, 22 July 1875, 148 CTS 416; 66 BFSP 19; 3 Martens (2d) 614; 57 LNTS 201; (1913) AJIL Supp. 276 (Conv. Arts. 1-3, 5-8, 11-12 and 17 only).

4 Radio Telegraphic Convention, Final Protocol and Regulations, Berlin, 3 November 1906, 1909 UKTS 8, Cd. 4559; 37 Stat. 15665, TS 568; 203 CTS 101; 99 BFSP 321; (1906) 3 AJIL Supp. 330-40; 3 Martens (3d) 147; 1 Bevans 556. See Chapter 3 at n. 16.

5 International Radio-Telegraph Convention, Final Protocol and Service Regulations, London, 1912: 216 CTS 244; 1 LNTS 135; 191; 81 BFSP 79; (1912) UKTS 10, Cd. 6873; 38 Stat. 1672, USTS 581; (1913) AJIL Supp. 229; 1 Bevans 883 (Convention only); (1923) 3 Malloy 3048 (Convention with station codes and short coding for ship messages).

6 Chapter 2 at nn. 73, 74.

7 Chapter 3, c. nn. 67, 70.

faced an immense task particularly in relation to radio, for the War had had its usual effect in forcing the development of technologies. The usable spectrum had increased; its use had become anarchic. Then within ten years of the 1947 ITU getting down to work, Sputnik I was launched and the space age began, adding to its responsibilities and burdens. New, and often developing, countries came into being, requiring account to be taken of their interests. Successive plenipotentiary conferences tackled various aspects of the problems of new technologies and new interests.[8] But procedures became too slow and mechanisms sclerotic. Eventually it was accepted that the old ITU had to be replaced. By the late 1980s a new structure was required.

The Telecommunication Convention and Regulations, Madrid, 1932

In 1932 the International Telegraph Union and the International Radio Union fused and the International Telecommunication Union was formed by the Madrid Telecommunication Convention and related Regulations.[9] The previous multilateral treaties, agreements and Regulations that governed the international system were formally abrogated and replaced (Conv. Art. 8). Since this was a development of fundamental importance I go into somewhat more detail than we will for a number of later conventions.

The process of fusion was both complex and simple.[10] Wired and wireless services had intertwined. New technologies were displacing the need for specialised operators. Multiplex systems had been brought into service. Teleprinter links were being installed. Radio was providing long-distance telegraphic facilities, for example between London and Sydney, Australia, and Madrid and Santiago in Chile. Broadcasting was booming, and both that service and traditional radiotelegraphy needed agreement on new frequencies to be fixed across the international community to avoid interference. But precisely how the wireless and

8 F. Molina Negro and J-M. Novillo-Fertrell y Paredes, 'The International Telecommunication Convention from Madrid (1932) to Nairobi (1982): half a century in the life of the Union' (1982) 49 *Telecom. J.* 814.

9 Telecommunication Convention, General Radio Regulations, Additional Radio Regulations, Final Protocol to the General Radio Regulations, and Additional Protocol (European) to the Radio Regulations, Telegraph Regulations and Telephone Regulations, Madrid, 9 December 1932; 151 LNTS 4; 49 Stat. 2393, TS 867; 6 Hudson 109; 3 Bevans 65. See http://www.itu.int/en/history/plenipotentiaryconferences/Pages/1932Madrid.aspx.

10 For detail of the Conference see Codding I, 131-57; I. Stewart, 'The Madrid International Telecommunication Convention' (1934) 5 *Air L. Rev.* 236; cf. V. Morailles Mora, 'The Plenipotentiary Conference, Madrid, 1932: A Historical Perspective' (1982) 49 *Telecom. J.* 811.

wired regulatory agencies might be brought together was a conundrum, and views differed as to its solution.[11]

Each Union simultaneously held plenipotentiary conferences at Madrid. Both Conferences started on 3 September 1932. The Radiotelegraph Conference ran to 9 December while the Telegraph Union concluded its business one day later. The new Convention was signed on 9 December, the General Radio Regulations and Additional Radio Regulations also on 9 December, and the Telegraph Regulations and the Telephone Regulations on 10 December, 1932.[12] In addition, taking account of some specific European difficulties, a Final Protocol to the General Radio Regulations and an Additional Protocol (European) to the Acts of the Radiotelegraphic Conference were signed on 9 December.

In their respective Plenary Assemblies each Union dealt with the matters of their individual remit but the major preoccupation in the discussion among the conference participants was the union of the Unions.[13] By this time both organisations were firmly of the view that a single Telecommunication Union was the way forward. The questions were how to bring this about, and what the structure and functioning of the new body should be. Unfortunately neither Union had done preparatory work on these questions, whether through a preliminary conference or even by setting up a working group to consider how its area of competence might be served within a single united agency. Since there was no united position within either the wired or wireless services a number of parties including seventeen individual states brought proposals to Madrid. Some of these proposals were wide-ranging, while others concentrated on particular areas of detail. The International Telegraph Bureau prepared a report on the proposals,

---

11 Cf. R. Homburg, 'The Next World Conference at Madrid and the International Regulation of Electric and Radio-Electric Communications' (1931) 1 *J. Radio L.* 220. At 222-6 Homburg writes of the provisions common to Telegraphy and Radiocommunication and then of provisions peculiar to each of Telegraphy, Telephony and Radiocommunication.

12 Lest the dating sequence seem odd, remember that the Convention and various Regulations could come into force only after going through the domestic ratification procedures of the parties. The several instruments all came into force on 1 January 1934.

13 Codding I, 131, notes that eighty countries and sixty-two private companies together with other private and international organisations attended the Telegraph Conference, while sixty-five countries and sixty-four private and international organisations attended the Radiotelegraph Conference. How far there was overlap between the non-state attenders at the conferences is unclear. Cf. O. Kučera, 'Legal Problems of the Madrid International Radio Conference' (1932) 2 *J. Radio L.* 473 (written before the conference and translated from 5 *Archiv Für Funkrecht*, 1931). Kučera notes the intended presence at the Radiotelegraph Conference of the League of Nations Committee on Communications and Transit, the International Broadcasting Union, the International Committee on Air Navigation (CINA), the International Committee on Radio, the International Shipping Federation, the International Organisation of Criminal Police, the International Amateur Radio Union, the International Federation of Wireless Telegraphers, and the International Air Traffic Association.

systematising and grouping them.[14] In addition, complete draft Conventions were submitted by Greece, Italy, the *Comité international de télégraphie sans fil* and the International Bureau itself.[15]

Additional to their 'domestic' meetings the Plenary Assemblies of the Unions held joint meetings. A Joint Convention Committee was formed to consider proposals for the new Convention but it was symptomatic of deep divisions that a separate Joint Committee on the Right to Vote had to discuss the important question of the representation and voting weight to be afforded to each state participant. There the usual questions arose as to whether a 'colonial' power should be able to vote for the various territories which it in effect represented.[16] The practice of allowing 'experts' to participate in discussions, albeit without vote, was thought likely to cause difficulties since there were many groups which wanted to express their views.[17]

Another question at Madrid was the language of debate. This ran into the tradition that French had been the language of diplomacy in the 1800s.[18] In

---

14 Kučera, *supra*, n. 13, 473 notes that originally 1371 proposals were commented on by the International Bureau, but that report was supplemented just prior to the Conferences. Stewart, *supra*, n. 10, at 238, states that initially 1433 proposals were submitted for the radio conference but exceeded 1665 by its end, while 1479 proposals had been made by the start of the telegraph conference and exceeded 1670 by its end. The respective Volumes II of the Proceedings of each conference run to 922 and 930 pages respectively.

15 L. Boulanger, Vice-Director of the International Bureau, had published a draft combination of the basic documents of the two Unions in 1930, and this proved influential. See (1930) *Journal Télégraphique* 117-25. The International Bureau suggested that proposals should be based on that draft: I. Stewart, *supra*, n. 10, at 237. Boulanger prepared a further draft for the conferences which was used in the actual discussions.

16 The Joint Committee on the Right to Vote sat from 7 September to 15 November, 1932, an indication of the depth of disagreement, the demands of respective prestige, posturing and (?)horse-trading. For detail see Stewart, *supra*, n. 10, at 245-57. Eventually Art. 21 of the Rules of Procedure for joint meetings of the Unions was adopted. It listed those entitled to vote but only for the purposes of the Madrid Conferences (Codding I, 134-5). As Codding I, 136 wryly observes it was clear that 'the principle of colonial voting was too entrenched to be eliminated.' Germany, which had lost its colonies at Versailles, but which had retained 6+1 votes at the Washington Radio Telegraph conference (see Chapter 3 at n. 72) and the USSR (which had sought separate votes for a number of its constituent 'republics') were 'exceptionally' allowed one extra vote each (Art. 21.2). Parties to only the Telegraph or the Radiotelegraph Regulations were allowed to vote only in respect of the Regulations to which they were parties (Art. 21.3).

17 Operators and manufacturers sought a voice, the latter so that they could build equipment that would meet international requirements which, with their expertise, they had helped to set.

18 See Stewart, *supra*, n. 10, at 257-61. The use of English was the main question. It was also suggested that contributions be made in Spanish, Portuguese, Italian and German, though these were not persisted with. Given the later ITU debates over 'official languages' and the slow acceptance of the present arrangements under which there are five official

fact there was no formal decision on language, French and English both being used with translation from and into English being dealt with courtesy of the US delegation. However, as far as the documentation was concerned Art. 21.1 of the eventual Convention provided that the Acts of conferences of the Union and all its documents should be in French. Of greater importance was the compass of the eventual agreements. Over the decades since the first general Telegraph Convention of 1865 international communications had become complex. War had done its work in developing technologies. Interests varied.[19] The domestic arrangement of communications within states could be very different. In some states communications were firmly a part of government, in others there was governmental responsibility, and in yet others governmental power was minimal. In some, government did not have the power to intervene. The USSR had never been party to the radiotelegraph arrangements and did not wish the radio elements to have any place within the general treaty. The answer was a single convention bringing together the principles common to the telegraph, the telephone and the radio, but with the detailed regulation of each of the three media contained in separate documents by which governments might or might not agree to be bound. Finally there was a question as to the name of the new organisation. Some still hankered after the 'telegraph' roots of history.

The Madrid Convention, 1932

Article 1.1 gets straight to the point. The parties 'form the International Telecommunication Union' which is to be governed by the provisions of the Convention. The new Union is to replace the International Telegraph Union. The 'International Radio Union' is not mentioned because, as we have seen, as a matter of formal law it never existed. To make matters even clearer, further on into the text the old arrangements were expressly cancelled by Art. 8 and replaced as between the parties by the new Convention. Article 8 specifically abrogated 'the International Telegraph Conventions of Paris (1865), Vienna (1868), Rome (1872) and St Petersburg (1875) together with the Regulations annexed thereto, as well as the International Radiotelegraph Conventions of Berlin (1906), London (1912) and Washington (1927) and the Regulations annexed thereto'. This formulation, however, left open the useful possibility that a state not ratifying the new Convention or relevant Regulations might in its relations with others remain

---

languages, it is amusing to find argument as to the expense of translation, the delay it could cause and the point seriously made that by 1932 English was the major language in international communications traffic.

19 Cf. W.S. Rogers, 'International Electrical Communications' (1922-1923) 1 *For. Aff.* 144; G.S. Shoup, 'The Control of International Radio Communication' (1929) 142 *Annals Am. Acad. Pol. & Soc. Sc.* 95.

bound by a previous set of obligations. So long as the old and new obligations did not conflict international cooperation could continue.

After the affirmation of Art. 1.1, Art. 1.2. pitched into a matter of detail, establishing a set of definitions of terms by way of reference to the Annex to the Convention.[20] In particular, 'telecommunication' was defined for the first time, it being 'Any telegraph or telephone communication of signs, signals, writings, images and sounds of any nature, by wire, radio, or other systems or processes of electric or visual (semaphore) signaling'. 'Radio communication' was defined as 'any telecommunication by means of Hertzian waves'.

By Art. 2.1 the Convention was 'completed' by the Telegraph Regulations, the Telephone Regulations, and the Radio Regulations (General Regulations and Additional Regulations). These Regulations bound only the governments that accepted them, and applied only as between governments so accepting (Art. 2.1). Every party to the Convention was required to sign at least one of the sets of Regulations, though the Additional Radio Regulations could be signed only by those signing the General Radio Regulations (Art. 2.2). Further, it was expressly provided that a party was to be bound only in respect of those service regulations which it had signed: the requirements from one set of rules were not to 'creep' over to bind a state which had not accepted them (Art. 2.3). Articles 3-14 then mostly dealt with technical questions of ratification, adhesion, reservation and denunciation of both the Convention and the Service Regulations and relationship with non-parties to the Madrid arrangements. Article 9 on the execution of the Convention and Regulations contained the duty on parties to impose the requirements of the Convention and relevant Regulations on offices and stations established or operated by them which were open to public correspondence, on their broadcasting services, and to special services governed by the Regulations (Art. 9.1). These requirements were also to be imposed on private operating agencies authorised by the parties to establish and operate international services whether or not they were open to public correspondence (Art. 9.2). Article 13 made allowance for special arrangements under which private operating agencies and others could agree on service matters provided the arrangements remained within the terms of the Convention and Regulations and as regards any interference which they might cause to the services of other countries.[21] This provision resulted

20 Annex: Definition of Terms Used in the International Telecommunication Convention, Telecommunication Convention; 151 LNTS 4; 49 Stat. 2391, TS 867; 6 Hudson 109 at 132; 3 Bevans 65 at 82.

21 Under Art. 13 on 'Special Arrangements' agreement was reached also on a 'Regional Arrangement concerning Maritime Beacons' [in the Western Europe area, roughly between the Loire in France and the top of Norway and including the UK and Ireland], Paris, 8 July 1933, 6 Hudson 420, and the 'Regional Arrangement concerning Maritime Radio Beacons' [in the Baltic and the Kattegat and Skagerrak], Stockholm, 20 September 1933, 6 Hudson 446. These replaced previous arrangements arrived at under the Washington Radio Regulations of 1927. Cf. the 'Regional Arrangement on Maritime

in an arrangement attached to the Little Entente of 1934,[22] the Agreement on an African Telecommunication Union in 1935,[23] a similar one for South America also in 1935,[24] and the regional Baltic Agreement of 1936.[25] Article 14 authorised parties and their recognised operating agencies to conclude agreements with non-parties to the Convention (Art. 14.1), but a message transiting or entering the territory or service of a party from a non-party was subject to the rates provisions of the Convention and relevant Regulation (Art. 14.2). Article 15 provided for the arbitration of disputes between the parties as to the Convention or Regulations should the matter not be solved by normal diplomatic means.

One major difference from the later ITU is to be found in Arts. 16-7. No supervisory body, whether standing committee, council or other group, was created in 1932 for the new organisation. There was no body that could effectively deal with problems that might arise in the intervals between conferences, or contemporaneously oversee or scrutinise the working of the Union. Instead the continuation of the consultative committee structures of the predecessor Unions and the International Bureau was provided for. Article 16.1 allowed the existence of standing committees to study questions of telecommunication services; their exact composition, duties and functioning were defined by the relevant Service Regulations (Art. 16.2). This therefore effectively permitted the continuance of the International Consultative Committees on the Telegraph (CCIT),[26] on the Telephone (CCIF)[27] and Radio (CCIR).[28] However, it may be noted that Art. 16 itself neither named nor constituted these consultative committees. It merely facilitated their creation. By contrast Art. 17 specifically provided for the continued existence of the

---

Beacons' Bordeaux, 28 April 1934, 6 Hudson 851, and the 'Regional Arrangement on the Radiotelephone Service of Ships in the North Sea', 8 October 1934, 6 Hudson 943.

22 Treaty of Entente and Collaboration between the Baltic States, Geneva, 12 September 1934, 166 LNTS 75, 6 Hudson 936, and related Special Arrangement for Cooperation with regard to Posts and Telecommunications, Belgrade, 24 September 1934, 6 Hudson 940, replaced by the Special Arrangement for Cooperation with regard to Posts and Telecommunications, Bucharest, 12 October 1936; 7 Hudson 422.

23 African Telecommunication Union Agreement, Pretoria, 30 October 1935, 189 LNTS 51, 7 Hudson 180, with related Telegraph Regulations, 189 LNTS 83; 7 Hudson 195 (the Portuguese African Colonies did not accept the Agreement, 8 Hudson 233): revised by the African Telecommunication Union Agreement, Cape Town, 20 January 1939, 8 Hudson 241, and its Working Arrangements for various services, 8 Hudson 257-9.

24 South American Regional Agreement on Radiocommunications, Buenos Aires, 10 April 1935, 7 Hudson, 47, revised by the South American Regional Agreement on Radiocommunications, Rio de Janiero, 20 June 1937, 7 Hudson 767, with the Internal Regulations of the South American Radiocommunications, 7 Hudson 780.

25 Agreement concerning Telecommunications, Stockholm, 15 December 1936, 7 Hudson 492.

26 See *infra*, n. 40.

27 See *infra*, nn. 44, 45.

28 See *infra*, n. 51.

International Bureau, which had formerly formally signally served the International Telegraph Union, and, albeit under less formal arrangements, the International Radio Union. Under the supervision of Switzerland (Art. 17.4) the Bureau was to continue in its service for conferences (Art. 17.1.a-d), and in the collection and publication of telecommunications data (Art. 17.1.c) including an official journal (Art. 17.1.2). At the request of parties it was also to provide information and opinions on telecommunications matters, which, given its location at the centre of an information network, it was in a good position to obtain and form (Art. 17.1.3). Its general functioning and duties in respect of plenipotentiary conferences were financed by the contribution of the parties, based on their selection of one of the six unit classes carried forward from the previous treaties (Art. 17.3).[29] However, its servicing of administrative conferences and of the requirements of the separate sets of Regulations were separately budgeted, and contributions thereto assessed and apportioned in terms of the unit classes selected by their different parties (Art. 17.3.2). Separate accounting was put in place for the wired and wireless services and costs duly apportioned (Art. 17.3.3).

Chapter II (Arts. 18-21) dealt with conferences. Article 18 was important for two reasons. First, it dealt with the revision of the Convention and Regulations, providing that the Convention itself could be revised by plenipotentiary Conference (Art. 18.1) held either as fixed by a previous conference or on the request of at least twenty parties, it being officially notified to the Swiss government (Art. 18.2). Administrative conferences of delegates from the parties were to revise the various Regulations, these setting the date and place of subsequent conferences (Art. 18.3). However, conference dates and locations could be changed (Art. 19). The second important aspect of Art. 18 lies in Art. 18.4, which for the first time specifically permitted the participation in the administrative conferences of private operating agencies authorised by their home states. Their participation was, however, to be in an advisory capacity only. Of course, as we have seen in previous chapters, the inclusion of 'experts' in delegations and their non-voting voice in administrative deliberations had happened. Madrid Art. 18.4 regularised the practice. It was only reasonable that, since private or non-governmental operators handled much of the international traffic, they should contribute to the development of practice and rules. They best knew the operational problems. The internal regulation of a conference was a matter for that conference and its first item of business (Art. 20.1), although the rules of the relevant regulations were to be taken as a model to be departed from only as deemed advisable (Art. 20.2). French was to be the language of drafting and of the official documents of the ITU (Art. 21.1). However, English or French could be used in the discussions and debates, interpretation being provided by official interpreters from the International Bureau (Art. 21.2.1-2). Other languages might also be used in conference documents provided that the delegates producing them arranged for their translation into French or English

29 As before the classes were Class 1, 25 units; Class 2, 20 units; Class 3, 15 units; Class 4, 10 units, Class 5, 5 units and Class 6, 3 units.

(Art. 21.2.3). Translation of speeches in French or English into other languages was the responsibility of those desiring such translation (Art. 20.4).

Chapter III of the Convention (Arts. 22-33) laid out important generalities, many already familiar from the agreements of the preceding decades. Telecommunication was a public service, and the public had the right to use the international services (Art. 22) though governments undertook no responsibility to users (Art. 23). The secrecy of communications using the international telecommunication services was assured (Art. 24.1) although the parties might communicate the content of messages to appropriate authorities to comply with local internal legislation or with international treaties (Art. 24.2).[30] The parties undertook to establish and maintain the international networks so as to provide the rapid and uninterrupted exchange of messages (Art. 25.1 and 3-4). In so doing the best methods and procedures were to be used, and systems kept abreast of scientific and technical progress (Art. 25.2). All these obligations were also to be imposed on private operators within the jurisdiction of each party (Art. 25.5). However, the parties accepted no responsibility for the international services (Art. 23). Secret language was competent (Art. 31.1-2) and parties which disallowed the internal use of secret language had nonetheless to permit such messages to transit their systems (Art. 31.3). Governmental messages had a priority, but individual parties might waive that right (Art. 30). Stoppage of telegraphic communications might occur where the content was contrary to public order or decency (Art. 26.1), with a similar possibility for telephonic communications (Art. 26.2). In the case of telegrams notice of stoppage had to be given to the sender unless the notice might be contrary to the safety of the state (Art. 26.1). In the telephonic case danger to the safety of the state, contrariness to local law or to public decency were the relevant criteria (Art. 26.2). Beyond such reasons the suspension of international services was competent should a state deem it necessary (without further specification as to 'necessity') provided only that the other parties were informed (Art. 27). Article 28 provided for violations of the Convention to be made known to parties, but without providing either for penalty or for the solution of problems. The rates and franking privileges for communications were to be set in the relevant Service Regulations (Art. 29). The French gold franc weighing 10/31 of a gram and of millesimal fineness 0.900 was set as the accounting unit for the setting of rates and settling of accounts (Art. 32) and the parties agreed mutually to account for the charges collected by their respective systems (Art. 33). Articles 26 and 31 dealt respectively with the elements that composed an international tariff and for the fixing and notification of monetary equivalents in local currencies. This was to produce difficulties.

Special provisions for radio were contained in Chapter IV, Arts. 34-9. By Art. 9 the parties had agreed to impose the Convention requirements on all telecommunication services open to international correspondence, 'to the

30 Kučera, *supra*, n. 13, at 474 noted that questions of secrecy might collide with the need to deal with international opium trafficking.

broadcasting service, or to the special services governed by the Regulations' and also on private operating agencies which they authorised whether these were open to public correspondence or not. That said, most of Chapter IV related to the mobile service.[31] Carrying on from the previous radio conventions intercommunication was required. By Art. 34.1 stations in the mobile service were bound to exchange radio communication irrespective of the radio systems used. However, systems incapable of intercommunication with other systems were permitted provided that that was due to the specific nature of the system and not through their being adopted solely to prevent intercommunication (Art. 34.2). Distress messages were to be accepted from any source and appropriate action taken (Art. 36). False or deceptive messages including distress messages were to be prevented (Art. 37). Included under that heading was the use of a call signal not regularly assigned to the transmitting station (Art. 37). Limited service was competent (Art. 38).

Radio interference was the subject of a separate article, Art. 35. This had become an increasing problem as technologies advanced and more and more radio stations came into operation.[32] Regardless of their purpose all radio stations were to be operated so as not to interfere with the radio services of other parties or of their authorised operating agencies (Art. 35.1-2).

Notwithstanding all the foregoing, but entirely understandable in the wake of the World War, Art. 39 exempted national defence radio installations from the requirements of the Convention and Regulations, allowing 'full freedom' to the parties to organise such installations as they thought fit (Art. 39.1). However, such installations had, so far as possible, to comply with the requirements as to distress messages, to avoid interference, 'to the extent possible' to comply with the rules as to equipment and frequencies (Art. 39.3), and, when engaged in services of public correspondence, military stations were to comply with the Convention and relevant Regulations (Art. 39.4).

The Telegraph Regulations, Madrid, 1932

The Service Regulations adopted for the Telegraph at Madrid were drafted by the delegates to the Plenipotentiary Conference of the International Telegraph Union.[33] The bulk of the Regulations were devoted to practical and finance-related matters,

31 Mobile service was defined in the Annex of Definitions as being a service 'carried out between mobile and land stations and by mobile stations communicating among themselves, special services [a service used only by specified persons or for specified purposes] being excluded'. In fact 'mobile service' had been extended to cover aeroplanes since the 1912 London Radiotelegraph Convention.

32 The French text heads Art. 35 'Brouillages' – literally fogginess, or the making of fog, a very informative term for the phenomenon. See also Madrid GRR Art. 20.

33 Convention Art. 16, and Telegraph Regulations, Madrid, 9 December 1932; 151 LNTS 50; 49 Stat. 2391, TS 867; 6 Hudson 200; 3 Bevans 65.

including in particular the elements of charges. According to Codding I, 141-4 there were few arguments as to their content, the prior Regulations having been adopted by the previous Union as recently as 1925, and these themselves having been the product of decades.[34] One innovation (present also in the Telephone and Radio Regulations) was the consecutive numbering of paragraphs for ease of reference, a practice now common in ITU agreements including the present Convention and Constitution. New and old services were to be covered.

By Chapter I (Art. 1) the Telegraph Regulations applied also to radiotelegraphy insofar as they dealt with objects common to the telegraph and telephony and their provisions were not contrary to those of Telephone Regulations (Art. 1.1). Chapter II (Art. 2-4) set out the provisions as to the composition, maintenance and use of the international system, Chapter III (Arts. 5-6) dealing with the nature and hours of service. The single Art. 7 of Chapter IV allowed operators to require proof of the identity of the sender and recipient of a telegram. Chapter V (Arts. 8-17) covered the preparation and handing in of a telegram. This included provision as to code language (Art. 10) and cypher language (Art. 11), over which there was some contention.[35] The 1928 Brussels re-classification of coded messages into Category A and Category B depending on the length of their words and placement of vowels was departed from and a simpler system adopted including a maximum word length of five letters per word (Art. 10.2.2).[36] Article 12 set out the characters that might be used in a telegram, while Art. 13 required the message to be composed in the order: paid service indication, address, text, signature. Article 14 then listed the various 'paid service' indicators. Article 15 established how the address was to be expressed.[37] Article 16 required the text of a telegram to be written in accordance with Arts. 8-12, and forbad the sending of a telegram that consisted only of an address (Art. 16.2). However, a signature was not compulsory (Art. 17.1), doubtless thus saving money, an important consideration, for the next seven Articles (Chapter VI, Arts. 18-24) covering in all paras 78-128 (6 columns of the Hudson text), dealt with the counting of words. Chapter VII (Arts. 25-31) dealt with tarification, Chapter VIII (Arts. 32-4) with the collection of charges and Chapter XXVIII with accounting. Articles in other Chapters dealt with a variety of technical matters including the routing (Art. 47), interruption and diversion (Arts. 48-9), cancellation (Art. 50), stoppage (Art. 51), and the delivery of a telegram (Arts. 52-3). Specific provision was made for money orders (Art. 67),

---

34 International Service Regulations annexed to the International Telegraph Convention of July 22 1875, Paris, 29 October 1925; 57 LNTS 201; 3 Hudson 1695. See http://www.itu.int/en/history/administrativeconferences/Pages/1925Paris.aspx. See also *supra*, Chapter 2.

35 Codding I, 153-4.

36 Arts. 10, 20 and 26 of the Madrid Telegraph Regulations, 151 LNTS 51; 6 Hudson 200. On the Brussels provisions see Chapter 2 at n. 95.

37 In telegrams to China groups of four figures could 'be used to designate the name and abode of the addressee' (Art. 15.3).

for press telegrams (Arts. 68-72), for meteorological telegrams (Arts. 73), and for governmental telegrams (Art. 78). Intriguingly, Art. 64 of the Regulations made provision for photo-telegrams between Administrations willing to organise such a service,[38] while Art. 65 continued the traditional provisions as to semaphore telegrams, and Arts. 66 and 74 the same for radiotelegrams.

One point of issue at Madrid was the equivalence of currencies for the calculation of rates and accounting. As indicated above, Conv. Art. 32 stipulated the French gold franc as the monetary unit to be employed. In 1925 the UK had resumed the gold standard, but this had been disastrous and in 1931 it went back off the gold standard. The UK pound immediately deflated and its international value varied. However, the UK had not notified an equivalent value in its currency for the purpose of rates for international telegraphy. In the 'Final Protocol of the Telegraph Regulations' the UK, Australia and New Zealand declared they would not be bound by the requirement to notify local equivalent values (Decls. 1-3), and thirty-nine other parties (including British India) made a similar declaration (Decl. 4). However, this last group apparently made it know that their reservation would persist only so long as any other signatory maintained a similar reservation.[39]

Article 94 of the Telegraph Regulations used the power given by Conv. Art. 16 to establish/continue the Consultative Committee on the Telegraph (CCIT). Under its Rules of Procedure[40] the CCIT had a plenary assembly and committees (Rules, Art. 3). However its secretariat and the organisation of its meetings were in the hands of a 'Managing Administration', which was selected by successive meetings (Rules, Art. 12.3), its duties lasting from five months after the closing of the preceding CCIT meeting to five months after the meeting which it organised (Rules, Art. 1). There was therefore no continuing body involved, although the International Bureau collaborated with successive secretariats and provided some base of operations (Rules, Arts. 4 and 8). The CCIT plenary assembly was composed of representatives of Administrations, each having one vote (Rules, Art. 13). CCIT committees studied matters approved by the plenary assembly (Rules, Arts. 12.1 and 13.1) and might invite representatives of private enterprises and industries to assist them in their work (Rules, Art. 11.3). The reports of the studies of the committees were for the plenary assembly to approve, and if approved they were circulated to Administrations by the International Bureau (Rules, Art. 12.2). Approved reports might be influential but were not legally binding.

Finally, Chapter XXX, Arts. 91-3, dealt with the relationship of the telegraph and telephone elements of the new Union with the International Bureau, fleshing out the provision made in Conv. Art. 17. Reflecting a concern for value for money that has recurred in the ITU down the years, Art. 91 set the budget of the Bureau

38 Such a system allowed the transmission of pictures through the use of pixellation.

39 The history of this dispute is but a small part of the general problems of currency stability following the First World War.

40 See also the 'Rules of Procedure of the International Telegraph Consultative Committee (CCIT), Annex II to the Telegraph Regulations'; 151 LNTS 215; 6 Hudson 250.

for telegraph and telephone matters as not to exceed 200,000 gold francs, though an overspend on printing in one year could be met by an underspend in the next, and provided that total spend might be altered by the unanimous consent of all parties between two conferences (Art. 91.3). Administrations contributed to this sum according to the units which they had taken up in accordance with Conv. Art. 17. Article 92 then laid out the duties of Administrations to keep each other informed on telephone and telegraph matters through the medium of the Bureau. By Art. 93 it was the duty of the Bureau to publicise such matters as well as to gather and publish information on the international network, statistics, lists of telegraph offices including radiotelegraph offices, and related matters. The publications involved were to be distributed to Administrations in proportion to their contribution to the expenses of the Union in terms of Conv. Art. 17. Additional copies were charged at cost, and were available for purchase (Art. 93.6).

The Telephone Regulations, Madrid, 1932

Like the Telegraph Regulations the Madrid Telephone Regulations were also drafted by the conference of the International Telegraph Union.[41] They represented two significant developments. First, telephony was separated from telegraphy and made the subject of a separate set of Regulations. This was reasonable given the progress in telephone technology. Second, another factor had called for the regulation of telephony separate from telegraphy. The previous Telephone Regulations as part of the Telegraph Regulations had applied only to a specified group, the European system (Art. 1.1). At first sight that area might appear to be more or less 'Europe', but Madrid Art. 1.2 further defined that area to comprise 'all the countries of Europe and countries situated outside Europe the Administrations of which declare that they belong to this system'. As Codding observes (I, 155) in practice the European system applied across much of the world since it was in use in Africa, fourteen Latin American countries, India, Japan and Turkey, all of which now declared they belonged to it.[42] Telephony within the 'European system' was subject to the Telephone Regulations if conducted using only channels set up by members of the system (Art. 1.2). Telephony outwith the European system was subject to agreement between Administrations and/or private entities providing the service (Art. 1.3).

The Madrid Telephone Regulations were necessarily much more extensive than their predecessor provisions. As in the other sets of Regulations the paragraphs of the Telephone Regulations were numbered consecutively for ease of reference. The new Telegraph Regulations were applicable to telephony insofar as they dealt

41 Convention Art. 16 and Telephone Regulations, Madrid 1932; 151 LNTS 226; 6 Hudson 257.

42 See also the list of countries which did not sign the Telephone Regulations, *infra*, at n. 73.

with objects common to the telegraph and telephony and their provisions were not contrary to those of Telephone Regulations (Art. 1.4), but the new Regulations had much to deal with. After Chapter I (Art. 1) restricting the applicability of the Regulations to the 'European system' as noted above, Chapter II (Art. 2) established definitions for terms and procedures such as a 'telephone exchange', a 'telephone circuit', a 'direct call', a 'transit call' and 'booking a call'. Chapter III (Arts. 3-4) covered the establishment and maintenance of the international system. Chapter IV (Arts. 5-6) set the direction of the international service, leaving opening hours of exchanges to the discretion of the relevant Administration (Art. 5.1). However, whatever the opening hours, where an exchange was not permanently open it had to remain active for twelve minutes after its normal closing time to deal with calls in process and any booked calls which had not yet been dealt with (Art. 5.2). By Art. 6 the 'time' of an exchange had to be that of the country concerned, change in that time (e.g. daylight saving[43]) being notified to parties in advance of its application. Under Chapter V (Arts. 7-8) telephone directories were to be compiled and supplied to Administrations and private companies operating the international service. Chapter VI classified different types of calls, ranging from private calls and urgent private calls through government calls and service calls to stock exchange calls. The booking of calls was the subject of Chapter VII (Arts. 20-24) while Chapter VIII (Arts. 25-27) dealt with priorities between calls (Art. 25), the establishing and disconnection of calls (Art. 26) and their duration (Art. 27). Chapters IX (Arts. 28-31) and X (Arts. 32-5) set out the arrangements for charging and accounting between the telephone administrations. Importantly, while there were some rules as to charges for some specific calls, in contra-distinction to the provisions for telegraphy Art. 30 effectively gave telephone administrations complete freedom as to setting charges.

Chapter XI was devoted to institutionalities. The relationship with the International Bureau was set out, it being responsible for publishing general statistics, a list of the international telephony circuits and appropriate maps (Art. 36). Article 37 created/continued the International Telephone Consultative Committee (CCIF) as part of the new ITU and, notably within it, gave a role to private companies as well as to Administrations.[44] Composed of experts drawn from both Administrations and private enterprises which wished to take part in it (Art. 37.2.1), the CCIF was to study both technical questions and 'questions of exploitation and tarification submitted to it both by Administrations and by private enterprises' (Art. 37.1). In principle the CCIF was to meet biennially, but this could

---

43 'Daylight saving' alterations to local time were first proposed in New Zealand in 1895, and in England in 1907. 'Daylight saving time' was introduced in Germany in 1916 to help in the War effort, and most other European countries soon followed suit. See the Wikipedia entry 'Daylight saving time'.

44 Art. 37, Telephone Regulations, Madrid 1932; 151 LNTS 227; 6 Hudson 257, and 'Internal Regulation of the International Telephone Consultative Committee (CCIF)' annexed to the Telephone Regulations, 151 LNTS 275; 6 Hudson 274.

be varied on the request of ten Administrations and dependent on the number and nature of the questions to be examined (Art. 37.3). The CCIF plenary meeting was called by an Administration, the place and date being set by the previous meeting (Internal Regs. (*infra*) Art. 2.2). The Director of the International Bureau and representatives of the CCIR and CCIT had the right to attend CCIF meetings, but only in a consultative capacity (Art. 37.5). In decisions or recommendations each Administration had a single vote, but if an Administration were not present delegates from its private companies were entitled to a single vote (Art. 37.4.2). CCIF expenses were to be borne by participating Administrations in proportion to their contribution to the International Bureau (Art. 37.2.2). However, if only representatives of private companies attended from a particular state, they between them were to contribute the sums due (Art. 37.2.3) and each Administration or private company was responsible for the personal expenses of experts they might send to CCIF meetings. These provisions were further fleshed out by 'Internal Regulations'.[45] Under these the CCIF consisted of four elements, a plenary assembly, committees of reporters, a laboratory serving as a point of reference for telephone transmission, and a general secretariat and general secretary paid for out of the CCIF dues (Internal Regs. Art. 1). The secretariat was responsible for managing CCIF business, including the organisation of the assemblies (Internal Regs. Art. 5). Decisions of the plenary assembly ('*avis*') might be unanimous or reached by a majority (Internal Regs. Art. 2.7). These decisions were issued to the International Bureau, which then published those deemed the 'most interesting' (Internal Regs. Art. 2.8). Such decisions had considerable weight, particularly if unanimous. In other words, a standing organ of the new ITU monitored what was going on in the 'European system' of telephony and in effect could make or amend international practice within its field.

The General Radio Regulations, Additional Regulations and Related Protocols, Madrid, 1932

Madrid Conv. Chapter IV (Arts. 34-9) made special provision for radio. The General Radio Regulations (GRR),[46] the Additional Regulations,[47] the related

45 'Internal Regulation of the International Telephone Consultative Committee (CCIF)' annexed to the Telephone Regulations, 6 Hudson 274 (not yet available on ITU History Portal).

46 General Radiocommunication Regulations, Madrid, 1932, 151 LNTS 278; 6 Hudson 133. Also available as 'General Radiocommunication Regulations, Final Protocol and Additional Radiocommunication Regulations' via link at http://www.itu.int/en/history/radioconferences/Pages/1932MadridRadio.aspx.

47 Additional Radio Regulations, Madrid 1932, 151 LNTS 448; 6 Hudson 185. The Additional Regulations covering certain operating details and charges were separated out from the General Regulations as Canada and the US could not agree to them because of how their radio services were established. The Additional Regulations could be accepted only

Final Protocol[48] and the Additional Protocol (European)[49] provided much more detail. Drafted by the members of the International Radio Union conference, the GRR largely repeated the provisions of the Washington Radiotelegraph Regulations of 1927.[50] The Additional Radio Regulations and protocols made provision for special instances. As in the other sets of Regulations the paragraphs of the General Regulations were numbered consecutively for ease of reference and this numbering was carried seriatim on through the Additional Regulations.

The General Radio Regulations, Madrid, 1932

In terms of structure the GRR made use of the power given under Conv. Art. 16 to create/continue the International Radio Consulting Committee (CCIR) within the new ITU.[51] Meeting in principle every five years, although that might be varied (Art. 31.3), the CCIR was charged with the study of technical questions and problems soluble basically by technical means that might be referred to it by Administrations or operating companies (Art. 31.1). The CCIR was composed of experts from Administrations and radio operating companies which wished to be represented and were authorised by their national state (Art. 31.2).[52] In addition, international organisations might be permitted to participate if designated by a previous plenipotentiary or administrative conference and provided they contributed to the expense of the meeting (Art. 31.2), and the Directors of the International Bureau and of the CCIF and CCIT could take part, but only in an advisory capacity (Art.31.5). Voting was to follow the rules used by the last plenipotentiary or administrative conference held before a CCIR meeting (Art. 31.4.1). Effectively each administration had one vote but if the state was not represented the operating companies from it could exercise that single vote (Art. 31.4.2). The expenses of experts were a matter for the sending authority, whether state, company or organisation (Art. 31.3). The expenses of the CCIR itself were capped ordinarily at 200,000 gold francs annually, although that sum might be raised and exceptional expenses could occur if necessary (Art. 32). Like the CCIT, but unlike the CCIF, the responsibility for managing the CCIR rested

---

along with the General Regulations, but the General Regulations could be accepted without accepting the Additional Regulations (Conv. Art. 2.2).

48 Final Protocol to the General Radio Regulations, Madrid 1932, Madrid, 1932, 151 LNTS 445; 6 Hudson 182.

49 Additional Protocol (European), Madrid, 1932, 151 LNTS 467; 6 Hudson 192.

50 Codding I, 146, notes that the Madrid Radio Regulations dropped the word 'telegraph' from its title. He also notes that while the Washington Regulations had thirty-four articles, the Madrid General Regulations had thirty-three, the difference being occasioned through the relocation of the Washington provisions as to the International Bureau from the Radio Regulations to the Convention (*supra*, Madrid Conv. Art. 17).

51 Reference point, n. 28 *supra*. The name was changed at Cairo in 1938.

52 Note, manufacturing companies were not included.

with the 'Managing Administration' under the CCIR Rules of Procedure,[53] aided by an International Bureau (Rules, Arts. 1 and 4). The Managing Administration was selected by successive administrative conferences (Rules, Art. 9.4) and had jurisdiction from five months after the previous CCIR meeting to five months after the meeting which it organised (Rules, Art. 1).

The GRR began with a list of definitions (GRR Art. 1).[54] Many of the Regulations were technical as to the operation of services, the availability of mobile and land stations to the public, call signs and calling, amateur stations, mobile traffic and distress traffic.[55] The secrecy of radio communications not intended for public general use was provided for (GRR Art. 2). No transmitting station was to operate without being licensed by its national state (GRR Art. 3).

The GRR then turned to technical questions. The choice of transmitting and receiving apparatus was unrestricted provided that the requirements of the Regulations were met (GRR Art. 4.1). However, that choice had to be guided by the most recent technical progress 'as shown, notably, in the Opinions of the CCIR' (GRR Art. 4.2). Various measures sought to cope with the problem of radio interference. However, the quarter of a century since the 1906 Berlin Convention had seen swift development in radio, the War and the emergence of broadcasting being major contributing factors.[56] Methods of regulation that were adaptable to technical progress were necessary. The characteristic of permissible emissions (transmissions) were set out, divided into two classes, 'Continuous Waves' and 'Damped Waves' (GRR Art. 5.1-4), the wavelength being indicated in kilocycles with the metric equivalent bracketed thereafter (GRR Art. 5.5). The quality of emissions had to be kept to the authorised frequency as 'exactly as the state of the art' permitted, their radiation being kept 'as free as practicably possible from all emissions not essential to the type of communications carried on' (GRR Art. 6.1).[57] Administrations were required to police compliance with these requirements having regards to the Appendices on Frequency Tolerances and on Band Widths (GRR Art. 6.2-4).

Much time and effort at Madrid went into the discussion of GRR Art. 7, the 'Allocation and Use of Frequencies (Wavelengths) and of Types of Emission'. The Washington Convention and its Radio Regulations of 1927 had done much

53 'Rules of Procedure of the International Consulting Committee on Radiocommunication (CCIR), Madrid, 1932, 151 LNTS 439; 6 Hudson 178. See also I. Stewart, 'The International Technical Consulting Committee on Radio Communication' (1931) 25 AJIL 684.

54 Intriguingly for 1932, Art. 1 (para 13) defines a 'Visual broadcasting service' as 'A service carrying on the broadcasting of visual images, either fixed or moving, primarily intended to be received by the general public'. Public television was very new in 1932.

55 It is interesting to see many provisions as to aircraft.

56 See Chapter 3.

57 'Frequency tolerance: The frequency tolerance is the maximum permissible separation between the frequency assigned to a station and the actual frequency of emission.' General Radio Regulations, Madrid 1932, Art. 1, para 18.

of the work,[58] but there was still pressure to include additional services in the uses of existing wave-bands. New wave-bands had to be considered. Short-wave broadcasting had come on the scene, as had general broadcasting services. New stations were already operating in frequencies not contemplated by the Washington agreements, let alone those of London of 1912.[59] Again the USSR had not been at the Washington conference since it was not then recognised by the US government. The USSR radio duties and rights remained those set under the 1912 London Convention, so its interests had to be accommodated within the new Regulations.

Madrid hardened the international duties as to radio. GRR Art. 7 makes it clear that the Madrid Table of Allocations was an agreed plan, not merely a guide for licensing Administrations (GRR Art. 7.7). While as a matter of law Administrations technically retained entire freedom as to assignment of frequencies and type of radio wave used, the assignments they made were to be made 'on the sole condition that no interference with any service of another country' might result from the use of the assignment (GRR Art. 7.1). Deviation from the Table of Allocations in GRR Art. 7 would make interference the more likely. The principle of 'no interference' with foreign radio services thus so clearly spelled out at Madrid remains integral to the current ITU arrangements.[60] Similarly, the requirement in GRR Art. 7.5 that assignments be notified to the International Bureau with a view to their publication continues in the present activities of the Radiocommunication Bureau of ITU-R.[61] Assignments were to be notified sufficiently in advance to allow other administrations 'to take any action which they may deem necessary to insure the efficient operation of their services' (GRR Art. 7.5.1). Assignments outwith the bands authorised for a service by the Regulations had to be notified to the International Bureau at least six months before being put into service, or, in urgent cases, at least three months prior to use (GRR Art. 7.5.2.a). Further, any increase in power of an operating station or change in a station operating outside the bands authorised for the service it provided had similarly to be notified to the Bureau (GRR Art. 7.5.2.b). All these notifications were added to the data on the 'Berne List' of radio stations which the Bureau had been operating and publishing since before the Washington arrangements of 1927.

Although the result of debates and negotiation, the 'Allocation and Use of Frequencies (Wavelengths) and of Types of Emission' (GRR Art. 7) was a lengthy and detailed text running to sixty-six numbered paragraphs. That Article was, however, unable to deal with all the problems faced by the Madrid conference. In particular radio broadcasting within Europe remained insoluble. Accordingly provision was made for these problems to be dealt with by agreement within

58 See Chapter 3, c. n. 76ff.

59 These stations were not to be closed down, but the frequencies which they had been assigned to use had to be notified to the International Bureau (Art. 7.5.2.c).

60 Current ITU Constitution, Art. 45 (197-199). See Chapter 5.

61 See Chapter 5 at n. 105, and 'The Radio Regulations' at n. 183.

Europe provided that services authorised by other administrations elsewhere were not caused interference (GRR Art. 7.5.a-d). An Additional Protocol expanded this provision.[62] The result was the calling of a regional European conference and the adoption of a broadcasting plan for Europe at Lucerne in 1933.[63]

It is all very well to have a plan and an international reporting procedure for station assignments but Madrid recognised interference as nonetheless likely to remain a problem. As noted above, a specific article of the Convention, Art. 35, laid down broad duties regarding interference. GRR Art. 20 made further provision as to the reduction or mitigation of interference. Unnecessary signals or messages were forbidden (GRR Art. 20.1). The testing of equipment and experiment in radio technology were allowed provided that no interference was caused (GRR Art. 20.2).[64] In the mobile services the minimum power required to ensure good communication had to be used (GRR Art. 20.3). All administrations were to take whatever steps 'they deem advisable and are in keeping with their domestic legislation so that electrical apparatus capable of serious interference with an authorised radio service' would be 'used in such a manner as to avoid such interference' (GRR Art. 20.8). However, all such steps could not eliminate the possibility of interference. Accordingly GRR Art. 20.7 provided for complaints. An administration or enterprise making a complaint had to support and justify its complaint, specify the characteristics of the interference,[65] state that the station interfered with was using its assigned frequency, and that it 'regularly uses equipment equivalent to the best used in the current practice of the service concerned.' Failing satisfactory resolution of the complaint the matter could be taken to arbitration in terms of Conv. Art. 15.

The Madrid scheme was reasonably comprehensive. Duties as to frequency tolerances and band widths were set. The Table of Allocations was adopted. A variety of notifications to the International Bureau were required. And the Bureau had a duty to publish the data. However, a major flaw in the scheme was that there was no real provision for an enforcement mechanism and the arbitration provision of Conv. Art. 15 was weak. Further, the Final Protocol to the GRR contained a number of reservations.[66] Thus Germany reserved its position as to radiotelephony for press purposes and the Dutch East Indies reserved its position as to mobile stations. Perhaps more importantly the USSR reserved a number of frequencies for broadcasting and other services, which provoked counter-reservations by

62 Additional Protocol (European), Madrid, 1932, 151 LNTS 467; 6 Hudson 192.

63 The European Broadcasting Convention, *infra*, n. 68.

64 GRR Arts. 20.1.2, 5 and 6 placed further restrictions on testing, calibration and experiment.

65 Such could include the frequency, variation in adjustment, call signal of the interferer, but the list ends 'etc.'.

66 Final Protocol to the General Radio Regulations, Madrid, 9 December, 1932, 151 LNTS 445; 6 Hudson 182.

China, Hungary, Japan, Poland and Romania, safeguarding their ability to take appropriate measures.

The Additional Radio Regulations, Madrid, 1932

The Additional Radio Regulations (ARR) contained measures to which certain countries could not accede had their provisions been incorporated in the GRR.[67] To deal with some problems the ARR contained detailed regulation for the radiotelegraph service which was unacceptable *inter alios* to states where the messaging services were provided by private companies (notably Canada and the US), while others had other objections. Putting these measures into the ARR meant that willing parties could sign up to them, while the generality of the GRR was secured.

The Additional Protocol (European), Madrid, 1932

Finally, based on GRR (Art. 7.5.a-d) the Additional Protocol (European) (AP/E) to the Madrid Acts was also signed on 9 December 1932. It provided that a conference would be held before the GRRs came into force to agree an allocation of frequencies for broadcasting stations within Europe (AP/E Art. 1.1). Its members were to consist of European states which had acceded to the Berlin and London radio conventions, and the Washington Radio Regulations of 1927 (AP/E Art. 1.1). In addition, any non-European state could send observers and take part in discussions of matters which they considered might affect their services (AP/E Art. 1.1). The International Broadcasting Union (UIR), the International Commission for Air Navigation (CINA), the International Radio-Maritime Committee (CIR), the International Scientific Radioelectric Union (URSI) and the International Shipping Confederation were allowed to request to attend the conference, but might be present only in a consultative capacity (AP/E Art. 1.1). The conference was to take account of the needs of all countries in the European region (AP/E Art. 3.1) and 'do its utmost' to assign frequencies to permit each state to ensure a national broadcasting service of reasonable quality, but regard had to be had to the existing situation (AP/E Art. 3.2). In particular: 'The undersigned governments recognise that in order to attain this result, it may be necessary for them to consent to sacrifices in the common interest' (AP/E Art. 3.4). While the GRRs had to be complied with, particular provisions were made for power limits (AP/E Art. 7), for the possibility that an agreed frequency might have been reserved for another European service (AP/E Art. 8) or that of another state (AP/E Art. 9) and for account to be taken of the USSR reservation to the GRR as to certain frequencies

67 Additional Radio Regulations annexed to the Telecommunication Convention, Madrid, 9 December 1932, 151 LNTS 449, USTS 867; 6 Hudson 185. Those not acceding to the ARR (and therefore the objectors to their inclusion in the GRR) were Afghanistan, Albania, Bolivia, Canada, Dominica, Ethiopia, Greece, Luxemburg, the US, and Yemen.

for broadcasting, radio beaconing and aeronautical services (AP/E Art. 10.1). In the USSR case, however, the Additional Protocol specifically stated that that recognition had 'its origin in considerations of a special character, and cannot serve as a precedent in any other case' (AP/E Art. 10.2). In the meantime there were to be negotiations between all relevant governments, including that of the USSR, to bring about a unified organisation of radio in Europe, with the 'special aim [of] the elimination of interference between stations' (AP/E Art. 10.3). The Swiss government was charged with making arrangements (AP/E Art. 4). The result was the adoption of a broadcasting plan for Europe at Lucerne in 1933, the first of a sequence of European Broadcasting plans.[68]

The Madrid Result

Seventy-two delegations signed the Madrid Convention.[69] Sixty-eight signed the General Radio Regulations[70] and the Additional Radio Regulations.[71] Sixty-eight signed the Telegraph Regulations.[72] Sixty signed the Telephone Regulations.[73] The Madrid packages came into force on 1 January 1934.

The ITU Administrative Conferences, Cairo 1938

There was to be no further plenipotentiary conference of the ITU until after the Second World War. Administrative conferences were held for the telegraph and telephone and for radio at Cairo from 1 February to 8 April 1938. Both conferences agreed to use English as a conference language, with the International Bureau to be responsible for translation in future radio conferences.[74]

Seventy-eight states and forty-five private companies took part in the Telegraph and Telephone conference where the wired services Regulations were considered.[75]

68 European Broadcasting Convention, Lucerne, 19 June, 1933; 154 LNTS 133; 6 Hudson 345.

69 Paraguay did not sign. In addition to the formal parties twenty-seven private companies also effectively acceded to the Convention as was permitted under Art. 13 on 'Special Arrangements'.

70 Ethiopia, Luxemburg, Mexico and Persia did not sign the GRR.

71 Canada, Ethiopia, Luxemburg, Mexico, Nicaragua, Persia and the US did not sign the ARR.

72 Canada, Liberia, Nicaragua and the US did not sign the Telegraph Regulations.

73 Australia, Canada, China, Ethiopia, French colonies, Liberia, Mexico, New Zealand, Nicaragua, Persia, the US and Venezuela did not sign the Telephone Regulations.

74 The US provided English translation services at both Cairo conferences.

75 International Telegraph Regulations; International Telephone Regulations, Cairo, 1938 (both available via link at http://www.itu.int/en/history/administrativeconferences/Pages/1938Cairo.aspx); summarised 8 Hudson 36 and 38; F.C. de Wolf, 'The Cairo Telecommunication Conferences' (1939) 10 *Air L. Rev.* 298; and his 'The Cairo

English was permitted as a conference language. One important step was that the Telephone and the Telegraph Regulations were agreed to be published as independent documents. Intra-European telegraph rates were unified, but progress on telegraph rates outwith Europe was deferred for further consideration and report to the next conference which was scheduled for Rome, 1942. The organisation of the CCIT (telegraph) was altered to bring its functioning into correspondence with that of the CCIF (telephone). Its remit was expanded to cover the study of tariff questions submitted to it by future conferences, plenipotentiary or administrative, or by twelve Administrations.[76] It was also to classify telegraph messages similarly to the system used by the telephone services.[77]

An indicator of the burgeoning importance of radio was that the Cairo Radio conference was attended by eighty-six states and seventy-one private companies, considerably more than the wired services conference. The conference revised the Radio Regulations and made some progress.[78] Spectrum was becoming congested so higher technical standards were set for transmitters as to tolerance, and older transmitters were required to meet the new requirements by 1944.[79] The use of spark transmission (damped waves, type B waves) was limited with a view to its abolition by 1 January 1940.[80] The CCIR was reorganised, its remit being extended to cover both technical and operational matters (GRR Art. 33 (771-81)), and to take account of the speed of development in radio the interval between its main meetings was reduced from five to three years (GRR Art. 33.5 (780)). Participants in the CCIR met their own expenses, but the expenses of the meetings of the CCIR itself were to be defrayed by a unit system of four classes which related to the unit classes established by Art. 17 of the Madrid ITU Convention itself.[81]

Telecommunication Conferences' (1938) 32 AJIL 562. See also H.S. LeRoy, 'Treaty Regulation of International Radio and Short Wave Broadcasting' (1938) 32 AJIL 719.

76 Art. 103.1, International Telegraph Regulations, Cairo, 1938.

77 Arts. 9-20, International Telephone Regulations, Cairo, 1938. 'Reversed charge' calls were introduced by Art. 20.

78 General Radiocommunication Regulations and Additional Radiocommunication Regulations, Cairo, 8 April 1938, 54 Stat. 1417, TS 948, 8 Hudson 41; 3 Bevans 518, also via the link at http://www.itu.int/en/history/radiconferences/Pages/ListRadiConferences.aspx.

79 GRR Art. 6, 'Quality of Emissions', and App. 1, 'Table of Frequency Tolerances', Cairo, 1938.

80 Art. 7.10, (161-162) General Radiocommunication Regulations, Cairo, 1938. Ship stations were exceptionally permitted to use damped waves (spark transmission) on three frequencies, 375 Kc/s (800 m) for direction finding, 425 Kc/s (706 m) for traffic, and 500 Kc/s (600 m) unrestricted as to use (Art. 7.10.1 (161)). That permission was to diminish from 1 January 1940 except for ships using less than 300 watts (Art. 7.10.2 (162)), and Administrations were to 'endeavour to abandon, as soon as possible' the use of type B waves at other than 500 Kc/s (600 m) (Art. 7.10.3 (163)).

81 GRR Art. 10, Appendix 16, 'Rules of Procedure of the CCIR', Cairo, 1938.

With the exception of a new version of GRR Art. 7, which came into force on 1 September 1939,[82] the various Regulations adopted at Cairo came into force on 1 January 1939.

War intervened.

The Second World War

The Second World War caused the indefinite postponement of administrative conferences for the telegraph, telephone and radio which the Cairo meetings had scheduled to be held in Rome in 1942. Once more the conflict demonstrated that technological innovation is a result of hostilities, whether actual or planned. The results, particularly in radio, were to provide but part of the matériel involved in the post-War reconstruction of the ITU.

Naturally during the Second World War, as in the First, the International Bureau did not have very much to do. However, technically, at least, the ITU Bureau continued to function impartially throughout the War, thanks in part to being located in neutral Switzerland. As a matter of legal history it is interesting that in the midst of the War some of the niceties of international legal order were being preserved. In October 1942 a regional European Postal and Telecommunication Union was created at Vienna and its existence duly publicised by the ITU International Bureau.[83] Basing itself on the 'Special Arrangements' permission of Art. 13 of the 1932 Madrid Convention and the equivalent Art. 5 of the 1939 Universal Postal Union Convention, the parties to the Vienna agreement were Albania, Bulgaria, Croatia, Denmark, Finland, Germany, Hungary, Italy, The Netherlands, Norway, Romania, San Marino and Slovakia. Intriguingly France was not a party. The Vienna Union operated through separate permanent committees on the postal service, on telecommunications services and on telecommunication techniques (Art. 4). Its own International Bureau was headquartered in Vienna (Art. 5) and its official languages were German and Italian (Art. 5.2). The postal and telecommunications services committees held sessions in 1943, but the Vienna Union was overtaken by events.

82 GRR Art. 7, 'Distribution and use of Frequencies (Wave-lengths) and Types of Emissions'.

83 Agreement concerning a European Postal and Telecommunication Union, Vienna, 19 October 1942, 9 Hudson 43. Art. 9 maintained application of the ITU Convention insofar as not contradictory to the Vienna agreement. Hudson notes that the ITU International Bureau printed a French translation in (1942) 9 *Journal des télécommunications* 162.

The International Convention on Telecommunications, Atlantic City, 1947

In the aftermath of the Second World War a number of regional agreements attempted to provide some immediate stability and order for international telecommunications.[84] Preceded by a number of conferences between various parties, of which the most important was held in Moscow in 1946,[85] reconstruction of the ITU came through the Atlantic City Conferences that ran from 15 May to 2 October 1947.[86] The tasks faced were immense. However, the 'wired' services were not the subject of major consideration. The 'wired' services were swept in to the newly structured Union, but the provisions of the Telegraph and Telephone Regulations were not reconsidered until 1949.[87] Second only to questions of structure, it was radio that was the major problem at Atlantic City. During the War the military on both sides had employed frequencies without regard to the allocations made by Art. 7 of the Radio Regulations of Madrid, 1932, or of Washington, 1927, or to the 'Berne List' of radio stations published by the International Bureau since before the 1912 London conference.[88] In pursuit of success the military paid no attention to such matters. The radio spectrum usable by new and expanded technologies had been significantly extended. Interference was rife. New stations, new frequencies, new services had to be accommodated. Order had to be imposed and secured.

---

84 E.g. 1: The Inter-American Telecommunication Convention, Rio de Janeiro, 27 September 1945, 9 Hudson 663. The parties were Argentina, Bolivia, Brazil, Canada, Chile, Colombia, Costa Rica, Dominica, Ecuador, El Salvador, Guatemala, Haiti, Honduras, Mexico, Nicaragua, Panama, Paraguay, Peru, the US, Uruguay and Venezuela. E.g. 2: the Agreement concerning Telecommunications, Bermuda, 4 December 1945, 9 UNTS 101; (1946) UKTS 17, Cmd, 6837, 9 Hudson 815. The parties were the US, UK, Canada, Australia, New Zealand, South Africa, India and Southern Rhodesia (Burma later acceded).

85 Codding I, 197-204.

86 International Convention on Telecommunications, Atlantic City, 2 October 1947; 193 UNTS 191; 1950 UKTS 76, Cmd. 8124; 148 BFSP 684; 63 Stat. 1399, TIAS 1901; 4 Bevans 470. See Codding I, 205-328. Three Conferences were held, though not entirely simultaneously: a Telecommunications Conference to revise the Madrid Convention (began 1 July), an Administrative Radio Conference to revise the Cairo Radio Regulations (began 15 May), and a High Frequency Radio Conference to deal with problems arising from access to higher frequencies not contemplated prior to the War (began 16 August). Radio Regulations annexed to the Convention: 194 UNTS 5, with Appendices, 195 UNTS 5; Additional Radio Regulations, 195 UNTS 119; Additional Protocol, 195 UNTS 153; Recommendations and Resolutions adopted by the International Radio Conference, 195 UNTS 175. See also http://www.itu.int/en/history/plenipotentiaryconferences/Pages/1947AtlanticCity.aspx.

87 The International Telegraph and Telephone Conference, Paris, 1949, *infra,* at n. 122.

88 See Chapter 3, c. n. 59.

A major question was which states were to participate in the Conferences.[89] In fact officially seventy-six of seventy-eight ITU member states attended. Before the Madrid Convention 'contracting states' had the right to attend the plenipotentiary conferences of the two Unions and the conferences themselves (whether plenipotentiary or administrative) had always sorted out voting questions at each particular conference. At Madrid such questions had been left unconsidered and the Madrid Conv. had no provision as to membership of the ITU under the post-War circumstances. Its Art. 1.1 had simply provided that the parties to the ITU Convention formed the Union, while Arts. 3-5 dealt with later adhesion, which was without any need for approval by other members. Parties might withdraw (Arts. 10-12), but the Madrid Conv. was silent on expulsion, suspension or how membership might be challenged. Post-War that lack of provision caused difficulties. Unsurprisingly Germany and Japan were not present.[90] However, other states that had been 'on the other side' attended, including Hungary and Italy, and their presence was not questioned. Mongolia had adhered to the Madrid arrangements early in May 1947 and was admitted to the Radio Conference although it was not recognised by many states. Could it be a member of the new ITU? The decision was that it could not.[91] Estonia, Latvia and Lithuania had been members of the Madrid arrangements but had been absorbed by the USSR in 1940. Even so, as a technical matter, did they still exist as ITU members, able to attend and vote?[92] Again, what to do about Spain, which was on the list of initial invitees, but whose invitation had been opposed at Moscow? Spain was another member of the Madrid Convention – indeed it had hosted the Madrid conferences. The Madrid Convention still existed. Until abrogated it constituted the only existent body of ITU rules, and these had no provision for the exclusion of a member. However, the UN had set its face against the Franco regime which had been supported by Hitler and Mussolini during the Spanish Civil War.[93] Spain was excluded. On the other hand Pakistan, which came into being only during the

89 Codding I, 208-28.

90 Germany and Japan were occupied territories. Additional Protocol II to the Atlantic City Convention provided that they could accede to the Convention 'at such time as the responsible authorities consider such accession appropriate'.

91 The Plenary Assembly of the Telecommunications Conference voted 32 to 28 for the admission of Mongolia, but because the Conference Rules of Procedure required a two-thirds majority, its case failed: Codding I, 215-7.

92 The Plenary Assembly of the Telecommunications Conference voted 41 to 16 against: Codding I, 217-9.

93 Hugh Thomas, *The Spanish Civil War*, 3rd ed. (London: Penguin, 1990): Codding I, 219-22. UNGA Res. 39 (1) on 'Relations of Members of the United Nations with Spain' had recommended that: 'the Franco Government of Spain be debarred from membership in international agencies' connected with the UN. Additional Protocol III to the Atlantic City Convention provided that Spain and its territories could accede to the Convention when UNGA Res. 39 (I) was abrogated or ceased to be applicable. Spain was admitted to the UN in 1955.

Atlantic City conferences, was easily recognised as a member along with India, the two states being successors to the previous Indian membership of the ITU. Other questions emerged as to voting. Should qualified majorities be required or just a simple majority, and should voting be by show of hands (as before) or by secret ballot?[94]

The resultant provisions were extensive and complex. Conv. Annex 2 defined many terms used in the ITU documentation, including the Convention itself. Annex 4 contained 'General Regulations' having the same force and duration as the Convention. These laid down general provisions regarding conferences and their procedures,[95] and the working of the International Consultative Committees. More fundamentally the Convention was 'completed' by the Administrative Regulations which comprised the Telegraph Regulations, the Telephone Regulations, the Radio Regulations and the Additional Radio Regulations (Art. 13.2).[96] These were to bind all State Members and Associate Members (we are coming to membership) subject to their approval by individual Members (Art. 13.2-3). In the case of any inconsistency between their provision and the Convention, the Convention was to prevail (Art. 13.4).

In a Preamble acknowledging (genuflecting to?) the right of 'each country to regulate its telecommunication' the 'Contracting Governments' nonetheless agreed to the Atlantic City Convention 'with a view to ensuring the effectiveness of telecommunications'. In other words they tacitly recognised that in the absence of agreement and cooperation international telecommunication systems would not function properly.

Membership

Membership had to be settled. In the light of the Atlantic City debates on participation and attendance just outlined, and the failure of the Madrid Convention to have fully dealt with the matter, this was essential. Two types of membership were constituted, Members and Associate Members (Art. 1.1). There were three routes to 'full' membership. Members were first, the states listed in Annex 1 (the states which attended the Atlantic City conferences and signed the Convention) upon their ratification of the Convention (Art. 2.1.a), second, states which became members of the UN and then acceded to the Convention (Art. 1.2.b) and, third, states not so qualifying but which acceded to the Convention having been

94 Qualified majorities were introduced for major matters. Secret ballots were allowed at the request of a minimum of five delegations. Cf. the case of Mongolia, *supra*, n. 91.

95 Under Conv. Art. 12, conferences were to adopt their own rules of procedures, but were to take the General Regulations as their basis.

96 Although the Radio Regulations were considered at Atlantic City (*supra*, n. 86), the Telegraph and Telephone Regulations were not revised until 1949 (*infra*, n. 122).

approved for membership by a two-thirds majority of the Members (Art. 2.1.c).[97] All Member States had the right to take part in all ITU conferences and to be elected to any of its organs (Art. 1.3.1). A Member was also entitled to vote at any conference or meeting of any ITU organ of which it was a member (Art. 3.2).[98]

'Associate Members' were first, other states approved to hold the status by a simple majority of Members (Art. 1.4.a), second, territories not fully responsible for their own international relations and whose application for Associate Membership was sponsored by the state that was so responsible, subject to approval by a simple majority of Members (Art. 1.4.b), and third, trust territories sponsored by the UN (Art. 1.4.c). Associate Members had rights of participation in ITU meetings, but not of voting or of being elected to any ITU organ (Art. 1.5).[99]

Purposes

Article 3 set out the Purposes of the Union. These included international cooperation for the improvement and rational use of all kinds of telecommunication, the promotion of technical facilities, their efficient use, and the international harmonisation of telecommunications (Art. 4.1.a-c). The allocation of radio frequencies and the registration of assignments so as to avoid harmful interference to the radio services of different countries was particularly specified as a Purpose (Art. 3.2.a). Additional Purposes in Art. 3 were the fostering of collaboration so

97 Switzerland, which did not join the UN until 10 September 2002, is the obvious example.

98 Naturally membership was to present difficulties for the ITU in the future. The representation of China caused problems subsequent to the proclamation of the 'People's Republic of China' by Chairman Mao in Peking on 1 October 1949, and the withdrawal to Taiwan of the 'Chiang Kai-shek' government of the 'Republic of China'. The replacement of the 'China' representative did not come until 1972, following upon UNGA Res. 2758 (XXVI) (1971) 'Restoration of the lawful rights of the People's Republic of China in the United Nations'. See Codding I, 417-9, Codding II, 39, 62; H.G. Schermers and N.M. Blokker, *International Institutional Law*, 4th rev.ed.(Boston/Leiden: Nijhoff, 2003); C.W. Jenks, *The Proper Law of International Organisations* (London: Stevens, 1962); N. Blokker, 'International Organisations and their Members' (2004) *Int. Org. L.R.* 139; H. Aufricht, 'Principles and Practices of Recognition by International Organisations' (1949) 43 AJIL 679; S.S. Kim, 'The People's Republic of China and the Charter-based International Legal Order' (1978) 72 AJIL 317. The total exclusion of delegations from such as Spain, South Africa and Southern Rhodesia from ITU meetings had different motivation.

Cf. the survey of practice as to state succession carried out by the International Law Commission down to 1970 (which includes data on the ITU), at 1970 YBILC II, 63 ff. See also the 'Vienna Convention on the Succession of States in respect of Treaties', 1978, 1946 UNTS 3; (1978) 17 ILM 1488; (1978) 72 AJIL 971 (in force 6 November 1996, 22 parties, 26 signatories).

99 This form of 'Associate Membership' was abolished in 1973 by the Malaga-Torremolinos Convention, *infra*, following n. 142.

as to establish service rates as low as possible consonant with efficiency, and the need to ensure the sound financial basis of telecommunications (Art. 3.2.b), the safety of life at sea (Art. 3.2.c), the undertaking of studies, formulation of recommendations and the collection and publication of relevant data (Art. 3.2.d). As in the case of its predecessors, Chapter IV affirmed the right of the public to use the international telecommunication services (Art. 28), and the secrecy of those communications (Art. 32). Secret language was competent for government and service communications (Art. 37.7), but might also be permitted by individual states for private communications (Art. 37.2). Coded messages in transit by wire could not be stopped by states which did not domestically permit the use of codes or cyphers (Art. 37.3). As previously in the Telegraph Conventions, the parties to the new Convention disavowed responsibility for the working of the international system (Art. 31), but affirmed a right to stop wired communications for reasons including state security, public order or decency (Art. 29.1-2). Services might also be suspended (Art. 30). Charges were to conform to the relevant Regulations (Art. 35). Inter-state accounting and appropriate settlement of accounts was required (Art. 38), the international accounting unit being the gold franc of 100 centimes of weight 10/31 of a gram and fineness of 0.900 (Art. 39).

Structure

To carry out its tasks a new ITU structure was put in place. By Art. 4 the ITU was to consist of a Plenipotentiary Conference as its supreme organ, Administrative Conferences and six permanent organs: an Administrative Council, a General Secretariat, an International Frequency Registration Board (IFRB), the International Telegraph Consultative Committee (CCIT), the International Telephone Consultative Committee (CCIF), and the International Radio Consultative Committee (CCIR) (Art. 4.1-3). Of these the Administrative Council and IFRB were new, and the General Secretariat was a much altered version of the International Bureau. Departing from the Berne location of the former International Bureau, the seat of the Union and the permanent organs were to be at Geneva (Art. 2).

Plenipotentiary and Administrative Conferences

The Plenipotentiary Conference was ordinarily to meet every five years, the time and place of meeting being determined by the preceding conference although this timing could be altered at the instance of twenty members or the Administrative Council (Art. 10.2-3). The function of the Plenipotentiary Conference was to consider the report of the Administrative Council on the activities of the Union since the last plenipotentiary conference, to establish budgets and approve accounts, to elect the members of the Administrative Council, to enter into arrangements with other international organisations, to revise the Convention, if necessary to enter into or revise agreements with any other international body, and deal with other telecommunications questions as needed (Art. 10.1.a-g).

Administrative conferences of the constituent elements of the Union were able to revise the Regulations with which each was concerned (Art. 11.1.1). They were ordinarily to meet along with the quinquennial plenipotentiary conference, but that timing could be departed from either on the decision of a plenipotentiary conference, or at the request of twenty Members, or on the proposal of the Administrative Council (Art. 11.3). Regional administrative conferences were also competent, provided that any agreement resulting therefrom did not conflict with the Convention (Art. 41).

General Secretariat

The General Secretariat was headed by a Secretary General and two Assistant Secretaries General appointed by Administrative Council (Art. 5.11.c). Staff were to be appointed by the Secretary General with due regard to recruitment on as wide a geographic basis as possible, the paramount consideration being high efficiency, competence and integrity (Art. 9.5). Its duties were more extensive than that of the former International Bureau but can be summarised as servicing the administrative requirements of the organs of the Union, including the plenipotentiary conference and Administrative Council, together with the collection and publication of data relevant to telecommunications (Art. 9.2), all of which were matters for which the Secretary General was ultimately responsible to the Administrative Council (Art. 9.1).

Administrative Council

The Administrative Council was a major innovation. It was a permanent body, able to enter into agreements on behalf of the Union and thus allowing the ITU to become a member of the UN 'family of agencies'.[100] Meeting annually, or otherwise as necessary, or at the request of six of its members (Art. 5.5), its eighteen members were elected by the Plenipotentiary Conference with 'due regard to the need for equitable representation of all parts of the world' (Art. 1.1).[101] Members

100 For the ITU/UN Agreement see *infra*, n. 120.

101 The main Atlantic City conference sought 'equitable representation' by using the four regions adopted by the Radio Conference for elections to the IFRB (*infra*, n. 108), Regions A, B and D each having five seats, and Region C three seats. The result was: Region A (Americas) Argentina, Brazil, Canada, Columbia and the US; Region B (Western Europe and Africa) France, Italy, Portugal, UK and Switzerland; Region C (East Europe and North Asia) Poland, USSR and Yugoslavia; Region D (Southern Asia and Pacific) China, Egypt, Lebanon, Pakistan and Turkey. Clearly this was unbalanced. There was no African state (except Egypt apparently as part of Southern Asia); no state from South East Asia; nor were India, Pakistan, Australia or New Zealand represented.

elected held office until a successor was appointed, re-election being competent (Art. 5.1.1). Were a vacancy to occur the Member having the next highest vote in the relevant region, but unelected at the last plenipotentiary, took over (Art. 5.1.2).[102] Every Member elected was to appoint 'a person qualified in the field of telecommunication services' to serve on its behalf (Art. 5.1.2).

The Administrative Council was to act on behalf of the Plenipotentiary Conference between the meetings of that conference, but only within the limits of power that might be delegated to it (Art. 5.8). Broadly this meant supervising, facilitating and coordinating the work of the Union, including its financial affairs (Art. 5.10-11). It was also responsible for the calling of the Plenipotentiary Conference and administrative conferences (Art. 5.11.g). Each Council Member had one vote (Art. 5.3.1), the rules as to majorities being those of the General Regulations or as adopted by the Council itself should the Regulations be silent on the instance (Art. 5.3.2). The Chairman of the IFRB, the Directors of the CCIs, together with the Vice-Director of the CCIR, were entitled to take part in its deliberations, although exceptionally the Council might determine otherwise. These officials, however, had no voting rights (Art. 5.6).

The International Frequency Registration Board (IFRB)

The other major innovation of Atlantic City was the creation by Art. 6 of the International Frequency Registration Board, the IFRB.[103] Placing this provision immediately after that for the Administrative Council (Art. 5) demonstrated the importance of the new body, and reflected the need to deal with the chaotic situation of radio after the War.[104] Another justification for the IFRB, though one certainly not explicitly listed in its constituent documentation, was to develop over its life. This was the instilling and maintenance of confidence in the international radio regulatory arrangements. Fundamentally, the IFRB gave a credibility to the international system. Its presence and actions came to induce confidence, particularly among those countries less able in telecommunications matters. The Atlantic City Conferences had recognised that an international body was needed to administer the system. It had to be independent and trustworthy. But was it

102 As to 'relevant region' see n. 101 *supra*.

103 On the creation of the IFRB see Codding I, 241-52; Leive 29, 55-65. On its working down to their dates see Leive *passim*; Codding II, 117-37. Cf. F. Lyall, *Law and Space Telecommunications* (Aldershot, Hants: Dartmouth, 1989); R.L. and H.L. White, *The Law and Regulation of International Space Communication* (Boston: Artech House, 1988). For discussion as to its role in later years see Leive, 310-19. On opposition to its replacement in 1992 see F. Lyall, 'The International Frequency Registration Board' (1992) 33 *Proc. IISL* 394-9.

104 The right of the IFRB Chairman together with the Director and Vice-Director of the CCIR to take part in meetings of the Administrative Council (Art. 5.5) also reflected the importance of radio in the new ITU.

merely to record, or to be more active?[105] As radio became more complex, and particularly with the opening of space, the Board was to become more active than many in 1947 expected. There had been many different expectations of the IFRB when it was set up. Some thought the IFRB was to act as a witness and nothing more in the operation of the system of registration of frequency allocations.[106] As it developed, however, it even came to be spoken of as an analogue of the US Federal Communications Commission, a World Communications Commission established with some of the characteristics of the International Court of Justice.[107] That was too visionary, although the duties of the Board were, in part, of extreme technical complexity and in part effectively judicial. We should not underestimate its advisory role particularly (but not exclusively) for the 'weaker' Members of the Union.

IFRB members were to be elected by ordinary administrative radio conference (Arts. 6.3 and 11.1.2), each successive radio conference determining their number and adopting a system that would ensure a balanced selection of members from various parts of the world (Art. 6.2; RR 10.3.3).[108] It was to be composed of nationals from different member states (Art. 6.2). Members of the Board were 'to serve not as representative of their respective countries, or a region, but as custodians of an international public trust' (Art. 6.5.1). They were not to seek or accept instructions from any government or any private organisation or any person, and Members were to respect their independence (Art. 6.5.2). It was to be thoroughly independent. 'No member of the Board or its staff' was to 'participate in any manner or have any financial interest whatsoever in any branch of telecommunication, apart from the work of the Board' (Art. 6.5.3, RR Art. 10.3.5).

---

105 On the creation of the IFRB see Codding I, 241-52; Leive.

106 See the Chairman of the Working Group which drew up the IFRB procedure as quoted by Codding I at 245.

107 Cf. Leive, 25; H.K. Jacobson 'The International Telecommunication Union: ITU's Structure and Functions', App. C to *Global Communications in the Space Age: Toward a New ITU* (New York: Markle Foundation and Twentieth Century Fund, 1973) cited by Codding II, 119; F. Lyall, 1. 'The International Telecommunication Union: A World Communications Commission?' (1994) 37 *Proc. IISL* 42-7; and 2. 'The Rational, Efficient and Economic Use of Space: Three Suggestions', in M. Benko (ed.), *Air and Space Law in the 21st Century: Liber Amicorum K-H Bocksteigel* (Cologne: Carl Heymann Verlag, 2002) 386.

108 At Atlantic City eleven members were elected to the IFRB (RR 10.3.1). The requirement as to a balanced selection from various parts of the world was met by the Radio Conference dividing the world into four regions and attaching a certain number of IFRB seats to each. The result was: Region A (the Americas) 3 seats – Argentina, Cuba, US; Region B (West Europe and Africa) 3 seats – France, South Africa, UK; Region C (East Europe and North Asia) 2 seats – Czechoslovakia and USSR; Region D (Remainder of the World) 3 seats – Australia, China, India. See Codding I, 241-52. Note the 'four regions' pattern for the IFRB elections was different from the three regions determined by RR Art. 5 and Appendix 16 for the purposes of frequency allocation, as discussed *infra*, n. 111.

Members were to be technically trained in radio and experienced in frequency assignment (RR Art. 10.3.2). They were to perform their functions on a world-wide basis, in the interests of the most effective use of the radio spectrum, and were to decide on frequency assignments 'solely on an engineering basis' (RR Art. 10.3.3). They were 'custodians of a public trust' (RR Art. 10.3.4). They were to meet as frequently as necessary, and normally at least once a week (RR Art. 12.2). Each member had one vote and majority decisions were competent, but identification of the voters was not to be made public. Proxy or correspondence voting was disallowed (RR Art. 12.3.1-2). Finally, RR Art. 12.5 required the Board to maintain records and minutes archiving them with the Secretary General.

Under Conv. Art. 6 and RR Art. 10 the IFRB had two main sets of duties. First, it was to see to the orderly recording of frequency assignments made by members, establishing their date, purpose and technical characteristics in accordance with the Radio Regulations (RR)[109] 'with a view to ensuring the formal international recognition thereof' (Art. 6.1.a). Second, it was to advise Members and Associate Members so that the maximum practicable number of radio channels could be operated in portions of the radio spectrum where harmful interference might occur (Art. 6.1.b). The procedures for notification of assignments, their evaluation and entry on the Master International Frequency Register (MIFR) were contained in RR Art. 11. RR Art. 5 set out an extensive Table of Frequency Allocations in the range 10 Kc/s-10,500 Mc/s setting out the services authorised to use particular frequency bands within that section of the radio spectrum. These allocations to services were occasionally made on a world-wide basis, but more often for a region, three regions for the purpose being defined in RR Art. 5.3 and Appendix 16.[110] In effecting the orderly registration of frequency assignments the IFRB built on work done by a Provisional Frequency Board which had been established to investigate both the use of new frequencies and the transmitting stations that had been brought into operation since the 1938 Radio Conference and during the War.

The 'essential duties' of the IFRB set out in Art. 6 can be further dissected. There were six important classes of function. First, it maintained the Master International Frequency Register (MIFR). Second, and intimately connected with that, it developed and maintained rules of procedure for the regulation and operation of international radio services. Although nominally technical standards and procedures were and are adopted by Members of the Union, in the main what the IFRB suggested was enacted. Third, and particularly important in relation to space (a development that was only ten years away in 1947) the advice or approval of the IFRB for the design of a proposed radio system was a good basis on which to proceed – a factor important in finding funding. Fourth, the Board functioned as a quality control on the work of its Specialised Secretariat, the body that carried through the routine work of checking and recording assignments. Fifth and sixth go together: fifth was the function of interpreting the RR in particular instances,

109 For the 1947 Radio Regulations see 194 UNTS 5.

110 Appendix 16 is at 195 UNTS 113.

merging into sixth – the quasi-judicial advice given in truly difficult cases, albeit that in the last analysis the right to assign remained (and remains) with each Member of the Union.

Under the RR the IFRB had the duty to investigate cases of harmful interference and make recommendations concerning it, but only at the request of one of the parties involved.[111] In so doing the Board sought a technical solution and did not act as judge. In appropriate cases after study it might suggest alternatives for the parties to consider but any findings were not legally binding.[112] However, given that the IFRB has been replaced it is unnecessary to explore its function and functioning further.[113]

Consultative Committees

Article 8 of the Convention continued the three Consultative Committees, empowering them to study technical and operating questions, and issue appropriate recommendations.[114] In the cases of the CCIT (telegraph) and CCIF (telephone) Arts. 8.1.1 and 2 allowed them also to deal with tariff matters. The CCIR (radio) did not deal with tariffs.[115] Each CCI operated through a Plenary Assembly, meeting normally every two years at a location and date set by its predecessor meeting, together with appropriate study groups (Art. 8.4.a-c). The relevant Plenary Assembly elected the Director of each CCI for an indefinite period (though the Director could resign) and he was assisted by an appropriate Secretariat (Art. 8.4.c-d). While each CCI might adopt additional rules, they were required in their meetings and working to observe the General Regulations annexed to the Convention.[116]

Language

At Atlantic City the question of the official language or languages of the Union had once more to be settled. In 1932 the Madrid Convention had set English and French as the official ITU languages. By 1947 to have only two official languages was unacceptable. Chinese, English, French and Russian were the official languages of

111 Leive, 128-33, 137-43. Each country with a direct interest could send a representative to appear at the relevant Board meeting (RR Art. 12.6).

112 RR Art. 11.17-19.

113 For further information see Leive, 128-33, 137-43 for procedures, 190-201 for ten case studies on the IFRB and cases of harmful interference, and 282-319 for his proposals of 1970 for the enhancement of IFRB powers. See also Codding II, 117-37 and RR Arts. 10-12 (194 UNTS 5).

114 The Union had the power to set up laboratories or technical installations for CCI use (Art. 8.4.e).

115 RR Art. 46 spelled out the duties, powers and procedures of the CCIR.

116 ITU Convention, Annex 4: 'General Regulations annexed to the International Telecommunication Convention'.

the UN.[117] The ITU went one better, agreeing Chinese, English, French, Russian and Spanish as official languages (Art. 15.1.1) with French as the authentic text of the Convention in case of dispute (Art. 15.1.2). However, while the service documents of the Union were to be published in the five official languages (Art. 15.3), for other documentation the working languages of the Union were to be English, French and Spanish only (Art. 15.3.1 and 3). At conferences these three were to be the languages of discourse with appropriate translation services into Russian and Chinese provided as part of the expenses of the Union (Arts. 15.4.1 and 15.5). Other languages might be used provided that those using a non-official language provided and paid for the cost of translation into at least one of the official languages (Art. 15.4.2). The costing and charging for language services for conferences and meetings of the organs of the Union were to be worked out by the Administrative Council (Art. 15.5). However, it was for the Secretary General to calculate the pricing for other ITU documents (Art. 15.5) – a power which later allowed the Secretariat to ensure the publications division was sufficiently profitable to provide a useful income stream.

Infringements and Disputes

Of course such a complex system was likely to produce dissension. Article 34 provided for Members to inform each other of infringements of the Convention or Regulations, but clearly that might not be enough to solve matters. Accordingly Art. 25.1 provided for the settlement of disputes between Members and Associate Members to be arranged either through diplomatic channels or any relevant bilateral or multilateral agreements to which they were parties. Failing such settlement the matter could go to arbitration conducted in terms of Conv. Annex Three (Art.25.2). Arbitration was to be initiated by a party sending notice to the other party. The arbitration itself might be by individuals, administrations or governments as decided by the parties, or, failing agreement within one month of the notice, by governments (Annex 3, cl.4). No arbiter could be a national of a disputant, be domiciled in a disputant or be employed by a disputant (Annex 3, cl.3). Where the dispute related to any of the Regulations and was to be decided by administrations or governments the arbiters had to be parties to the agreement on which the dispute centered (Annex 3, cl. 4). A single arbiter might be selected by agreement of the parties or by each party nominating an arbitrator, the actual appointment being determined by lot (Annex 3, cl. 8). Multiple arbiters were

117 UN General Assembly, Rules of Procedure, Art. 51; UN Security Council, Rules of Procedure, Art. 41. Spanish was added as official UN language in 1948 by UNGA Res. 262 (III). Arabic was added as a GA official language in 1973 by UNGA Res. 3190 (XXVIII), and in the subsidiary organs of the GA, the Security Council and in the Economic and Social Council by UNGA Res. 35/219 of 1980. See also UNGA Res. 3191 (XXVIII), 1973, as to the amendment of the GA Rules of Procedure. Arabic became an official language in the Security Council in 1982 by SC Res. 528.

possible, each party or group of parties sharing a common position appointing a single arbiter and these two a third in a bilateral dispute. Where agreement as to the third was not forthcoming the two appointed arbiters each nominated a third, and the appointment of the third was again settled by lot (Annex 3, cl. 7). The arbiter or arbiters determined the procedure to be followed (Annex 3, cl. 9), the Union providing all information that might be needed (Annex 3, cl. 12). Parties bore their own costs and that of the arbitration (Annex 3, cl. 11). The decision, which might be by a majority, was final and binding (Annex 3, cl. 11). That said, the procedure was never used in the period 1947-92.[118] Perhaps this was because of the 'final and binding' element, which might make compromise more attractive. Perhaps not.[119]

UN Connection

Consequent upon the Atlantic City arrangements the ITU became a member of the UN family of Specialised Agencies as contemplated by Arts. 57 and 63 of the UN Charter. Annex Five to the Atlantic City Convention included an Agreement between the United Nations and the International Telecommunication Union, which was binding on the ITU in terms of Conv. Art. 26.1.[120] Under Art. 26.2 the ITU/UN Agreement extended the rights and duties under the ITU Convention and related Regulations to the UNO and entitled it to attend all meetings, albeit in a consultative capacity only and without eligibility for election to any ITU organ whose membership was by election by a plenipotentiary or administrative

118 However, the role of the IFRB expressing its views on disagreements as to the use of the RR was to become important. See *supra*, n. 113. Leive, 136 n. 90, notes a dispute dealt with under the equivalent provision of the Madrid Convention, 1932, regarding Egypt's suspension of the operation of Radio Orient within its jurisdiction. See 'Affaire de la Société Radio-Orient' (1950) III RIAA 1871-81; 'Arbitral Decision: In the Matter of the Suspension of the Operation of the French Company Radio-Orient in Egypt' (1943) 37 AJIL 341-50.

119 Later the Montreux PP, 1965, replaced Annex Three by an 'Optional Additional Protocol on the Compulsory Settlement of Disputes' under which arbitration became compulsory between its parties at the request of one if a dispute was not settled through diplomatic channels or mediation. The 'final and binding' element was retained therein. Not all Members signed. The 'Optional Protocol' remains an option (2011). It has never been used.

120 The Agreement between the United Nations and the International Telecommunication Union was approved by the Plenipotentiary Telecommunication Conference on 4 September 1947 and by the UNGA on 15 November 1947. The Protocol as to its entry into force was signed on 26 April 1949, 30 UNTS 316. However, in terms of its Art. XV the ITU/UN Agreement was applied provisionally immediately on signature and came into force along with the new ITU Convention. The Agreement is the basis of the privileges and immunities of the ITU recommended in Part D of UNGA Res. 22 (I), of 13 February 1946.

conference. Reciprocally, under Art. I of the Agreement the UN recognised the ITU as the specialised agency in the areas delineated by the constituent documents of the Union. Other provisions set out the relationship between the two organisations in great detail. This Agreement remained in force under subsequent metamorphoses of the ITU and now for the current (2011) Constitution and Convention. In addition the ITU was also admitted to the security of the UN Convention on the Privileges and Immunities of the Specialised Agencies, thus basically making its senior officials members of the international civil service.[121]

Postponed Matters

Finally, as noted above, although the Convention was 'completed' by the Administrative Regulations comprising the Telegraph Regulations, the Telephone Regulations, the Radio Regulations and the Additional Radio Regulations (Art. 13.2), the Telegraph and Telephone Regulations were not revised at Atlantic City. Those revisions came with the International Telegraph and Telephone Conference of Paris, 18 May to 4 August 1949.[122] That Conference amended detail, but not principle.

The International Telecommunication Convention, Buenos Aires, 1952

The ITU next met in plenipotentiary conference in the Faculty of Law of the University of Buenos Aires on 3 October 1952, the Convention, the Final Protocol and other documents being signed on 22 December.[123] The organisation had

---

121 See Annex IX to the Convention on the Privileges and Immunities of the Specialised Agencies of the United Nations, New York, 21 November 1947; 33 UNTS 261; 1959 UKTS 69, Cmnd. 855. (Curiously the ITU was itself excluded from the privileged treatment in respect of communications accorded to other UN Specialised Agencies. Over the years there has been debate over official UN and UN agency communications.) Cf. the General Convention on the Privileges and Immunities of the United Nations, New York, 13 February 1946, 1 UNTS 15 (with corrigendum at 90 UNTS 327); 1950 UKTS 10, Cmd. 7891; 21 UST 1418, TIAS 6900; 1946 UNGA Res. 22 (I); 9 Hudson 499.

122 The International Telegraph and Telephone Conference, Paris, 18 May-4 August 1949; Telegraph Regulations (Paris Revision, 1949) annexed to the Final Protocol to the International Telecommunication Convention (Atlantic City, 1947) (Geneva: ITU, 1949); Telephone Regulations (Paris Revision, 1949) annexed to the International Telecommunication Convention (Atlantic City, 1947) (Geneva: ITU, 1949) both at http://www.itu.int/en/history/administrativeconferences/Pages/1949Paris.aspx.

123 The International Telecommunication Convention, Buenos Aires, 22 December 1952, 1958 UKTS 36, Cmnd. 520; 6 UST 1213, TIAS 3266; also available at http://www.itu.int/en/history/plenipotentiaryconferences/Pages/1952BuenosAires.aspx. Given the terms of Art. 102 of the UN Charter, it is curious to find that the 1952 Convention was not registered with the UN.

grown to eighty-nine members, of which eighty-three attended.[124] However, as Codding and Rutkowski note, circumstances were not auspicious.[125] At the time the 'Cold War' was intense, so dispassionate and objective discussion was meagre. Notwithstanding, it should be noted that from 1952 technical cooperation began to be fostered by the ITU as a matter of practical action.

Atlantic City had made major changes to the ITU structure and functioning, and only five years later and in Cold War conditions there was a reluctance to revisit controverted matters since the institution seemed to be working adequately. That said, the Buenos Aires conference did make some changes to the Atlantic City arrangements. The elected officials, the Secretary General, the Assistant Secretaries General, the Directors of the three Consultative Committees and the Vice-Director of the CCIR were newly required each to be of different nationalities (respectively Arts. 8.1.1 and 7.5). The duties and procedures of the Administrative Council were more clearly defined and expanded (Art. 5). Despite the increase in ITU membership, the size of the Council was retained at eighteen, with, as always, due regard to its geographic distribution (Art. 5.1.1). Each state elected to the Council was required to appoint a person 'qualified in the field of telecommunication services' to act on its behalf (Art. 5.2).

Changes to the IFRB were adopted that both reflected the importance of radio and brought it more under control of the plenipotentiary conference, partly by bringing provisions from the RR into the Convention. Imposing order on the international registration of frequencies had proved extremely difficult. The role of the IFRB had therefore had to expand.[126] Under the Atlantic City arrangements the members of the IFRB had been elected by the Administrative Radio Conference which also set their number.[127] This was altered. Previously the administrative radio conference had elected individuals to the Board. By Art. 6.3.1 of the new Convention the administrative radio conference was to elect not individuals but member states, and these were to nominate a national to serve on the IFRB.[128] IFRB members normally remained in office until their successors determined by the following plenipotentiary conference took up their duties (Art. 6.3.4). A nominated person had to meet the qualifications for individual IFRB members which were moved from the Radio Regulations to the Convention. Conv. Art. 6 was expanded to provide that Board members had to be 'thoroughly qualified by technical training in the field of radio and shall possess practical experience in the assignment and utilisation of frequencies' (Art. 6.2.2). Further, to ensure that the Board members understood the problems it would encounter, Art. 6.3.3 required

124 These figures are taken from Codding II, 38. However Codding II, 61, gives an attendance figure of 82 out of 87 members.

125 Codding II, 38-9.

126 Leive, 67-72.

127 See *supra*, at n. 108.

128 Cf. election to the Administrative Council, *supra*, n. 101. Countries elected to nominate an IFRB member were eligible to be re-elected (Art. 6.3.3).

each member nominated by his home state to 'be familiar with geographic economic and demographic conditions within a particular area of the world'. However, there was no formal procedure in the Buenos Aires Convention for the testing of these qualifications, for compliance with the requirements, or for others to object to a nomination. If a Board member resigned or was absent for more than three months without good cause, his place had to be filled by another nomination by the relevant state within three months. Failing such timeous nomination the right to nominate a national devolved on the state having the next highest vote at the relevant administrative conference (Art. 6.3.5).

The duties of the IFRB newly listed in the Convention were extended and in measure altered. In the orderly recording of frequency assignments Art. 6.1.a added a requirement to comply with any decisions taken by competent conferences of the Union. Again the Board was 'to perform any additional duties, concerned with the assignment and utilisation of frequencies prescribed by a competent conference of the Union, or by the Administrative Council with the consent of the majority of the Members of the Union in preparation for or in pursuance of the decisions of such a conference' (Art. 6.2.c). IFRB duties (and in effect its powers and influence) were thereby extended but were to be spelled out by plenipotentiary conference, not the radio conferences.

An important decision related to the Consultative Committees. Although Conv. Arts. 4 and 7 provided for the continuation of the CCIT (telegraph), the CCIF (telephone) and the CCIR (radio), Additional Protocol II dealt with the 'Possible Amalgamation of the International Telegraph Consultative Committee and the International Telephone Consultative Committee'. This authorised the Administrative Telegraph and Telephone Conference to be held in 1954 to approve the amalgamation of the CCIT and CCIF from a date not earlier than 1 January 1955, and made appropriate prospective amendments to Arts. 4 and 7 of the Convention in the event of that fusion.[129] The step was taken in 1956, and thereafter the former responsibilities of the two committees were handled by the International Telegraph and Telephone Consultative Committee (CCITT).

The International Telecommunication Convention, Geneva, 1959

The 1952 Convention had set the intervals between plenipotentiary conferences as normally five years, but left the timing and location of the next plenipotentiary conference for determination by either the previous conference (1952 Conv. Art. 9.2) (alterable by consent of a majority of State Members on the proposal of twenty members) or the decision of the Administrative Council (1952 Conv. Art.9.3). In fact it was seven years before the Union again convened in plenipotentiary conference.

129 The Administrative Council was authorised to implement such a fusion and Additional Protocol II in the event that the 1954 conference was postponed beyond that year. The conference was held in 1958.

This was held in Geneva in 1959, concluding its business on 21 December.[130] Eighty-five of the ninety-six ITU members were represented.[131] Before outlining its result we may note one practical, if technical, change to practice. Copying a practice introduced in the 1947 Radio Regulations the resultant Convention had its paragraphs numbered additional to the normal mode of division into articles and paragraphs etc., a great aid in simplifying reference and cross-reference.[132]

At Geneva the membership of the Administrative Council was increased from eighteen to twenty-five, reflecting the increase in numbers of members to ninety-six (Art. 9.1.1 (78)). As noted above the CCIT and CCIF had been merged in 1956 to form the CCITT. This was reflected in Arts. 5.4.b and c (32-3) and 13 (176-191) of the new Convention. Organisationally the ITU was assimilated to the common UN system as to working conditions, salaries, pensions and other benefits. Conference Resolution 25 formally instructed the Union to provide technical assistance to developing countries, and the development of their telecommunications was included as a purpose of the Union (Art. 4.2.d (24)).

Finally it should be noted that the 1959 plenipotentiary conference took place simultaneously and collocationally with a major administrative radio conference. WARC-59 substantially revised the Radio Regulations, including within the new rules allocations for services concerned with the possibilities emergent in the exploration and use of outer space.[133]

---

130 The International Telecommunication Convention, Geneva, 21 December 1959, with Annexes, Final Protocols and Additional Protocols, 1961 UKTS 74, Cmnd. 1484; 12 UST 1761, TIAS 4892. Also available via link at http://www.itu.int/en/history/plenipotentiaryconferences/Pages/1959Geneva.aspx. Once more, given the terms of Art. 102 of the UN Charter, it is curious to find that the 1959 Convention was not registered with the UN.

131 Codding II at 61 gives an attendance of 88 out of 96 members. According to Codding II, 39, dispute about who should represent China following the Communist takeover of power earlier in the year was settled by secret ballot, the 'People's Republic of China' which had been proclaimed by Chairman Mao on 1 October 1949 being denied representation. The Taiwan based Government of the Republic of China held the seat as well as its place on the Administrative Council until 1971. See *supra*, n. 98.

132 Cf. Arts. 7.3.2 and 12.2.1 and 3 which refer to numbered paragraphs elsewhere in the Convention rather than the formal 'Art., paragraph' involved. The practice continues. In the following text the number in brackets after the formal citation of an article or part of an article gives these numbers.

133 The World Administrative Radio Conference (WARC), Geneva 1959, amended the Radio Regulations to include definitions of 'space station', 'earth station', 'space service' and 'earth/space service'. To avoid confusion it should be explained that 'space-station' in this context refers to a transmitter station, and not to the later manned 'space stations' such as Skylab, MIR and the International Space Station (ISS), although these had and have an ITU 'space-station' on board.

The International Telecommunication Convention, Montreux, 1965

Like its predecessor, the 1959 Convention did not set an interval between plenipotentiary conferences, but left the timing and location of the next plenipotentiary conference for determination by the preceding conference (1959 Conv. Art. 6.3. (44)), or by the Administrative Council with the consent of a majority of members (1959 Conv. Art. 6.4.1-2 (45-8)). In fact the next plenipotentiary conference was not held for six years. There was a special celebration of the 'centenary' of the Union in Paris on 17 May 1965, but the formal PP did not convene until October in Montreux, the final session being on 12 November 1965.[134] Membership had risen from ninety-six to one hundred and twenty-nine, of which one hundred and twenty-two sent delegations.[135] There was debate over South Africa, and, although it formally remained an ITU member, the conference voted to exclude the South African delegation from all ITU conferences because of its apartheid policies, and this was to remain the position for many years.[136] In addition it may be noted that the next year the Administrative Council decided that Southern Rhodesia, by then in dispute with the UK, and which had unilaterally declared its independence, was an illegal regime, and deleted its signature from the 1965 Convention.[137]

The composition of the Administrative Council was raised again from twenty-five to twenty-nine to reflect the increased membership of the Union (Art. 9.1.1 (78)). Council membership was, of course, still to 'have due regard to' the need for an 'equitable representation of all parts of the world' (Art. 9.1.1 (78)). Accordingly the Council suggested that within the informal 'regional' division of the world the four 'extra' seats were allocated three to the 'Africa' element and one to the 'Asia' element of the Union. That decision reflected the location of the bulk of the new members.

At the Montreux Plenipotentiary the US and others proposed the abolition of the IFRB on the main ground that it had by then completed compiling the International Master Frequency List from among the wartime chaos, and that

134 The International Telecommunication Convention, Montreux, 12 November 1965, 1967 UKTS 41, Cmnd. 3383; 18 UST 575, TIAS 6267; also available via link at http://www.itu.int/en/history/plenipotentiaryconferences/Pages/1965Montreux.aspx. As with the 1959 Convention, given the terms of Art. 102 of the UN Charter, it is curious to find that the 1965 Convention was not registered with the UN.

135 Codding II, 61.

136 Conf. Res. 44 and 45. South Africa was restored to participation in the ITU by Res. 1955 of the Council and Res. PLEN/10 of the Kyoto Plenipotentiary Conference, 1994. Apartheid had gone, elections had been held earlier in 1994, and a National Government formed.

137 'Situation Concerning Rhodesia', ITU Admin. Council Res. 599, 18 UST 675. For action within the UN see particularly the 'Question of Southern Rhodesia' UNGA Res. 2012, 2022 and 2024 of 1965 (XX), 2138 and 2151 of 1966 (XXI) and 2262 of 1967 (XXII). See also UNSC Res. 216 and 217 (1965) and 221 and 232 (1966).

the remaining function of recording assignments could be done simply by administrators located within the General Secretariat.[138] This was opposed mainly by the developing nations who stood out for the IFRB, perceiving it as useful to them as an impartial voice in arguments as to frequency allocation, and as a source of disinterested advice. However, membership of the IFRB was reduced from eleven to five (Art. 13.2.1 (169)). IFRB members were to be 'thoroughly qualified by technical training in the field of radio', and were to 'possess practical experience in the assignment and utilisation of frequencies' (Art. 13.2.2 (170)). A change was that members were to be elected at intervals of not less than five years by world administrative radio conference from among candidates sponsored by their national states, which might propose only one candidate each (Art. 13.3.1 (172)). In other words the election was now not blind as to the individuals who might actually serve, as it had been under the 1952 arrangements where states were elected and they then nominated a person to serve. Each member was to be 'familiar with the geographic, economic and demographic conditions within a particular area of the world' (Art. 13.2.3 (171)) and the election procedures were as before required 'to ensure equitable representation of the various parts of the world' (Art. 13.3.2 (173)).[139] Re-election was competent (Art. 13.3.3 (174)).

By the mid 1960s telecommunications had increased in complexity. Regional unions were being constituted to deal with localised problems, and the emergence of space raised world-wide problems of the use of radio frequencies. Accordingly Art. 7 (49-76) split the arrangements for administrative conferences, world administrative conferences dealing with matters of world-wide concern, and regional administrative conference covering matters of regional importance.

At Montreux the status and function of the constituent documents was a matter of discussion, some suggesting the introduction of a permanent constitution and a general assembly of members which would replace the practice of irregular plenipotentiaries, with the adoption of a new Convention at each plenipotentiary. PP Res. 35 'Preparation of a Draft Constitutional Charter' instructed the setting up of a study group on the matter. The idea was to bear fruit nearly three decades later, the next step coming with the next convention, that of 1973.

The International Telecommunication Convention, Malaga-Torremolinos, 1973

The plenipotentiary conference held at Malaga-Torremolinos lasted from 14 September to 25 October 1973, the new Telecommunication Convention and

138 Codding II, 44-5, 121-2; Leive, 27, 73-80. Codding II at 44 notes the curiosity that the USSR had opposed the very creation of the IFRB while the US had advocated it. These positions were reversed in the 1965 debates. The major narrative and discussion of the work of the IFRB down to its date is Leive, *passim*.

139 The election of the members resulted in one member from each of the five ITU regions, a pattern that was to persist until the IFRB disappeared in the 1992/4 reconstruction.

related Protocols etc. being signed by delegations on the last day.[140] The new Convention began a process of dividing the basic instrument of the ITU. Without actually splitting the Convention, it had two distinct sections. The 'First Part, Basic Provisions' (Preamble and Arts. 1-52 (1-170)) contained provisions considered less likely to require amendment in the future, while the 'Second Part, General Regulations' (Arts. 53-82 (201-571)) contained provisions likely to be more mutable.[141] The 'First Part' is couched in general terms declaring fundamental principles, while the 'Second Part', entitled 'General Regulations', fills these out with greater detail. By Art. 41 (146) in the event of inconsistency between the two Parts the provision made in the First Part was to prevail. According to Codding II, 204, however, this development was less than the Montreux conference had had in contemplation.

By 1973 ITU membership had grown to one hundred and forty-six, from which one hundred and thirty-one delegations attended the conference. Although to do so was arguably legally dubious Portugal and South Africa (once more) were excluded from attendance at all ITU meetings because of their racial and colonial policies.[142] The actual membership of the Union was revised. The category of 'Associate Member' that had been introduced by the Atlantic City Convention was dropped from Art. 1. Now, 'having regard to the principle of universality and the desirability of universal participation in the Union', membership was open to the states listed in Annex 1 (the members of the previous Convention), to UN members, and to others approved by two-thirds of the members (Art. 1.1-2 (2-6)). The rights and duties of Members were then set out in Art. 2 (7-10). However, although the Malaga-Torremolinos Convention and the various Regulations were clearly directed to their telecommunication purposes, the influence of the newer State Members can be seen in the exclusion of Portugal and South Africa mentioned above. It is also clear in some of the Convention language, and particularly in Conference Resolutions 16-25 and Opinion 2, which were designed to favour the interests of developing countries and the improvement of their telecommunication facilities.[143]

140 International Telecommunication Convention, Malaga-Torremolinos, 25 October 1973, 1209 UNTS 255; 1975 UKTS 104, Cmnd. 6219; 28 UST 2495, TIAS 8572; also available via link at http://www.itu.int/en/history/plenipotentiaryconferences/Pages/1973 MalagaTorremolinos.aspx. The ITU itself published the Convention, Final Protocol, Additional Protocols, Resolutions, Recommendations and Opinions in 1974.

141 You will see there is discontinuity in the numbering of the Parts. This was to allow for future change. In the current instruments (2011) resort has had to be made to suffixes to numbers, designating new introductions as A, B, C, or *bis*, *ter*, *quater*, etc., as this is considered preferable to renumbering familiar provisions.

142 See respectively Conf. Res. 30 and 31 (Malaga-Torremolinos, 1973).

143 'Participation of the Union in the UN Development Programme' (Res. 16); Improvement of Union facilities for rendering technical assistance to developing countries' (Res. 17); 'Application of science and telecommunications technology in the interest of developing countries' (Res. 18); 'Special measures for the least developed countries' (Res. 19);

That eight years had elapsed since the Montreux PP was a worry. The pace of innovation in telecommunications was swift. Accordingly Art. 53.1.1 (201) called for the PP to be 'convened at regular intervals and normally every five years'. If practicable the previous conference would set the date and place of its successor, which failing the Administrative Council could do so with the concurrence of a majority of members of the Union (Art. 55.1.2 (202)). As had previously been the case, arrangements could, however, be modified (Art. 53.2 (203-5)). The intention was good, but the execution faulty. It was to be nine years before the next PP was to convene in 1982 in Nairobi.

The World Administrative Radio Conference (WARC), 1979

In 1979 a major World Administrative Radio Conference (WARC) met at Geneva to revise the Radio Regulations.[144] The process took ten weeks, running from 24 September to 6 December. One hundred and forty-seven delegations took part, there being about two thousand individual delegates. About one hundred and twenty working groups were employed to consider some fifteen thousand proposals, of which twelve thousand related to the allocation of frequencies to particular uses. While much discussion related to technicalities, the requirements and demands of the developing countries were also the subject of major debate.[145]

The International Telecommunication Convention, Nairobi, 1982

Despite the Malaga reversion to the idea that plenipotentiary conferences 'shall be convened a regular intervals and normally every five years' (1973 Conv. Art.

'Inter-country projects financed by UNDP in the field of telecommunications' (Res. 20); 'Special Fund for Technical Cooperation' (Res. 21); 'Recruitment of experts for technical cooperation projects' (Res. 22); 'Training standards' (Res. 23); 'Training of refugees' (Res. 24); 'Seminars' (Res. 25); 'Favourable treatment for developing Countries' Opinion No. 2.

144 Final Acts of the World Administrative Radio Conference, Geneva, 1979 (Geneva: ITU, 1980). The 1979 conference was of major importance, but it should be noted that regular administrative radio conferences, often dealing with a region or a particular service, were held over the years. (See list at http://www.itu.int/en/history/radioconferences/Pages/ListRadioConferences.aspx.) The 1979 WARC was, however, of general importance both in its revision of procedures and the decisions it made as to the use of frequencies. See http://www.itu.int/en/history/radioconferences/Pages/1979-WARC.aspx.

145 G.O. Robinson, 'Regulating the International Airwaves: The 1979 WARC', (1980) 21 *Virg. J. Int. L.* 1; T. Hart, Jr., 'A Review of WARC-79 and Its Implications for the Development of Satellite communication Services' (1980) 12 *Lawyer of the Americas* 442; A.M. Rutkowski, 'The 1979 World Administrative Radio Conference: The ITU in a Changing World', (1979) 13 *Int. Lawyer* 289; D.B. Fenkell, 'US Preparation for ITU Conferences: WARC'79, a Case Study' (1984) 5 *Mich. YB Int. Leg. Stud.* 319.

53.1.1 (201)), it was nine years before the next PP was held in Nairobi, Kenya. One explanation for the delay may be the rigours of the series of radio conferences in the 1970s, most notably the 1979 WARC, but other factors may also have been in play.

The 1982 PP ran from 28 September to 6 November 1982.[146] Many considered that its business, though heavy, could have been discharged in four weeks.[147] During its six weeks, however, much pith, effort and unofficial discussions were occupied by political argument and manoeuvring particularly about the presence of Israel and its membership of the ITU. Between 16 and 18 September, ten days before the Conference convened, there had been a massacre of Lebanese and Palestinian civilians at the Sabra and Shatila refugee camps outside Beirut. The Israeli Defence Force (IDF) had invaded Lebanon and at the time appeared to be in control of the area. It was alleged that the IDF had allowed Christian forces access to the camps, and that these had carried out the massacre over a period of three days (16-18 September) without IDF intervention to prevent it.[148] At Nairobi a number of Arab states therefore called for the exclusion of Israel from the conference and from all future ITU conferences, pressing for this in draft Resolution 120.[149] The US delegation was instructed to walk out should the exclusion of Israel be agreed. An informal group discussed the matter and no less than three Plenary Meetings of the Conference were consumed by debate on the question.[150] The legality of draft Resolution 120 was questioned, and the opinion of the Legal Adviser sought. Dr Nöll's fully argued opinion was that the Convention

146 International Telecommunication Convention, Nairobi, 6 November 1982, 1531 UNTS 320, 1985 UKTS 33, Cmnd 9557; US Tr. Doc. 99-6; also available via link at http://www.itu.int/en/history/plenipotentiaryconferences/Pages/1982Nairobi.aspx. F. Lyall, 'The International Telecommunication Union, Nairobi, 1982' (1983) 4 *J. Media L.* 224.

147 Res. 4 (Kyoto, 1994) limited the Plenipotentiary Conference to a maximum of four weeks unless there was 'a pressing need otherwise'. As revised at Guadalajara, 2010, and still subject to 'pressing need', the 'maximum' has been dropped and duration is re-set as three to four weeks. The Secretary General is to take steps to 'facilitate the most efficient use of time and resources' during conferences.

148 The Sabra/Shatila events remain a matter of contention. Cf. S. MacBride et al., *Israel in Lebanon: The Report of the International Commission to enquire into reported violations of International Law by Israel during its invasion of the Lebanon* (London: Ithaca Press, 1983); and *The Report of the Kahan Commission*, at http://www.mfa.gov.il/MFA/Foreign%20Relations/Israels%20Foreign%20Relations%20since%201947/1982-1984/104%20Report%20of%20the%20Commission%20of%20Inquiry%20into%20the%20e. Cf. 'The Situation in the Middle East', UNGA Res. 37/123.

149 *Minutes of the Plenipotentiary Conference of the International Telecommunication Union, Nairobi 1982* (Geneva: ITU, 1983), delegation statements of Algeria (37-8), Iran (41), Syria (259-60).

150 *Minutes of the Plenipotentiary Conference of the International Telecommunication Union, Nairobi 1982* (Geneva: ITU, 1983), Plenary Meetings 15 (Doc. 456, *Minutes*, 261-71), 16 (Doc. 457, *Minutes*, 273-80) and 18 (Doc. 459, *Minutes*, 287-90).

allowed for only the sanction of the removal of voting privileges in the case of a failure timeously to ratify the Convention or through falling seriously into arrears in financial contribution. Exclusion of a member state was not competent.[151] A group of Western European states, together with Canada and Australia, sought to mediate in the argument. Eventually a resolution condemnatory of the Israeli action/inaction but without excluding Israel, coupled with ITU action to restore Lebanon's shattered telecommunications facilities, was adopted.[152]

The major significance of the Nairobi meetings lies in the clear effect of the growingly vocal developing countries.[153] Although that effect can be seen in the Malaga-Torremolinos arrangements, it was accentuated at Nairobi. The 1960s and 70s had seen a considerable increase in the number of states in the world, independence being granted and/or achieved by many elements of former colonial empires.[154] Many of these new states found, however, that their new status as 'sovereign' was not as unfettered as they had thought, or expected. New states, whose assets were natural resources, often found the exploitation of these resources was tied up by contracts and concessions that favoured international businesses, and often commercial and other entities which were nationals of their former colonial masters. Others found that basic infrastructures such as railways and electricity generating and supply companies were similarly outwith their control. Nationalisations and expropriations occurred, and, while some instances were resolved by agreement, in others disputes proliferated.[155]

---

151 See 'Exclusion of a Member from the Plenipotentiary Conference and all other Conferences and meetings of the International Telecommunication Union: Opinion of the Legal Adviser to the Plenipotentiary Conference of the International Telecommunication Union on 18 December 1982' (1982) UN Jur, Y.B. 214.

152 After a series of procedural votes, Nairobi Conf. Res. 74 'Resolution adopted by the Plenipotentiary Conference regarding Israel and assistance to Lebanon' was adopted in a secret ballot by a vote of 85 to 41, with 13 abstentions, countered by Israel Reservation 28. See 1531 UNTS 501; Legal Adviser's opinion (*supra*, n. 151, at 217). See also M.R. Gardner, US Delegation Chairman, *Report of the US Delegation to the Plenipotentiary Conference of the International Telecommunication union, Nairobi, Kenya, September 28-November 6, 1982*, 1983, at 4-6. Cf. S.E. Probst, 'The Plenipotentiary Conference of the International Telecommunication Union, Nairobi, 1982: A Summary of Results' (1983) 77 *Proc. Am. Soc. Int. L.* 354 at 358. Probst was working from conference documents. His para numbering of the Convention is not the same as the final text as edited by the ITU Secretariat and as found in the UNTS and other official series.

153 J.G. Savage, *The Politics of International Telecommunication Regulation* (Boulder, CO: Westview, 1989); B.E. Harris, 'The New Telecommunications Development Bureau of the International Telecommunication Union' (1991) 7 *Am. U.J. Int. L.& Pol.* 83 at 87-9.

154 Cf. the dates of admission of states to membership of the United Nations at http://www.un.org/en/members/index.shtml. In 1959, and apart from Egypt, only one independent African state, Ghana, was a member of the ITU. By Nairobi there were forty-six.

155 See from that time B.A. Wortley, *Expropriation in Public International Law* (Cambridge: Cambridge UP, 1959); G. White, *Nationalisation of Foreign Property*

The new states all became members of the UN and the ITU. To highlight the interests of the new states, and the importance of their development, the UN proposed various 'World Years' and 'regional years'.[156] On the recommendation of the Economic and Social Council (ECOSOC Res. 1981/60), UNGA Res. 36/40 (1981) proclaimed 1983 as 'World Communications Year: Development of Communications Infra-structures' with the ITU to be the lead agency, and gave it responsibility for coordinating the inter-organisational aspects of related programmes and activities of other agencies. With that spur it was not surprising that the developing countries had an influence on the Nairobi discussions.[157] Some account of their interests had already been taken at Malaga-Torremolinos as we have seen, but by 1982 more specific language in the ITU Convention was required.

The Nairobi Convention included language recognising the world interest in good telecommunications and clearly established that the ITU could and should act towards the development of telecommunications in the developing countries. The Preamble to the Convention was amended *inter alia* to include reference to 'the growing importance of telecommunication for the preservation of peace and the social and economic development of all countries'. Further reference was made to 'peaceful purposes' and to 'economic and social development'. The listing of the Purposes of the Union was added to. It now included 'to promote and to offer technical assistance to developing countries in the field of telecommunications' (Art. 4.1.a (14)). The fostering of 'international cooperation in the delivery of technical assistance to the developing countries' was appended to the creation and improvement of telecommunications through participation in UN programmes (Art. 4.2.c (20)), and the use of ITU resources was added to that activity. A new paragraph – 'technical cooperation and assistance provided to the developing countries' – was added to the list of permissible ITU expenses (Art. 15.1.c (110)). The IFRB powers to advise were extended, allowing it to take special account of

(London: Stevens, 1961). Cf. UNGA Res. 1803 (XVII) (1962) on 'Permanent sovereignty over natural resources', and UNGA Res. 3281 (XXIX) (1974) the 'Charter of Economic Rights and Duties of States'. Cf. also US Congress, 'Legislative Reference Service Report on Expropriation of American-Owned Property by Foreign Governments', (1963) 2 ILM 1066.

156 Cf. The 'Transport and Development Decade in Africa' (UNGA. Res.32/160, 1977), the 'World Development Decade' (UNGA Res. 35/56, 1980). See also UNGA Decision 35/424, 1980 on 'Guidelines for international years and anniversaries', UNGA Res. 53/199, 1998, on 'Proclamation of International Years' and related ECOSOC Res. 1980/67 and 1998/1. The texts of ECSOC Res. 1980/67 and UNGA Decision 35/424 are not electronically available on the UN website, but see *inter alia* UNESCO http://portal.unesco.org/en/ev.php-URL_ID=32568&URL_DO=DO_TOPIC&URL_SECTION=201.html and less formally http://www.iym.uhi.ac.uk/whatafter.htm. In fact the Malaga-Torremolins-Aires Res. 46 in 1973 had set 17 May as 'World Telecommunication Day', 17 May being the date of the adoption of the International Telegraph Union Convention in 1865.

157 Note also that Codding II was published in 1982 prior to the ITU conference.

the needs of developing countries (Art. 10.4.c (79)). The 'geographical situation' of particular countries (Art. 10.4.c (79)) and the 'equitable utilisation of the geostationary orbit' (Art. 10.4.d (80)) were added as matters to be taken into consideration in ITU action and decisions. While all this stopped short of making the interests of the developing countries overriding, it did for the first time include these elements as formal legitimate ITU concerns.

Apart from the formal legal inclusion of 'development', various Resolutions and Opinions of the Nairobi Conference underscored the message. Resolution 24, 'Telecommunication Infra-structure and Socio-Economic Development' (1531 UNTS 464) set a base, elaborated in other documents. Thus *inter alia* Res. 16 called for continued cooperation with UNDP,[158] Resols. 17 and 18 for the review and continuation of financial measures,[159] and Res. 19 for voluntary technical cooperation.[160] Res. 34 called for the ITU to work with other international bodies in developing world telecommunications,[161] and Res. 73 for participation in the programmes of the UN World Communications Year, which was in part to be directed towards developing countries.[162] Conference Opinion No. 2 called for developed countries to re-think their attitudes to requests from developing countries for favourable treatment.[163] In addition, a Commission was set up further to investigate and report on telecommunications development.[164] UNGA Res. 36/40 (1981), 'World Communications Year: Development of Communications Infrastructures' was cited among other documents as the reasons for this step.[165]

158 Res. 16, 'Participation of the Union in the United Nations Development Programme (UNDP) and in Other Programmes of the UN System', 1531 UNTS 454.

159 Res. 17, 'Inter-Country Projects Financed by the United Nations Development Programme (UNDP) in the Field of Telecommunications', 1531 UNTS 455; Res. 18, 'Budgetary and Organizational Aspects of Technical cooperation and Assistance of the Union', 1531 UNTS 455.

160 Res. 19, 'Special Voluntary Programme for Technical Cooperation', 1531 UNTS 458; cf. Res. 21, 'Review of the Overall Management and Operation of Technical Cooperation and Assistance Activities', 1531 UNTS 460; Res 22, 'Improvement of Union Facilities for Rendering Technical Assistance to developing countries', 1531 UNTS 461; and Res. 23, 'Recruitment of Experts for Technical cooperation projects', 1531 UNTS 463.

161 Res. 34, 'The Role of the International Telecommunication Union in the Development of World Telecommunications', 153 UNTS 474.

162 Res. 73, 'World Communications Year. Development of Communications Infra-structures', 1531 UNTS 500.

163 Opinion No. 2, 'Favourable Treatment for Developing Countries', 1531 UNTS 503.

164 Res. 20, 'Establishment of the Independent International Commission for World-Wide Telecommunications development', 1531 UNTS 459.

165 The UN itself was, of course, increasingly active in relation to the developing countries. Cf. UNGA Res. 35/202 (1980) on 'Technical Cooperation Among Developing Countries' and UNGA Res. 35/205 (1980) on the 'United Nations Conference on the Least Developed Nations'.

The Commission, the 'Maitland Commission', reported in December 1984.[166] It noted the disparity between the developed and the developing world in their access to the benefits of good telecommunication services. It identified the importance of telecommunications in the modern world, not only for emergency, health and social service communications, but also for commerce and economic growth. It therefore called for governments and development aid agencies to give a higher priority to investment in telecommunications, for existing telecommunications systems to be made more effective, including through the use of new technologies, for the financing for these efforts to take account of the difficulties faced by developing countries in accessing foreign exchange, and in various ways for the ITU to play a more effective role in the attainment of these objectives. These aims were to echo down the years, and remain important for the current ITU.

In contrast, the 'legal' changes to the ITU at Nairobi were slender. Structurally, the membership of the Administrative Council was increased from thirty-six to forty-one (Art. 8.1.1 (57)). The power of the PP was also increased. Thirty years earlier, in 1952, Buenos Aires had changed the election arrangements for the IFRB. States, not individuals were to be elected to nominate a national as an IFRB member, and that the election of nominating states was to be by PP, not the administrative radio conference. That had been partly reversed at Montreux in 1965, the PP electing individuals, not countries, as IFRB members. At Nairobi provision was now made for the Directors of the CCITT and CCIR also to be elected by the next Plenipotentiary Conference and not as previously by the Plenary Assemblies of those organs. Last, Arabic was added to the official languages of the Union.[167]

Financial matters were discussed in some detail. The increase in ITU membership, particularly through the accession of smaller states, presented problems. Resolution 8 of the 1973 Malaga-Torremolinos PP had remitted the question of the financial basis of the ITU to the Administrative Council for study and report. At Nairobi a step favouring the smaller countries was the extension of the contributory unit classes to a 1/4 and a 1/8 unit class, the latter being restricted to least developed countries according to the relevant UN lists and approved by the Administrative Council (Art. 15.2 (111)). The extension of the top end of the unit classes to a 40 and a 35 unit class might have been thought unduly hopeful, but that opportunity was indeed taken up, as was the option of contributing more than 40 units, effectively through the USSR contributing for Mongolia. However, although other steps were taken to secure budgetary control, it was obvious that the budget was going to be under considerable strain through the extension of the powers and duties of the Union.

Finally, because of the nine-year gap between the Nairobi conference and its predecessor, the provision as to the interval between PPs was tightened. Article 6.1

---

166 *The Missing Link: Report of the Independent Commission for World-wide Telecommunications Development* (Geneva: ITU, 1985); the 'Maitland Commission'.

167 Cf. *supra*, n. 117. See UNGA Res. 35/219 (1980) as to the use of Arabic in the subsidiary and other organs of the UN.

(34) still required that the plenipotentiary conference meet 'normally' every five years but added that 'in any case the interval between successive Plenipotentiary Conferences shall not exceed six years'.

The World Administrative Telegraph and Telephone Conference (WATTC-88), 1988

Throughout the post-War period conferences at Paris and Geneva revised the Telegraph Regulations and the Telephone Regulations.[168] These need not now detain us.

At Melbourne in 1988 a CCITT conference made major changes to the regulations dealing with the Telegraph and the Telephone.[169] By 1988 a number of telecommunications providers were undergoing privatisation of one kind and another. In addition, what we now know as 'convergence' was starting as broadcasting, data exchange, information services and computer technologies etc. came to be disseminated on the traditional telecommunication infrastructures. These developments were unevenly spread among the ITU members, so it took time before compromise was arrived at. However, as the related note on the Melbourne Conference in the ITU website indicates, the Regulations that were then agreed, very reluctantly by some, have facilitated the privatisation process that is to be seen in the last twenty years, together with the liberalisation of the telecommunication market.

In brief, the International Telecommunications Regulations (ITRs) adopted at Melbourne in 1988 replaced both the former Telegraph and the Telephone Regulations. The Telegraph had lost its position within communications in general, and there was felt no longer to be the need for detailed regulation for both international telephone and telegraph services. Since the Melbourne ITRs are still in force, I consider them no further here. They will be outlined in Chapter 5.

---

168 International Telegraph and Telephone Conference, Paris, 1949; International Telegraph and Telephone Conference, Geneva, 1958. Both available from the ITU website via respectively http://www.itu.int/en/history/administrativeconferences/Pages/1949Paris.aspx and http://www.itu.int/en/history/administrativeconferences/Pages/1958Geneva.aspx.

169 International Telecommunication Regulations: Final Acts of the World Administrative Telegraph and Telephone Conference, Melbourne, 1988 (Geneva; ITU, 1989). See http://www.itu.int/en/history/administrativeconferences/Pages/1988Melbourne.aspx.

The International Telecommunication Constitution and Convention, Nice, 1989

The maximum six year interval between PPs set by Nairobi Conv. Art. 6.1 (34) was almost complied with. The Nice PP met from 23 May to 19 June 1989.[170]

At Nice a major structural change to the basic ITU documentation was the formal division of the former single ITU Convention into a separate Constitution and a Convention, the division being close to the differentiation between the First and Second Parts of the Malaga-Torremolinos (1973) and the Nairobi (1982) Conventions. Another innovation was the creation by Art. 14 of a new Bureau, a Telecommunications Development Bureau. This was to be a permanent organ of the ITU, and directed towards both telecommunication cooperation and technical assistance. It was intended to shoulder the ITU responsibilities as a UN specialised agency in these areas, and to implement telecommunication projects under the wider UN development system (Art. 14.1 (112)).

As it turned out, although the Nice documents are interesting, bulky and detailed, probably the most significant step taken at Nice is to be found in Res. 55, on the 'Review of the Structure and Functioning of the International Telecommunication Union'. This called for the constituting of a High-Level Committee of fifteen to twenty-one persons, 'composed, with due regard to equitable geographic representation'. The personnel of the Committee were to be nominated by State Members, which were to 'designate representatives enjoying the highest reputation in international telecommunications and having broad ITU experience.'[171] Resolution 55 is long and complex, citing many past resolutions, decisions and documents. In short the Committee was to review all the functioning of the ITU in relation to its immediate and future tasks and to make recommendations. It was to work swiftly, but was subject to financial constraints. Expenditure on its task was to be kept as low as possible.[172] The Committee could call on the services of outside consultants, but subject to these being selected by the Administrative Council and their fees staying within budgetary limits set by the Council.[173] Finally, the Committee itself was to work on a voluntary basis, 'on

---

170 Final Acts of the Plenipotentiary Conference, Nice 1989: Constitution and Convention of the International Telecommunication Union, Optional Protocol, Decisions, Resolutions, Recommendations and Opinions (ITU: Geneva, 1990); also available via link at http://www.itu.int/en/history/plenipotentiaryconferences/Pages/1989Nice.aspx.

171 PP-89, Nice, Res. 55, 'Review of the Structure and Functioning of the International Telecommunication Union', *resolves* 2. The selection of the nominating Members was made by the Administrative Council meeting in November 1989, *ibid.*, *instructs* 1. Twenty-one Members were selected: Algeria, Australia, Brazil, Canada, China, Colombia, Denmark, France, Germany, India, Indonesia, Japan, Mali, Morocco, Senegal, Saudi Arabia, UK, US, USSR, Yugoslavia and Zimbabwe.

172 Ibid., *resolves* 5. Expenses were drawn from the ordinary ITU budget under the supervision of the Administrative Council.

173 Ibid., *resolves* 3.

the understanding that, where necessary, they shall be given financial assistance to enable them to attend Committee meetings'.[174]

It was time for such a move. Concern over the structure and organisational abilities of the Union had been building for a long time, coming to a climax in the 1980s. The globalisation of telecommunications, the increased and increasing pace of technological change, the development of the information economy and its interaction with society and societies around the world, had rendered the slow mechanisms of the ITU obsolescent, if not obsolete. The swiftly changing telecommunications environment really did require that the ITU alter its structures and procedures. The Consultative Committee system was under strain. Both the CCITT and CCIR were having trouble coping with swift developments in their respective fields. Built into the CCITT procedures were concerns that had been appropriate in the Nineteenth century, with an overlay of reactions to Twentieth century history. The CCIR, having struggled with the massive development of radio in and after the Second World War, was now having to cope with space telecommunications in addition to its terrestrial responsibilities. The whole ITU system was moving too slowly, the intervals between its plenipotentiary conference being symptomatic. Only six such conferences had been held since the Union had last been properly reconsidered at Atlantic City in 1947: Buenos Aires 1952; Geneva, 1959; Montreux, 1965; Malaga-Torremolinos, 1973; Nairobi, 1982; Nice, 1989. There were also problems of internal institutional relationships. In particular there was friction between the IFRB and other organs. As Codding II, 133-5, points out, the Board did not report to the Administrative Council, but sent it a report for its information. Although in terms of vacancies, appointment and salary the Specialised Secretariat of the IFRB was the budget responsibility of the Secretary General,[175] IFRB duties were set by the RR and the radio conferences and the Board made its own decisions. In short, much dissatisfaction with the operation of the Union had built up, and suggestions and proposals for change had been made at intervals over a good number of years.[176]

174 Ibid., *resolves* 4.

175 Nairobi Conv. Art. 56.1.c. This remains the case: see Chapter 5, at n. 91.

176 Cf. *The Missing Link* (the Report of the Maitland Commission) 1985, (*supra*, n. 166), and *The Report of the Secretary General's Advisory Group on the Changing Telecommunications Environment* (the 'Hansen Committee') (Geneva: ITU, 1989). See also Codding II, *passim*; J.H. Glazer, 'Infelix ITU - The Need for Space Age Revisions to the International Telecommunication Convention' (1963) 23 *Fed. B.J.* 1; D.M. Leive, 'The Future of the International Telecommunication Union: A Report for the 1973 Plenipotentiary Conference', with Appendix by S.D. Estep; 'Panel on International Telecommunications Policy of the American Society of International Law' (1972) 3 *Stud. Transnat'l Legal Pol.* i-vii and 1-67; A.L. Allison, 'Meeting the Challenges of Change: The Reform of the International Telecommunication Union' (1991-1992) 45 *Fed. Comm. L.J.* 492.

The International Telecommunication Constitution and Convention, Geneva, 1992: and the Final Acts of the Plenipotentiary Conference of the International Telecommunication Union, Kyoto, 1994

The High Level Committee appointed at Nice acted swiftly, its Report, *Tomorrow's ITU*, being issued in April 1991.[177] Its recommendations were far-reaching and widely welcomed. Accordingly, and since by the time the Report was published only six countries had ratified the 1989 Nice constitutional documents, the Administrative Council decided to press ahead with reform.[178] It arranged that an Additional Plenipotentiary Conference would convene in Geneva in December 1992 before the Nice arrangements were to come into force. This, the 'Extra-Ordinary Plenipotentiary Conference of the International Telecommunication Union', while retaining certain elements of Nice, 1989, put in place major structural changes.[179] However, even before the Geneva Final Acts came into force they were in their turn revised, albeit not fundamentally, by the 1994 Kyoto Plenipotentiary Conference.[180] Coming into force in 1996, the resultant Geneva/Kyoto arrangements have set the pattern of the modern ITU. Subsequent PPs have amended the Geneva Constitution and Convention, but the basic ITU structure has not been altered. All the subsequent PPs have amended the Geneva documents. They have not adopted a new ITU Constitution and Convention.[181]

---

177 *Tomorrow's ITU: The Challenges of Change: the Report of the High Level Committee to review the structure and functioning of the International Telecommunication Union (ITU)* (Geneva: ITU, 1991).

178 This was authorised by PP-89, Nice, Res. 55 (*supra*, n. 171), *instructs the Administrative Council*, 8, and *instructs the Secretary-General*, 6.

179 Constitution and Convention of the International Telecommunication Union: Final Acts of the Additional Plenipotentiary Conference, Geneva, 22 December 1992 (Geneva: ITU, 1993), 1825 UNTS 331; 1996 UKTS 24, Cm. 3145; US Tr. Doc. 104-35; available via link at http://www.itu.int/en/history/plenipotentiaryconferences/Pages/1992Geneva.aspx.

G.A. Codding, 'The International Telecommunication Union: 130 Years of Telecommunications Regulation' (1995) 23 *Denv. J. Int. L. & Pol.* 501-11; F. Lyall, 'The International Telecommunication Union Reconstructed' (1993) 36 *Proc. IISL* 78-88; R. L. and H.L. White, 'The Impact of New Communication Technologies on International Telecommunication Law and Policy: Cyberspace and the Restructuring of the International Telecommunication Union' (1995) 32 *Cal. West. L. Rev.* 1-30; A.L. Allison, 'Meeting the Challenges of Change: Reform of the International Telecommunication Union' (1993) 45 *Fed. Comm. L.J.* 491-540.

180 Final Acts of the Plenipotentiary Conference of the International Telecommunication Union, Kyoto, 14 October 1994 (Geneva: ITU, 1994); US Tr. Doc. 104-34; also available via link at http://www.itu.int/en/history/plenipotentiaryconferences/Pages/1994Kyoto.aspx.

181 While the Final Acts of the Conferences exist in published form, the ITU published in 1999, 2003 and 2007 versions of a *Collection of the basic texts of the International Telecommunication Union adopted by the Plenipotentiary Conference* consolidating the amendments with the Geneva texts, updating the Resolutions and Recommendations in

In the new system the division of the constitutional instruments of the Union into a Constitution and Convention adopted at Nice was retained. The 'relegation' of the regulations of the wired and wireless services to 'administrative regulations' continues, albeit these documents are of status equal to that of the CS and CV. The working arrangements of the Union have been largely recast. The Plenipotentiary Conference and Secretariat carry on, but the 'Consultative Committees', the CCITT and CCIR, have disappeared. Three new organs, named 'Sectors', replace them – the Telecommunication Development Sector (ITU-D[182]), the Telecommunication Standardisation Sector (ITU-T[183]) and the Radiocommunication Sector (ITU-R). The five-member full-time IFRB has gone, part of its role being transferred to a nine-member part-time Radio Regulations Board, the rest apportioned mainly to the new ITU-R and the remainder to ITU-T.

As indicated above, the Geneva/Kyoto arrangements have been further revised by Plenipotentiary Conferences held in Minneapolis, USA, in 1998;[184] at Marrakesh, Morocco, in 2002;[185] in Antalya, Turkey in 2006;[186] and at Guadalajara, Mexico, in 2010.[187] These conferences have refined the basic texts, made minor improvements and introduced further reforms, but they have not altered the fundamental changes of 1992. Simplification of the basic texts continues.

---

force at the time of publication, and very usefully indexing the whole. A new fourth edition, including the changes made by the Guadalajara PP of 2010, is now available on the ITU website.

182 Successor of the Telecommunications Development Bureau, Nice 1989.

183 Confusingly for English-speakers the form 'ITU-T' reflects its French title.

184 Final Acts of the Plenipotentiary Conference, Minneapolis, 1998: Instruments Amending the Constitution and the Convention of the International Telecommunication Union (Geneva, 1992) as amended by the Plenipotentiary Conference (Kyoto, 1994) (Geneva: ITU, 1998); Constitution, 2133 UNTS 313; Convention, 2134 UNTS 222; available via link at http://www.itu.int/en/history/plenipotentiaryconferences/Pages/1998Minneapolis.aspx.

185 Final Acts of the Plenipotentiary Conference, Marrakesh, 2002: Instruments amending the Constitution and the Convention of the International Telecommunication Union (Geneva, 1992) as amended by the Plenipotentiary Conference (Kyoto, 1994) and the Plenipotentiary Conference (Minneapolis, 1998) (Geneva: ITU, 2003); US Tr. Doc. 109-11; Constitution, 2260 UNTS 2; Convention 2261 UNTS 72; available via link at http://www.itu.int/en/history/plenipotentiaryconferences/Pages/2002Marrakesh.aspx.

186 Final Acts of the Plenipotentiary Conference, Antalya, 2006: Instruments amending the Constitution and the Convention of the International Telecommunication Union (Geneva, 1992) as amended by the Plenipotentiary Conference (Kyoto, 1994), the Plenipotentiary Conference (Minneapolis, 1998) and the Plenipotentiary Conference (Marrakesh, 2002) (Geneva: ITU, 2007); US Tr. Doc. 110-16.

187 Final Acts of the Plenipotentiary Conference, Guadalajara, 2010: Instruments amending the Constitution and the Convention of the International Telecommunication Union (Geneva, 1992) as amended by the Plenipotentiary Conference (Kyoto, 1994), the Plenipotentiary Conference (Minneapolis, 1998) and the Plenipotentiary Conference (Marrakesh, 2002) and the Plenipotentiary Conference (Guadalajara, 2010) (Geneva: ITU, 2011).

It would be otiose here to go through the subsequent amendments to the Geneva CS and CV in detail, but some comment is required. Most notably it is clear that the introduction of a regular four year interval between plenipotentiary conferences has had a significant effect. That the meetings of the other organs of the Union are intercalated within that four year cycle has required them to adopt a regular regime of deliberation and action. The tasks of the Union being clearly seen as 'work-in-progress' has encouraged a willingness to respond to the changing telecommunications environment. As noted, the 1994 Kyoto plenipotentiary conference made little change to the main pattern of Geneva, 1992. However, the tenor of the discussions represented by its Resolutions and Recommendations indicate an invigoration of atmosphere within the Union. A schedule was set for the period through 1999 for the future world conferences of the Union and the Sectors (PP-94 Kyoto, Res. 3). A Strategic Plan was adopted for the work of the Union for next four years *inter alia* setting priorities for the Sectors (PP-94, Res. 1). Other Resolutions included strengthening the regional presence of the ITU (PP-94 Res. 25), and establishing a series of World Telecommunications Fora within which members, whether states or lesser sector members[188] would meet to discuss and exchange information (PP-94 Kyoto, Res. 11). The patterns thus established have continued.

We now turn to the current ITU.

188 Non-state 'sector members' are considered in the next chapter.

Chapter 5
The Modern ITU

Preliminary Note

The modern ITU remains the sole international agency through which international electrical communications, whether wireless or wired, are regulated by agreement of its members, which include all the members of the UN.[1] This remains its basic function. However, as was seen in the previous chapter, pressure has grown for the ITU also to act as a body through which technical developments are brought to states that are less technologically privileged. I will therefore deal first with the structural elements of the ITU – those relating to its basic function and incorporated in its constituent documents – before turning to sketch the efforts to develop communications through such activities as ITU Telecom, WSIS (the World Summit on the Information Society) and others.

This chapter considers the ITU as it is in the period 2012-2015. It assumes that the Final Acts of the Guadalajara Plenipotentiary Conference come into force on 1 January 2012 as they provide. The ruling constitutional documents are therefore the Constitution (CS) and Convention (CV) adopted at the Additional Plenipotentiary Conference held in Geneva in 1992, as amended. The CS and the CV are 'completed' by the Administrative Regulations which share their status.

It is now common practice to cite provisions of the Constitution as 'CS' and those of the Convention as 'CV'. These indicators are followed first by the technical treaty citation 'Article, paragraph, sub-paragraph, etc.' as is the practice in other treaties, and then by a number in brackets. The bracketed numbering runs consecutively through each of the CS and CV, and facilitates reference to particular provisions. Numbers are editorially supplied by the ITU Secretariat following the relevant conference. However, numbers that related to deleted provisions are retained: change including deletion does not involve a renumbering. This practice is sensible as it allows clarity in reference down through the years. New provisions within a numbered paragraph may require 'A', 'B', etc. to be added to the basic number, with '*bis*', '*ter*', etc. used for new subsections. Decisions are cited as 'Dec.', Resolutions as 'Res.'

1 The ITU remains the UN specialised agency for international telecommunications. See Annex IX to the Convention on the Privileges and Immunities of the Specialised Agencies of the United Nations, New York, 21 November 1947; 33 UNTS 261; 1959 UKTS 69, Cmnd 855 and *supra*, Chapter 4, nn. 121-2. Non-UN members may be ITU members, e.g. the case of Switzerland until it joined the UN in October 2002. See *infra* 'Membership: State Membership'.

and Recommendations as 'Rec.', with a note in brackets of the Conferences adopting or revising them. The numbering of Decisions, Resolutions and Recommendations runs from the 1994 plenipotentiary conference. Abrogated Decisions, Resolutions and Recommendations are simply dropped, but their numbers are not reused. At first sight surprising, this practice again makes for clarity in citation and discussion as a user does not have to track any re-numbering or re-ordering of these materials.

Finally, Plenipotentiary Conferences are designated 'PP' with, if necessary, the year involved (e.g. PP-94). An Additional Plenipotentiary Conference is designated 'APP', (e.g. APP-92). The Radio Regulations are commonly denoted by the abbreviation 'RR'.

* * *

The Final Acts of the Additional Plenipotentiary Conference of the International Telecommunication Union, Geneva, 1992, contain the Constitution and Convention of the Union, as well as the Decisions, Resolutions and Recommendations of the Conference.[2] Both CS and CV have been amended by PPs held in 1994 at Kyoto, Japan;[3] in 1998 at Minneapolis, US;[4] in 2002 at Marrakesh, Morocco;[5] in 2006

2 Constitution and Convention of the International Telecommunication Union: Final Acts of the Additional Plenipotentiary Conference, Geneva, 22 December 1992 (Geneva: ITU, 1993). Constitution, 1825 UNTS 331; Convention, 1825 UNTS 390; 1996 UKTS 24, Cm. 3145; US Tr. Doc. 103-35; US Tr. Doc. 104-34; also available via link at http://www.itu.int/en/history/plenipotentiaryconferences/Pages/1992Geneva.aspx.

3 Final Acts of the Plenipotentiary Conference, Kyoto, 1994: Instruments Amending the Constitution and Convention of the International Telecommunication Union (Geneva, 1992), Decisions, Resolutions and Recommendations (ITU: Geneva, 1994); 1997 UKTS 65, Cm. 3779; US Tr. Doc. 104-34 (CS at 297, CV at 319); also available via link at http://www.itu.int/en/history/plenipotentiaryconferences/Pages/1994Kyoto.aspx.

4 Final Acts of the Plenipotentiary Conference, Minneapolis, 1998: Instruments Amending the Constitution and the Convention of the International Telecommunication Union (Geneva, 1992) as amended by the Plenipotentiary Conference (Kyoto, 1994) (Geneva: ITU, 1998); Constitution, 2133 UNTS 313; Convention, 2134 UNTS 222; also available via link at http://www.itu.int/en/history/plenipotentiaryconferences/Pages/1998Minneapolis.aspx.

5 Final Acts of the Plenipotentiary Conference, Marrakesh, 2002: Instruments amending the Constitution and the Convention of the International Telecommunication Union (Geneva, 1992) as amended by the Plenipotentiary Conference (Kyoto, 1994) and the Plenipotentiary Conference (Minneapolis, 1998) (Geneva: ITU, 2003); US Tr. Doc. 109-11; Constitution, 2260 UNTS 224; Convention 2261 UNTS 72; also available via link at http://www.itu.int/en/history/plenipotentiaryconferences/Pages/2002Marrakesh.aspx.

at Antalya, Turkey;[6] and in 2010 at Guadalajara, Mexico,[7] the Final Acts of the last coming into force on 1 January 2012. Various general points should be noted. First, there has been a significant change from the practice of the pre-1992 period. The ITU no longer replaces the previous treaty arrangements: the later PPs amend the 1992 arrangements. Second, the number of alterations, and their weight, has diminished over time as the 1992 arrangements have been proven by experience and adapted as necessary. Kyoto improved the Geneva text. Minneapolis was a bulkier exercise, tweaking a variety of provisions. The Marrakesh, Antalya and Guadalajara conferences made relatively few further changes. In short, while the post-1992 amendments introduced some additional reforms, improved the 1992 text and ironed out problems, they have not seriously departed from the fundamental changes of 1992/1994. Simplification is desired.[8] Indeed, rather than change to the CS or CV, in many ways the most significant output of the later conferences is to be found in their Decisions, Resolutions, and Recommendations that largely relate to the work of the Union, not to its structure and procedures.

The Final Acts of the Geneva, Kyoto, Minneapolis, Marrakesh, Antalya and Guadalajara PPs are published as separate volumes by the ITU, on the ITU website and in the UNTS and other official series as footnoted above. In what follows, the texts of the 1992 CS and CV are taken as amended down to 2010. Most useful is the 'clean text' provided in the *Collection* authorised by Res. 75 of the Minneapolis PP.[9] Technically an internal ITU compilation and without formal legal standing, the *Collection* (and its Index) are extraordinarily helpful.

---

6 Final Acts of the Plenipotentiary Conference, Antalya, 2006: Instruments amending the Constitution and the Convention of the International Telecommunication Union (Geneva, 1992) as amended by the Plenipotentiary Conference (Kyoto, 1994), the Plenipotentiary Conference (Minneapolis, 1998) and the Plenipotentiary Conference (Marrakesh, 2002) (Geneva: ITU, 2007); US Tr. Doc. 110-16; also available via link at http://www.itu.int/en/history/plenipotentiaryconferences/Pages/2006Antalya.aspx.

7 Final Acts of the Plenipotentiary Conference, Guadalajara, 2010: Instruments amending the Constitution and the Convention of the International Telecommunication Union (Geneva, 1992) as amended by the Plenipotentiary Conference (Kyoto, 1994), the Plenipotentiary Conference (Minneapolis, 1998), the Plenipotentiary Conference (Marrakesh, 2002) and the Plenipotentiary Conference (Antalya, 2006) (Geneva: ITU, 2011); also available at http://www.itu.int/pub/S-CONF-ACTF-2010/en.

8 The process of simplification continues. The Marrakesh Plenipotentiary Conference, 2002, moved many of the rules as to the calling of conferences and their rules of procedure to a separate document, 'General Rules of Conferences, Assemblies and Meetings of the Union', and suppressed the previous provision in CV Arts. 26-30 (299-323). Detailed Rules are now a matter for the particular conferences and assemblies concerned but these are always adopted within the context of the 'General Rules'.

9 *Collection of the basic texts of the International Telecommunication Union adopted by the Plenipotentiary Conference* (Geneva: ITU, 2011) available as a CD ROM or as http://www.itu.int/pub/S-CONF-PLEN-2011/en. Previous editions were published in softback

***

To recap: as constituted under the Atlantic City Convention of 1947,[10] and down to the Nairobi Convention of 1982,[11] the structure and operation of the ITU were conditioned by its evolution through more than a century. Three organs met at intervals – the Plenipotentiary Conference, Administrative Conferences and the Administrative Council. Four permanent organs were charged with the detailed business of the Union. These were the General Secretariat, the International Frequency Registration Board (IFRB), the International Radio Consultative Committee (CCIR) and the International Telegraph and Telephone Consultative Committee (CCITT).[12]

In the 1960s and 70s the ITU grew quickly as new countries came into existence and joined. They had their own views and interests. Technology developed increasingly swiftly. Space communications came on the scene. The old structures and functioning became sclerotic. Dissatisfaction grew. At Nice in 1989 it was arranged that a High Level Committee should review the ITU. This Committee acted speedily, and largely on the basis of its Report[13] an Additional Plenipotentiary Conference held in Geneva in 1992 made major changes to the Union which were refined at the Kyoto PP in 1994. The ITU Convention, the previous basic single constitutional document, was split into a Constitution and a Convention.[14] The ITU was given its present form, including the re-allocation of major areas of responsibility to three new Sectors. A new four-year cycle of PPs was established within which its organs work, conferences are intercalated, and the Sectors and their sub-groups function.[15] The intention was efficiency, cost effectiveness, and an ability more swiftly to respond to the regulatory needs of a rapidly changing international telecommunications environment. Nonetheless the traditional substantive duties that undergirded the institution remain fundamental to the current arrangements.

in 1999, 2003 and 2007 following the PPs of Minneapolis, 1998, Marrakesh, 2002 and Antalya, 2006. These remain useful for history.

10 International Convention on Telecommunications, Atlantic City, 2 October 1947; 193 UNTS 188, 194 UNTS 3; 1950 UKTS 76, Cmd. 8124; 63 Stat. 1399, TIAS 1901; 4 Bevans 470. See http://www.itu.int/en/history/plenipotentiaryconferences/Pages/1947AtlanticCity.aspx.

11 International Telecommunication Convention, Nairobi, 6 November 1982; 1531 UNTS 320 (E); 1985 UKTS 33, Cmnd 9557; US Tr. Doc. 99-6; also available via link at http://www.itu.int/en/history/plenipotentiaryconferences/Pages/1982Nairobi.aspx.

12 Nairobi Convention, *supra*, n. 11, Art. 5.

13 Tomorrow's ITU: The Challenges of Change: the Report of the High Level Committee to review the structure and functioning of the International Telecommunication Union (ITU) (Geneva: ITU, 1991).

14 The Final Acts of the Nice Plenipotentiary Conference of 1989 had made that split, but its provisions had not come into force, and were overtaken by the 1992 decisions.

15 Some ITU 'operations' run to a four-year timetable and others to a two-year cycle. Non-cyclical meetings etc. are scheduled as needed or desirable.

Traditional Substantive Duties

Although the mechanics of the ITU have altered greatly, the original purpose of the institution remains its bedrock. International telecommunications require international agreement as to their technical arrangements. Both predecessor elements of the ITU therefore laid on their parties significant rights and duties directed to the facilitating of international services. Retained throughout the history of the Union these are now to be found in CS Chapter VI (Arts. 33-43 (179-94) and CV Chapter V (Arts. 36-40 (496-506)), special provision for radio being also found in CS Chapter VII (Arts. 44-8 (195-204)). The precise scope of these rights and duties is further spelled out within the Administrative Regulations, to which we will come. Details have altered, but the objective remains. For example, there has to be agreement on the division of the payment made for the service provided. That requires two computations, the size of the message and the distance travelled within each jurisdiction. At the first the basic rate for an international telegram depended on the counting of words in a message. There had also to be agreement on what constituted a 'word'. Only then could 'distance' be brought into play. Now telecommunication traffic counts 'bits' – binary digits – a simpler process, but conceptually the same operation.

As we saw in Chapters 2 and 3, the purpose of the original agreements was the establishment and maintenance of international telecommunications on a general basis. That did not exclude the possibility of bilateral or regional arrangements being entered into by their parties, a freedom now preserved in CS Art. 43 (194) and RR Art. 6, subject to these alternative arrangements being not in conflict with the CS or CV. Except in relation to exempt services,[16] Member States are to abide by the CS, the CV and the Administrative Regulations in the operation of telecommunication offices, or stations engaged in international services, or stations that may cause harmful interference to the radio services of other countries (CS Art. 6.1 (37)). Member States are further required to impose these obligations on operating agencies which they may license (CS Art. 38.2 (38)). Despite these duties Member States 'accept no responsibility towards the users of international telecommunication services, particularly as regards claims for damages' (CS Art. 36 (183)).[17]

The duty of interconnection – the establishment and maintenance of international telecommunication networks – is contained in CS Art. 38 (186-189A). To 'carry on the rapid and uninterrupted exchange of international telecommunications' Member States are to take all necessary steps to ensure the establishment under the best technical conditions of necessary installations and channels (CS Art. 38.1 (186)) and to safeguard those that lie within their jurisdictions (CS Art. 38.3 (188)).

16 I.e. military stations, for which see *infra*, at n. 22.

17 This exclusion, of course, does not bar a user claiming in respect of a failure by a private telecommunications provider, but that liability may be excluded by the contract between the user and the provider concerned.

Installations and channels are so far as possible to be operated by methods and procedures shown by practical experience to be best (CS Art. 38.2 (187)). They are to be maintained 'in proper operating condition and kept abreast of scientific and technical progress' (CS Art. 38.2 (187) *ad fin*). Particularly, each Member State is to maintain the sections of international networks within its control unless other conditions are laid down by special arrangements (CS Art. 38.4 (189)).[18] Members also recognise the necessity to take 'practical measures to prevent the operation of electrical apparatus and installations of all kinds from disrupting the operation of telecommunication installations in other states' (CS Art. 38.5 (189A)).

Correlative to the maintenance and operation of the international telecommunications system is the question of the payment of charges for its use. As seen in Chapters 3 and 4, that has always been a matter of concern, at one time involving complex rules defining what counted as a 'word' together with the computation of the distance a message was transmitted. The current provisions as to charges and free services (such as service communications) are contained in CV Arts. 37-8 (496-9) and in the International Telecommunication Regulations (ITR), to which we will come in more detail. The rendering and settlement of accounts between Member States are 'current transactions' (CV Art. 37.1 (497)). The administrations of Member States and Sector Members operating international telecommunication services are required to agree their mutual debits and credits (CV Art. 37.2 (498)). Statements are drawn up in accordance with the ITRs unless other arrangements have been agreed between the entities involved (CV Art. 37.3 (499)). Settlement is effected in accordance with any special arrangement between the parties, failing which the ITR provisions apply (CV Art. 37.1 (497) and CS Art. 42 (193)). In the absence of special agreement the monetary unit used in rendering and settling accounts is either that of the International Monetary Fund or the French gold franc (CV Art. 38 (500); ITR Art. 6.3 (48-9)).

The right of the public to access to and use of 'the international service of public correspondence' is recognised by Member States (CS Art. 33 (179)). Charges and safeguards are to be the same for all users in each category of correspondence (CS Art. 33 (179)). There is no priority or preference among private messages (CS Art. 33 (179)). Member States are to take all possible measures to ensure the secrecy of international correspondence (CS Art. 37.1 (184)). However, they also reserve the right to communicate that correspondence to any competent authorities to ensure compliance with national law or with relevant international conventions (CS Art. 37.2 (185)). The old rules remain as to the ability of a state in accordance with its national law to stop the 'transmission of any private telegram' which may appear dangerous to the security of the state, to be contrary to its law or to public order or decency (CS Art. 34.1 (180)). The only requirement thereanent is that the stopping of a telegram should be reported to the sending origin of the message, unless that notification itself might appear to endanger state security. The

18 For example, a trans-ocean cable agreement may contain special provisions as to the maintenance of the cable.

power to stop on these grounds also extends to any private telecommunications (CS Art. 34.2 (181)). Short of stoppage Member States reserve the right to suspend telecommunications generally, or in relation to certain types of messages, in whole or in part, whether incoming, outgoing or in transit, providing only that such suspension is notified to other Member States through the ITU Secretary General (CS Art. 35 (182)).[19]

Messages concerning safety of life, whether at sea, on land, in the air or in outer space, together with 'epidemiological telecommunications of exceptional urgency of the World Health Organisation' are to be given absolute priority (CS Art. 40 (191)). In radio communication, distress messages are to be accorded priority irrespective of their origin. Radio stations are to accept such messages, to reply, and to take whatever action may be required (CS Art. 46 (200)). The corollary is that Member States are required to 'prevent the transmission or circulation of false or deceptive distress, urgency, safety or identification signals, and to collaborate in locating and identifying stations under their jurisdiction transmitting such signals' (CS Art. 47 (201)).

Specifically in relation to radio one finds provisions that conceptually go right back to the Berlin Convention of 1906. All 'stations, whatever their purpose, are to be operated in such a manner not to cause harmful interference to the radio service or communications of other Member States' or to other radio users operating in accordance with the RR (CS Art. 45.1 (197)). Member States are required to impose correlative duties on radio users that they license (CS Art. 45.2 (198)). Beyond that, Member States recognise the need to take 'all practicable steps' to prevent electrical apparatus and installations of all kinds 'from causing harmful interference to the services or communications' of other members (CS Art. 45.3 (199)). Article 44.1 (195) requires Member States to try to limit the number of radio frequencies and spectrum bandwidths used by themselves and those they license 'to the minimum essential to provide in a satisfactory manner the necessary services. To that end they shall endeavour to apply the latest technical advances as soon as possible'.[20] Article 44.2 (196) further both recognises and requires Member States to bear in mind that, contrary to general opinion, radio frequencies and, in relation to space, any associated orbits (including the geostationary satellite orbit), are 'limited natural resources'. They must be used 'rationally, efficiently and economically' in accordance with the Radio Regulations.[21]

---

19 How this applies in relation to access to information websites is uncertain.

20 Note that Art. 44.1 (195) requires 'endeavours' to be made, a term that allows of some wriggle-room.

21 F. Lyall, 'The Rational, Efficient and Economic Use of Space: Three Suggestions', in M. Benkö and W. Kroll (eds), *Air and Space Law in the 21st Century: Liber Amicorum K-H Böckstiegel* (Cologne: Carl Heymanns Verlag, 2002) p. 386. ITU-R, the Radiocommunication Sector, is the major agency through which the radio provisions are implemented: as to which see *infra*, n. 103.

National defence service systems and installations sit ambiguously with these requirements.[22] Member States 'retain their entire freedom with regard to military radio installations' (CS Art. 48.1 (202)). Nonetheless such installations must 'so far as possible' comply with duties as to distress messages, the prevention of harmful interference, and, depending on the service provided, with the Administrative Regulations as to emission types and frequencies used (CS Art. 48.2 (203)). Further, when a military radio station provides public correspondence services or other services which are governed by the Administrative Regulations, it must in general comply with the regulatory provisions made for the conduct of those services (CS Art. 48.3 (204)).

The Constitution (CS) and the Convention (CV)

The instruments of the Union are the Constitution (CS), the Convention (CV) and the Administrative Regulations (CS Art. 4.1 (29)), the CS being the basic instrument (CS Art. 4.2 (30)). The CS and CV were drawn up in Arabic, Chinese, English, French, Russian and Spanish, which are the official languages of the Union (Art. 21.1.1 (171)). In the case of a discrepancy the French version is final (CS Art. 58.5 (242)).[23] The Administrative Regulations comprise the International Telecommunication Regulations (ITRs) and the Radio Regulations (RR). These regulate international telecommunications. They 'further complement' the CS and CV, having equal status with those documents (CS Art. 4.3 (31)).

The CS and the CV were adopted by the Geneva Additional Plenipotentiary Conference in 1992, and each has been amended by subsequent PPs including, before they came into force, the further amendments made at Kyoto in 1994. The CS and CV are not equal in status. The CS is the basic instrument (CS Art. 4.2 (30)). This is reflected in two ways. First, if there is an inconsistency between the CS, the CV or the Administrative Regulations, the CS prevails (CS Art. 4.4 (32)). Second, an amendment to the CS requires approval by at least a two-thirds majority in a plenary meeting of the PP (CS Art. 55.4 (227)), the quorum for which is at least one-half of the accredited delegations. An amendment to the CV requires only a simple majority in the PP (CV Art. 42.4 (522)), subject to the same requirements as to quorum (CV Art. 42.3 (521)). Amendments proposed to either the CS or the CV must be notified to the ITU Secretary-General not later than eight months before the opening of a PP, and published at least six months prior to it (CS Art. 55.1 (224); CV Art. 42.1 (519)). However, a modification to a duly

22 Reference point, *supra*, n. 16.

23 The French alphabetical order is used for the seating of delegations at conferences (GR 9 (48), for roll-call votes GR 25.1.b (125)) and in the listing for the elections of the Secretary General, the Deputy Secretary General and the Directors of the Sector Bureaux (GR 32.3.a-b (181-3)), of the Radio Regulations Board (GR 33.2.a-b (176-8)), and to Council (GR 34.2.a-b (208-10)).

proposed amendment can itself be put forward at any stage thereafter, including during the relevant conference (CS Art. 55.2 (225); CV Art. 42.2 (520)). The Council may 'consider and adopt, if appropriate,' a proposal for the amendment of the CS or the CV, and put it forward to the next PP (CS Art. 8.2.i (57)).

The 1992 CS and CV as amended in 1994 were subject to simultaneous ratification, approval or acceptance as a single instrument by the appropriate constitutional procedures of each Member State (CS Art. 52.1 (208)). They came into force for their ratifiers on 1 January 1994 (CS Art. 58.1 (238)) and for their ratifiers abrogated and replaced the ITU Convention of Nairobi 1982 (CS Art. 58.2 (239)). After the entry into force of the two documents a non-ratifying State Member enjoyed full rights in the Union for two further years within which it might approve the revised texts. After that period a non-ratifying member might continue to attend all ITU meetings, but lost the right to vote at them or in any consultation (CS Art. 52.2-3 (209-210); CS Art. 55.8 (231)).[24]

Amendments to the CS or CV are adopted as a single instrument and come into force on a date specified by the PP which adopts them (CS Art. 55.6 (229); CV Art. 42.6 (524)). An amending instrument must be accepted as a whole, acceptance of only a part being excluded (CS Art. 55.6 (229); CV Art. 42.6 (524)). Should an amendment to the CV be required by a modification of the CS, it cannot come into force until the related amendment to the CS comes into force (CV Art. 42.7 (525)).

Accession

A non-Member state eligible for membership can accede to the CS and CV at any time by depositing an instrument of accession with the Secretary General, but must do so in a single instrument covering both documents. An instrument of accession comes into effect immediately on its deposit or on such date as it may specify (CS Art. 53.1-3 (212-4)).[25]

Denunciation

Denunciation of the CS and CV is competent. Denunciation can only be in respect of both documents simultaneously and in a single instrument. It takes effect one year after its deposit with the Secretary General (CS Art. 57.1-2 (236-7)). A denouncing state remains liable for its financial contributions to the Union until the denunciation takes effect (CV Art. 33.2.2 (473)).

---

24 As at July 2010 Antigua and Barbuda, Nauru, the Solomon Islands and Sierra Leone had not acceded to the Geneva CS and CV, and Grenada, while a signatory, had not yet ratified or approved the CS and CV: see 'Loss of the Right to Vote', Note by ITU Sec. Gen., PP-10, Doc. 60.

25 See *infra*, 'Membership: State Membership'.

A Sector Member may denounce its participation or a State Member may denounce on behalf of a Sector Member on six month's notice.[26] It remains liable for its financial contribution for the period in which it remains a Sector Member (CV Arts. 19.10 (240) and 33.2.2 (473)).

Declarations and Reservations

Not all multilateral agreements permit 'declarations and reservations' to their substantive provisions.[27] As noted above, no reservations can be made to the substantive provisions of the CS and CV or to amendments to them, although reservations to the Administrative Regulations are competent (CS Art. 54.2 (216) and CV Art. 32B (340D-G)). The ITU Final Acts, however, are always accompanied by statements, declarations or reservations made by delegations on signature or sometimes when a state later transmits its notification of its ratification of the documents.[28] In 1947 many of the relatively few declarations and reservations had to do with a non-acceptance of the Telephone or Telegraph Regulations. Later, other considerations appear. In the Final Acts affecting the CS or CV some reserve the right to make further reservations responding to those made by others. A blanket refusal to accept any consequences deriving from the reservations made by other states is common. Often there is a reservation of the power to take any steps necessary to safeguard state interests should other parties fail to comply with their obligations. Frequently there is a refusal to accept any increase in financial commitment should others fail to pay their dues. Some reservations simply state

26 For Sector Members see *infra*, 'Membership: Sector Membership'.

27 Thus Art. 309 of the Convention on the Law of the Sea, Montego Bay, 1984 (1833 UNTS 3; (1999) UKTS 81, Cm. 4524; (1982) 21 ILM 1261) permits no reservations and exceptions to the Convention unless expressly allowed by specific articles of the Convention. Again, the current UPU Constitution and General Regulations do not permit reservations to them, although reservations to other UPU Agreements are permitted. See UPU Constitution, Arts. 22.1, 2 and 6, and Chapter 8, 'Acts of the Union'.

For the general rules as to reservations to multilateral treaties see Art. 2.1.d, and Arts. 19-23 of the Convention on the Law of Treaties, Vienna, 1969, 1155 UNTS 155; 1980 UKTS 58, Cmnd. 7964; 8 ILM 679; (1969) 63 AJIL 875. See also M.H. Mendelson, 'Reservations to the Constitutions of International Organizations' (1971) 45 BYIL 137.

28 See the ITU publication of the various Final Acts noted in the previous Chapter. Sometimes these statements appear in the UNTS version. See Atlantic City, 1947, 193 UNTS 296; Buenos Aires, 1952, 1958 UKTS 36, Cmnd. 520; 6 UST 1213, TIAS 3266: Geneva, 1959, 1961 UKTS 74, Cmnd. 1484; 12 UST 1761, TIAS 4892; Montreux, 1965, 1967 UKTS 41, Cmnd. 3383; 18 UST 575, TIAS 6267; Malaga-Torremolinos, 1973, 1209 UNTS 32, 255; 1975 UKTS 104, Cmnd. 6289; 28 UST 2495, TIAS 8572; Nairobi, 1982, 1531 UNTS 320 (E), 1985 UKTS 33, Cmnd 9557; US Tr. Doc. 99-6. Notwithstanding Art. 102 of the UN Charter, the 1952, 1959 and 1965 Conventions were not registered with the UN.

What follows uses 'Decl.' as the abbreviation for both Declarations and Statements.

that their makers maintain reservations made to the 1992 documents and related amending Final Acts.[29] Recently some declarations and reservations have included statements that the ITU obligations would be met within the context of other multilateral arrangements.[30] Sometimes a declaration or reservation can seem, to an outsider, odd.[31] Some declarations and reservations relate to territorial claims. For example, at Montreux, 1965, by Decl. V Argentina objected to the UK signing the Final Acts in respect of the Falkland Island Dependencies and the British Antarctic Territories, the UK signature having no effect on Argentine sovereignty over the Malvinas, the South Sandwich and the South Georgia Islands, which had been 'occupied by the UK by an act of force never accepted by' Argentina, or as to territories lying in the Argentine Sector of the Antarctic. This was countered by the UK in Decl. L. Similar Declarations followed, the most recent being Argentina's Decl. 20 to the Guadalajara Final Acts countered by UK Decl. 90. At Malaga-Torremolinos (1973), Chile (Res. VIII) objected to any suggestion that 'British Antarctic Territories' could include sections of Antarctica claimed by Chile, while Argentina made a similar but wider Declaration (Decl. LXXXVII) objecting to the UK signature including for the Falkland Islands, South Georgia and the South Sandwich Islands as well as for the UK Antarctic mainland area.[32] These were 'noted' and rejected in the UK counter (Decl. CII). Similar content may be found in Chilean and Argentinian reservations to later Final Acts.[33] ITU Final Acts have also seen a succession of reservations based on 'sovereignty' or 'sovereign rights' in or over the geostationary orbit that are founded on the Bogota Declaration of 1976.[34] Some reservations or declarations concern the propriety of another

29 E.g. Minneapolis, Final Acts, Decl. 66 by Cyprus, Denmark, Estonia, Finland, Germany, Ireland, Iceland, Italy, Latvia, Liechtenstein, Malta, The Netherlands, Norway, Romania, Switzerland and the UK. Antalya Decl. 73 contains the same Declaration by 36, and Guadalajara Decl. 39 by 33 European states. Cf. Guadalajara Decls. 27 (Viet Nam), 70 (Mexico).

30 E.g. Antalya (2006) Decl. 33 by members of the European Economic Area, Decl. 51 by members of the European Union, and Guadalajara Decl. 23.

31 By Antalya Decl. 36 (repeated in Guadalajara Decl. 10) Belgium states that: 'Signature by members of the delegation shall be equally binding on the French Community, the Flemish Community and the German-speaking community', perhaps reflecting strains within the Kingdom of the Belgians. In Nice, Decl. 43, Burkina Faso safeguards its financial and other positions should others default, and concludes 'Fatherland or Death', a phrase not repeated in its reservations to later Final Acts.

32 Cf. Nice, Final Acts, 1989, Decls. 75 (Argentina) and 109 (UK); Geneva, 1992, Decls. 49 (Argentina) and 80 (UK reply).

33 Nairobi, Final Acts, 1982, Decls. 10 (Argentina) and 59 (Chile), countered by Decl. No. 102 (UK).

34 The Declaration of the First Meeting of the Equatorial States, Bogota, 1976 (1978) 6 J. Sp. Law 193-6; Manual on Space Law, N. Jasentuliyana and R.S.K. Lee (eds), (Dobbs Ferry, NY: Oceana, 1979-81) Vol. 2, 383-7. Eight equatorial states (Brazil, Colombia, Congo, Ecuador, Indonesia, Kenya, Uganda and Zaire) claimed sovereign rights in the geostationary

signatory to the Final Acts.[35] Israel, the most common target of such reservations, always enters a counter-reservation.[36] Others may comment on matters of current

---

orbit over their respective territories. On the Declaration see Lyall/Larsen 61-2 and 253-6; T. Gangale, 'Who Owns the Geostationary Orbit?' (2006) 31 AASL 425-46.

Nairobi Decl. 90 jointly by Colombia, Congo, Ecuador, Gabon, Indonesia, Kenya, Uganda and Somalia incorporated by reference their Res. 40, 42 and 79 based on the Bogota assertions to the Final Acts of the 1979 Administrative Radio Conference. That was rejected by twenty-four delegations by their Decl. 104. This process was repeated at Nice, 1989, by Decls. 4 (Congo), 6 (Ecuador), 69 (Kenya) and 83 (Colombia), which were rejected by twenty-four delegations in Res. 110 and separately by Afghanistan in Decl. 3. At Geneva, 1992, Colombia (Decl. 48) and Kenya (Decl. 53) again reserved their position as to sovereignty in the geostationary orbit. This attempt was rejected separately by Afghanistan (Decl. 6) and by twenty-seven other delegations (Decl. 73). At Minneapolis, 1998, by Decl. 111 twenty-five delegations rejected a similar claim by Columbia in its Decl. 50. At Marrakesh, 2002, Columbia (Decl. 45) again stated its position on the geostationary orbit. This, and any similar statement in other reservations, was rejected by twenty-eight other delegations (Decl. 101). At Antalya, 2006, Colombia (Decl. 58) again reserved the question and this and similar statements were rejected by thirty-one delegations (Decl. 98). Of these, nine made a further counter reservation (Decl. 106) to those of Mexico (Decl. 34), Ecuador (Decl. 55) and Columbia (Decl. 58) which in effect had reference to orbits over the Americas. Cf. Guadalajara, Mexico Decl. 70 and response by 32 other countries in Decl. 85. The Guadalajara reservations may indicate that the cycle has ended.

35 Montreux, 1965, Decl. IV by many African states declared that their signature of the Final Acts did not imply recognition of the then South African government or entail any obligation towards it. By Decl. X Byelorussia, the Ukraine and the USSR objected to signatures by the government located in Taipei, Taiwan, for China, and Saigon for VietNam. By Decl. XIV Bulgaria, Cuba, Hungary, Mongolia, Romania and Czechoslovakia denied the right of the Chiang Kai-shek government to sign for China. By Decl. XI the then Soviet bloc objected to the 'Saigon Administration' signing on behalf of Viet-Nam, and to South Korea signing for Korea (the latter objection repeated in Nairobi, 1982, Decl. XV). By Decl. XXXIII Indonesia disclaimed any recognition of Malaysia, China or any other government which it did not recognise. By Malaga-Torremolinos, 1973, Decl. LIX China stated the 'traitorous Lon Nol clique is a handful of Cambodian national scum and is illegal from the very beginning'. It therefore had no right to sign for Cambodia. China went on to question the signatures of the 'Saigon Administration' for VietNam and by South Korea for Korea.

36 At Montreux, 1965, by Decl. III eleven Arab states indicated that their signature of the Final Acts and possible subsequent ratification were not to imply recognition of Israel. This was countered by Israel by Decl. XXXV. At Malaga-Torremolinos 17 Muslim states repeated this in Decl. XXXVII, countered by Israel in Decl. LXXII. At Nairobi, 1982 (unsurprisingly given the debate as to Israel at the conference (see Chapter 4 following n. 147)), the language was more pointed. Malaysia (Decl. 6) and 22 other Muslim states objected to the signature by the 'Zionist-Entity' and stated that their participation did not imply its recognition. Israel replied by Decl. 97. By Nice Decl. 15 23 Arab and Muslim delegations (and Malaysia, Decl. 11) stated that their signature of the Final Acts and their possible ratification were not valid with respect to 'the so-called "Israel"', and did not imply

international concern.[37] A running set of declarations, reservations and counter-reservations is made by Cuba and the US as to Guantanamo Bay and also regarding US broadcasting directed towards Cuba.[38] Finally, occasionally a reservation may be made in the Final Acts to a Conference Resolution,[39] including as to the interpretation of an instruction as to the internal working of the Union.[40]

Membership

In membership the ITU has 'regard to the principle of universality and the desirability of universal participation in the Union' (CS Art. 2 (20)). Membership has two forms, State membership and Sector membership. The latter is what it says it is – membership of an element of the Union. State membership is full membership of the Union. These apart there are also other arrangements under which certain other entities take some part in ITU activities.

State Membership

Only a state can be a State Member of the Union.[41] Three avenues to that status are provided in CS Art. 2 (20-3): any state a member of any ITU Convention prior to the 1992 CS and CV; any UN member acceding to the 1992 arrangements;[42] and

its recognition. Israel replied by Res. 107. In Minneapolis Decl. 40 14 Muslim states made the same objection to 'Israel' which responded by Res. 98, the process being continued by Antalya Decl. 59 by 12 Arab states, and responded to by Israel Decl. 90. At Guadalajara 2010 17 Muslim and Arab states objected to Israel in Decl. 35, which countered by Decl. 71.

37 By Nairobi, 1982, Decl. 93, Zimbabwe condemned apartheid in South Africa together with its then current activities in Namibia, as well as Israel's 'aggressive activities against its neighbours'.

38 E.g. Nice, 1989, Decls. 63 and 113; Antalya, 2006, Decls. 80 and 114; Guadalajara Decls. 32 and 84.

39 Cf. Malaga-Torremolinos, 1973, when Israel (Decl. XCIX) objected to Conference Res. 48 blaming it for a submarine cable break off Beirut. The Resolution had been adopted on a Saturday when Israel was absent. Unusually, the Chairman of the Conference defended his rulings in Decl. CV. In Nice, 1989, by Decl. 67 Israel rejected condemnation of its practices vis-à-vis Palestine in Conf. Res. 64. At Antalya by Decl. 79 Iran expressed some doubts with regard to Conf. Res. 102 anent the Internet, but considered it 'fairly acceptable'.

40 E.g. by Minneapolis Decl. 97 Germany, India, Japan and the UK considered that an instruction in Conf. Res. 78 as to internal invoicing for BDT activities had not been properly debated although it had significant management implications. They therefore considered the Resolution not to bind the Secretary General or the Directors of the Bureaux.

41 'Member State: A State which is considered to be a Member of the International Telecommunication Union in application of article 2 of this Constitution' (CS Annex, (1001A)).

42 See *supra*, 'Accession'.

any non-UN member which applies for membership, secures the approval of two-thirds of the existing ITU members, and then accedes to the 1992 arrangements.[43] The ordinary rules as to state succession may apply, and, for example, the Peoples' Republic of China now acts for the former UK colony of Hong Kong, and for Macao, the former colony of Portugal, subsequent to their transfer to China.[44]

In the main these provisions work well. As noted in Chapter 4 above, there have been occasions when there has been dispute/discussion as to the representation of a particular state member,[45] and to whether a partly recognised 'state' could be a member.[46] Combining these there is the instance of Taiwan. As a matter of history at Atlantic City in 1947 China was represented by the KMT government. The (Communist) People's Republic of China was proclaimed in 1949 but while the KMT government had withdrawn to Taiwan it continued to represent China until displaced from that UN status in 1971, the Beijing government taking its place in the ITU Council in May 1972.[47] Thereafter, while 'China, Taiwan' has figured in, for example, ITU reports on World Telecommunication Development and in the World Summit on the Information Society (WSIS), 'China, Taiwan' is not an actual ITU Member. Clearly the non-status of Taiwan within the ITU system is anomalous.[48]

The rights of State Members are set out in CS Art. 3.2 (25-8). All State Members can take part in all conferences, are eligible for election to the ITU Council, and can nominate nationals as candidates for election as officials of the Union or as members of the Radio Regulations Board (CS Art. 3.2.a (26)). Subject to the rules as to loss of vote, State Members each have one vote at world conferences and assemblies, and in Council if a member of that body. Only members of that region have a vote at regional conferences (CS Art. 3.2.b (26)). Similar voting provisions apply in the case of consultations carried out by correspondence (CS Art. 3.2.c (27)).

43 An application can be made between PPs in which case the matter is dealt with by correspondence. Any member state which does not respond to the relevant consultation letter from the Secretary General is deemed to have abstained (CS Art. 2.c (23)).

44 Cf. the survey of practice as to state succession carried out by the International Law Commission down to 1970, which includes data on the ITU: 1970 YBILC II, 63ff. See also the Note 'China' in US *Treaties in Force*, 2010, 51-2. See also the 'Vienna Convention on the succession of States in respect of treaties', 1978, 1946 UNTS 3; (1978) 17 ILM 1488; (1978) 72 AJIL 971.

45 See Chapter 4 at nn. 93, 137, 142, for the instances of Spain, Southern Rhodesia and South Africa.

46 See the instances of Palestine, *infra*, nn. 58-62, and of Taiwan, *infra*, n. 64.

47 UNGA Res. 2758 (XXVI) (1971) 'Restoration of the lawful rights of the People's Republic of China in the United Nations'; S.S. Kim, 'The People's Republic of China and the Charter-based International Legal Order' (1978) 72 AJIL 317.

48 See further below, 'Other Arrangements', and Chapter 6, 'Membership'.

Sector Membership

Sector membership is membership of one or more of the three Sectors established by the 1992/1994 reconstruction through which much of the work of the Union is carried through.[49] A Sector Member may be a full member (open to state and non-state entities) or an Associate Sector Member (*infra*). Since much of the practical work of the ITU is carried out through working and study groups within the Sectors the involvement of Sector Members is crucial. The ITU needs to involve persons and entities active in relevant industries, businesses and other interests in its work. CV Art. 19 (228-241) therefore now requires the Secretary General and the Directors of the Sectors to encourage such participation, increased access to ITU materials being offered as an inducement to join (CV Art. 19.1. (228-231), Art. 19.3-4 (234-234C)).

Sector membership consists of all State Members together with non-state entities that have been granted that membership. The participation of a State Member in the work of a Sector is not compulsory, but State Members are Sector Members as of right (CS Art. 12.3.a (87) (ITU-R); CS Art. 17.3.a (111) (ITU-T); CS Art. 17.3.a (135) (ITU-D)). Non-state entities that wish to become Sector Members must be authorised by an appropriate State Member. Such authorisation may be accorded in individual cases or a State Member may generally authorise entities under its jurisdiction to apply direct to the Secretary General to be a member of a particular Sector.[50] As at 1 June 2011 there were 555 Sector Members.[51]

Full Sector Members take part in the works of their sector, subject to some restraints. They may provide chairmen and vice-chairmen of Sector assemblies and meetings and of world telecommunication development conferences. Within limits they help formulate the questions and recommendations the Sector deals with and have a role in decisions as to the working methods and procedures of the Sector (CS Art. 3.3.a-b (28A-28C)).

Minneapolis PP-98 introduced the category of Associate Member of a particular sector for non-state entities. This status is available by permission of the Sector concerned to otherwise duly authorised non-state entities which wish to

49 'Sector Member: An entity or organization authorised in accordance with Article 19 of this Constitution to participate in the activities of a Sector' (CS Annex (1001B)). The current membership of each Sector is available on their several websites: see links at www.itu.int.

50 CS Art. 3 (24-28C), Art. 12.3 (86-88), Art. 21.4 (134-136), Art. 17.3 (110-112).

51 The ITU website (www.itu.int) provides lists of State, Sector and Associate members. As at 1 January 2011 there were 555 Sector Members, viz. ITU-R 247, ITU-T 264 and ITU-D 313. On 1 January 2011 there had been 535 Sector members, viz. ITU-R 249, ITU-T 270 and ITU-D 306. On 1 January 2008 there were 608 Sector Members: ITU-R 285, ITU-T 314 and ITU-D 327. In 2005 the figures were ITU-R 300, ITU-T 357, ITU-D 219. The figures do not add up because of multiple memberships.

take part in the work of only one Study Group within that Sector (CV Art. 19.12 (241A-E)).[52]

The expenses of the Sectors are met by contribution set at one-fifth of the contributory units from each ITU Member State (CV Art. 3.5 (480)).[53] Non-state Sector Members pay a fee for their participation and meet their own costs. A non-state Sector Member selects its level of contribution, and the fee level for an Associate Member of a Sector is less than that required of a non-state Sector Member.[54] In appropriate cases, and subject to reciprocity, the Council may exempt an international organisation wishing to become a Sector Member from the requirement to help defray conference and other sector expenses.[55]

Other Arrangements

Apart from these 'rules' as to state and non-state membership the Union has been able to extend its ambit to a variety of entities, albeit that this might provoke some dissension, even apoplexy. The practice antedates the current arrangements and works on the basis that so far as possible the ITU should have a 'universal character'. For example, by Additional Protocol IV to the Malaga-Torremolinos Convention of 1973,[56] 'to protect the Rights of Papua New Guinea' the status of that country was preserved as an Associate Member, notwithstanding that the new Convention abolished the status of Associate Member of the ITU.[57] More contentiously, by Res. 6 (Kyoto, 1994) liberation organisations recognised by the UN may 'attend at any time conferences, assemblies and meetings' of the ITU, albeit only as observers.[58]

52 As at 1 February 2011 the ITU website recorded a total of 146 Associate Members of Sectors: ITU-R 22, ITU-T 123 and ITU-D 7. However, by 1 June 2011 these totals had dropped to: ITU-R 5, ITU-T 7 and ITU-D 0. Res. 169 (Guadalajara, 2010) admitted duly authorised academia, universities and associated research establishments to the work of the Sectors for a trial period until the next PP. As at 1 June 2011 there were nineteen such members, the Sectors involved being ITU-R 9, ITU-T 14, ITU-D 7. The fee for these is set as 1/16 of that of Associate Members from the least developed countries. See *infra*, n. 168.

53 For the 'contributory unit' system see Chapter 4, and *infra*, 'Finance'. The Council sets the value of the contributory unit every two years.

54 The minimum of the contributory unit for an Associate Member (other than academe) in ITU-R and ITU-D is 1/2 unit. ITU-D Sector Members may choose 1/8 or 1/4 unit with a possible 1/16 unit reserved for Sector Members from developing countries only.

55 See http://www.itu.int/members/sectmem/fees.html.

56 The International Telecommunication Convention, Malaga-Torremolinos, 25 October 1973, 1209 UNTS 255; 1975 UKTS 104, Cmnd. 6219; 28 UST 2495, TIAS 8572.

57 Associate membership for countries, territories and trust territories had been instituted by Art. 1.4 of the Atlantic City Convention, 193 UNTS 188, 194 UNTS 3; 1950 UKTS 76, Cmd. 8124; 63 Stat. 1399, TIAS 1901; 4 Bevans 470. See *supra*, Chapter 4 at n. 99. Papua New Guinea became a full member of the ITU in 1975.

58 Observer status in the UN is given by the UNGA to named liberation movements on a case by case basis. The UN Charter is silent on such matters. Cf. UNGA Res. 3237

Particular provision is made for Palestine, which is a 'partly-recognised' state, but which, in the face of a potential US veto in the Security Council, is unlikely to be a full UN member in the immediate future.[59] By Res. 99 (Rev. Guadalajara), 'The status of Palestine in ITU', Palestine is subject to the Administrative Regulations as if it were an ordinary administration, has the right to attend ITU meetings, to raise points of order on Middle East issues,[60] to take part in debate and to reply, to sponsor draft resolutions and decisions on Middle East issues,[61] and to speak on non-Middle East issues after all other speakers. Palestinian entities may become Sector or Associate Sector Members.[62] Israel has entered reservations to the successive versions of Res. 99 in the Final Acts of the recent PPs.[63] Given the importance of Taiwan in modern communications technology and business, and that the island has a population of some 22 million, it seems anomalous that similar arrangements have not been made for its participation in the ITU.[64]

Purpose and Means

The Preamble of the ITU CS (1) 'fully' recognises the sovereign right of states to regulate their telecommunications. It also identifies the importance of telecommunications in preserving peace and in the economic and social development of all states. It notes that efficient telecommunication services facilitate peaceful relations, international cooperation and economic and social

(XXIX) (1974) 'Observer status for the Palestine Liberation Organization'; UNGA Res. 35/167 (1980) on 'Observer status of national liberation movements recognised by the Organization of African Unity and/or by the League of Arab States'; and the 1998 UNGA Res. on Palestine (*infra*, n. 59). See also the 'Convention on the Representation of States in Their Relations with International Organizations of a Universal Character', Vienna, 1975, A/CONF.67/16; (1975) 69 AJIL 730 (not in force). This Convention requires 35 ratifications to come into force. As at 15 March 2010 it had 34 ratifications and 20 signatures. Most states housing such organizations either voted against or abstained. See J.G. Fennessy, 'The 1975 Vienna Convention on the Representation of States in Their Relations with International Organizations of a Universal Character' (1976) 70 AJIL 62.

59 See UNGA Res. 52/250 (1998) on 'Participation of Palestine in the work of the United Nations'; ITU Res. 99 (Rev. Guadalajara, 2010) 'Status of Palestine in ITU'.

60 Though not to challenge the decision of the presiding officer.

61 Though only a Member State may press for a vote. Palestine took part in the RRC, Geneva, 2006, and is to take part in the digital broadcasting plan. See *supra*, n. 59.

62 Though not as to policy and regulatory measures, or as to the working methods of the Sector.

63 See Res. 41 (Israel) to the Antalya Final Acts, 2006, and its Decl. 71 in the Guadalajara Final Acts.

64 See Chapter 4, n. 98, and Chapter 6, nn. 18-20. Cf. C.H. Lin, 'The International Telecommunication Union and the Republic of China (Taiwan): Prospect of Taiwan's Participation' (2004) 10 *Ann. Surv. Int. & Comp. L.* 233.

development. Members have agreed the CS and CV and other more detailed regulation and procedures to achieve these ends. Tacitly, therefore, Members have in the international interest each effectively given up (suspended?) their 'sovereign rights' under normal conditions, although they retain the option of denunciation of the CS and CV and withdrawal from the Union (CS. Art. 57.1-2 (236-7)). Member States have reserved the right separately to make regional arrangements and form regional telecommunications organisations. However, the results of any regional arrangement they enter into must not conflict with the CS or CV (CS Art. 43 (194)).

CS Art. 1 (2-19) sets out the purposes of the Union and outlines the means by which these are to be pursued. Purposes include maintaining and extending international cooperation, promoting and offering technical assistance to developing countries, promoting the development of technical facilities and their efficient operation so as to increase their usefulness, and making them generally available to the public, extending the benefits of new technologies, promoting the use of telecommunications to facilitate peaceful relations, harmonising the actions of members to attain these purposes, and, through cooperation with other organisations (including non-governmental organisations), promoting a broad approach to telecommunications issues in the global information economy and society.

Curiously, the first two means identified for the attaining of these purposes relate to radio. The ITU is to allocate radio-frequency bands, allot them, register their assignment, including, in the case of space services, orbital positions on the geostationary orbit and associated characteristics of other satellites, so as to avoid harmful interference, to coordinate the elimination of harmful interference between the radio services of different countries and to improve the use made of the radio spectrum and of the geostationary and other orbits (CS Art. 1.2.a-b (10-12)).[65] The remainder of CS Art. 1 then turns to list in particular: standardisation as a means of facilitating a satisfactory quality of telecommunications service, 'cooperation and solidarity' in delivering technical assistance to developing countries, coordinating technical developments to take full advantage of them (including in space services), fostering cooperation to keep telecommunication rates as low as possible consistent with efficiency and a sound business basis, promoting measures directed to the safety of life at sea, carrying out studies, regulating and recommending, publishing information, promoting favourable lines of credit for social projects *inter alia* for extending telecommunications in remote areas and, last, getting appropriate entities to take part in the activities of the Union (CS Art. 1.2.c-j (13-19A)).[66]

From CS Art. 1 all else follows.

---

65 The presence of radio at the start of the listing of 'means' reflects its overriding importance in telecommunications and the fact that, unlike wired services, radio is unconfined in the distribution of the signal.

66 In passing, note the many references to development and the developing countries in CS Arts.1.1 and 2.

ITU Structure

For its current incarnation, CS Art. 7 (37-46) provides that the ITU comprises:

1. the Plenipotentiary Conference;
2. the Council;
3. world conferences on international telecommunication;
4. the Radiocommunication Sector (ITU-R);
5. the Telecommunication Standardisation Sector (ITU-T);
6. the Telecommunication Development Sector (ITU-D);
7. the General Secretariat.

While in legislative terms the above order makes sense, I deal with the Plenipotentiary Conference, the Council and the General Secretariat before turning to the individual Sectors.

Obviously the ITU organisation is complex. It is therefore useful that a Coordination Committee, composed of the Secretary General (Chairman), the Deputy Secretary General and the Directors of the Bureaux of the three Sectors, acts as an internal management team (CS Art. 26 (145-6); CV Art. 6 (106-111)). The Coordination Committee tries to act unanimously. Should the Chairman not be supported by a majority the matter ultimately goes to the Council (CV Art. 6.2 (109)). However, the Guadalajara PP has, in addition, chosen to conform to UN recommendations for the UN family, and has asked the Council to establish an Independent Management Advisory Committee for a trial period of four years.[67]

Plenipotentiary Conference

As we have seen in Chapter 4, before the reforms of 1992/1994 PPs had been held irregularly.[68] Article 8.1 (47) of the present CS provides that the PP 'shall be convened every four years'. This is a useful constraint and effectively introduces a timetable for the activities of the organisation which helps fit the ITU for coping with swift technological developments. Exceptionally an additional PP may be held between two 'ordinary' PPs with an agenda restricted to specific matters. An additional meeting may be decided upon by a previous PP (as in the case of the Geneva APP, 1992, sanctioned by the Nice PP, 1989) or it may be convened at the request of two-thirds of the State Members, or on the proposal of the Council supported by two-thirds of the State membership (CS Art. 8.3 (59A-D)).

The meeting of a PP is determined, if possible, as to both location and dates by the previous PP, which failing these are fixed by the Council with the concurrence of a majority of Member States (CV Art. 1.2 (2)). Location and/or dates may be

67 Res. 162 (Guadalajara, 2010) 'Independent Management Advisory Committee'.

68 See the dates of the conferences listed *supra*, n. 28.

changed on the proposal of at least one quarter of the Member States or by the Council itself. However, any change as to a set location or dates must be approved by at least a majority of the Member States (CV Art. 1.2 (2-6)). Res. 4 (Kyoto, 1994), 'Duration of the plenipotentiary conferences of the Union', limited the PP to a maximum of four weeks unless there was 'a pressing need otherwise'. While still allowing for 'pressing need', Guadalajara, 2010 dropped the 'maximum' and re-set the duration of a PP as 'three to four weeks', the Secretary General working to 'facilitate the most efficient use of time and resources'.

The Plenipotentiary Conference is the supreme organ of the Union (CS Art. 7.a (40)). It is composed of delegations representing all Member States (CS Art. 8.1 (47)). A delegation is the totality of the delegates sent by a Member, including advisers and interpreters (if any), and can include persons belonging to any entity or organisation authorised by the ITU (CS Annex (1005)).[69] The credentials of a delegation to a PP must be signed by the Head of State, Head of Government or the Minister for Foreign Affairs (CV Art. 31.2.1 (325)).[70] Credentials must confer full powers on the delegation, or authorise the delegation to represent its government without restriction, or give it (or designated members) power to sign the Final Acts (CV. 31.2.3 (328-31)). Provisional accreditation is possible, subject to confirmation before the signature of Final Acts (CV Art. 31.2.3 (327)). Credentials are scrutinised by a PP committee which reports to a plenary meeting. Subject to any other loss of vote for other reasons, until its credentials have been accepted a delegation can neither vote nor sign the Final Acts (CV Art. 31.4.9 (332-8)).[71] Delegations (usually the Head of Delegation) may make policy statements to a PP but only during the first week and are limited to five minutes.[72] Finally, two ITU staff members may attend and present staff views on staff-relevant matters.[73]

Every Member State has one vote at a PP (CS Art. 3,2.b (27); CV Art. 32A.1 (340A)).[74] Normally each Member State sends its own delegation to a PP but it can give the delegation of another Member State power to vote and sign for it provided that this is notified to the conference by one of those otherwise authorised

69 This means that personnel from non-state Sector Members may be included in the delegation of a Member State. See *supra*, 'Sector Membership'.

70 The credentials of a delegation to a world conference on telecommunications or to a radio communication conference may be signed by the Head of Government, the Minister for Foreign Affairs, or by any other Minister responsible for the questions to be dealt with by that conference (CV Art. 31.2.2 (326)).

71 A state may lose the right to vote through not having timeously ratified the CS and CV (*supra*, n. 24) or through being in arrears in its contributions (*infra*, n. 163).

72 Rec. 4 (Marrakesh, 2002). The full text of such statements are electronically available. Justification for these limits can be found in the *Minutes of the Plenipotentiary Conference of the International Telecommunication Union, Nairobi 1982* (Geneva: ITU, 1983).

73 'Staff participation in conferences of the Union', Res. 51 (Rev. Minneapolis, 1998).

74 Cf. *supra*, n. 71. Any right to vote is subject to having ratified, accepted or approved the CS and CV (CS Art. 3.2.b (37)).

to accredit its delegation (CS Art. 31.6 (335)). Further, during a conference a delegation may mandate another delegation to record a vote on its behalf on a matter to be determined at a meeting which it cannot attend, provided that the Chairman of the Conference has been so notified in writing in good time (CV Art. 31.7 (336)). No delegation may exercise more than one proxy vote (CV Art. 31.8 (337)). Telegrams are not acceptable to constitute a proxy or transfer powers unless in reply to a query from the conference authorities (CV Art. 31.9 (338)).

The many responsibilities of the PP are set out in CS Art. 8 (47-59). They include the determination of general policies, establishing the basis of the budget of the Union and related financial limits, giving general directives as to staffing, and the examination of the accounts of the Union. It can set salaries, salary scales, allowances and pensions for all ITU staff (CS Art. 8.2.d (52)). It elects the Member States which are to nominate individuals to serve on the Council (CS Art. 8.2.f (54)). It elects the Secretary General, Deputy Secretary General and the Directors of the Bureaux of the Sectors of the Union (CS Art. 8.2.g (55)), and the members of the Radio Regulations Board (CS Art. 8.2.h (56)). It considers and, if appropriate, adopts proposals for the amendment of the ITU CS and CV (CS Art. 8.2.i (57)). It adopts and amends the general rules for ITU conferences, assemblies and other meetings (CS. Art. 8.2.j*bis* (58A)).[75] It also approves the Strategic Plan for the Union, which is prepared for each quadrennium by the Secretariat and Sectors and is submitted to the PP by the Council.[76]

The Council

The major provisions as to the ITU Council are contained in CS Art. 10 (65-72) and CV Art. 4 (50-82). Members of the Council are elected by the PP (CS Art 8.2.f (54)) with 'due regard to the need for equitable distribution of the seats on the Council among all regions of the world' (CS Art.9.1.a (61)).[77] Member States so elected appoint one person to serve on the Council, who may be assisted by

---

75 By CS Art. 32 (177-8) the General Rules of Conferences, Assemblies and Meetings of the Union (GR) apply to all meetings of the Union, including as to elections. Additional rules may be adopted by the relevant bodies. The General Rules were removed from the Constitution and Convention and transposed to a separate document by the Minneapolis PP, 1996.

76 The ITU Strategic Plan is adopted as Res. 71 and replaced by successive PPs.

77 On the use of regional allocation of representation in international organisations see J.K. Cogan, 'Representation and Power in International Organization: The Operational Constitution and its Critics' (2009) 103 AJIL 209. The five ITU regions are the Americas, Western Europe, Eastern Europe, Africa, and Asia and Australasia. Rec. 6 (Marrakesh, 2002) suggested that although there is no formal requirement, regional and sub-regional areas should confer bi- and multi-laterally to facilitate a rotation of Council membership on a voluntary basis so as to encourage and to tap the potential of Member States to contribute to the work of the Union. This had some effect in the 2006 and 2010 elections to Council.

up to two advisers (CS Art. 10.1.2 (66)). Council members hold office until the next Council takes up its duties and may be re-elected (CV Art. 2.1 (7)). The 1992 provisions set the membership of the Council at forty-three (Geneva CV Art. 4.1 (55)). This was amended at Kyoto to give power to the PP to re-determine the number of members every four years (CV Art. 4.1 (55)). However, an upper limit was established, Kyoto providing that membership of the Council is not to exceed twenty-five per cent of the total number of member states (CV Art 4.1.2 (50A)).[78] For the period 2011-14 the Council consists of forty-eight Member States, an increase of two from the previous quadrennium and a step anticipated in 2006.[79] A seat on the Council is considered vacant if the representative of an elected

The three 'regions' for RR purposes are different, their detailed delimitation being set out in Arts. 5.2-5.9 of the RR (as to which see *infra*).

78 This limit was introduced by the Minneapolis PP in 1998. As at 1 January 2011 there were 192 ITU member states: 25% = 48.

79 Cf. Antalya Res. 134 'Number of Council Member States', which also indicated that the regional allocation of seats might be revised. At Guadalajara 2010 an extra seat was added to each of Region A (Americas) and Region E (Asia and Australia). See further: 'Allocation of Seats of Council Member States', Res. 164 (Guadalajara, 2010) for how the number of seats per region is set.

For the period 2011-14 the 48-member Council is composed of: Region A (Americas): 9 seats – Argentina, Brazil, Canada, Costa Rica, Cuba, Mexico, Paraguay, the US and Venezuela; Region B (Western Europe): 8 seats – France, Germany, Greece, Italy, Spain, Sweden, Switzerland and Turkey; Region C (Eastern Europe and Northern Asia): 5 seats – Bulgaria, Czech Republic, Poland, Romania, and the Russian Federation; Region D (Africa): 13 seats – Algeria, Burkina Faso, Cameroon, Egypt, Ghana, Kenya, Mali, Morocco, Nigeria, Senegal, Rwanda, South Africa, and Tunisia; Region E (Asia and Australasia): 13 seats – Australia, Bangladesh, China, India, Indonesia, Japan, South Korea, Kuwait, Malaysia, Philippines, Saudi Arabia, Thailand, and the United Arab Emirates.

In 2007-10 the 46 Council members were: Region A (the Americas): 8 seats – Argentina, Brazil, Canada, Cuba, Mexico, Trinidad and Tobago, United States, Venezuela; Region B (Western Europe): 8 seats – France, Germany, Italy, Portugal, Spain, Sweden, Switzerland, Turkey; Region C (Eastern Europe): 5 seats – Bulgaria, Czech Republic, Romania, Russian Federation, Ukraine; Region D (Africa): 13 seats – Algeria, Burkina Faso, Cameroon, Egypt, Ghana, Kenya, Mali, Morocco, Nigeria, Senegal, South Africa, Tanzania, Tunisia; Region E (Asia and Australasia): 12 seats – Australia, China, India, Indonesia, Japan, Republic of Korea, Malaysia, Pakistan, Philippines, Saudi Arabia, Thailand, United Arab Emirates.

In the period 2003-7 the 46 Council members were: Region A (the Americas): 8 seats – Argentina, Brazil, Canada, Cuba, Mexico, Surinam, United States and Venezuela; Region B (Western Europe) 8 seats – France, Germany, Italy, Norway, Portugal, Spain, Switzerland and Turkey; Region C (Eastern Europe) 5 seats – Bulgaria, the Czech Republic, Poland, Romania and Russia; Region D (Africa) 13 seats – Algeria, Burkina Faso, Cameroon, Egypt, Ghana, Kenya, Mali, Morocco, Nigeria, Senegal, South Africa, Tunisia and Uganda; Region E (Asia and Australasia) 12 seats – Australia, China, India, Indonesia, Iran, Japan, the Republic of Korea, Malaysia, Pakistan, Saudi Arabia, Thailand and Vietnam.

Member State is not in attendance for two consecutive ordinary meetings of the Council or if it resigns its membership (CV Art. 2.3.a-b (10-12)). If a vacancy occurs the seat passes for the remainder of that Council term to the Member State which had the highest number of votes for the relevant region but was not elected (CV Art. 2.2.1 (8)). If this is not possible (as where no candidate for election in the relevant region was unelected) the Chairman of the Council invites Member States of the relevant region to stand for election within one month of his invitation and, if necessary, an election by all Member States is held by secret ballot by correspondence. A Member State so elected holds the seat until the next election for the Council (CS Art. 2.2.2 (9)).

The rules for the election of the Council are found in GR Chapter III, Sec. 34 (207-218). Each Member State can cast votes for up to the number determined by the PP to be available for each ITU region, and is not restricted to voting for only its own region.[80] Elections may be electronic or by paper ballot. Ballots which contain votes exceeding the number set for a region are invalid in respect of that region (GR 34.4 (214)). In the case of paper ballots the rules are strict, only an 'X' within an appropriate box is permitted, a ballot paper with any other mark being invalid (GR 34.3.b and 4 (213-4)). The states receiving the highest number of votes for a region are elected until the seat allocation for that region has been filled (GR Sec. 34.4-6 (214-6)). In the event of a tie for last place in a region a further special ballot is held six hours later, unless the conference decides otherwise, and if that does not produce a 'winner' the Chairman of the conference draws lots to determine which Member State (or States) is elected (GR Sec. 34.7-8 (217-8)).

The Council meets annually in Geneva, although an extra or additional session is competent (CV Art. 4.2.1-3 (51-53)). Each ordinary session of the Council elects its chairman and vice-chairman 'taking account of the principle of rotation between the regions'. These hold office until the next ordinary meeting (i.e. for one year) and are not eligible for re-election (CV Art. 4.4 (55)). The Council normally takes decisions only when in session, although it can decide to decide a specific matter by correspondence (CV Art. 4.3 (54)). It adopts its own rules of procedure (CV Art. 4.10*ter* (61B)) and carries out a number of tasks through working groups.[81] From 2001, pursuant to Council Res. 1181 a 'troika' of three Council representatives, working largely by electronic means, has overseen such matters as the transition between Chairmen of the Council and liaised with the Secretariat to make sure that proper preparation is made for Council sessions.

80 The number of states in a region alters with changes in the membership of the Union. Under 'Allocation of Seats of Council Member States', Res. 164 (Guadalajara, 2010), the Secretary General informs members of changes in regional numbers. Res. 164 also applies the 25% representation rule to the allocation of seats to regions. See also n. 79, *supra*.

81 The working group system has caused difficulties in staffing and scheduling (perhaps through *ad hoc* creation). Dec. 22 (Guadalajara, 2012) 'Creation and management of Council working groups' calls for its systematic revision.

The ITU Secretary General, Deputy Secretary General and the Directors of the Sector Bureaux usually take part in Council deliberations as of right, but without vote, although Council may decide to hold meetings of representatives of Member States only (CV Art. 10.9 (60)). Any Member State not elected to the Council may, having given prior notice to the Secretary General, send an observer at its own expense to meetings of the Council, its committees and working groups. An observer does not have the right to vote (CV Art 4.9*bis* (60A)). Sector members may also similarly be represented as observers at meetings of the Council, its committees and working groups (CV Art 4.9*ter* (60B)). Two staff members may also attend to provide the views of staff on staff-relevant matters.[82]

The general functions of the Council include facilitating the implementation of the CS, CV and the Administrative Regulations, much of which is done through its resolutions and decisions.[83] It also sees to the implementation of the will of the PP and of other conferences as these may be required (CS Art. 10.4 (69-72)). In the interval between PPs and within the powers delegated to it (i.e. *intra vires*), the Council acts on behalf of the PP as the governing body of the Union (CS Art.10.3.b (68)). The functions of the Council are more extensively laid out in CV Section 2 (CV Art. 4 (50-82)). In particular Council supervises the overall management and administration of the Union, approves staff and financial regulations (CV Art. 4.11 (62-68)), decides on the implementation of decisions taken by conferences of the Union that have financial implications (CV Art. 4.11.11 (77)), and takes any other action necessary for the proper functioning of the Union. It oversees the implementation of the Strategic Plan for the period, and, within limits, may amend it (CV Art. 4.10-10*bis* (61-61A)). In so doing it is constrained by the CS, CV and Administrative Regulations (CV Art. 4.11.12 (78)), and by financial considerations. The annual Report to Council on the implementation of the Strategic Plan together with actions taken by the Council thereanent prepared by the Secretary General is a very useful source of information on what the ITU is doing on a year to year basis (CV Art. 4.10 (61-61A)).

Officials and Staff: the Secretary General, General Secretariat, Directors of Sector Bureaux, the Radio Regulations Board, and Other Staff

Elections and Appointment

The officials: election Given the importance of telecommunications the selection of the leaders of the ITU is crucial. The major ITU officials are the Secretary General, the Deputy Secretary General, and the Directors of the three ITU Sector Bureaux. There are also the members of the Radio Regulations Board. Officials

82 'Staff participation in conferences of the Union', Res. 51 (Rev. Minneapolis, 1998).

83 See Resolutions and Decisions of the Council of the International Telecommunication Union (Geneva: ITU, 2009).

are elected by PP, candidates for each post being nominated by their national Member State.[84] No candidate may stand for election to more than one post (GR 32.2 (180)). Election may be by electronic means or by paper ballot. Blank ballots are considered as abstentions and ballots bearing any mark other than an 'X' in the appropriate box, or with other marks on the ballot paper, are invalid (GR 32.6 (188)). Abstentions are not considered in the computation of a majority (GR 32.6 (188)) unless there is a majority of abstentions over votes cast, in which case the outcome of the ballot is deferred until a later vote at which abstentions are not counted (GR 32.7 (189) and 21.4 (121)). If no candidate achieves a majority on the first ballot, a second and, if necessary, a third is held at intervals of six hours unless the conference decides otherwise (GR 32.9 (191)). If there is no clear result in a third ballot a fourth ballot is held between the candidates with the highest numbers of votes (GR 32.10 (192)). However, in the event of a tie such that there are not two candidates to proceed to a fourth and final ballot, further ballots are held after intervals of six hours to resolve the situation (again unless conference decides otherwise). Eventually, and curiously, if no ballot additional to the 'fourth' provides a result, the oldest candidate still in contention is declared elected (GR 32.11 (193)). Fortunately, fully shared birthdays are statistically rare.

In the election of officials due regard is given to an equitable geographic distribution amongst the regions of the world, while also paying due regard to the 'paramount consideration' of 'the necessity of securing for the Union the highest standards of efficiency, competence and integrity' (CS Art 27.2 (154)). The Secretary General, the Deputy Secretary General and the Directors of the three ITU Sectoral Bureaux must be nationals of different countries and are nominated by the home state of each (CS Art. 9.1.b (62)). Candidates for the Radio Regulations Board (RRB) are also nominated by their national Member States. RRB members are elected in their individual capacity, again with due regard to their experience and an equitable geographic distribution.[85] In the case of the RRB the sole 'nationality' restriction now is that no RRB member may have the same nationality as the ITU-R Director (CS Art. 9.1.c (63)).[86] The Antalya PP

84 Detailed 'Election Procedures' are contained in GR Chapter III. Elections are by secret ballot (GR 31.7 (174)), and carried out in the order: 1) *seriatim* Secretary General, Deputy Secretary General, Directors of the Bureaux of the Sectors; 2) members of the RRB; 3) Member States of the Council (GR 31.6 (173)). No election for an official post can begin until the election for the previous position is concluded (GR 32.1 (178-9)). For proxy voting see *supra*, following n. 74.

85 The number of the members of the RRB is set by PP, as is the proportion of the membership allocated to the various ITU regions (GR Sec. 33.1 (195)). A Member State may nominate only one candidate for the RRB (CS Art. 9.1.c (63)).

86 Until the Marrakesh PP, 2002, CS Art. 9.1.b (62) required that the Secretary General, Deputy Secretary General, the Directors of the three ITU Sector Bureaux and the members of the RRB were required all to be nationals of different countries. That was clearly excessive. As to the RRB see *infra*, 'The Radiocommunication Sector: Radio Regulations Board'.

amended CV Art. 2 (13) and (20) to make it clear that an elected official may be re-elected only once to the same post, whether the second elected term is for a term consecutive with the first or not.[87] Whether this formulation is satisfactory has been doubted since it allows one individual to be elected successively to a variety of posts, as has indeed happened. While this could allow the building of expertise within the Union, it might be in the greater general interest to refresh the pool of talent by limiting an elected official to a total of only two terms whether in the same or in any of the full-time posts.[88]

Elected officials: vacancy Of course there is a possibility that a vacancy in an 'official' post occurs between plenipotentiaries. Various provisions deal with this situation. The Deputy Secretary General succeeds the Secretary General and remains in office until a date determined by the next PP (CV Art. 2, Elected Officials 2 (14)). If, whether by succession to the vacant Secretary Generalship, or otherwise, the office of Deputy Secretary General falls vacant more than one hundred and eighty days before the next PP, the Council appoints a Deputy Secretary General for the remainder of the term (CV Art. 2, Elected Officials 3 (15)). If the offices of Secretary General and Deputy Secretary General fall simultaneously vacant the Sector Director who has been longest in office acts as Secretary General for ninety days. Council then appoints a Secretary General and, if the vacancies occur more than one hundred and eighty days before the next PP, a Deputy Secretary General. Officials so appointed serve until the expiry of the term for which the predecessor was appointed (CV Art. 2 Elected Officials 4 (16)). In the case of the vacancy of a Sector Directorship the Secretary General ensures that the duties of the Director are carried out until Council appoints a successor at its next ordinary meeting (CV Art. 2 Elected Officials 5 (17)). In making any of the above appointments the Council acts at its next ordinary meeting if it is within ninety days of the vacancy occurring, or at a session convened within the indicated one hundred and eighty days before a PP (CV Art, 2 Elected Officials 6 (18)). Finally, when an individual non-elected official is appointed to fill a vacancy that period of service does not affect eligibility for election or re-election to that post (CV Art. 2 Elected Officials 7 (19)).

Elected officials: criteria CS Art. 27 (150-4) lays down general principles as to elected officials and staff. In terms derived from Art. 9.5 of the Atlantic City Convention, the paramount consideration in the election of officials and of staff recruitment is 'the necessity of securing for the Union the highest standards of

---

87 However, as outlined in the next paragraph, if an official is appointed to fill a vacancy the period of service in that 'vacancy' does not affect eligibility for election or re-election to that post (CV Art. 2 Elected Officials 7 (19)).

88 Cf. 'Proposal to Stabilize the Basic Instruments of the Union', Contribution of Australia, Council Doc. C10/43, Appendix, para CG1/05. Cf. also the rules as to the Director and Deputy Director of the UPU International Bureau outlined in Chapter 8.

efficiency, competence and integrity' while bearing in mind the 'importance of recruiting the staff on as wide a geographic basis as possible' (CS Art 27.2 (154)).[89] Further, in terms deriving from Arts. 6.5 and 9.6 of the Atlantic City Convention on the IFRB, no elected official or staff should seek or accept any instructions from their home state or any other entity (CS Art. 27.1.1. (550)), nor should any Member or Sector Member seek to influence them (CS Art. 27.1.2 (551)). While elected officials or staff should not have any financial interest in telecommunications, entitlements from previous employment are exempt (CS Art. 27.1.3 (152)). Excluding the RRB, Member States are to refrain from recalling between PPs any national who has been elected to an ITU post (CS Art. 27.1.4 (153)).

The Secretary General, Deputy Secretary General and the three Directors of the Bureaux of the Sectors partake of the privileges of the 1947 Convention on the Privileges and Immunities of the Specialised Agencies, as it may have been incorporated into national legislation.[90] Subject to the municipal legislation of Member States members of the RRB enjoy 'functional privileges and immunities equivalent to those granted to the elected officials of the Union by each Member State' in the exercise of their ITU duties or while on mission for the Union. This is for the purposes of the Union only and not for personal advantage, and the privilege may be withdrawn by the Union (CV Art. 10.4*bis* (142A)).

The detailed responsibilities of the Secretary General and the General Secretariat are laid out in CS Art. 11 (73-77) and CV Art. 5 (83-105) (*infra*). Those of the Sector Bureaux and the RRB are dealt with *seriatim* below.

Other staff Staff other than the elected officials are chosen by the segment of the Union which is to employ them. They are, however, appointed (and dismissed) by the Secretary General.[91] The general principles of CS Art. 27 (150-4) outlined immediately above (Elected officials: criteria) apply to staff. Staff efficiency, competence and integrity as well as the recruitment of staff on a wide geographic basis are important, as is the independence of staff from outside influence. Staff development and training is provided for.[92] In common with other UN agencies the Administrative Tribunal of the International Labour Office is the final recourse in cases of appeal or complaint. Staff are members of the UN Joint Staff Pension Fund

89 Can all the requirements of this sentence always be simultaneously met? This question seems to highlight a problem common throughout the UN and its family of agencies. Geographic distribution may mask incompetence.

90 Convention on the Privileges and Immunities of the Specialised Agencies, New York, 1947: 33 UNTS 261; http://www.uia.org/legal/app51.php; cf. the UK Specialized Agencies of the United Nations (Immunities and Privileges) Order 1974, 1974 SI 1260, as amended, made under the International Organisations Act, 1968, c. 48.

91 Secretariat, CV Art. 5.1.d and e (87, 88); ITU-R, CV Art. 12.3 (182); ITU-T, CV Art. 15.3 (206); ITU-D, CV Art. 18.5 (226).

92 'Human resources management and development', Res. 48 (Rev. Guadalajara, 2010); 'Organizational structure and grading in ITU', Res. 49 (Kyoto, 1994).

(CV Art. 4.11.6 (72)). As noted above, in recognition of the value of staff input to staff-relevant matters, up to two representatives of staff may attend Council and PPs to present the views of staff.[93]

The Secretary General, Deputy Secretary General and the Secretariat

The Secretary General, assisted by a single Deputy Secretary General (CS Art 11.1.1 (73)), and the General Secretariat, coordinates the activities of the Union, reports to the Council on policies and the working of the Strategic Plan, coordinates the implementation of that Plan, and takes all actions required to ensure the economic use of the resources of the Union (CS Art 11.1 (73-75)). He or she also acts as the legal representative of the Union (CS Art 11.1 (76*bis*)). The Deputy Secretary General assists the Secretary General, including in matters specifically entrusted to him.[94] He acts as Secretary General when the 'real' Secretary General is absent (CS Art. 11.2 (77)) and succeeds him in the event of a vacancy.[95]

The Directors of the Bureaux of the Sectors and the Radio Regulations Board

The duties of the Directors of the Bureaux of the three Sectors, ITU-R, ITU-T and ITU-D are outlined under the relevant Sectors immediately following. Those of the Radio Regulations Board are covered within the discussion of the ITU-R.

The Sectors

Introduction

The 1992/1994 reconstruction abolished three major former ITU organs, the Consultative Committee for Telephone and Telegraph (CCITT), the Consultative Committee for Radio (CCIR) and the International Frequency Registration Board (IFRB). The work of these bodies is now carried out through three 'Sectors' whose responsibilities do not equate exactly with those of their forerunners. They are the Radiocommunication Sector (ITU-R), the Telecommunication Standardisation Sector (ITU-T)[96] and the Telecommunication Development Sector (ITU-D). Close cooperation between all three sectors is called for, particularly in CS Arts. 12.1.2 (79), 17.1.2 (105) and 21.1.2 (119) as well as elsewhere.

---

93 'Staff participation in conferences of the Union', Res. 51 (Rev. Minneapolis, 1998).

94 This general provision has been extended to require the Secretary General to issue specific directives to the Deputy Secretary General, and to report them to Council and to staff: Res. 148 (Antalya, 2006) 'Tasks and functions of the Deputy Secretary-General'.

95 For the procedure in a vacancy see *supra*, 'Elected officials: vacancy'.

96 The acronym ITU-T derives from its French title.

Provisions Common to the Sectors

Structure The Bureau of each Sector[97] is headed by a Director[98] who is elected by the PP (CS Art. 8.2.g (55)) and may be re-elected once only to that post whether that re-election is consecutive or at a later time (CV Art. 2.3.1 (13)).[99] In addition to its Bureau each Sector carries out its remit through a variety of working groups, study groups, regional conferences (except in the case of ITU-D), world conferences and assemblies. The ITU-R and ITU-T Assemblies and ITU-D conference may each adopt its own working methods so long as these are compatible with the CS and CV and the Administrative Regulations (CS Ch. IVA (145)). CV Sec. 8 (CV Arts. 19-22 (228-254)) contains provisions common to the three Sectors as to participation in the work of the Sectors, and their abilities to refer matters to each other and to other international organisations. ITU-R and ITU-T are also specifically to provide technical assistance to ITU-D (CV Arts. 12.4 (183), 15.4 (207)), and all three Sectors are required to cooperate and mutually coordinate their activities including the distribution and sharing of work.[100] Study groups are constrained as to the questions on which they work and make recommendations particularly if these have regulatory and policy aspects and/or financial implications (CV Art. 22.5*bis*.4 (246D-H)). The working methods of radiocommunication assemblies, standardisation assemblies and world development conferences (to all of which we are coming) that put the results of study groups into practice must be compatible with the CS, the CV and the Administrative Regulations (CS Chapter IVA (145A)). Conferences and sector meetings may be attended by the Secretary General, Deputy Secretary General, the Directors of the other Sectors and members of the RRB, but in an advisory capacity only (CV Art. 22.2 (253)). If invited, representatives of a Sector may attend the meetings of another international organisation, but in an advisory capacity only (CV Art. 22.3 (254)).

---

97 ITU-R, CS Art. 12 2.e (85); ITU-T, CS Art. 17.2.c (109); ITU-D, CS Art. 21.3.c (133).

98 ITU-R, CS Art. 12 2.e (85); ITU-T, CS Art. 17.2.c (109); ITU-D, CS Art. 21.3.c (133).

The title 'Director' was reconsidered by Council prior to the 2010 Guadalajara conference, but no change was recommended. The point in question was whether the title might better reflect the true status of the Director of a Sector within the ITU structure, and eliminate any impression of independence being given to authorities and individuals external to the Union. However, a) a change in title would require the amendment of CS and CV, and b) possible alternatives were cumbersome (and in my view open to ridicule as unduly grandiose – though pretentious/grandiloquent job-titles seem to be in vogue in many organisations).

99 See *supra*, n. 87.

100 CS Arts. 12.1.2 (79), 17.1.2 (105), 21.1.2 (119); CV Arts. 11.5 (158), 11.7 (160) 14.2 (195), 14.4 (197) and 17.2 (215).

Study groups and recommendations The study groups of the three Sectors conduct their business in accordance with CV Art. 20 (242-9). Joint meetings of study groups from different Sectors can be arranged on matters of common interest, their recommendations being passed to the assemblies and conferences of the relevant Sector (CV Art. 22.1 (252.1)).

With due regard to competence, equitable geographic distribution and 'to the need to promote more effective participation by the developing countries' radiocommunication assemblies, standardisation assemblies and world development conferences appoint the Chairman and one or more Vice-Chairman (if needed) for each study group within their particular sector (CV Art. 20.1-2 (242-3)). Between assemblies or conferences the Vice-Chairman succeeds the Chairman if necessary, but if there is more than one Vice-Chairman the study group elects one as its Chairman at its next meeting. A similar process applies for the replacement of vice-chairmen (CV Art. 20.3 (244)).

Study groups work 'as far as possible by correspondence using modern means of communication' (CV Art. 20.4 (245)). On the basis of the decisions of an assembly or conference the relevant Director draws up the general plan for study group meetings after consulting the Secretary General and coordinating as the CS and CV requires, including with other Sectors (CV Art. 20.5 (246)). Joint working groups are competent where expertise from different study groups is required (CV Art. 20.7 (248)). An Associate Member takes part in the study group to which it has been admitted but without taking part in decisions (CV Art. 20.7*ter* (248B)).[101] Organisations that are not members of a Sector may be invited to participate in the discussion of specific matters (CV Art. 20.7*bis* (248A)).

Study groups tackle questions set by the appropriate Sector Assembly or conference. Usually these originate within the Sector, but any ITU assembly or conference may submit recommendations to another conference on a matter within its competence (CV Art. 21 (251-2)). The relevant sector assembly or conference sets the procedures to be used by the study group, and should also indicate whether any resultant recommendations are to be the subject of formal consultation with the sector's State Members. Recommendations not requiring consultation are considered as being approved when made (CV Art. 20.5*bis*.1-3 (246A-C)).[102] Recommendations that are approved by this process have the same status as those that are formally approved by State Members (CV Art. 20.6*bis* (247A)). However, as noted above, these provisions do not apply to questions and recommendations that have policy or financial implications (CV Art. 20.5.4 (246D)). Examples given in the CV include: for ITU-R, questions and recommendations relevant to radiocommunication conferences or that can be decided by radiocommunication assemblies; for ITU-T, questions and recommendations relating to tariffs and accounting or to numbering and addressing; and for ITU-D, questions and

---

101 For Associate Sector Membership see *supra*, 'Sector Membership'.

102 Between two assemblies or conferences a study group may initiate any approval process by procedures set by the relevant superior body (CV Art. 20.6 (247)).

recommendations relating to regulatory, policy or financial issues (CV Art. 50.54.a-d (246E-G)). Finally, for clarity, the provisions as to when questions and recommendations are not referred to State Members for approval do not apply when there is any doubt as to their scope (CV Art. 20.4.d (246F)).

Meetings: conferences, assemblies etc. Meetings and conferences of the Sectors or their components are subject to a variety of rules. Of these the broadest compilation is in the *General Rules of Conferences, Assemblies and Meetings of the Union* (GR). These used to be in the CV but were largely removed to a separate document at Minneapolis in 2002, although some elements were retained in the CV. The GR include provisions as to invitations to meetings and conferences, their convening, re-timing or relocation or cancellation, the making of proposals, time limits, the seating of delegations (the French ordering of Member States is used), committees, debate, amendments, voting, reports, elections and press relations. Within the constraints of the CS, CV and Administrative Regulations, however, some departure from the General Rules is permitted (GR 1-2 (1-2)).

The Radiocommunication Sector (ITU-R)

The major responsibilities of the Radiocommunication Sector (ITU-R) relate to the RR,[103] together with some elements of standardisation in the sphere of radiocommunication. Structurally the Sector has two elements, its Bureau headed by its Director,[104] and the RRB – the new creation that to an extent takes the place of the old International Frequency Registration Board (IFRB).

The Radiocommunication Sector is dealt with in CS Chapter II (CS Arts. 12-16 (78-103)) and CV Section 5 (CV Arts. 7-12 (112-183)) together with the common sectoral provisions noted immediately above (CV Sec. 8, Arts. 19-22 (228-254)). Its purpose is to ensure 'the rational, equitable, efficient and economical use of the radio frequency spectrum by all radiocommunication services, including those using the geostationary satellite orbit, and to carry out studies without limit of frequency range' (CS Art. 12.1.1 (78)). This has two aspects. First, part of its remit is fulfilled through studies and work on the RR. The RR, adopted and amended by world and regional conferences, are of quasi-legislative character as we will see.[105] In addition, the Sector adopts Recommendations on radiocommunications on the basis of studies carried out within the Sector study groups (CS Art. 12.1.1 (78)). The second element of its remit is the administration of the Master International Frequency Register (MIFR), to which we will also come in due course.[106]

---

103 See *infra*, 'Administrative Regulations: The Radio Regulations'.

104 As noted above the Director is elected by PP (CS Art. 8.2.g (55)) and may be re-elected only once (not necessarily consecutively) (CV Art. 2.1 (13)).

105 *Infra*, 'Administrative Regulations: The Radio Regulations'.

106 Ibid.

Members of the Sector include all State Members of the Union as of right, together with any properly authorised entity or organisation (CS Art. 12.3 (86-88)).[107] Associated membership is also competent.[108] The Sector operates through World and Regional Radiocommunication Conferences, Radiocommunication Assemblies (frequently associated with world radiocommunication conferences), the Radiocommunication Advisory Group (RAG), study groups and the Radiocommunication Bureau operating under the Director (CS Art. 12.2 (80-85)).

World Radiocommunication Conferences (WRC) (previously known as World Administrative Radio Conferences (WARC)) are normally held every three to four years, although that may be varied through the scheduling of an additional or the omission of a conference (CS Art. 13.2 (90); CV Art. 3.1.a (24)).[109] A WRC is held by decision of the PP (CV Art. 3.3.a (32)), or of the Council (CV Art. 3.3.d (35)), or on the recommendation of a previous WRC or a study group if approved by Council (CV Art. 3.3.b (33)). A WRC may also be held at the request of at least one quarter of the State Members (CV Art. 3.3.c (34)). The date and place of a WRC is set by the PP (CV Art. 3.5.1 (41)), which failing it is set by Council after consultation with State Members (CV Art. 3.5.2 (42)).[110] The date and location may be later changed after further consultation with the State Members and support by a majority (CV Art. 3.7 (47)).

The powers and duties of a WRC are elaborated in CS Art. 13 (89-92) and CV Art. 7 (112-128). A WRC may partially, or in exceptional cases completely, revise the RR (CS Art. 13.1 (89)).[111] It can also deal with any question of a worldwide character (CS Art. 13.1 (89); CV Art. 7.2.1 (113-117)). A WRC may instruct the RRB or the Radiocommunication Bureau. It may put matters on the agenda of future world conferences, and may refer questions to the Radiocommunication Assembly (CV Art. 7.2.1.c (116)). Given the importance of the RR it is not surprising that the general scope of the agenda of a WRC should be established four to six years in advance, and the final agenda established by the ITU Council

107 *Supra*, 'Sector Membership'.

108 For Associate Sector Membership see *supra*, 'Sector Membership'.

109 Financial considerations have tended to limit the frequency of conferences. Few WRCs have been written up in legal periodicals. Cf. M.L. Smith, 'Space WARC 1985: The Quest for Equitable Access' (1986) 3 *Boston Univ. I.L.J* 229; S.E. Doyle, 'Regulating the Geostationary Orbit: The ITU's Warc-Orb 85-88' (1987) 15 *J. Sp. L.* 1; S.E. Doyle, 'Space Law and the Geostationary Orbit: The ITU's Warc-Orb 85-88 Concluded' (1989) 17 *J. Sp. L.* 13.

110 Consultation is subject to rules and time limits. States which do not reply within the limits are not taken into account in compiling the majority. If the number of responses is less than one-half of the total ITU membership the consultation is re-run and the result is decisive irrespective of the number of states taking part (CV Art. 3.7 (47)).

111 The 1979 RR was a major overhaul of the system: q.v. see Chapter 4. Subsequent WRCs have tended to revise and modify what was then agreed. Most change and development in the RR has come in response to the needs of space communications. Provisions as to terrestrial radio have been more stable.

'preferably' two years ahead of the conference (CV Art. 7.2.2 (118)).[112] The agenda for a WRC must include any matter which the PP directs (CV Art. 7.2.3 (119)) but broadly the agenda consists of proposals from Member States.[113] The agenda can be changed on the proposal of the Council or at the request of one-quarter of the Member States. However, a proposed change cannot finally be adopted until a majority of Member States so agree.[114]

Regional radio conferences (RRC) are competent. As the name implies they deal with the concerns of a particular region (CS Art. 12.2.a (81); CS Art. 13.4 (92), CS Art. 43 (194)). They are called pursuant to the decision of a PP, or on the recommendation of a previous world or regional radio conference if approved by Council, or at the request of at least one quarter of the State Members in the region concerned, or on the proposal of the Council (CV Art. 3.4 (36-40)). Regional conferences adopt or revise RR provisions, including, for example, an 'allotment plan' for a particular type of broadcasting in the region concerned.[115] A RRC can only consider matters which are included on its agenda (CV Art. 9 (138)). However, apart from the official ITU RRC, there remains the possibility for Members to enter into regional or other special arrangements outwith the ITU, provided that they do not conflict with the CS or CV (CS Art. 42 (194)).

Radiocommunication Assemblies (RA) are normally convened every three to four years to provide the technical basis for the work of world conferences (CS Art. 13.3 (91); CV Art. 8.2.5-6 (135-136)). A RA usually acts on the basis of the reports of study groups (CV Art. 8.2 (130-136)) and deals with and issues recommendations on questions adopted through its own procedures, or which are referred to it by a PP, by any other conference, by the Council or by the RRB (CV Arts. 8.1 (129) and 8.2 (130-136B)). Particularly important is the ability of a RA to terminate study groups and to create new ones, allocating the questions to be dealt with by them (CV Art. 8.2.3 (133)).

---

112 'Principles for establishing agendas for world radiocommunication conferences' (with its Annexes), Res. COM6/3 (WRC-07), World Radiocommunication Conference Provisional Final Acts: Geneva 22 October - 16 November 2007 (Geneva: ITU, 2008). Res. 805 [COM 6/7] of the 2007 WRC (WRC-07) (Geneva) recommended to Council the agenda for the WRC to be held in 2011 (now January 2012), and Res. 806 [COM6/22] (WRC-07) laid out a preliminary agenda for the 2015 WRC.

113 See 'Report of the First Session of the Conference Preparatory Meeting for WRC-11', Annex 4 to Rad. Bur. Admin. Circ. CA/171, 20 December 2007.

114 On consultation see *supra*, n. 110.

115 E.g. the 'European Broadcasting Plan', Stockholm, 1961, as revised. See J-M. Paquet, 'The Stockholm 1961 Agreement', http://www.itu.int/ITUR/conferences/seminars/geneva-2006/docs/E/05-Terrestrial_Plan_ST61_JMP.doc. The first European Broadcasting Plan was the 'Long and Medium Frequency Plan' adopted by 29 European countries in 1929. Cf. J. Doeven, 'Revision of ST61 – Lessons from History' (2002) 290 *EBU Tech. Rev.*, http://www.ebu.ch/en/technical/trev/trev_290-doeven.html. The 'European Broadcasting Area' is defined in RR 5.14.

The Radiocommunication Advisory Group (RAG) was added to the Sector by the 1998 Minneapolis PP by CS Art. 12.2.d*bis* (84A) and CV Art. 11A (160A-160H). RAG membership is open to all Member States, to representatives of Sector Members and to the chairmen of study and other groups (CV Art. 11A.1 (160A)). Meeting annually the RAG advises the Director through reviewing the ITU-R priorities and strategies as well as monitoring the progress and guiding the work of study groups. The RAG also plays a role in fostering cooperation within the ITU.

Radiocommunication study groups are regulated by CV Art. 11 (148-160). Members are appointed by an RA, which also determines their remit. ITU-R study groups deal with matters including the use of the radio-frequency spectrum in terrestrial and space radiocommunication and from/in the geostationary and other satellite orbits, the characteristics and performance of radio systems, the operation of radio stations, and radiocommunication aspects of distress and safety (CV Art. 11.2.a-d (151-4)).[116] Studies and reports are also prepared for WRCs and RRCs (CV Art. 11.3 (156)). ITU-R study groups can take economic factors into consideration only when comparing technical or operational alternatives, and may not discuss general economic questions (CV Art. 11.2.3 (155)).

The Radio Regulations Board

The Radio Regulations Board (RRB) replaced the International Frequency Registration Board (IFRB) in the 1992/4 reconstruction.[117] Back in 1965 at the Montreux PP it was argued that the IFRB should be abolished since the task of imposing order on the use of the radio spectrum through the RR and the MIFR had been completed. It was suggested that all that was needed thereafter was the simple bureaucratic exercise of maintaining the list of assigned and notified frequencies. But to have done away with the Board would have been to eliminate something important, if unacknowledged. The root justification of the IFRB then (and now to an extent of the RRB) is the instilling and maintenance of confidence in the international radio regulatory system. In 1965 at Montreux it was mainly

116 Res. ITU-R 4-5 'Structure of Radiocommunication Study Groups' of the Radiocommunication Assembly (RA-07) Geneva, 2007, continued six study groups. Group 1 – Spectrum Management; Group 3 - Radio-wave Propagation; Group 4 – Satellite Services; Group 5 – Terrestrial Services; Group 6 – Broadcasting Services; Group 7 – Science Services. Some joint activities and collaboration is anticipated. See also Res. ITU-R 5-5, 'Work programme and Questions of Radiocommunication Study Groups'. Note: discontinued study groups do not result in a re-numbering of the remainder.

117 On the creation of the IFRB see Codding I, 241-52. On its working see Leive, and his 'Regulating the Use of the Radio Spectrum' (1970) 5 *Stan. J. Int., Stud.* 21-52; Lyall, 321-2, 341-2; F. Lyall, 'The Use of the Radio Spectrum: The Role of the IFRB' 1969 *Jur. Rev.* 233; R.L. and H.L. White, *The Law and Regulation of International Space Communication* (Boston: Artech House, 1988). On the 1992 proposals see F. Lyall, 'The International Frequency Registration Board' (1992) 33 *Proc. IISL* 394.

the developing nations that stood out for the IFRB, perceiving it useful to them as an impartial voice in arguments as to frequency allocation, and as a source of disinterested advice. Even with the inception of ITU-D these justifications of the RRB continue and have increased with the advent of satellite communications.

RRB members serve part-time (CS Art. 14.1 (93)), only their travelling, subsistence and insurance expenses being met by the Union (CV Art. 10.4 (142)). In their election regard is had to 'equitable geographic distribution' (CS Art. 9.1.c (63)). As in the IFRB, members serve 'not as representing their respective Member States, or a region, but as custodians of an international public trust' (CS Art. 14.3.1 (98)), a statement traceable back to the Atlantic City Convention of 1947.[118] In 1947 there was some hope that the notion of 'public trust' would result in the election of members of the original IFRB on merit alone, but, following a practice then already emergent in the UN, a regional distribution of membership was adopted. Now, by CS Art. 14.1 (93) RRB members are to be 'thoroughly qualified in the field of radiocommunications' and possess 'practical experience in the assignment and utilization of frequencies' (CS Art. 14.1 (93)).[119] RRB Members must be nationals of different countries and not of the same nationality as the ITU-R Director (CS Art. 9.1.c (63)). Each is to be 'familiar with the geographic, economic and demographic conditions within a particular area of the world' (CS Art. 14.1 (93)) and to be of the highest efficiency, competence and integrity (CS Art. 27.2 (154)).

The composition of the RRB is not more than the greater of twelve, or six per cent of the total state membership of the ITU (CS Art. 14.1bis (93A)).[120] Members are elected by the PP (CS Art. 8.2.h (56)) under the specific rules of procedure of GR Sec. 33. The PP allocates a number of seats on the Board to the different ITU RR regions (GR 33.1 (195)),[121] and any Member State within the relevant region may propose one of its nationals for election (CS Art. 9.1.c (63)). All State Members vote on the RRB membership, being able to vote up to the maximum of the number of seats permitted for their region (GR Sec. 33.3 (199)), the rules for RRB elections being as for other elected officials.[122] Re-election is competent, but only for one further term whether the re-election is consecutive to the first election

118 Art. 6.5.1, International Convention on Telecommunications, Atlantic City, 2 October 1947; 193 UNTS 188, 194 UNTS 3; 1950 UKTS 76, Cmd. 8124; 63 Stat. 1399, TIAS 1901; 4 Bevans 470.

119 This statement of qualification was an innovation in 1992/4. Members of the previous IFRB were all technically qualified (cf. Art. 57.1.1 of the Nairobi Convention, (*supra*, n. 11) and its predecessors). 'Practical experience in the assignment and utilization of frequencies' opens the door to those with only administrative experience and (or even) only of the commercial and political side of telecommunications.

120 As of 1 January 2011 there are 192 ITU state members: 6%= 11.46. The 1992/4 version of the Constitution provided for 9 RRB members, and this was increased to 12 in 1998.

121 There are three RR regions. See *infra*, n. 190.

122 See *supra*, 'The officials: election'.

or not (CV Art. 2: Members of the Radio Regulations Board 1 (20)). Should a Board member resign, or otherwise become unable to pursue his or her duties,[123] much depends on the date of that occurrence. If the vacancy occurs more than ninety days before a Council session or after the last Council session before a PP, the relevant Member State nominates a replacement to act until the next session of the Council (which will elect a replacement) or of the PP (which will be electing the whole RRB). In other cases the Member States of the region concerned are invited to nominate candidates for the vacancy, and the Council elects a replacement at its next meeting. Service as such a 'replacement' does not count for the 'two elections limit' rule (CV Art. 2: Members of the Radio Regulations Board 2 (21)).

That RRB membership is part-time (CS Art. 14.1 (93)) might be thought to detract from independence since, presumably, given the other requirements as to competence and that only expenses are paid to its members, they are likely otherwise to be employed, most probably in telecommunications.[124] However, a member of the Board may not intervene in decisions concerning his home state (CS Art. 14.3.1 (98)), and CS Art. 14.3.2 (99) prohibits the seeking or taking of instructions from anyone, or doing anything incompatible with the independent status of the Board. Correlatively CS Art. 14.3.3 (100) requires State Members of the Union to respect the international character of the duties of the Board, and not attempt to influence its members.[125]

The RRB meets up to four times a year and for up to five days at a time, usually at Geneva, at which meetings at least two-thirds of the membership are to be present (CV Art. 10.5.2 (145)).[126] However, the Board 'may carry out its duties using modern means of communication' (CV Art. 10.5.2 (145)). In general the Board is to seek unanimity, failing which it may make a decision by vote, with at least two-thirds of the membership voting in favour; proxy voting is not permitted (CV Art. 10.5.3 (146)). The RRB Chairman and Vice-Chairman are elected by the Board from its members to serve for one year, the Vice-Chairman succeeding the Chairman (CV Art 10.5.1 (145)). In the absence of both, a temporary Chairman is elected for a particular meeting from among the attenders by those present (CV Art. 10.5.1 (145)).

The duties of the RRB are wide-ranging (CS Art. 14.2 (94-7); CV Art. 10.2 (140-141A)). It approves the Rules of Procedure under which the registration of

---

123 A Board member is deemed unable to pursue his duties if absent from three consecutive meetings of the Board (CV Art. 2, Members of the Radio Regulations Board 3 (22)).

124 Cf. F. Lyall, 'The International Frequency Registration Board' (1992) 33 *Proc. IISL*, 394.

125 The language is traceable to Art. 6.5.1 of the Atlantic City Convention.

126 More than four meetings, and sessions of up to two weeks, are possible if the matters under consideration so require (CV Art. 10.5.2 (145)). However, compliant with Option 18 of Annex 2 to Antalya PP Decision 5, as part of the general reduction of ITU expenditure the RRB has reduced its meetings to three a year.

frequency assignments is made.[127] These Rules can be commented on by Members of the Union, and, in the case of a continuing dispute as to their terms, the matter is referred to a WRC (CS Art. 14.2.a (95)). The RRB also considers matters which cannot be solved by the application of the Rules by the Director and the Sector Bureau. Board members take part in an advisory capacity in Radiocommunication Conferences. Two RRB members are designated by the Board to advise at PPs and RAs. Board members so designated are barred from membership of their national delegations (CV Art. 10.3-3*bis* (141-141A)).

The IFRB had a major role in acting in disputes between administrations in respect of proposed and actual assignments, and the operation of transmitters. This continues. By CV Art. 10.2.1 (140) the RRB considers reports from the Director of ITU-R on cases of harmful interference that have been investigated at the instance of an interested administration, and adopts recommendations on the case. Further, independent of the ITU-R Bureau, the RRB can, at the instance of one or more of the interested administrations, consider an appeal against a decision of the Bureau regarding a notified frequency assignment (CV Art. 10.2.2 (140)).[128]

The Telecommunication Standardisation Sector (ITU-T)

The Telecommunication Standardisation Sector (ITU-T)[129] is provided for by CS Chapter III (CS Arts. 17-20 (104-117)) and CV Section 6 (CV Arts. 13-15 (184-207)), together with the provisions noted above as common to all Sectors (CV Sec. 8, Arts. 19-22 (228-254)).

The Telecommunication Standardisation Bureau is headed by a Director (CV Art. 17.2.c (109)) who is elected by the PP (CS Art. 8.1.g (55)).[130] Members of the Sector include all State Members of the Union as of right, together with any entity or organisation authorised by the appropriate procedures to be a member of the sector (CS Art. 21.4 (134-136)).[131] The Sector works through World Telecommunication Standardisation Assemblies (WTSA), study groups, a Telecommunication Standardisation Advisory Group (TSAG) (CS Art. 19 (116) and CV Arts. 17 (214-5A) and 17A (215C-G)), and the Sector Bureau (CS Art. 17.2 (106-112)). The Sector complies with the provisions common to all Sectors

127 For radio frequency assignment and registration see *infra*, 'Radio Regulations'.

128 For other dispute resolution see *infra*, 'Disputes: Arbitration and Settlement'.

129 The designator ITU-T may confuse English speakers. It derives from the French text.

130 As a matter of history, but showing that the CCITT, not the CCIR, was the major standardisation agency within the ITU before the new system was adopted, Geneva APP 1992 Res. PLEN/8, 'Provisional Application of Certain Parts of the Constitution and the Convention of the International Telecommunication Union' provided that the then CCITT Director was to act as Director of ITU-T until the post was filled by election by the Kyoto PP in 1994.

131 See *supra*, 'Sector Membership', n. 49 and following.

indicated above (CV Sec. 8, Arts. 19-22 (228-254)). Its responsibilities cover technical, operating and tariff questions. It adopts Recommendations on such matters with a view to their standardisation on a world-wide basis (CS Art. 17.1.1 (104)).

As we have seen in Chapter 2, it was the need for standard international procedures and practices, for compatibility between equipment, and for operating protocols that gave the initial impetus towards international agreement on telecommunication matters in the Nineteenth century. It was quite simply necessary that standards were adopted as common between the different telecommunications systems so that messages could be passed across borders and from one system to the next. Fundamentally the position is no different today. Common standards for equipment and protocols and procedures for their operation are essential in the modern international electronic community. Manufacturers want assurance that their products fit international requirements and therefore will sell. Occasionally a question of 'standard' is left to the decisions of the market place. Because of a lack of 'standardisation' we have the fact that in video and television the PAL/NSTC and SECAM systems operate in different parts of the world. Again the collision in video recorder standards between the Betamax and VHS system was abrupt and dispositive. The more recent options as to blue or red ray high definition television and DVD systems may similarly soon have been clarified by market forces. But, while some matters can be left to the market place, many questions of telecommunication standards and procedure are better settled internationally by discussion and agreement. The effect that even a substantial (let alone a consensus) view formed by a standardisation agency of the status of the ITU should not be underestimated, especially given manufacturers' desire for market reasons to follow such advice. Naturally in this process political and economic interests also play major and obvious roles.[132] In particular as an operational example it may be noted that international dialling codes and access protocols are set out in ITU-T Recommendation E.164.1-3. They are not binding, but are largely complied with.

The ITU had served as a forum for such discussions down through the years, through the conferences and the work of Study Groups of both the CCITT and the CCIR. Regulations adopted by Administrative Conferences of the Union, and the Recommendations of the CCIs, contained standards for the operation of telecommunications, and for mechanisms affecting the operation of telecommunications equipment. However, the elaboration of standards under the CCITT and CCIR became slow and cumbersome. The separation of the 'wire' and 'wireless' CCIs together with the involvement of the CCIs with other aspects of ITU work contributed to a deceleration in standard setting. Other international

132 J.G. Savage, *The Politics of International Telecommunications Regulation* (Boulder, Co. and London: Westview Press, 1989). See also the journal *Telecommunications Policy*.

global and regional standard-setting *fora* therefore emerged.[133] There was a risk (some would have said already a practice by the late 1980s) that the ITU would be bypassed on matters which properly ought to lie within its competence. All this was known before the 1990 High Level Committee began reviewing the structure and functioning of the ITU and was among the reasons why the High Level Committee was given its task.[134]

Standards adopted under the new system and those referred to as part of the ITU Administrative Regulations, particularly the ITR to which we will come, are legal rulings for ITU members. Recommendations and Administrative Regulations established under the former ITU remain in force under the present arrangements until they are amended or repealed. Even so the newer process could (and can) be slower than modern conditions require. In response, in 2000 the WTSA adopted an 'alternative approval' system to provide a fast-track system by which informal approval of new 'standards' can be obtained relatively quickly.[135] 'Alternative approvals' are not binding but their existence has considerably increased the speed at which ITU-T reacts to swiftly developing technologies.

WTSAs are convened every four years with the possibility of an additional conference being intercalated if necessary (CS Art. 18.2 (114)). Dissimilar to ITU-R, there is no provision for regional ITU-T conferences. A WTSA deals with specific matters related to telecommunications (CV Art. 13 (184-191D)). Questions to be studied and on which recommendations may be issued may be generated from within the Sector or referred to it by a PP, by other conferences, or by the Council (CV Art. 13.2 (185)). Steps are being taken to improve the role and effectiveness of ITU-T.[136] There is also concern in the Sector as to an emergent gap between developed and developing countries in the matter of standardisation, and steps are being taken to address the problem.[137]

The Geneva Conference of 1992 did not take a sword to the Gordian tangle of questions and responsibilities for standardisation within the pre-1992 ITU structure. In compliance with CS Arts. 12.1.2 (79) and 17.1.2 (105), the precise responsibilities of ITU-T and ITU-R have been subject to continuing review as to

---

133 G. Wallenstein, *Setting Global Telecommunication Standards* (Boston and London: Artech House, 1990). Cf. the European Telecommunication Standards Institute, set up in 1988 as a joint project by the then European Community and the European Postal and Telecommunication Conference (CEPT) (http://www.etsi.org/) to publish telecommunications standards for Europe. Not all standard-setting institutions are intergovernmental or international.

134 *Supra*, at n. 13.

135 See now 'Alternative approval process for new and revised ITU-T Recommendations', Recommendation ITU-T A.8 (10/2008).

136 See 'The evolving role of the World Telecommunication Standardisation Assembly', Res. 122 (Rev. Guadalajara, 2010). See also *infra*, 'The Administrative Regulations: The International Telecommunication Regulations'.

137 See Res. 123 (Rev. Guadalajara, 2010), 'Bridging the standardisation gap between developing and developed countries'.

matters of common interest. Duplication of effort (not to say conflict of interest) between the Study Groups of ITU-T and ITU-R had been foreseen as a possible problem, as it had been for the CCITT and the CCIR. CV Arts 11.5 (158) and 14.2 (193) therefore provide for a continuing review and possible change or transfer of responsibilities between the Sectors and relevant Study Groups, and that in case of failure to reach timely and effective agreement, the matter is referred to the PP through the Council.[138] Over the years this has produced some adjustment between ITU-T and ITU-R.

ITU-T is active in considering what areas of telecommunications should have, or would benefit from, standardisation. To that end it operates a 'Technology Watch', assessing relevant new technologies both as to future standardisation and as to their impact on existing standards. ITU-T issues Technology Watch Alerts,[139] publishes reports, and under that heading has run events and symposia. So far sixteen reports have been issued.[140] Reports are the responsibility of their authors, and are not binding but may indicate possible future areas of activity for ITU-T.

The Telecommunication Development Sector (ITU-D)

The phrase 'economic and social development' appears twice in the Preamble (1) of the ITU Constitution.[141] The concept appears both formally and by implication in various paragraphs of CS Art. 1 which sets out the purposes of the Union (CS Arts. 1.b-g (4-9), 2.d-e (14-5), 2.i (19)). ITU-D is the main (though not the only) channel through which the ITU seeks the development of world telecommunications and in particular recognises the interests of the developing countries. Article 5 of the Nice Constitution, 1989, had added a Telecommunications Development Bureau to the organs of the Union, but this had not properly started to function before the 1992/1994 revisions were adopted. Its role was taken over by the new Sector.

---

138 CV Art. 11.5 (158). Of all the United Nations agencies, the ITU has a history of a pragmatic approach to problems.

139 1. Mobile Applications (2009); 2. Batteries for portable ICT devices (2010).

140 1. Intelligent Transport Systems and CALM (2007); 2. Telepresence: High Performance video-conferencing (2007); 3. ICTs and Climate Change (2007); Ubiquitous Sensor Networks (2008); 5. Remote collaboration tools (2008); 6. Technical aspects of Lawful Interception (LI) (2008); 7. Next Generation Networks (NGNs) and energy efficiency (2008); 8. Standardisation Activities for Intelligent Transport Systems (2008); 9. Distributed Computing: Utilities, Grids and Clouds (2009); 10. The Future Internet (2009); 11. ICTS and Food Security (2009); 12. Biometrics and Standards (2009); 13. Decreasing Driver Distraction (2009); 14. ICT as Enabler for Smart Water Management (2010); 15. Using Submarine communications Networks to Monitor the Climate (2010); 16. Standards and eHealth (2011).

141 See F. Lyall, 'Space Telecommunications and the Developing Countries' (1989) 32 *Proc. IISL*, 242, and 'The International Telecommunication Union and Development' (1994) 22 *J. Sp. L.* 23.

Development first became a major factor at Malaga-Torremolinos in 1973 resulting in various programmes.[142] That was taken further at Nairobi, development appearing in the Preamble of the Nairobi Convention of 1982.[143] The post-Nairobi ITU was to 'promote and to offer technical assistance to developing countries in the field of telecommunications' (Nairobi, Art. 4.1.a (14)), and foster 'international cooperation in the delivery of technical assistance to the developing countries' through participation in UN programmes (Nairobi, Art. 4.2.c (20)). '[T] echnical cooperation and assistance provided to the developing countries' was added to permissible ITU expenses (Nairobi, Art. 15.1.c (110)), and the powers of the then IFRB to advise were extended to take special account of the needs of developing countries (Nairobi, Art. 10.4.c (79)). The geographical situation of particular countries (Nairobi, Art. 10.4.c (79)) and the 'equitable utilisation of the geostationary orbit' were included as matters to be taken into consideration in ITU action and decisions (Nairobi, Art. 10.4.d (80)).

Nairobi had been a wake-up call to the generality of the ITU community. Although foreshadowed by Malaga-Torremolinos, during the Nairobi conference the developing countries had made it clear that what had been originally constituted as an organisation directed to facilitating technicalities should expand its remit to include the fostering of their telecommunications.[144] There was, of course, argument whether this was a departure from the basic purposes of the organisation. There were even suggestions that those who disapproved of such an extended remit might peel off and form another international organisation in which technical regulation would remain paramount.[145] Certainly on the face of things telecommunications development would seem more properly to be the function of

142 See Chapter 4, 'The International Telecommunication Convention, Malaga-Torremolinos, 1973'. See above, pp. 112-4.

143 'While fully recognizing the sovereign right of each country to regulate its telecommunications and having regard to the growing importance of telecommunication for the preservation of peace and the social and economic development of all countries, the plenipotentiaries of the Contracting Governments, with the object of facilitating peaceful relations, international co-operation and economic and social development among peoples by means of efficient telecommunication services, have agreed to establish this Convention, which is the basic instrument of the International Telecommunication Union.' Preamble, International Telecommunication Convention, Nairobi, 6 November 1982, 1531 UNTS 320, 1985 UKTS 33, Cmnd 9557; US Tr. Doc. 99-6. With minor variation the 1992 CS retains this phraseology, adapted to include reference to the associated CV. 'Social and economic' development is reversed in the 1992 version. I do not know whether this is merely for consistency with the later use of the phrase in the paragraph or is an important variation. See above, pp. 114ff.

144 B.E. Harris, 'The New Telecommunications Development Bureau of the International Telecommunication Union' (1991) 7 *Am. U.J. Int. L. & Pol.* 83 at 87-9. See also Chapter 4, 'The International Telecommunication Constitution and Convention, Nice, 1989'.

145 Harris, *supra*, n. 144; Lyall *supra*, n. 141.

the UN Development Program (UNDP) (http://www.undp.org/). History has gone down the other trouser-leg.

In the reconstruction of the Union there was therefore no doubt that development would be an important purpose of the ITU.[146] The ITU was already running programmes to help developing countries establish good telecommunications facilities.[147] The Nice CS and CV therefore had included the creation of a new Bureau, the Telecommunications Development Bureau (TDB).[148] The list of its specific functions in Nice CS Art. 14.2 (113-20) was extensive and remarkably detailed. However, as we have seen the Nice drafts did not come into force, being overtaken by the decisions of the 1992 Geneva APP.

Geneva CS Art. 1 lists among the purposes of the Union the promotion of technical development including providing technical assistance to developing countries (CS Art. 1.1.1.b (4)), developments to make telecommunication facilities 'so far as possible generally available to the public' (CS Art. 1.1.c (5)), and 'the extension of the benefits of new communications technologies to all the world's inhabitants' (CS Art 1.1.d (6)). The ITU is to 'foster international cooperation and solidarity in the delivery of technical assistance to the developing countries and the creation, development and improvement of telecommunication equipment and networks in developing countries by every means at its disposal …' (CS Art. 1.2.d (14)). An innovation was the inclusion of a duty 'in particular' as to the promotion 'with international financial and development organisations' of 'the establishment of preferential and favourable lines of credit to be used for the development of social projects aimed, *inter alia*, at extending telecommunication services to the most isolated areas in countries' (CS Art 1.2.i (19)).[149]

Though based in Geneva, ITU-D has regional offices to help achieve its objectives. The Sector operates under CS Chapter IV (CS Arts. 21-24 (118-145)) and CV Section 7 (CV Arts. 16-18 (207A-226)) as well as the already noted provisions common to all Sectors (CV Section 8, Arts. 19-22 (228-254)). So much for the documentation. However, the 1992/1994 reforms went much

146 See Chapter 4, nn. 155-66. *The Missing Link: Report of the Independent Commission for World-wide Telecommunications Development* (Geneva: ITU, 1985) (the 'Maitland Commission') had stressed the importance of 'development'.

147 See *supra*, n. 146. Apart from such formal programmes, before 1992/1994 the ITU did undertake a certain amount of 'development' work through facilitating cooperation between ordinary commercial undertakings and developing countries. In addition the IFRB conducted training courses and workshops for officials responsible for radio matters in newly emergent nations.

148 Final Acts of the Plenipotentiary Conference, Nice 1989: Constitution and Convention of the International Telecommunication Union, Optional Protocol, Decisions, Resolutions, Recommendations and Opinions (Geneva : ITU, 1990); http://www.itu.int/en/history/plenipotentiaryconferences/Pages/1989Nice.aspx. Constitution, Art. 14 (112-24). Harris, *supra*, n. 144.

149 This is without prejudice to the just mentioned generalities of CS Arts. 1.1.b (4), 1.2.d (14) and 1.2.i (19).

further than previously authorised 'development' activities. This has not been entirely welcomed by all countries and the funding of the Sector has been under constraint.[150]

Like the other Sectors, ITU-D consists of a Bureau (CV Art. 18 (216-226)) headed by a Director elected by the PP (CS Art. 8.1.g (55)) whose duties are laid out in CV Art. 18 (216-226). Members of the Sector and the various groups through which it works include the State Members of the Union as of right, together with any entity or organisation authorised by the appropriate procedures to be a member of the sector (CS Art. 21.4 (134-136)).[151] Subsidiary groups include a Telecommunication Development Advisory Group (TDAG) which reviews the work of the Sector, including the implementation of its operational plan, and suggests any necessary corrective measures (CV Art 17A (215C-215K)). TDAG also prepares reports for ITU-D conferences.

While ITU-D does much of its work through study groups (CV Art. 17 (214-215B)), courses and workshops, an important element of its activity is carried out through the Telecommunication Development Conferences (TDC) (CS Art. 22 (137-43)). These, governed by CV Art 16 (208-213A), are *fora* for discussion and providing guidance to ITU-D (CS Art. 22.1 (137)). TDCs take place within the ITU four-year cycle on a schedule of one world conference per cycle together with regional conferences, subject to priorities and the availability of resources (CS Art. 22.3 (141)). ITU-D conferences do not produce Final Acts (i.e. treaty-level binding agreements). Instead they adopt resolutions, decisions, recommendations and reports of variable cogency. These must, of course, all conform to the CS, CV and the WTDC Administrative Regulations. The foreseeable financial implications of any proposals made by a TDC must be taken into account and conferences may not adopt resolutions and decisions which might cause expenditure above limits set down by the ITU PP (CS Art. 22.4 (142)).

World Telecommunication Development Conferences (WTDCs) establish work programmes and guidelines giving direction and guidance for ITU-D as a whole (CV Art. 16.1.1.a (209)). Regional Conferences deal with matters specific to the region concerned (CV Art. 16.1.1.b (210)). At their meetings WTDCs fix objectives and strategies for a balanced world-wide and regional development of telecommunications (CV Art. 16.1.c (211)). In this the conferences should give 'particular consideration to the expansion and modernisation of the networks and services of the developing countries as well as the mobilisation of resources required for this purpose. They shall serve as a forum for the study of policy, organisational, operational, regulatory, technical and financial questions and related aspects, including the identification and implementation of new sources of funding' (CV Art. 16.1.c (211)). Channels of technical assistance and of financial aid for developing countries have therefore been opened up and existing

150 See also *infra*, 'Finance'.

151 See *supra*, 'Sector Membership'.

channels deepened in a way that would not have been possible under the pre-1992 arrangements.

The Sector has played a significant role in extending accessibility, affordability and infrastructure particularly in the developing countries. Major results have been the adoption of Declarations and an Action Plan at successive WTDCs: at Buenos Aires, Argentina, in 1994;[152] Valletta, Malta, 1998;[153] Istanbul, Turkey, 2002;[154] Doha, Qatar, 2006;[155] and Hyderabad, India, 2010.[156] The Valletta Plan, as amended, had particular chapters on the development of a global information infrastructure and a special programme for developing countries. The Istanbul Development Plan, which included a special programme for least developed countries, was divided into six programmes: (i) regulatory reform, (ii) technologies and telecommunication network development, (iii) E-strategies and E-services/applications, (iv) economic and finance, (v) human capacity building, and (vi) a special programme for the least developed countries.[157] The Istanbul WTDC also set further objectives to be attained by ITU-D within the ITU cycle for 2003-2007 and called for regional preparatory meetings to help shape the next WTDC. This device was reasonably successful and has been used subsequently. The Doha Declaration of 2006 indicated that most of the previous Action Plans had been implemented. However, it called for an increased pace in progress towards a truly global information society and further striving towards improving the position of the developing countries.[158] The Doha Action Plan took these matters further, and was able to build on the outcomes of the World Summit on the Information Society (WSIS, 2003-2005), which is outlined separately below. The Doha WTDC, 2006, called for the next WTDC to be preceded by regional gatherings to prepare for the world conference and this was done, Hyderabad 2010 adopting a variety of recommendations and resolutions together with the Hyderabad Declaration and Action Plan which had an impact on the Guadalajara PP.[159]

---

152 WTDC-94. The Buenos Aires Action Plan, 1994: see http://www.itu.int/ITU-D/bdtint/general/baapbrochure.htm. For the Buenos Aires Declaration, see http://www.itu.int/ITU-D/conferences/wtdc/1994/firstWTDC.html.

153 WTDC-98. The Valletta Action Plan, 1998: see http://www.itu.int/ITU-D/conferences/wtdc/1998/VAP.html.

154 World Telecommunication Development Conference (WTDC-02, Istanbul) – Final Report (Geneva: ITU, 2002): see http://www.itu.int/ITU-D/isap/WTDC-02FinalReport/index.html.

155 World Telecommunication Development Conference (WTDC-06-Doha) – Final Report: http://www.itu.int/dms_pub/itu-d/opb/tdc/D-TDC-WTDC-2006-TOC-HTM-E.htm.

156 World Telecommunication Development Conference (WTDC-10-Hyderabad) – Final Report: http://www.itu.int/publ/D-TDC-WTDC-2010/en.

157 See Istanbul Final Report (n. 154) at 22.

158 See Doha, Final Report (n. 155) and the Doha Declaration at http://www.itu.int/ITU-D/conferences/wtdc/2006/DohaDeclaration.html.

159 See *supra*, n. 156. The Hyderabad Declaration is at http://www.itu.int/ITU-D/conferences/wtdc/2010/index.html. For a survey of WSIS progress see *WSIS+5: Report on*

Finance

The financial arrangements of the ITU remain unusual within the family of UN agencies. Like the UPU (q.v.) it retains the 'contributory unit' system that was first instituted within the International Telegraph Union by the Vienna Convention of 1868.[160] The relevant provisions are now found in CS Art. 28 (155-70) and CV Art. 33 (468-87). Finance, and value for money, remains a concern within the Union, the financial plan being adopted by the PP but operated on biennial budgets approved by Council.[161] The complex process by which the value of the 'contributory unit' is established and Members select their class of contribution reflects that concern.

All State Members and Sector Members contribute to the expenses of the Union in accordance with the number of contributory units which they have chosen (CS Arts. 28.2.2*bis* (159C) and 28.3.1 (160)). Payment is made annually in advance on the basis of the biennial budget as adjusted by Council (CS Art. 28.8 (168)).[162] The 'new' rate of contribution applies from the date at which the first biennial budget after a PP takes effect. A State Member which falls into arrears equal to or more than two years of its contribution loses its right to vote in all ITU meetings and consultations, including the Council should it have been elected a member of that body (CS Art. 28.8 (169)).[163]

The procedures whereby the State and Sector Members select their class of contribution vary. State Members make their choice at the PP (CS Art. 28.3.2 (161)). This choice is not wholly uninformed. Nor, as we see below, is it entirely unrestricted. Prior to each PP, Council sets a provisional figure for the contributory

---

the World Summit on Information Society Plus Five (Geneva: ITU, 2010).

160 International Telegraph Convention, Vienna, 21 July 1868, 136 CTS 122 and 292: 59 BFSP 322; 10 De Clercq 121. See Chapter 2 at n. 47.

161 See successive versions of PP Decision 5, 'Expenditure of the Union for the period ...'.

162 The contribution of a new State or Sector Member is calculated from the first day of the month of its accession or admission (CV Art. 33.2.1 (472)). Should a State Member or a Sector Member withdraw from the Union it remains liable for payment of its contribution calculated up to the last day of the month on which its withdrawal becomes effective (CV Art. 33.2.2 (473)).

163 As at July 2010 nineteen members, Antigua and Barbuda, the Central African Republic, Chad, Dominica, the Gambia, Grenada, Equatorial Guinea, Guinea-Bissau, Haiti, Liberia, the Marshall Islands, Nauru, Nicaragua, the Democratic Republic of the Congo, St Kitts and Nevis, the Solomon Islands, Somalia, Tajikistan, Turkmenistan and Tuvalu were in arrears of at least two years of contribution: see 'Loss of the Right to Vote', Note by ITU Sec. Gen., PP-10, Doc. 60. In addition, Antigua and Barbuda, Nauru, the Solomon Islands and Sierra Leone had not yet acceded to the Geneva CS and CV, and Grenada, while a signatory, had not deposited its instrument of ratification or acceptance. Grenada and Sierra Leone were not in arrears of contribution. By 11 October 2010 Chad, The Gambia, Grenada and Haiti had rectified their situations: see Rev. 4 to PP Doc. 60, *supra*.

unit based on the draft financial plan and the total number of units currently selected (CS Art. 28.3*bis*.1 (161B)). Then, no later than four weeks before the conference, the Secretary General asks Member States what class of contributory unit they have provisionally chosen (CS Art. 28.3*bis*.2 (161C)). Thereafter during the conference this information is juggled with to fix first, a provisional upper limit for the contributory unit, and then a definitive figure for that value. On the basis of the definitive value Member States should by at the latest the Monday of the final week of the conference indicate their final choice of class of contribution (CS Art. 28.3*bis*.3-4 (161D-E)). The financial plan for the ensuing period is then approved taking account of the total of contributory units selected (CS Art. 28.3*bis*.6 (161G)). Member States which do not timeously select their class of contribution retain that for the previous quadrennium (CS Art. 28.3*bis*.5 (161F)). A State Member may at any time choose a class of contribution higher than the one it has already adopted (CS Art. 28.5*ter* (165B)), but there are restrictions on the right to decrease its class. Until Guadalajara, generally a Member State could not reduce its contribution by more than two classes of contribution. That provision was altered at PP-10 to reflect the forty-five contributory classes system that was there adopted. The revised provision still allows a Member State to reduce the number of units it selects, but not by more than fifteen per cent of the number of units it chose for the period preceding the reduction, rounding down to the nearest lower number of units for contributions of three or more units, or by more than one unit class for contributions below three units. When a State Member makes a reduction Council indicates to it how that reduction may be phased in or implemented over the period between PPs, a provision which allows the ITU to balance its cash-flow (CS Art. 28.5 (165)). However, PP may authorise a greater reduction where a Member State shows exceptional circumstances such that it cannot maintain its original choice of class (e.g. a natural disaster that requires international aid) (CS Art. 28.5 (165)). Between PPs Council may authorise a reduction on the same grounds (CS Art. 28.5*bis* (165A)).

Mutatis mutandis much of the preceding paragraph applies to the Sector Members. Each Sector Member selects its class of contribution and is given three months from the close of the PP to indicate its choice. Should it fail to do so it retains its previous level of contributory class (CS Art. 28.3*ter* (161H-63)). The value of the contributory unit for a Sector Member is normally one-fifth of the contributory unit paid by Member States (CV Art. 33.5 (480)). However, to encourage their participation the Guadalajara conference made exceptional provision for Sector Members from developing countries, allowing them to take part in the work of ITU-T and ITU-R with a contribution of one-sixteenth of a contributory unit.[164]

---

164 Res. 170 (Guadalajara, 2010), 'Admission of Sector Members from developing countries to participate in the work of the ITU Telecommunication Standardization Sector and the ITU Radiocommunication Sector'. Such a sector member must not be a subsidiary of a multinational company which is headquartered in a developed country, must not already be a Sector Member of either ITU-T or ITU-R, and its 'parent' developing country

Ordinary contributions by Sector Members are part of the ordinary ITU income (CV Art. 33.5 (480)) but are identified as being made to the relevant Sector (CV Art. 33.5*bis* (480A)). A reduction in contribution may be authorised by Council in exceptional circumstances where a Sector Member cannot maintain its obligations (CV Art. 33.5*ter* (480B)).

The contribution made by an Associate Member to the Sector to which it is admitted is set by Council (CV Art. 33.4bis (483A)).

The contributory unit and the selection of contributory classes are, of course, at the heart of ITU income. As we have seen the value of the unit is set by the PP having regard to the financial plan and the likely take-up by Member States of the various classes of contribution. In 2006 at Antalya, CV Art. 33.1 (468) set twenty-four classes of contribution ranging from a 40 unit class to a 1/16 unit class. In 2010 the Guadalajara PP significantly altered this range by introducing single unit steps from 40 units to 2 units while retaining the 1 1/2, 1, 1/2, 1/4, 1/8 and 1/16 unit classes below that. There are therefore now forty-five classes of contribution, albeit that the ratio between potentially largest to smallest remains 480:1.[165] It was and remains competent for a State Member to contribute more than 40 units (CV Art. 33.1.2 (469)). However, the tendency has been for State Members to reduce their contributory class.[166] State Members are restricted as to the unit selection. Only states listed as least developed by the UN or accepted as such by Council may select the 1/8 and 1/16 unit classes (CV Art. 33.1.1*bis* (468A)), and Sector Members may not select a unit class lower than 1/2 except in the case of ITU-D where a Sector Member may select the 1/4 or 1/8 classes. In addition a State Member of ITU-D may choose the 1/16 unit class provided that it is both on a list of least developed countries maintained by the UN Development Programme (UNDP) and that the selection is accepted by ITU Council (CV Art. 33.1.1*ter* (468B)).[167] The other exceptional provision is in ITU-T where, following Res. 71 of the 2008 WTSA, the 2010 PP allowed academic and similar research establishments and institutions to be admitted as Sector Members for a trial period of four years with a minimum contribution level of 1/32 unit (roughly CHF 2000 = GBP 1329 or USD 2161, as at early 2011).[168]

must fall within the UNDP 'low-income' category with an annual per capita income not more than USD 2000.

165 The actual ratio of largest to smallest contributory unit take up in 2010 prior to the Guadalajara PP was 360:1.

166 It would be interesting to know how far that reduction has affected the purchasing power of contributions in real terms.

167 From PP-2002 access to the 1/8 and 1/16 unit classes was based on a calculation involving population and GDP per capita which produced a set figure for general UN purposes and was used by ITU. That figure did not vary with time. The Secretary General proposed to the 2010 Council that instead reference should be made to whatever the current UN figure might be: 'Criteria Applicable for the Choice of Class of Contribution', C10/67.

168 'Admission of academia, universities and their associated research establishments to participate in the work of the three Sectors of the Union', Res. 169 (Guadalajara 2010).

Income from 'subscriptions' is not the sole source of finance for the Union. Subsequent to, and triggered by, the financial and other difficulties encountered by ITU-R in dealing with a massive increase in notifications of assignments in respect of satellites, the ITU took power to recover the cost of providing certain of its products and services from those requiring them (CV Art. 33.5 (484)).[169] In particular, costs are at least partially recovered in relation to processing of satellite notifications.[170]

In its financial operations the ITU abides by normal practice. It is required to maintain a reserve sufficient to meet essential expenditures and, so far as possible, is to avoid resorting to loans. This is supervised by Council as part of its duties (CV Art. 33.6 (485)). Extra-ordinary expenditures such as the building of the Montbrilliant Building in Geneva were handled separately.[171]

The Administrative Regulations

CS Art. 4.1 (29) lists the instruments of the Union as comprising the CS, the CV and the Administrative Regulations. CS Art. 4.3 (31) states that the CS and CV are 'further complemented' by the Administrative Regulations, these being the International Telecommunication Regulations (ITRs) and the Radio Regulations (RR), which 'regulate the use of telecommunications' and are 'binding on all Member States'. By CS Art. 6 Member States are bound to comply with the CS, the CV and the Administrative Regulations in their own operations (CS Art. 6.1 (37)), and to impose observance of these instruments on the providers of international telecommunication services which they license, as well as on any radio stations

By 1 June 2011 nineteen such institutions had been admitted to Sectors: see *supra*, n. 52.

169 'Cost recovery for some ITU products and services', Res. 91 (Rev. Guadalajara, 2010). In the original 1992 Convention the equivalent of CV Art. 33.13 (484) required that in pricing ITU publications the Secretary General should in general seek to cover the cost of printing and distribution. Its current form dates from Minneapolis, 1998. (The paragraphing of Art. 33 was re-numbered at Kyoto.)

170 'Processing charges for satellite network filings and administrative procedures' Res. 88, now subsumed into Res. 91, 2010 (*supra*, n. 169). See also Res. [COM 5/2] (WRC-07) as to the entry into force of provisions regarding the non-payment of cost-recovery fees.

In Decl. 91 to the 1998 Minneapolis Final Acts the US sought to distinguish between government and other space networks in the application of cost recovery. This was rejected by Austria, Belgium, Denmark, Estonia, Finland, France, Germany, Greece, Ireland, Italy, Liechtenstein, Luxembourg, The Netherlands, Norway, Portugal, Slovakia, Spain, Sweden, Switzerland, Turkey and the UK in Decl. 112.

Leive, 317-8, notes that at the 1959 Geneva PP J. Gracie, then Vice-Chairman of the IFRB, suggested that a 'registration fee' be charged to cover all the IFRB costs for processing the notification of an assignment. Good ideas take time to germinate.

171 Cf. Kyoto Res. 61, 'Premises of the Seat of the Union: Construction of the "Montbrilliant Building"', (abrogated Minneapolis, PP-98).

capable of causing harmful interference to those of other countries (CS Art. 6.2 (38)). Where there is any inconsistency between these instruments the provisions of the CS prevail over both the CV and the Administrative Regulations, and those of the CV prevail over the Administrative Regulations (CS Art. 4.4 (32)).

The Administrative Regulations are further dealt with in CS Art. 54. Repeating the provision of CS Art. 4.3 (31), CS Art. 54.1 (215) again states that the Administrative Regulations are binding international instruments, subject to the provisions of the CS and CV. Ratification, acceptance or approval of the CS and CV under CS Art. 52 (208-11) or accession under CS Art. 53 (212-4) carries with it consent to be bound by the Administrative Regulations adopted by competent world conferences prior to a state joining the Union, but subject to any reservation which it may make at the time (CS Art. 54.2 (216)). Thereafter State Members have to ratify later amendments (whether partial and complete) to the Administrative Regulations (CS Art. 54.2*bis*-3*quater* (216A-217C)). Reservations to revisions of the Administrative Regulations are competent under the normal rules of the Law of Treaties (CS Art. 53.5*ter* (221B)).[172] Recognising that the ratification processes of various countries can move slowly, and that revisions to the Administrative Regulations may require to be applied more speedily, revisions are applied provisionally to all states from the date at which the relevant provisions of Final Acts come into force except in the case of states which indicate their opposition when the revising document is signed (CS Art. 54.2.3*penter* (217D)). Provisional application persists until a state communicates its decision as to its consent or otherwise to an amendment (CS Art. 54.4 (218)). A state which has timeously indicated opposition but does not notify its objection within thirty-six months of the entry into force of an amendment is deemed to have consented to that amendment (CS Art. 54.5*bis* (221A)).

The International Telecommunication Regulations (ITR)

Main responsibility for the International Telecommunication Regulations lies with the Standardisation Sector, ITU-T. The current (2011) ITRs were adopted by the World Administrative Telegraph and Telephone Conference held in Melbourne, South Australia, in 1988, four years before the 1992/1994 reconstruction.[173] The Antalya PP of 2006 decided that they should be reviewed.[174] With that explanation

172 Arts. 19-23, Convention on the Law of Treaties, Vienna, 1969, 1155 UNTS 155; 1980 UKTS 58, Cmnd. 7964; 8 ILM 679.

173 International Telecommunication Regulations: Final Acts of the World Administrative Telegraph and Telephone Conference, Melbourne, 1988 (Geneva; ITU, 1989). See also http://www.itu.int/en/history/administrativeconferences/Pages/1988Melbourne.aspx.

174 See Res. 146 (Antalya, 2006) 'Review of the International Telecommunication Regulations', and Res. 171 (Guadalajara, 2010) on 'Preparations for the 2012 World Conference on International Telecommunications'.

and the caveat that what follows is very likely to be departed from in measure when a new set of Regulations is adopted in 2012, the existing ITRs can be considered.

The modern ITRs are simpler than their predecessors and very much simpler than the RR. In their present form they run to fourteen pages setting out ten Articles with an Appendix on Accounting (five pages), and appendices on additional provisions on maritime telecommunications and on service and 'privilege' telecommunications – a total of twenty-three well-spaced pages.

The Preamble (1) to the ITR recognises the sovereign right of states to regulate telecommunications in terms redolent of the Preamble to the CS. Article 1 then declares that their purpose is to establish general principles on the provision and operation of public international telecommunication services and the underlying means through which these services are carried (ITR Art. 1.1.a (2)). However, ITR Art. 1.1.b (3) immediately recognises the right of ITU member states to allow special arrangements under ITR Art. 9 (58-60). ITR Art. 1.3 (5) indicates further that the intention of the ITRs is to facilitate global interconnection and interoperability and 'the harmonious development and efficient operation of technical facilities, as well as the efficiency, usefulness and availability to the public on international telecommunication services' are to be promoted. To that end ITR Art. 1.6 (8) states that Administrations should to the greatest extent practicable comply with the relevant CCITT Recommendations including any Instructions thereanent.[175] However, ITR Art. 1.4 (6) provides that reference to these in the ITRs does not give them the same legal status as the ITRs, and ITR Art. 1.5 (7) states that within the framework set out by the ITRs 'the provision and operation of international telecommunication services in each relation is pursuant to mutual agreement between administrations'. This, taken with the already mention Art. 9 allowance of special arrangements means that administrations can (and do) enter into a multiplicity of mutual arrangements, and this is likely to continue.

ITR Art. 2 (13-27) is a schedule of definitions, but for the purposes of the ITRs only. In broad they seem clear, indeed obvious. ITR Art. 3 requires Members to ensure that administrations cooperate in the creation, operation and maintenance of the international telecommunication network to provide a satisfactory quality of service and enough facilities sufficiently to meet the requirements of the service and demands for it (ITR Art. 3.1-2 (29-30)). The routing of an international service is by mutual agreement of administrations except that where there is no direct route the originating administration can choose the route (ITR Art. 3.3 (30)).[176] ITR Art. 3 concludes with the right of any user, subject to national law, to send a message, a satisfactory quality of service being again stated to be maintained 'to the greatest extent practicable' in accordance with CCITT Recommendations (ITR Art. 3.4 (31)).

175 CCITT Recommendations made prior to the coming into force of the 1992/1994 CS and CV remain valid until amended or repealed.

176 Notably this allows a service provider to choose whether to use a cable or satellite link.

ITR Art. 4 requires Members to promote the implementation of international services, and to make such available generally to the public through their national networks (ITR Art. 4.1 (32)). ITR Article 4.2-3 (33-8) goes on to require Members to see that administrations cooperate in providing a range of services of at least a minimum quality with access to these through terminals (provided these do not cause harm to technical facilities) (ITR Art. 4.3.a (33)), or through dedicated access points (ITR Art. 4.3.b (36)), and to provide 'at least a form of telecommunication' reasonably accessible to the public, including those who are not subscribers to a specific service (ITR Art. 4.3.c (37)). Interworking between different services is also to be provided (ITR Art. 4.3.d (38)). However, all these 'duties' are hedged by the recurrent 'to the greatest extent practicable', a phrase which rather reduces their effect. Where service is suspended (as is competent in terms of CS Art. 35 (182)) the ITU Secretary General is immediately to be informed, and he is to disseminate that information to all Members (ITR Art. 7 (55-6)).[177]

ITR Art. 5.1 (39) secures the absolute priority of and duty to transmit all telecommunications regarding safety of life. ITR Art. 5.2 (40) affords a degree of priority to government telecommunications, including UN messages, the priority of all other messages being set by CCITT (now ITU-T) Recommendations (Art. 5.3 (41)).

The ITR then pass to the important matters of charging and accounting, the latter being further dealt with in Appendix 1. Administrations set charges but are to endeavour to ensure that the cost of a message is approximately the same irrespective of the direction of travel (ITR Art. 6.1 (42-5)). Accounting rates for each service are to be agreed between administrations (ITR Art. 6.2 (46-7)). Unless otherwise agreed, the accounting unit is set by ITR Art. 6.3 (48-9) as either the monetary unit of the International Monetary Fund (in 1988 the Special Drawing Right) or the French gold franc (see also CV Art. 38 (500)). However, bilateral agreement as to the interaction of these accounting units is possible (ITR Art. 6.3.2 (50); CV Art. 38 (500)). ITR Appendix 1 further elaborates accounting requirements and procedures and includes provisions for the selection of the currencies to be used in the settlement of accounts.

ITR Art. 8 (57) states the duty of the ITU Secretary General to disseminate information about international telecommunication services, routes and statistics in terms which reflect those of CV Art. 5.1.o-p (98-9).

ITR Art. 9 (58-60) allows Members and their recognised operating agencies to enter into special arrangements *inter se* as to special networks for specialised services, provided that these do not concern Members in general. The language is opaque, but in fact allows the use of leased lines particularly for data and similar services. Intriguingly, under ITR Art. 9.1.b (59) any such arrangement 'should

177 See also now CS Art. 34.1-2 (180-1) and Art. 35 (182), *supra*, n. 19, as to suspension of service.

avoid technical harm to the operation of the telecommunication facilities of third countries'.[178]

Finally Appendix 1 further elaborates accounting procedures, Appendix 2 makes additional provision for maritime communications, and Appendix 3 for service and privilege communications.

As indicated above, the ITRs will be reviewed in the near future (probably in 2012).[179] Following discussions in ITU-T Study Groups 2 and 3 as well as in TSAG, an ITU-T Expert Group began work in 2007. Its remit was to identify duplication between the CS, the CV and the ITRs, to identify which ITR provisions ought to be in treaty-level instruments and which should remain as ITU-T Recommendations, to consider which operational provisions could be adequately reflected in ITU-T Recommendations, and to advise which provisions, if any, might be removed from the ITRs. The Expert Group was also to consider whether any ITR text should be amended or suppressed, the latter to include obsolete provisions. Finally, the review was also to investigate how the ITRs were used in actual practice by Member States to facilitate international telecommunications, in the provision of service, and in the timely settlement of accounts. The Expert Group was not to consider new or emergent issues which might warrant treaty-level provisions.[180] The Group reported to Council in 2009,[181] and by its Res. 1312 Council set up a further Working Group to prepare for a World Conference on International Telecommunications, now to be held in Geneva in November 2012.

Finally, the Expert Group reported that the prevailing view of their consultees was that the ITRs should remain a separate stand-alone Instrument of the Union, even though this might mean that they contained provisions identical or comparable to provisions found in the CS or CV. That seems sensible. In such a document it makes for clarity and ease of use to gather all relevant material within its text even if it repeats provisions from other documents, rather than that cross-reference is made to them. Whatever, if its recommendations are followed, the detailed report by the Expert Group indicates that the ITRs will undergo substantial revision in 2012.[182]

---

178 In the ITU publication of the ITR a related note reveals that the provision as to the 'avoidance of technical harm' was an attempt to cope with the possibility of internet viruses, one of the first, the 'Morris Worm', having been recognised just as the 1988 Melbourne conference convened. CS Art. 42 (193) on 'Special Arrangements' now contains similar language.

179 'Review of the International Telecommunication Regulations', Res. 146 (Antalya, 2006).

180 For its full Terms of Reference see ITU-T Circular 146, Annex 2, or the ITR Expert Group Doc. TD PL 1, 11 October 2007.

181 'Report to Council of the Expert Group on Review of the International Telecommunication Regulations (ITRs)', Doc. C09/6, with an Article-by-Article summary at C09/INF/1.

182 See *supra*, n. 181. Cf. Res. 171 (Guadalajara, 2010) 'Preparations for the 2012 World Conference on International Telecommunications'.

The Radio Regulations (RR)

The current (2011) Radio Regulations are those of Geneva, 1995 (WRC-95), as amended by subsequent radio conferences.[183] The next World Radio Conference was to be held in late 2011 but has been re-timed to January 2012 (WRC-12).

The RR contain the rules and procedures through which international protection against harmful interference is afforded to radio stations that provide particular services. They are the lineal descendants of the Berlin Radiotelegraph Convention of 1906, with its Art. 8 and the provisions of its Service Regulations as to interference, and of the 'Berne List' that gave notice of the frequencies in use.[184] Broadly, the radio stations now protected are those entered on the Master International Frequency Register (MIFR). The rules and procedures have evolved over the decades, the arrival of space services increasing the speed of that evolution. Indeed the speed with which the ITU recognised the new needs that space had is itself remarkable. The ITU took cognisance of the radio requirements of space research as early as 1959, only some eighteen months after Sputnik I, and began its more structured approach to the needs of space with the Extraordinary Administrative Radio Conference of 1963.[185]

The Articles of the RR are divided into nine Chapters. Chapter I deals with the terminology used in the RR and with technical characteristics of radio, Chapter II with radio frequencies, Chapter III with the questions of coordination, with the notification and recording of frequency assignments made by Member States and with the modifications of various Plans. Chapter IV deals with radio 'interferences' and their monitoring. Chapter V contains administrative provisions, including on secrecy, licensing, and station identification. It also covers service publications. Chapter VI sets out provisions for a variety of services including broadcasting, space and amateur services, radio astronomy, and radio-determination. Chapter VII contains the rules as to distress and safety communications, Chapter VIII those for aeronautical services and Chapter IX deals with maritime services. The RR are filled out by Appendices, Resolutions and Recommendations. The whole forms an extensive body of rules and practices, some of which is extremely (and to an outsider, extraordinarily) detailed.

---

183 WRC-97, Geneva (1997); WRC-2000, Istanbul (2000); WRC-07, Geneva (2007). For what follows Leive, though of 1970, is immensely informative.

184 Radio-telegraphic Convention, Final Protocol and Regulations, signed at Berlin 3 November 1906, 103 CTS 101; 1909 UKTS 8, Cd. 4559; 99 BFSP 321; (1906) UK Parl. Papers, HC 368; (US) 37 Stat. 15665, TS 568; (1906) 3 AJIL Supp. 330-40; (1923) 3 Malloy 2889; 1 Bevans 556; http://earlyradiohistory.us/1906conv.htm. See *supra*, Chapter 3, n. 59.

185 Partial Revision of the Radio Regulations: Final Acts of the Extraordinary Administrative Radio Conference to Allocate Frequency Bands for Space Radio Purposes, Geneva, 8 November 1963, 15 UST 887, TIAS 5603; (1964) 3 ILM 91. Part D of UNGA Res. 1721(XVI), 1961, acknowledged that the ITU would play a major role in 'International Cooperation on the Peaceful Uses of Outer Space'. Space-related provisions now form a large portion of the RR and a major part of the work of the ITU-R Bureau. See *infra*, at n. 187.

It is not feasible within the wordage available to me to cover the minutiae of the RR. They are extensive and complex, running to four volumes of A4 text, standing in stark contrast to the twenty-three pages of the International Telecommunication Regulations.[186] Their complexity is a known problem and attempts are under way towards their improvement, if not their simplification.[187] However, three of their ruling elements can be outlined, first, the allocation of frequencies to services, second, the extent to which some uses are 'planned', and last the protection afforded through RR procedures. These matters are important.

First, the allocation of frequencies to specific services has a long history. As we saw in Chapter 3, at the very beginning of the international regulation of radio Reg. II of the 1906 Berlin Regulations set aside the 300 (1000 Kc/s) and the 600 (500 Kc/s) metre bands for public correspondence and long distance use.[188] Now, for RR purposes RR 2.1 sub-divides the usable radio spectrum into nine frequency bands.[189] On the basis of that division RR 5 contains the 'Table of Allocations' under which frequencies within these bands are allocated to particular uses on either a world or a regional basis.[190] Broadly speaking the allocation to a service

186 The CD ROM version of the RR is easier to use since it is searchable.

187 Cf. Res. 86 (Rev. Marrakesh, 2002) 'Advance publication, coordination, notification and recording procedures for frequency assignments pertaining to satellite networks'. WRC Res. 951 (Rev. WRC-07), 'Enhancing the international spectrum regulatory framework', has called for the next WRC (January/February 2012) to consider the result of studies (on-going since WRC-03) as to improving the RR system. Regional preparations for WRC-12 have been held under the auspices of the African Telecommunications Union (ATU), the Arab Spectrum Management Group (ASMG), the Asia-Pacific Telecommunity (APT), the European Conference of Postal and Telecommunications Administrations (CEPT), the Inter-American Telecommunication Commission (CITEL) and the Regional Commonwealth in the Field of Communications (RCC). See http://www.itu.int/ITU-R/index.asp?category=conferences&rlink=wrc-12-regional&lang=en.

188 *Supra*, n. 184. See also Chapter 3, c. n. 31.

189 Nine frequency bands are designated by RR 2.1. They run from 3 Hz to 3000 GHz, designated in kilohertz (kHz) up to and including 3000 kHz, in megahertz (MHz) above 3 MHz up to and including 3000 MHz, and in gigahertz (GHz) above 3 GHz up to and including 3000 GHz (RR 2.1). The nine bands are VLF – Myriametric waves, 3-30 kHz; LF – Kilometric waves, 30-300 kHz; MF – Hectometric waves, 300-3000 kHz; HF – Decametric waves 3-30 MHz; VHF – Metric waves, 30-300 MHz; UHF – Decimetric waves, 300-3000 MHz; SHF – Centimetric waves, 3-30 GHz; EHF – Millimetric waves, 30-300 GHz; and THF – Decimillimetric waves, 300-3000 GHz. Frequencies are expressed in kHz up to and including 3000 kHz, in MHz from 3 MHz to 3000 MHz, and in GHz from 3 GHz to 3000 GHz. The Table of Allocations (RR 5) makes no allocations below 9 kHz. If a state authorises the use of a frequency below 9 kHz it must cause no harmful interference to services using the bands above 9 kHz (RR 5.53).

190 For RR purposes the world is divided into three Regions (RR 5.2), their boundaries being set out in RR 5.3-9. These are different from the five ITU regions designated for constitutional/electoral purposes. In addition there is the African Broadcasting Area, RR 5.10-3; the European Broadcasting Area, RR 5.14; the European Maritime Area, RR 5.15;

may be on a primary or a secondary basis.[191] Alternatively a particular use by a particular state or group of states may be permitted by way of a footnote to the main allocations as an additional allocation, as an alternative allocation, or as a different category of service.[192] As between the parties to the RR (i.e. all ITU Member States) all three possibilities have treaty status. Any exception to a particular allocation (for example for a small group of countries or even for a single state) is set out in a 'footnote'.[193]

Second, in the RR an 'allotment' may be given to a state or group of states in a particular region for a particular purpose (RR 1.17). A distinction is therefore to be drawn between 'planned' and 'un-planned' radio bands. In some regions and subregions an allotment (or a number of allotments) is made in respect of an agreed 'plan'.[194] Thus a broadcasting plan may be agreed for a region by which frequencies, signal strength and/or the location of transmitters are designated for particular broadcasting stations.[195] An allotment plan in respect of satellites was adopted by WARC-ORB 1985-8 and amended by WRC-03. Under it, for (but only for) direct satellite broadcast purposes, every state has been allocated a slot within a ten degree arc on the geostationary orbit together with uplink and downlink frequencies.[196] Unlike terrestrial allotment plans, until a state acts on this allotment

and the Tropical Zone, RR 5.16-21. A sub-Region consists of two or more countries in the same Region, RR 5.22.

191 A station transmitting on a secondary basis must not cause harmful interference to a station using a primary allocation, cannot claim protection from interference from such a station, but is protected from other stations using that secondary allocation (RR 5.28-31).

192 'Additional allocations': RR 5.34-7; 'Alternative allocations': RR 5.34-41. Either of these may have other restrictions placed on them. A 'different category of service' applies to named states in the 'category' and has either a primary or secondary status depending on its terms.

193 A 'footnote' allocation (or exemption from an allocation in the RR main text) is as authoritative as the provision of the main text. See 'Footnotes to the Table of Frequency Allocations in Article 5 of the Radio Regulations', RR Res. 26 (Rev. WRC-97).

194 Although separate regional arrangements between Members are allowed under CS Art. 43 (194), such a 'plan' is normally worked out through a RRC. Its implementation in respect of frequency allocations is a matter for a WRC revision of the RR.

195 E.g. the 'European Broadcasting Plan', Stockholm, 1961, as revised. See J-M. Paquet, 'The Stockholm 1961 Agreement', http://www.itu.int/ITUR/conferences/seminars/geneva-2006/docs/E/05-Terrestrial_Plan_ST61_JMP.doc. The first European Broadcasting Plan was the 'Long and Medium Frequency Plan' adopted by 29 European countries in 1929. Cf. J. Doeven, 'Revision of ST61 – Lessons from History' (2002) 290 *EBU Tech. Rev.*, http://www.ebu.ch/en/technical/trev/trev_290-doeven.html. The 'European Broadcasting Area' is defined in RR 5.14. Cf. the plans adopted by RRC-2006 for most of Region 1 for digital terrestrial broadcasting and the use of spectrum freed by the change.

196 For satellite services see RR Apps. 30, 30A and 30B. For procedures by which a new ITU member state can enter the allotment plan see RR App. 30B, Art.7. On the negotiation of WARC-ORB 85-88 see G.C. Staple, 'The New World Satellite Order: A Report from Geneva' (1986) 80 AJIL 699-720. See also E.D. DuCharme et al.,

others may place satellites in the slot in which its allotment is located. Orbits and frequencies are otherwise available on a 'first come, first served' basis, provided that the frequencies concerned are lawful within the service allocations set out in the Table of Allocations.

Third, 'first come, first served' brings us to the protection of frequency assignments through the ITU-R and RR procedures.

The Preamble (1) to the CS recognises 'the sovereign right of each state to regulate its telecommunication'. Accordingly, the 'assignment' of the use of a frequency to a particular radio station is the sovereign prerogative of the state having jurisdiction over the operator of the station (RR 1.18).[197] However, RR Chapter III (RR 7-14) sets out procedures by which an assignment by a state receives international protection from harmful interference. The result is that these procedures in effect require states to compromise their 'sovereign right'. If this is not accepted the Law of Physics will result in radio services being degraded, ultimately to unacceptable levels.[198]

Not all radio transmissions are subject to the international procedures. Only where the use of a frequency is likely to affect other countries do the RR procedures come into play. In this the Master International Frequency Register (MIFR), maintained by the ITU-R Bureau, is of crucial importance. Assignments that have been duly entered on the MIFR have a degree of international protection. The procedures vary depending on the frequency and service in question.[199] In broad summary the telecommunication administration of the state involved notifies ITU-R of its intention to assign the use of a particular frequency to a particular national user. When so doing it also supplies certain basic information.[200] This notification is published by ITU-R (advance publication) thus putting other states on notice of the intention.[201] The ITU-R Bureau examines the notification to check its conformity to the Table of Allocations (RR Art. 5). It also makes calculations based on the notification and the characteristics of existing assignments (data

'Direct Broadcasting by Satellite – The Development of the International, Technical and Administrative Regulatory Regime' (1984) 9 AASL 26787; Lyall/Larsen, 256-69.

197 See RR 1.18 and Resolution 1 (Rev. WRC-97) (RES1-1): 'unless specifically stipulated otherwise by special arrangements communicated to the Union by administrations, any notification of a frequency assignment to a station shall be made by the administration of the country on whose territory the station is located.'

198 The move to digital transmission exacerbates the effect of interference between two or more stations that use similar frequencies or signal characteristics.

199 RR Art. 11 sets out the requirements as to the notification of an assignment and details procedures for the different possible cases. For procedures prior to 1992/4 see Leive, and D. Leive, 'Regulating the Use of the Radio Spectrum' (1970) 5 *Stan. J. Int. Stud.* 21-52.

200 If the notification is incomplete, or is given too far ahead of the proposed use of the assignment, it is returned to sender. Periods vary.

201 Formerly a Weekly Circular, information is now available every two weeks in the form of a CD ROM as the BR International Frequency Information Circular (BR IFIC). Separate versions deal with Terrestrial and with Space Services.

which is already in the MIFR) to determine whether the proposed assignment would cause or receive 'harmful interference' to or from existing assignments. The result may be a 'favourable' or an 'unfavourable' finding. In the latter case the notification is returned to sender for revision or correction.[202] The most frequent correction required is the avoidance of 'harmful interference'. This involves consultation with any other potentially affected state to 'coordinate' assignments so that they do not cause each other 'harmful interference'.[203] In addition, other administrations may raise their concerns about a proposed assignment. Where a matter is unresolved by agreement the Bureau investigates the problem further and may make suggestions. In the ultimate it has to decide either to register the notified assignment or not. The decision of the Bureau may be reviewed (RR 14). Any affected disputant may appeal to the RRB against the decision of the Bureau (CV Art. 10.2 (140)) which makes a finding on the matter.[204] Later, actual interference may also occasion a reference by a state (not an operator) to the RRB procedures.

If there is no problem, or once problems have been resolved, the notified assignment is entered with a favourable finding on the MIFR. Thereafter it is entitled to protection through the operation of these procedures, other states being required to take it into account in order to avoid harmful interference to it from assignments which they may wish later to make (RR 8). An unregistered assignment is not so protected, and may incur harmful interference from a registered assignment, and *vice versa*. As noted above, the inexorable Laws of Physics impel compromise.

Normally a duly recorded assignment, which does not conflict with other assignments also duly recorded in the MIFR, is valid without limit of time. Codding II refers to such as a 'vested right' and in many ways it is. A duly registered terrestrial assignment may be altered, varied or departed from by consent of the relevant Member, by agreement between Members which wish to notify assignments that can be satisfied within an amended 'registration', or as the result of the adoption of a relevant 'Plan' as indicated above. However, particular provisions relate to the use of frequencies (and orbits) by satellite stations. Satellite frequencies and orbits are not 'vested' in that sense. Satellites are *ex natura* temporarily in their locations, and their replacements have to go through the registration process if their replacements have characteristics different from them (RR Res. 4).

202 This is separate from the normal negotiation between notifying administrations, from the arbitral procedures available under CS Art. 56 (233-235) and CV Art. 41 (507-518), and from the (never yet used) Optional Protocol on the Compulsory Settlement of Disputes, as to which see *infra*, n. 208.

203 For example, the frequencies involved may be altered or polarised, hours of use adjusted (cf. short-wave radio services), or transmitter power altered.

204 The Bureau prepares a report and draft recommendations for the Board to consider (CV Art. 12.2.f (171)). The RRB is to endeavour to take decisions unanimously, which failing a decision is valid only if at least two-thirds of the Board, being personally present, vote in favour. Proxy voting is not permitted (CV Art. 10.5.3 (146)).

Last, there is a continuing argument as to whether the use of the radio spectrum should be planned with frequencies and services pre-determined and allotted to each ITU Member for its telecommunication administration to implement. I return to this in the next chapter.

Disputes: Arbitration and Settlement

All international organisations should have procedures under which disputes between their members can be solved, mitigated or decided. The ITU is no exception. One possibility is for the PP or Council, authorised by the PP, in appropriate cases to ask for an Advisory Opinion from the International Court of Justice.[205] Short of that the CS provides for other mechanisms.

The settlement of disputes is dealt with by CS Art. 56 (233-235). CS Art. 56.1 (233) indicates that disputes relating to the interpretation or application of the CS, the CV or the Administrative Regulations (ITR and RR) may be settled by negotiation through diplomatic channels, or by bilateral or multilateral procedures, or by any other method to which the parties may agree. This statement is not unique to the ITU, but I would reiterate that in many ITU areas negotiation, compromise and agreement are bolstered by the existence of the Law of Physics. Some matters simply exist and cannot be altered. In these compromise is often the best recourse so that parties get some of what they wish. Accordingly, for example, ITU-R and the RRB can aid the attainment of acceptable solutions to questions of the use of radio frequencies.[206]

If negotiation fails, or is not resorted to, recourse may be had to arbitration (CS Art. 56.2 (234)), arbitral procedures being set out in CV Art. 41 (507-518).[207] Under these one party initiates the procedure by serving notice on the party with which it is in dispute (CV Art. 41.1 (507)). The parties then decide whether the arbitration will be conducted by individuals, administrations or governments, with governments serving if the parties cannot agree (CV Art. 41.2 (508)). Individual arbiters may not be nationals of, domiciled in, or employees of, a party (CV Art. 41.3 (508)). Arbitrating administrations or governments must be ITU members uninvolved in the dispute, but party to the agreement which is in contention (CV Art. 41.3 (509)). Within three months of the initial service of notice each party

205 'Request to the International Court of Justice for advisory opinions', Res. 59, (Kyoto, 1994).

206 RR Art. 15 deals with harmful interference. Its tenor is directed towards the swift elimination of interference when reported to the administration having jurisdiction over the cause. When this is ineffective ITU-R may be involved. The ITU-R Bureau can act only if a state so requests. It does not deal directly with disputes between telecommunications operators. It studies the dispute and issues non-binding recommendations to the parties. See *supra*, following n. 203.

207 CV Art. 41 in effect repeats the provisions of Annex 3 to the 1947 Atlantic City Final Acts.

appoints an arbiter, but where there is more than one party on each side these must make a single common appointment (CV Art. 41.4-5 (512-3)). The two arbiters then appoint a third, subject to the same requirements as to independence (CV Art. 41.7 (513)). Alternatively a single arbiter may be agreed, or the ITU Secretary General may be asked to draw lots to determine which of the two arbiters nominated by the parties should serve (CV Art. 41.8 (514)). The arbiter or arbiters decide on the venue and the procedure to be followed (CV Art. 41.9 (515)). The Union furnishes all the information which the panel may need in addition to the parties' submissions (CV Art. 41.12 (518)). The decision of a single arbiter is final and binding, as is that of the panel of three arbiters which may be reached by a majority (CV Art. 41.10 (516)). Parties bear their own expenses, and divide equally the other expenses of the arbitral procedure (CV Art. 41.11 (517)). Although CV Art. 41 is silent as to the giving of reasons for the decision, CV Art. 41.12 (518) provides for the decision being communicated to the ITU Secretary General for reference, if the parties so agree.

The final possibility is the Optional Protocol on the Compulsory Settlement of Disputes (CS Art. 56.3 (235)).[208] Broadly this applies the arbitration provisions of CV Art. 41 (507-518) as between its parties, but compulsorily. In the Optional Protocol CV Art. 41.5 (513) is extended, the Secretary General being empowered to appoint an arbiter at the request of a party should the other party fail to appoint one within the three month time limit (Op. Prot. Art. 1). As of 1 January 2011 the Optional Protocol had sixty-four parties. Withdrawal is competent upon one year's notice (Op. Prot. Art. 5). It is intriguing that the Optional Protocol, first instituted by the Montreux PP in 1965, has never been invoked.

* * *

The previous section dealt with the institutional structure of the ITU. However, as we saw in the later history of the 1932-1992 period, a growing demand arose, particularly from its newer members, that the ITU should assist, foster and encourage technical development as well as infrastructure and technical assistance. That process has continued in the reformed Union, as can be seen in many of the Resolutions and Recommendations of plenipotentiary and other conferences, in initiatives that the Union has taken, and in its cooperation with other agencies. What follows is not exhaustive of these activities, but certainly is evidence of the ITU commitment to the UNGA 'Millennium Declaration' of 2000,[209] and the 'Space Millennium: Vienna Declaration on Space and Human Development' of 1999.[210] The Final Acts of the 2010 PP contain the most recent versions of a

208 Available in *Collections*, and at http://www.itu.int/net/about/basic-texts/optional-protocol.aspx.

209 United Nations Millennium Declaration, UNGA Res. 55/2, 8 September 2000.

210 'Space Millennium: Vienna Declaration on Space and Human Development' adopted by the plenary meeting of the Third United Nations Conference on the Exploration

number of Resolutions directed towards technical assistance and development.[211] This carries on through the Strategic Plan for the 2011-2015 quadrennium adopted by the Guadalajara PP.[212] The 'Sectoral Objectives' there set contain significant elements directed towards improving the telecommunications of less-developed states. That said, it sometimes seems to outsiders that the demands of the less-developed can be strident and occasionally that the telecommunications of the 'developed' countries have been leap-frogged by some at least of those who have come later to modern systems. That may increasingly affect the willingness of the 'developed' to open their purse strings.

World Telecommunication Policy Forum

First held in 1996, the series of World Telecommunication Policy Forums has over the years brought together a variety of participants to discuss many areas of policy. Forums are called on the initiative of the Council. Topics so far dealt with include GMPCS (Global Mobile Personal Communications by Satellite) in 1996, trade in telecommunications in 1998, and IP Telephony in 1998. Participants include representatives of government, non-governmental organisations and stake-holders including manufacturers. The Forums may adopt Opinions. The last Forum was held in 2009 and considered convergence, public policy and regulatory issues, next-generation networks, and revision of the International Telecommunication Regulations.[213] It is not certain when the next will be called.[214]

---

and Peaceful Uses of Outer Space, Vienna, 30 July 1999: A/CONF.184/6, 30 July 1999; http:// www.oosa.unvienna.org/unisp-3/res/html/viennadecl.html.

211 E.g. all as revised at Guadalajara, 2010: Res. 25, 'Strengthening the regional presence'; Res. 30, 'Special measures for the least developed countries, small island developing states, landlocked developing countries and countries with economies in transition'; Res. 34, 'Assistance and support to countries in special need for rebuilding their telecommunication sector'; Res. 64, 'Non-discriminatory access to modern telecommunication/information and communication technology facilities, services and applications, including applied research and transfer of technology, on mutually agreed terms'; Res. 135, 'ITU's role in the development of telecommunications/information and communication technologies, in providing technical assistance and advice to developing countries, and in implementing relevant national, regional and interregional projects'; Res. 137, 'Next-generation network deployment in developing countries'; Res. 143, 'Extending the provisions in ITU documents relating to developing countries to apply to countries with economies in transition'.

212 Res. 71 (Rev. Guadalajara, 2010) 'Strategic plan for the Union for 2012-2015'.

213 See the now abrogated Dec. 9, Antalya, 'Fourth World Telecommunication Policy Forum'.

214 See Res. 2 (Rev. Guadalajara, 2010), 'World telecommunications/information and communication technology policy forum'.

Exhibitions: ITU Telecom

Telecommunication exhibitions under the auspices of the Union were first authorised by Opinion 3 of the Malaga-Torremolinos PP. ITU Telecom events are held to inform ITU members and others as to developments in technology. These have mostly been held in Geneva, but are not restricted to that venue.[215]

The Digital Divide

The Digital Divide has been a matter of major concern both to the Development Sector and to the ITU in general.[216] There is concern that a gulf might develop between countries whose telecommunications are analogue-based, and those whose telecommunications are increasingly moving over to digitally based technologies. WTDC Res. 37 (Istanbul 2002) took account of the matter, and by its Res. 123 the Marrakesh PP instructed the ITU-D Director to take measures to implement the Istanbul resolution and to take other related actions.[217] While the ITU is not the sole organisation active in standard setting, its role is significant in these matters.[218] Further efforts are being made through the WSIS process.

The World Summit on the Information Society (WSIS, 2003-2005), and Later

The World Summit on the Information Society (WSIS, 2003-2005) was an ITU initiative.[219] Its intention, and that of its follow-up activities, is the promotion and development of telecommunications for the information society and their spread to the less-privileged countries of the world. Good, up-to-date telecommunications systems are considered essential for all. In the first phase in 2003 one hundred and seventy-five countries meeting at Geneva adopted a 'Declaration of Principles' and

---

215 See Res. 11 (Rev. Guadalajara, 2010) 'ITU Telecom events'.

216 Cf. Nairobi PP Res. 24, 'Telecommunication Infrastructure and Socio-Economic Development', 1531 UNTS 464, and other materials cited Chapter 4 c. nn. 158-164. T. Kosuge, 'Bridging the Digital Divide in Asia' (2001) 5 *Sing. J. Int. & Comp. L.* 253.

217 Now Res. 123 (Rev. Guadalajara, 2010), 'Bridging the standardisation gap between developed and developing countries'. For the Istanbul Action Plan, see WTDC-02 Doc. 272; for the Istanbul Declaration see WTDC-02 Doc. 270. Cf. the Operational Plan of the ITU Development Sector, available from the Sector website. Cf. also Res. 124 (Rev. Antalaya, 2006): 'Support for the New Partnership for Africa's Development (NEPAD)'.

218 See, for example, the Okinawa Charter on Global Information Society adopted by the G-8 in 2000, and actions coordinated through the Digital Opportunity Task Force which it set up: www.dotforce.org.

219 WSIS Outcome Documents (Geneva: ITU 2005): http://www.itu.int/wsis/promotional/outcome.pdf.

a 'Plan of Action'.[220] The second phase, Tunis, 2005, saw a further 'Commitment' to the Geneva Principles and Plan.[221] The thrust of that Commitment is plain, particularly in its paras. 20-22 which call for special attention being given to the needs of: marginalised and vulnerable groups of society including migrants, internally displaced persons and refugees, unemployed and underprivileged people, minorities and nomadic people, older persons and persons with disabilities, to those of developing countries, countries with economies in transition, Least Developed Countries, Small Island Developing States, Landlocked Developing Countries, Highly Indebted Poor Countries, countries and territories under occupation, and countries recovering from conflict or natural disasters, and to the special situation of indigenous peoples, including the preservation of their heritage and their cultural legacy, the protection of children and the elimination of gender division. The 2005 Conference also adopted the 'Tunis Agenda for the Information Society' directed towards the implementation of the Commitment.[222] Since then the ITU has organised 'action lines' to secure the implementation of WSIS objectives, and held WSIS 'Forums' to encourage participants and facilitate action. There is much activity. It may be noted, however, that the WSIS and its follow-ups are not part of ordinary ITU expenditures but are funded by contributions from participants. The diversity in scale of contribution and the absence of some ITU Members makes a perusal of the list of contributors to the Tunis Phase of 2005 interesting, and perhaps revealing.[223]

The Internet

There is no space here to go into the legal history, regulation and functioning of the Internet and cyberspace. Suffice it to say that since the creation of the World-Wide Web, the development of the Internet has had an immense impact, opening up telecommunications to the general public and others in ways which our forebears would have had difficulties in envisioning. There are aspects of this development in which the ITU is and should be of significance. Indeed there may be an argument that it has not been as involved as it should have been, albeit that since Minneapolis in 1998 successive PPs have taken cognisance of the matter.[224]

220 Geneva Declaration of Principles: http://www.itu.int/wsis/docs/geneva/official/dop.html, and Plan of Action: http://www.itu.int/wsis/docs/geneva/official/poa.html.

221 'Tunis Commitment': http://www.itu.int/wsis/docs2/tunis/off/7.html.

222 'Tunis Agenda for the Information Society': http://www.itu.int/wsis/docs2/tunis/off/6rev1.html.

223 Second Phase, Tunis: Funding of WSIS 2005: http://www.itu.int/wsis/funding/contributors2.html.

224 Cf. successive versions of Res. 101, 'Internet Protocol (IP)-based networks' (first adopted 1998); Res. 102 on 'Management of Internet domain names and addresses' (first adopted 1998), renamed 'ITU's role with regard to public policy issues pertaining

In brief, the Web uses electrical communications channels. *De facto* ITU regulations are involved. However, two particular elements of that use should be mentioned: the protocols by which messages are routed, and the 'domain name'. Both are essential in the reception of messages through the locating of the intended recipient. A set of protocols exists for the routing of messages. Currently this set is in its fourth version IPv4, but is being replaced by IPv6.[225] The development of IPv6 was encouraged by the Johannesburg WTSA in 2008 (Res. 64), the Lisbon WTPF in 2009 (Opinion 5), and the Hyderabad WTDC in 2010 (Res. 63). That was taken further by the Guadalajara PP, which by Res. 180 instructed ITU-D to set up a study group, assist member states requiring support in implementation of IPv6, and invited member states to develop national policies, to encourage the spread and facilitation of IPv6, and to ensure new equipment has IPv6 capacity.[226]

Access to and the functioning of the Internet is consequent upon the individual identification of computers. Domain names are the familiar and usually relatively memorable names for internet computer systems, grouping similar computers within a particular network. In effect they translate (or more accurately are translated by) the relevant Internet protocol into the numerical address required for accurate transmission to an intended recipient. This requires the assignment of identifiers to particular computers. For users, however, the use of a 'name' is more convenient than a numerical string. This is done within separate 'domains', some of which are territorial and overseen by national Internet registries, and some of which are global, the national systems interacting with the global one – the 'Domain Name System' (DNS). Domains may be subdivided or hierarchical, and include country codes as well as codes for different types of organisation.[227] The allocation is accomplished through ICANN, the Internet Corporation for Assigned Names and Numbers,[228] formed by a Memorandum of Understanding between the US Department of Commerce and ICANN in 1998 and augmented by an 'Affirmation of Commitments' between the two in 2009.[229] ICANN is a

---

to the Internet, and the management of Internet resources, including domain names and addresses' in 2006; Res. 133, 'Role of administrations of Member States in the management of internationalized (multilingual) domain names' (first adopted 2002).

225 IPv5 was a series of experimental variations on IPv4 including the Internet Stream Protocol, none of which have been widely adopted.

226 'Facilitating the transition from IPv4 to IPv6', Res. 180 (Guadalajara, 2010). See also 'Internet Protocol-based networks', Res. 101 (Rev. Guadalajara, 2010).

227 Thus uk = United Kingdom; ca = Canada, and so on; org = organisation; net = network; int = international organisation; co = company; edu = US territory educational establishment; ac.co.uk = UK tertiary educational establishment; gov = government. Cf. the website references throughout this book.

228 For the ICANN constitution etc. see http://www.icann.org. [I have not seen M. L. Mueller, *Ruling the Root: Internet Governance and the Taming of Cyberspace* (Cambridge, Mass.: MIT Press, 2002) which is favourably cited in some journal discussions.]

229 See http://www.icann.org/en/affirmation/.

non-profit corporation first created and operating under the law of California though subsequently transferred elsewhere. ICANN coordinates the unique technical identifiers which users require to navigate the Internet.[230] The ITU has cooperated with ICANN on a variety of matters, ITU personnel being involved as technical liaison and cooperative agreements between the ITU and ICANN exist. However, there has been argument whether a private corporation should play such a role and as to the US position in such matters.[231] In case of conflict might a US company prefer the US interest to that of the world community as a whole?[232] The question arose during WSIS, but the only result was a request to the UN to set up an Internet Governance Forum which is limited to discussion of policy and the mutual exchange of information as to practice.[233] It would, however, be better that some, if not all, ICANN functions were transferred to the ITU, and probably sited within ITU-T. The ITU has already been working in this and related areas.[234]

Cybersecurity

Another area thrown up by the Internet, albeit not without relevance for other areas of telecommunications, is that of security, particularly cybersecurity. Beginning from 2002 the ITU Sectors have been active in considering such matters and making recommendations. The 2005 WSIS Tunis Agenda, particularly §§ 31 and 39, recognised the importance of Internet security. Thereafter the Doha Plan

---

230 ICANN: http://www.icann.org. See also R. Weber, 1. 'The Internet Corporation for Assigned Names and Numbers' in C. Tietje and A Brouder (eds), *Handbook of Transnational Economic Governance Regimes* (Leiden and Boston: Martinus Nijhoff, 2009), 538-53; 2. his 'Accountability in Internet Governance' (2009) *Int. J. of Comm. L. & Pol.* 152; and material cited in following notes.

231 Weber, *supra*, n. 230; W Kleinwächter, 'From Self-Governance to Public-Private Partnership: The Changing Role of Governments in the Management of the Internet's Core Resources' (2003) 36 *Loy. L.A.L. Rev.* 1103; S.P. Crawford, 'The ICANN Experiment' (2004) 12 *Cardozo J. Int. & Comp. L.* 409.

232 Weber, *supra*, n. 230. ICANN is subject to US law and supervision; M. Froomkin, 'Wrong Turn in Cyberspace: Using ICANN to Route Around the APA & the Constitution' (2000) 50 *Duke L.J.* 17; M. Froomkin and M.A. Lemley, 'ICANN and Antitrust' (2003) *U. Ill. L. Rev.* 1.

233 Weber, *supra*, n. 230. See Tunis Agenda §71 (*supra*, n. 222). Internet Governance Forum: http://www.intgovforum.org. Cf. W.J. Drake (ed.), *Internet Governance for All: Creating Opportunities for all: The Fourth Internet Governance Forum* (New York: UN, 2010).

234 See ITU PP Res. 102, 'ITU's role with regard to public policy issues pertaining to the Internet, and the management of Internet resources, including domain names and addresses'; Res. 133, 'Role of administrations of Member States in the management of internationalized (multilingual) domain names' (both Rev. Guadalajara 2010).

and Res. 45 (WTDC-06) established 'Mechanisms for enhancing cooperation on cybersecurity, including combatting spam'. Such matters will continue to be of importance in the ITU.[235]

235 See now the current formulation of the six page long Res. 130 (Rev. Guadalajara, 2010), 'Strengthening the role of ITU in building confidence and security in the use of information and communication technologies'. Cf. the Council of Europe Convention on Cybercrime, Budapest, 23 November, 2001, in force 1 July, 2004: 2296 UNTS 167; ETS 185, Additional Protocol, ETS 189.

Chapter 6
The Future of the ITU

What of the future?

There can be no doubt that the ITU will continue. If it did not exist something very like it would have to be invented. World-wide standardisation of the technical and administrative sides of electrical communication systems has had immense benefits. 'Wired services' are better dealt with multilaterally rather than by bilateral arrangement, even though individual cables are bilateral connections with their own ruling agreements as to ownership. It makes sense that wired messages are transmitted without the intervention or interruption of transfer to a system operating to different standards. In the 'wireless' realm the Laws of Physics require that radio services are internationally regulated and coordinated. Broadcasting, by its nature, can interfere with other broadcasts. Narrowcasting can disrupt the reception of other transmissions. Satellite frequencies require protection if the satellites are going to work.

In looking forward both new and newish factors have to be taken into account. The newish factor is now more than sixty years old – the role, interests, requirements and demands of the developing countries. Although evidenced earlier, the 1982 Nairobi plenipotentiary conference really marked the emergence of their voice. Most notably this factor has manifested in the last two decades with the inception of the Development Sector (ITU-D) and with the WSIS process (the World Summit on the Information Society). Now, however, it must be asked whether the increasing emphasis on the needs/requirements of the developing countries might unacceptably distort the functioning of what remains fundamentally an organisation dedicated to the technicalities of international telecommunications. While I recognise that I live in a 'first world' state (the UK) I remain concerned that, by strident insistence on what they consider to be their 'rights' or 'entitlements', the 'developing countries' may damage the institution and, as a result, their very own interests. That said, it is surely right that the developed countries do help the less-developed,[1] and those whose telecommunications infrastructure has been damaged by conflict or natural disaster.[2]

---

1 See most recently UNGA Res. 64/212, 'Science and technology for development'. Cf. Res. 30 (Rev. Guadalajara, 2010), 'Special measures for the least developed countries, small island developing states, landlocked developing countries and countries with economies in transition'; Res. 64 (Rev. Guadalajara, 2010) 'Non-discriminatory access to modern telecommunication/information and communication technology facilities, services and applications, including applied research and transfer of technology, on mutually agreed terms'.

2 Cf. Res.34 (Rev. Guadalajara, 2010), 'Assistance to countries in special need for rebuilding their telecommunication sector'. Countries named in its Annex are Afghanistan,

Another factor of major importance for the future is the change and variation in the character of telecommunications providers. Throughout the bulk of ITU history telecommunication services were provided by government or governmental entities. In the early Twenty-First century the privatisation in whole or in part of many important telecommunications providers has occurred and that process continues.[3] Private (i.e. non-state) companies exist to make profit for their shareholders, and their access to markets and their fluctuating market share therefore have importance. For reasons of wordage I cannot pursue that element much further, but it should be borne in mind. It goes along with the inclusion of telecommunications services in the regulation of international trade in services.[4] Are telecommunications a public service, or a service offered to the public which can be milked for as much profit as possible?

All that said, the Union could be improved. As indicated later, one way would be to constitute the ITU as a global telecommunications authority with full supervisory and licensing powers, but I recognise that that possibility partakes of the ethos of science fiction, not of practicality. It is passing unlikely that any state would be willing to surrender its sovereignty to that extent. However, as a lesser suggestion the possibility of regional decisions on telecommunications should be considered. I will return to that. Later we will come to the possibilities of additional responsibilities which the ITU could be asked to shoulder.

Constitutional Matters

The Constitution and Convention

The 1992 reconstruction divided the basic ITU treaty into the CS and the CV, the former being intended to contain provisions less likely to require future modification than the latter. Notwithstanding, until Guadalajara 2010 subsequent PPs amended both instruments, with each set of Final Acts requiring ratification by the Member States. Twenty years on from the discussions that led to the 1992 changes some questions may therefore be raised.

Burundi, Timor-Leste, Eritrea, Ethiopia, Guinea-Bissau, Liberia, Rwanda, Sierra Leone, Congo (Dem. Rep.), Iraq, Lebanon and Somalia. Res. 36 (Rev. Guadalajara, 2010), 'Telecommunications/information and communication technology in the service of humanitarian assistance'.

3 With one very minor exception the US has never had a state-owned telecommunications provider.

4 World Trade Organisation: Agreement on Telecommunications Services (Fourth Protocol to the General Agreement on Trade in Services) (1997) 36 ILM 354-95. M. Naftel and L.J. Spiwak, *The Telecoms Trade War: The United States, The European Union and the World Trade Organisation* (Oxford, UK and Portland, OR: Hart Publishing, 2000). Cf. P. Temin, *The Fall of the Bell System: a study in prices and politics* (New York: Cambridge UP, 1987).

While some amendments to the CS and CV since 1992 (particularly those of Minneapolis 1998) have been substantive, many later alterations look like tinkering without fundamental purpose – a honing of language rather than substantial advance.[5] Is this desirable? A contrast may be drawn with the success of the St Petersburg Convention of the International Telegraph Union of 1875, which remained unamended and in force throughout the remaining history of that Union, albeit its related Service Regulations were regularly updated.[6] The 2010 PP has set up another 'expert group' to draft the text of a further Constitution which would not be subject to such difficulties.[7]

The whole amendment process of the ITU CS and CV contains an anomaly. By CS Art. 52.2.2 (210) a Member State that did not ratify, accept or approve the new CS and CV within two years of their entry into force lost the right to vote within the Union, but not the other rights and privileges of membership. However, CS Art. 52.2.2 (210) applies only to the CS and CV in their 1992 formulation. The subsequent amending plenipotentiary Final Acts have no equivalent provision for the amendments they make. The *Collection* of the consolidated texts is useful,[8] but it does not itself have treaty status. Practice is that after the date set by each for the coming into force of successive Final Acts the Union proceeds on the basis of the 'provisional application' of the new arrangements.[9] In a way no harm is done, but as a matter of law this is not satisfactory.[10] The disparity in the levels of ratification, acceptance or approval of the

5 Cf. most of the long list of amendments proposed by Uzbekistan for the 2010 PP: PP-10, Doc. No. 33.

6 International Telegraph Convention, with annexed regulations and schedule of rates, St Petersburg, 22 July 1875, 148 CTS 416; 66 BFSP 19; 3 Martens (2d) 614; 57 LNTS 201; (1913) AJIL Supp. 276 (Conv. Arts. 1-3, 5-8, 11-12 and 17 only). See Chapter 2.

7 Res. 163 (Guadalajara, 2010), 'Establishment of a Council working group on a stable ITU Constitution' with 'Terms of Reference' annexed. Cf. 'Proposal to Stabilize the Basic Instruments of the Union', Contribution of Australia, Council Doc. C10/43. Supported by Russia (C10/54).

8 *Collection of the basic texts of the International Telecommunication Union adopted by the Plenipotentiary Conference*, 3d ed. 2007 (Geneva: ITU, 2007). The 4th ed. is available from the ITU website.

9 D. Sagar, 'Provisional Application in an International Organization', (1999) 27 *J. Sp. L.* 99; M.A. Rogoff and B.E. Gauditz, 'The Provisional Application of International Agreements', (1987) 39 *Maine L. Rev.* 29; A. Michie, 'The Provisional Application of Arms Control Treaties', (2005) 10 *J. Con. & Sec. L.* 345. Cf. the duty of a signatory state not to act in such a way as to contradict the object or purpose of an international agreement, a principle of customary international law articulated in Art. 18 of the Convention on the Law of Treaties, Vienna, 1969, 1155 UNTS 331; 1980 UKTS 58, Cmnd. 7964; (1969) 8 ILM 679; (1969) 63 AJIL 875.

10 At worst, were there to be a formal dispute, as a matter of law different State Members might be found to be bound by different texts of the CS or CV. The same might apply to the Administrative Regulations.

amending Final Acts is worrying.[11] Some allowance can made for the technicalities of ratification required by some national constitutions, including occasionally the necessity that the material to be considered is translated into a national language from one or other of the official languages of the text. However, that said, it does not really explain or excuse the long failure of many states to ratify, approve or accept the Final Acts after 1992.[12] Should another basic Constitution be proposed for adoption (perhaps by PP-2014) this is a matter its drafters should consider and, if possible, the new Constitution be rendered amendment-proof. Other organisations have managed to operate on a very rarely amended basic constitution supplemented by updatable subsequent other instruments.[13] However, the wisdom of C.W. Jenks should be remembered. A balance between rigidity and excessive flexibility must be struck in the interests of all members.[14]

Membership

The present rules as to ITU membership require a state connection, either through being a state or, in the case of Sector membership, through being authorised directly or indirectly by a relevant State Member to be member of a Sector.[15] Yet it is not that simple. Member States are states, but not all 'states' can be members. UN membership is conclusive, and the alternate possibility of acceptance by a majority of the ITU Member States exists. Just as in the UN, not all ITU State Members recognise each other, but that is so in many international organisations.[16]

---

11 The 'Introduction' to the Australian Proposal, *supra*, n. 7, notes that as at 26 February 2010 ratification levels were: Geneva Final Acts (1992) 186; Kyoto, 1994, 145; Minneapolis, 1998, 91; Marrakesh, 2002, 75; Antalya, 2006, 27. As at February 2011 there were 192 Member States. As at 22 December 2010 only 153 members had signed the Guadalajara Final Acts. Signatures and ratifications are awaited.

12 The data in the preceding note shows that less than half the membership had ratified the Minneapolis amendments in the twelve years following that conference.

13 E.g. the International Telegraph Union – Convention, St Petersburg, 1875, 148 CTS 416, 57 LNTS 201; the International Civil Aviation Organisation – Convention, Chicago, 1944, 15 UNTS 295; the Universal Postal Union – Convention, Vienna, 1964, 611 UNTS 64; 1966 UKTS 70, Cmnd. 3141; 16 UST 1291, TIAS 5881.

14 C.W. Jenks, 'Some Constitutional Problems of International Organizations' (1945) 22 BYIL 11 at 68. See *supra*, Chapter 1, at n. 14.

15 See Chapter 5, 'Membership'. A State Member may give a general authorisation to its national entities to apply direct to the Secretary General for membership of a particular Sector or any of them (CS Art. 3 (24-28C), Art. 12.3 (86-88), Art. 21.4 (134-136), Art. 17.3 (110-112)).

16 Cf. Chapter 5, 'Reservations'. E.g. Israel is not recognised by most Arab State Members. The implications of the ICJ Advisory Opinion on 'Accordance with International Law of the Unilateral Declaration of Independence in respect of Kosovo', 2010 ICJ, have yet to be determined. Cf. J.K. Cogan, 'Representation and Power in International Organization: The Operational Constitution and its Critics' (2009) 103 AJIL 209.

However, the current system can produce anomalies that are not helpful in the regulation of global telecommunications. Special arrangements have been made for Palestine although that is not particularly important for regulatory purposes.[17] Taiwan is different. It is not an ITU member, and under present rules it is unlikely to become one despite its importance for the telecommunications business. Taiwan enjoys a very limited recognition among the community of states. It is unlikely to gain UN membership because China would probably veto its application in the Security Council.[18] For similar reasons a direct application for ITU membership is unlikely to succeed were Taiwan to seek accession under the provisions of CS Art. 2.c (23) since such an application requires the approval of two-thirds of the existing Member States, many of which would defer to the views of China. But, pragmatically, Taiwan is a major producer of telecommunications equipment for the whole world. It would be sensible that it be formally brought within the ITU so that it could contribute to the ITU and make use of the ITU rights and privileges. The *quid pro quo* would be that it would also be subjected to the related duties including those of the International Telecommunications Regulations and the Radio Regulations.[19] The world community interest is that ITU membership be open to all with internationally significant impact in the field of telecommunications.[20] Should that suggestion remain difficult for extraneous and arguably irrelevant political reasons, at least Sector membership should be made available to Taiwan. Might some other mechanism be invented to permit Sector membership for Taiwanese entities?

As far as Sector membership is concerned, its extension to lesser bodies is to be welcomed. Might it go further?[21]

17 Chapter 5, nn. 55-63.

18 The Peoples' Republic of China took over the representation of China from the Taiwan government in 1971 ('Restoration of the lawful rights of the People's Republic of China in the United Nations', UNGA Res. 2758 (XXVI)). Thereafter for a decade and a half a group of small states tried to get the question of Taiwan re-opened in the UN, not so as to displace Beijing but to allow the admission of Taiwan. Admission to the UNGA requires the recommendation of the Security Council and a two-thirds majority vote in the General Assembly (UN Charter, Arts. 4.2 and 18.2).

19 A Falun Gong signal from a Taiwan transmitter is alleged to have overloaded an AsiaSat satellite in November 2004 and March 2005: http://www.chinadaily.com.cn/english/doc/2004-11/22/content_393776.htm; http://news.bbc.co.uk/1/hi/world/asia-pacific/4034209.stm. This is denied by the Falun Gong: http://www.infowars.com/articles/world/china_falun_gong_denies_pirate_signals.htm. But since Taiwan is not an ITU member, the matter could be taken no further.

20 'China, Taiwan' has figured in ITU reports on World Telecommunication Development and in the World Summit on the Information Society (WSIS). See also C.H. Lin, 'The International Telecommunication Union and the Republic of China (Taiwan): Prospect of Taiwan's Participation' (2004) 10 *Ann. Surv. Int. & Comp. L.* 233.

21 K. Irion, 'Separated Together: The International Telecommunications (sic) Union and Civil Society' (2009) 13 *Int. J. of Comm. L. & Pol.* 95.

Plenipotentiary and Other Conferences

Before the reforms of 1992/94 PPs were held irregularly.[22] CS Art. 8.1 (47) now provides that the PP 'shall be convened every four years'. This useful constraint helps the ITU to cope with the swiftly developing technologies, requiring its subsidiary meetings to be intercalated within the period. There has been concern, however, about the length and costs of conferences. The recent introduction of regional preparatory conferences is to be welcomed and should help restrict the period for which PP and other conferences need formally to meet. More should be done to foster regional collaboration, and to prepare for conferences by preliminary meetings as was done for PP-10. Regional views could be harmonised and on-site negotiations during the formal plenipotentiary meeting be thereby facilitated if not eliminated. The length and cost of PPs and other conferences could thereby be held static, if not diminished.[23]

The Council

The fundamental rules for the ITU Council are contained in CS Art. 10 (65-72) and CV Art. 4 (50-82). Members are elected by the PP (CS Art 8.2.f (54)) with 'due regard to the need for equitable distribution of the seats on the Council among all regions of the world' (CS Art.9.1.a (61)).[24] Membership of the Council may not exceed twenty-five per cent of the total number of member states (CV Art 4.1.2 (50a)).[25] With ITU membership now not far short of two hundred, that may be too large. The group dynamics of such a body are not always helpful, and some attenders may be merely passengers. Again, in the 2006 and 2010 Council elections the recommendation that regional and sub-regional areas should confer to facilitate rotation on a voluntary basis had some effect (Rec. 6 (Marrakesh, 2002)). Part of its justification was to help draw on the potential of all countries to contribute to the work of the Union, but the point of the size of the Council is not thereby dissolved. A more formal 'representation' of groups within a region

22 Atlantic City, 1947; Buenos Aires, 1952; Geneva, 1959; Montreux, 1965; Malaga-Torremolinos, 1973; Nairobi, 1982; Nice, 1989.

23 Res. 4 (Rev. Guadalajara, 2010) set the duration of PPs as three to four weeks 'unless there is a pressing need otherwise'. Cf. the ITU report: *Conference Preparatory Meeting for WRC 2012* (ITU, 2011).

24 For electoral purposes there are five ITU regions, the Americas, Western Europe, Eastern Europe, Africa, and Asia and Australasia. Plenary Conference Recommendation 6 (Marrakesh) is that although there is no formal requirement for a rotation of Council membership, regional and sub-regional areas should confer bilaterally and multilaterally to facilitate rotation on a voluntary basis. This had some effect in the 2006 and 2010 elections.

25 As at 1 January 2010 there were 192 ITU member states: 25% = 48. For the period 2011-14 Council has forty-seven members.

should be considered,[26] balanced by a prohibition on any individual appointed as a 'council representative' serving for more than two Councils (i.e. eight years). Finally, a really radical change would be to link voting weight within Council to the contribution made by the state or states represented by each individual Council member.[27]

Elections

In Chapter 1 I outlined the case for the involvement of experts in the negotiation of international arrangements that have a strong technical character. Parallel reasoning would call for a change in the election of the Directors of the Sectors and of the members of the Radio Regulations Board. At present these are elected by the plenipotentiary conference, a forum in which political considerations may intrude and voters may not have a clear idea of the work of the bodies concerned or of the qualifications and competence of the personnel standing for election. It would be better were the Sector Directors elected by the relevant Sector Assembly, and that the RRB be elected by the Radiocommunication Assembly. Those attending these bodies are more likely to be familiar with the actual work of the Sectors, and of the RRB, and therefore would make more informed choices.

Finance

An emphasis on costs recurs in the CS and CV, and the importance of keeping a tight rein on costs is plain throughout successive PP Resolutions. This is a particular concern of the major contributors to the Union, whose contribution is disproportionate to their voting weight. In 2010 it remained true that ninety per cent of the State Members paid ten per cent of the running costs of the Union or, putting it the other way round, ten per cent of the State Members paid ninety per cent of the ITU running costs. Notwithstanding that imbalance the Union runs on the 'one state, one vote' principle that is found in most international organisations. This produces stresses and strains.[28]

The unusual financing of the ITU is likely to remain unchanged. The number of unit classes from which State Members select their contribution was increased from twenty-four to forty-five by the Guadalajara PP.[29] With the single exception of the UPU, all other UN Specialised Agencies base the contribution exigible

26 Cf., by analogy, the Board Member in pre-privatisation INTELSAT. See Lyall/Larsen, 332; F. Lyall, *Law and Space Telecommunications* (Aldershot: Dartmouth, 1989), 97-104.

27 Ibid.

28 Cf. Res. 41 (Rev. Guadalajara, 2010) 'Arrears and special arrears accounts'.

29 CV Art. 33.1.1 as amended by the Guadalajara Final Acts, 'Instrument amending the Convention of the ITU'.

from members on Gross National Product, with some adjustment or variation.[30] Many consider that would be a fairer basis on which the ITU should operate. However, the recommendation put to and accepted by the 2010 PP was that the self-selecting system of contributions should remain. It has the advantage that no single contributor can severely affect the working of the Union by withholding its contribution.[31] It is possible, of course, that over time a Member may choose to reduce its class of contribution, but there are provisions which ordinarily prevent a reduction of more than two classes at any one time and in any case a reduction is normally phased in.[32] That said, it is noticeable that over the years a number of states have reduced their contributory unit choice, few have increased it, and no Member now selects the maximum class of contribution.[33] Even so, the increase in numbers over the last decades, coupled with the fact that most of the 'new' states fall into the 'developing' (i.e. lower contributory) category, has skewed the balance between contribution made and benefit received. Scanning the CS and CV as well as various Resolutions, the repetitive threnodic reference to the interests of the developing countries is excessive.[34] The developing countries have benefited well from the ITU. Dissatisfaction with the financial 'imbalance' might be ameliorated if, to some extent at least, it were reflected in some aspects of decision-making.[35] That said, however, the willingness of both sides to discuss and cooperate in practice may be undervalued. It would be interesting to have hard examples of word and action diverging.[36]

A financial strategy adopted for some particular ITU services is that of charging, thereby shifting their cost burden onto those who make use of them. 'Cost recovery' was originally introduced for publications sold to the general public or to Members above the number to which Members were (and are) entitled. Cost

30 There is sometimes a cap on the highest contribution, and often less or least developed countries enjoy very low levels of contribution.

31 Cf. the effect on the UN of the US withholding of its contribution in whole or in part during the period 1985-2009, and of the withdrawal of the UK and US from UNESCO. For the latter saga see Chapter 1, n. 10.

32 Generally a Member State cannot reduce its contribution by more than two classes of contribution, and even then Council indicates to it how that reduction may be phased within the period between PPs (CS Art. 28.5 (165)).

33 The UK reduced its contribution level when in 2002, having failed to be re-elected, it left Council.

34 Cf. 'the doctrine of repeated shouting' by G. Arangio-Ruiz, 'The Normative Role of the General Assembly of the United Nations and the Declaration of Principles of Friendly Relations', 137 *Hague Recueil* 1972-III, 419-572, at 476-7.

35 Cf. *supra*, n. 26. F. Lyall, 'Small States, Entrepreneurial States and Space' (2006) 49 *Proc. IISL* 382-90; Lyall/Larsen, 212-3. Cf. S. Zamora, 'Voting in International Economic Organizations' (1980) 74 AJIL 566.

36 Zamora, *supra*, n. 35. (That article is now 30 years old: is there a later study?).

recovery has been extended to satellite filings and other administrative activities.[37] However, the practice requires further scrutiny. States that impose costs on the ITU for requirements which are not of interest to the generality of the Union should bear the bulk (if not all) of the costs so generated. This would also have the benefit of making plainer, once more, the overriding importance of the technical activities of the ITU. In the ultimate it is the ITU facilitation of international telecommunications that is its justification.

Another possibility would be the introduction of a 'Resource Utilisation Fee' to be paid by those who make use of what is a general public asset, outer space.

Resource Utilisation Fee

Consideration should be given to the introduction of a 'resource utilisation fee' for some space systems. Commercialised and privatised entities make use of radio frequencies and orbital positions that are recognised as 'limited natural resources' (CS Art. 44.2 (196)). Their use should be paid for. The idea is not new.[38] A number of states generate domestic income through the sale or lease of spectrum space. Some have introduced 'bidding systems' for the allocation of licences for national terrestrial services.[39] In these states those who gain commercially have proven willing to stump up vast sums of money to use particular radio frequencies.[40] This forms part of their business costs that are passed on to customers and end-users. Such arrangements have not hitherto been considered in relation to space services: in fact they may be internationally illegal. This should change. Commercial entities own and operate satellite systems providing telecommunications and direct broadcasting services. Some operate commercial remote sensing systems. Other than for the national licensing process and ITU cost recovery such operations incur no charge, although presumably the owners of the businesses pay taxes somewhere. But why should this tax benefit be sporadic and patchy, depending on the willingness of a state to license the use of spectrum and orbits? Why should the

---

37 See 'Cost recovery for some ITU products and services', Res. 91 (Rev.Guadalajara, 2010).

38 H.J. Levin, *The Invisible Resource: Use and Regulation of the Radio Spectrum* (Baltimore MD: Johns Hopkins Press, 1971).

39 J.C. Thompson, 'Space for Rent: The International Telecommunication Union, Space Law and Orbit/Spectrum Leasing' (1996) 62 *J. Air Law and Comm.*, 279-311. In the UK, US and Australia, spectrum bands for terrestrial purposes have been auctioned. Cf. from an internal US (but otherwise useful) point of view, G.L. Rosston and J.S. Steinberg, 'Using Market-based Spectrum Policy to Promote the Public Interest', (1997) *Fed. Comm. L.J.* 87; E.P. Goodman, 'Spectrum Rights in the Telecosm to Come' (2004) 41 *San Diego L.Rev.* 269.

40 Cf. the auction of UK mobile phone licences: see 'The Auction of Radio Spectrum for the Third Generation of Mobile Telephones', (UK) National Audit Office, 2001, HC 233.

benefits be confined to states willing to facilitate a commercial business through licensing it and benefiting from the taxation of any resulting profit?[41] Again, why not open up the orbits and appropriate frequencies for commercial satellite systems for allotment by international auction?[42] Any 'rights' thus dealt with should be time-limited, say seven to ten years, and then reconsidered. In commercial space activities the resources used are general resources that are attributable to the world as a whole. A resource utilisation fee payable for the commercial use of a world resource is equitable.[43]

Various questions would arise. It might be argued that such a fee would be an unlawful tax on enterprise. Again, Article I of the Outer Space Treaty speaks of the use of space being 'free', but what does that mean? 'Free' in that context means nothing more than 'available to all'. A 'fee' is not excluded by the word 'free': to argue Art. I confers fiscal immunity is perverse. Commercial users of space should be required to pay a fee or fees, though some allowance could be given for 'public service' services if carried on the transponders of what otherwise is a commercial service satellite.

What would be the basis of assessment? A formula could be developed from the number of satellites in a system, their individual cost, the utility of the spectrum band used, a flat rate per 1000 MHz used, and the expected life of the system.[44]

Should a 'utilisation fee' be a one-off charge, or a continuing annual payment? The latter seems equitable throughout the operation of a commercial system. Who should administer it? The Bureau of ITU-R is the obvious candidate.

What should/could be done with the resultant income? Those subject to the fee would doubtless argue that, in appropriate cases, it should be returned to them

41 Many companies minimise their tax liabilities by using tax havens, and by constructing inter-locking series of companies for different purposes.

42 Cf. R.H. Coase, 'The Federal Communications Commission' (1959) 2 *J. Law & Econ.* 25; T.W. Hazlett, 'Assigning Property Rights to Radio Spectrum Users: Why did FCC License Auctions Take 67 Years?' (1998) 41 *J. Law & Econ.* 529; R.H. Coase, 'Comment on Thomas W. Hazlett, "Assigning Property Rights to Radio Spectrum Users: Why did FCC License Auctions Take 67 Years?"' (1998) 41 *J. Law & Econ.* 577.

43 Cf. the use of the resources of the Area under Part XI of the 1982 Convention on the Law of the Sea: Convention on the Law of the Sea, Montego Bay, 1984, 1833 UNTS 3; Part XI, the Deep Seabed, as revised by the Agreement to Implement Part IX of the Law of the Sea Convention, UNGA Res. 48/263, (1999) UKTS 82, Cm. 4524; (1994) 33 ILM 1309.

44 A UK/Luxemburg paper 'Due Diligence Considerations', submitted as part of the work of RAG-96 for the 1997 WARC, spoke in terms of a deposit of 2% of the cost of each satellite in the system multiplied by a charge for the amount of spectrum space sought computed in units of 1000 MHz, the deposit to be returned when the system became operational. Were the fee not to be returnable, it would be set somewhat differently, relating it clearly to processing cost. Exempted from the calculation would be the first 1000 MHz of spectrum sought only for a national service, or in the case of systems to be set up for the use of less-developed countries.

as subsidy for maintaining uneconomic services,[45] but that would merely invite abuse. Perhaps the income could be retained as part of ITU income, though that might also invite abuse, or conceal a failure in the ITU to maintain proper respect for cost-efficiency. So, with all due respect to the possibility of waste or what seems the ever-present corruption within the UN system, it might be best to make the resultant sums available to the UN, perhaps to foster development activities, the refugee programmes, disaster relief, or the work of such as World Health.[46]

Internet and Cyberspace

The ITU will continue to be active in Internet and cyberspace matters as outlined in the previous Chapter. Here it is enough to repeat the view that in the interests of objectivity the ITU should take over some of the functions of ICANN, the Internet Corporation for Assigned Names and Numbers.[47] Cybersecurity is another area of Internet in which the ITU will be involved. It is a major problem on which there is much discussion, some national legislation, but few international agreements.[48]

Radio

Current Responsibilities in Radio

It is the 'wireless' side of the ITU that has shown the most change since the Union was created in 1932. Technologies have altered and developed. More and more of the radio spectrum has become available for use and, particularly, the emergence of satellite services has complicated matters. The old arrangements, while satisfactory for terrestrial radio, could not cope with space. Indeed there is a strong argument that it was radio and the requirements of space communications that finally triggered the reconstruction of 1989/92/94.

---

45 Uneconomic services include low-traffic routes from and within some countries that depend on space links, and some, if not all, of the 'public services' discussed *infra*.

46 Cf. O. Stokke, *The UN and development: from aid to cooperation* (Bloomington, IN: Indiana UP, 2009).

47 See Chapter 5, following n. 224.

48 See Chapter 5, n. 235. I have not seen A. Rutkowski, 'Public international law of the international telecommunication instruments: cyber security treaty provisions since 1850' (2011) 13 *J. Policy, Regulation and Strategy for Telecommunications, Information and Media*, 13.

The Rights and Duties of States

Should all telecommunication administrations be able to register radio assignments with ITU-R? The CS Preamble (1) recognises the legal competence of states to regulate their telecommunications. In former days the 'recognition' of a state or a government might involve its 'willingness and ability' to fulfill its international obligations. Perhaps that test should be revived, at least with respect to telecommunications. 'Self-determination' has produced some odd fruit, and we now also have 'failed states'. Do all states have the technical competence properly to play their role in the international arrangements for telecommunications? Can all properly comply with the 'due diligence' requirements when reviewing applications for licence? Are all states willing honestly to execute their role in telecommunications?

'Ability' challenges the competence of civil servants of any state. The obligations under the RR form a daunting prospect both to understand and to implement. Both ITU-R and ITU-D mount training courses and this has had some beneficial effect. Efforts are made to involve personnel from the less-developed countries in ITU appointments and processes. However, a practical alternative which some states should consider is the fusion of their telecommunications administrations so that a larger territorial area is dealt with in a unified way, and, as a by-product, expertise can be shared, distributed and fostered to their mutual benefit. 'Willingness' is a different question, going to motivation.

'Willingness and ability' arises particularly in relation to outer space. By Art. VI of the Outer Space Treaty, 1967,[49] states are required to license and continuously supervise the activities of their national entities. First, entrepreneurial entities may seek to avoid proper or effective scrutiny of their activities by arranging for their space activities to be licensed by states that lack the technical competence properly to discharge that duty.[50] Second, a number of tiny states and jurisdictions seek to garner income through providing 'licensing and supervision' services for commercial space activities. Their ability to master and comply with the RR may be uncertain. We risk transferring the problem of 'flags of convenience' to space. The licensing of space activities that do not intrinsically concern national telecommunication requirements is depressing.[51] It would be reasonable that a

49 Treaty on Principles Governing the Activities of States in the Exploration and Use of Outer Space, including the Moon and other Celestial Bodies, 1967, 610 UNTS 205; (1968) UKTS 10, Cmnd. 3519; 18 UST 2410, TIAS 6347; 6 ILM 386; 61 AJIL 644.

50 The Bureau of ITU-D has produced a CD ROM 'Spectrum Management System for Developing Countries (SMS4DC)', now in its third version, which may to an extent alleviate this problem.

51 F. Lyall, 'Small States, Entrepreneurial States and Space', (2006) 49 *Proc. IISL* 382-90. Such as Nuie have advertised their willingness to license space systems, subject to an annual revenue from licensees.

state should register only assignments that relate to its own telecommunication and broadcasting requirements.[52]

The ITU-R Bureau should be given power to decline registration where the competence of the relevant state or its motivation in registering is dubious. There is a slim argument that the ITU could, without amendment to the CS or CV, refuse to process a filing on grounds of abuse of process, although no express power is given in the ITU basic documents. Beyond the express provisions of its constitution an international organisation has 'implied powers', comprising the powers necessary for its proper functioning.[53] To avoid doubt a power to decline to register an assignment on grounds of the competence or motivation of an administration should be expressly given to the ITU-R Bureau.

Of course such suggestions will be unacceptable to many. However, international law is opening up to the idea that the practical inequality of states should be recognised. In the field of environmental law, and particularly in relation to climate change, it is accepted that the responsibilities of some states must be differentiated from those of others.[54] The ITU CS, CV and conference resolutions are full of references to the needs of less-developed countries. A commitment to their needs should be mirrored by their recognition that they should not exercise the full rights of member states when they are unable properly to fulfill their responsibilities.

---

52 In the 1990s Tonga sought to register some 30 geostationary satellite positions. It was persuaded to withdraw all but six, and thereafter rented several via a network of companies to US entrepreneurs. Some of the Tongsat satellites were removed from the MIFR in 2010. See Lyall/Larsen 238-9; F. Lyall, 'Small States, Entrepreneurial States and Space' (2006) 49 *Proc. IISL* 382; D. Riddick, 'Why does Tonga own Outer Space?', (1994) 19 *Air & Sp. Law*, 1529; J.C. Thompson, 'Space for Rent: The International Telecommunication Union, Space Law and Orbit/Spectrum Leasing', (1996) 62 *J. Air L. & Comm.* 279; H. Wong, 'The "Paper Satellite" Chase: The ITU Prepares for its Final Exam in Resolution 18', (1998) *J. Air L. & Comm.* 849 at 853-4; F. Lyall, 'The International Telecommunication Union: A World Communications Commission?', (1994) 37 *Proc. IISL* 42-7; K.G. Gibbons, 'Orbital Saturation: The Necessity for International Regulation of Geosynchronous Orbits', (1979) 9 *Cal. W. Int. L.J.* 139-56; S. Cahill, 'Give Me My Space: Implications for Permitting National Appropriation of the Geostationary Orbit', (2000) 19 *Wisc. Int. L.J.* 231.

53 Cf. the Advisory Opinion of the ICJ on *Reparation for injuries suffered in the service of the United Nations*, 1949 ICJ Rep. 174; J.F. Hogg, 'The International Court: Rules of Treaty Interpretation', (1959) 43 *Minn. L. Rev.* 369.

54 D. French, 'Developing States and International Environmental Law: The Importance of Differentiated Responsibilities', (2000) 49 ICLQ 35; C.D. Stone, 'Common but Differentiated Responsibilities in International Law', (2004) 98 AJIL 268; N.E. Bufundo, 'Compliance with the Ozone Treaty: Weak States and the Principle of Common but Differentiated Responsibility', (2004) 21 *Am. U. Int. L. Rev.* 461; J. Katz, 'Noncompliance and the International Rule of Law', (2006) 31 *Yale J. Int. L.* 189. I have not seen A.M. Halvorssen *Equality among Unequals in International Environmental Law: Differential Treatment for Developing Countries* (Boulder CO: Westview, 1999).

First Come, First Served

As indicated in Chapter 5 there is argument over the protection afforded by entry on the Master International Frequency Register (MIFR). With very limited exception, under the present rules an earlier notification takes precedence over a later, and is entitled to protection from harmful interference that may be caused to it. Generally known as the 'first come, first served' principle it is contrasted with the notion of the 'engineered spectrum' by which the entire usable radio spectrum should be planned by international agreement so that the interests of all states are properly and equitably met. The 'first come, first served' principle, modified by regional agreement, works satisfactorily for most terrestrial frequency assignments. Regional and world conferences can and usually do sort out current and emergent terrestrial problems. The various terrestrial Broadcasting Plans cope. However, matters can be different in space. 'Space frequencies' and orbits were first used by the then space-competent states, and many of the most useful frequencies and orbits were 'taken' by them before other states were in a position to seek such for themselves. Some ITU Member States, including many of the less-developed countries, consider that they have thereby lost out.[55] The only concession to such views has been the adoption of the WARC-ORB Plan of 1985-88, now modified, under which every country has a right to a slot within a particular segment of the geostationary orbit and appropriate uplink and downlink spectrum for direct broadcast purposes.[56] Others continue to claim rights in the geostationary orbit notwithstanding that they have ratified the OST with its Art. II ban on sovereign rights in space.[57] Some of these complaints could be met by more attention being paid to the world public interest in certain services, a matter to which we will come.

55 See, for example, Minneapolis Final Acts (2134 UNTS at 272-3) Res. 33 by Algeria, Cameroon, Egypt, Jordan, Kuwait, Malta, Morocco, Mauritania, Oman, Pakistan, Saudi Arabia, Syria, Tunisia and the Yemen. These considered 'that their access to the common resources of the radio-frequency spectrum and orbits can only be safeguarded by planning which ensures equitable access for all Member States. Under no circumstances can they accept that existing entries in their names in the plans in Appendices 30 and 30A to the Radio Regulations, whether in respect of their implementation or of future modifications thereto to meet their legitimate requirements, should be affected by commercial systems.' This was countered by Austria, Belgium, the Czech Republic, Denmark, Estonia, Finland, France, Germany, Greece, Ireland, Italy, Luxembourg, The Netherlands, Norway, Poland, Portugal, the Slovak Republic, Spain, Sweden, Turkey and the UK which stated in Resn. 113 (2134 UNTS 298) that the Plans in Appendices 30 and 30A referred to administrations not to Member States and in Res. 112 (2134 UNTS 298) that no distinction should be made between commercial and other systems in considering their effect on registered systems.

56 See RR Apps. 30 and 30A-B.

57 See Chapter 5, n. 34.

Terrestrial Radio

To an outsider the procedures for terrestrial radio appear satisfactory. The RR and the various regional plans for terrestrial radio services work, as is testified to by the relative infrequency with which they are amended. However, WRC 2012 will have to consider whether the definitions on which the RR depend may be unsuited to the way in which convergence in telecommunications has occurred. Strict definitions that do not fit developing technologies hinder satisfactory regulatory processes. It may be that a greater degree of flexibility (or imprecision) will have to be introduced to accommodate the swift pace of developments.[58]

WRC-07 marked a significant development which will be implemented over the next few years. In particular the one hundred and twenty countries involved in the conference agreed a digital broadcasting plan (GE06). Digital broadcasting allows a number of television and several sound broadcasting programmes to be carried within one frequency channel, often with increased clarity of reproduction. As this plan is implemented over the next few years this will reduce the number and power of radio transmitters, ITU-R itself estimating that this might result in a tenfold reduction in numbers and power, with savings all round and probably with an effect on global warming. The use of the spectrum space thus freed has yet to be agreed and implemented by states.

Space Radio

The arrangements for space radio could be improved in various ways. Particular attention should be given to the points made above under the heading: 'The Rights and Duties of States' where I have used 'space' as an example, and to the points made as to 'first come, first served'. However, there are also some other inter-related elements to do with 'space'.

As recognised in CS Art. 44.2 (196), radio frequencies are a limited natural resource to be used rationally, efficiently and economically. Minneapolis 1998 extended this recognition to the orbits of radio-utilising satellites.[59] This was a welcome development. However, given that a satellite orbits the entire Earth its requirements for uplink and downlink frequencies are of interest to all states, and the 'first come, first served' principle discussed above can therefore cause conflict. Such questions will be discussed at WRC-12, as will alterations to frequency bands and definitions. Given 'convergence' there is a case for a looser approach to

58 Cf. (UK) Consultation paper, 'World Radiocommunication Conference, 2012 (WRC-12)', Ofcom, 2009, para 6.3; (US FCC) World Radiocommunication Conference (WRC-12), http://www.fcc.gov/ib/wrc-12/.

59 Previously CS Art. 44.2 (196) had identified only the geostationary as an orbital 'limited natural resource'. Minneapolis also amended the Purposes of the Union contained in Arts, 1.2.(a)-(b) (3-5) to reflect this increase in the ambit of the Union's concern and responsibilities.

definitions. Again, a better mechanism for purging the MIFR of unused and expired registrations must be devised. Another matter which must be settled in 2012 is what the 'bringing into use' of a service at a particular orbital location means. The current rules require clarification. Operators whose registered 'assignment' of an orbital location may expire before it can be fully activated may move a satellite briefly into the location, or test a newly launched satellite there before moving it elsewhere. They then argue that the assignment has been brought into use, thus complying with the RR requirements. 'Regular use' should mean a considerable period. Thirty to ninety days is being suggested. I would favour six months, as being more realistically related to language, and as lessening the temptation to abuse the system.

The World Public Interest

The 'world public interest' need not go as far as requiring a wholly planned use of the radio spectrum, nor particularly, one for the geostationary orbit. However, it is a matter that deserves recognition particularly in space. Developing countries have complained that the best frequencies and geostationary orbital slots have been taken before they were able to join in the use of space. Further there is the fear that states may license at the behest of and in the interest of those applying for a licence, which may not always result in the best use of spectrum and orbital resources. Certain frequencies and particular orbits can be the best for certain purposes. Through the ITU 'first come, first served' procedures these may, however, be taken up by commercial interests to provide whatever service is the content of their business. Thus a commercial telecommunications provider could occupy a geostationary position with relevant frequencies that could be better used to provide services between a sparsely populated state and the rest of the world, or within that state to provide domestic services. Again, the satellites of emergency systems such as the Global Maritime Distress and Safety Service (GMDSS) could be forced to orbital positions less useful for global coverage. Meteorological observations might be less accurate than would be possible if an orbit slot within a particular orbital arc were available.

Ex natura the decision of a state as to a space system has a global effect, occupying radio frequencies and orbital positions on a major regional basis in the case of geostationary orbits or on a world-wide basis in the case of non-geostationary orbits. However, 'world interest' is not a factor in national licensing processes. Despite Art. 44.2 (196) speaking of 'equitable access' and the needs of developing countries and particular locations, when licensing a space system and registering with ITU-R each state primarily seeks to secure the interests of its own nationals. Few national space laws mandate the serving of world interests and even when they do, one must question practice.[60] Can we be confident that the licensing of any satellite system by any national authority will be made on the basis of world interest to the exclusion or detriment of a national interest? The best use of orbits and frequencies in the general world interest will not necessarily be made while the 'first come' can secure commercial advantages merely by being 'first'. It is in the interests of all that the best use is made of the limited frequency and orbital resources. To modulate the language of CS Art. 44.2 (196), it would be rational, efficient and economic so to do. A new ITU organ, based on ITU-R and the RRB, should be empowered to disallow notifications of assignments that are not in the best 'world public interest'.

Public Services

The RR already set aside radio frequencies for purposes that serve the public interest, for example for time signals, for navigation and for meteorology. CS Art. 40 (191) imposes duties to give priority to messages concerning the safety of life at sea, on land or in outer space, as well as to epidemiological messages by such as the World Health Organisation. Recognition of public service issues should be extended particularly in the use of space. Appropriate radio frequencies and satellite orbits should be set aside for public service requirements, including non-commercial telecommunications, emergency and global positioning services, meteorology and other scientific investigation. An unrestricted 'first come, first served' system should not be allowed to impede this. Spectrum and orbits could be planned to accommodate the desirable requirements of a variety of public services, or at least to have regard to them when other services are under consideration. Orbits and frequencies particularly useful for public services that are not commercially viable should be set aside from the 'first come, first served' process. Such 'public services' should be guaranteed rationally selected orbits and frequencies that efficiently facilitate them. In particular the engineering of the geostationary orbit for such purposes should be undertaken. As in the case of WARC-ORB 1985-88, until a slot and the relevant frequencies are actually required for the pre-determined public service purpose they should remain available on the 'first come' basis, but they should be surrendered when required.

60 Cf. (US) National Aeronautics and Space Act 1958, Public Law 85-568, 72 Stat. 426, §102 where '[t]he Congress hereby declares that it is the policy of the United States that activities in space should be devoted to peaceful purposes for the benefit of all mankind'. See also A.B. Munir, 'Safeguarding the Concept of Public Service in View of Increasing Commercialisation and Privatisation of Space Activities, with Particular Attention to the Global Public Interest and the Needs of Developing Countries, (2001) 5 *Sing. J. Int. & Comp. L.* 103. R.S. Jakhu, Safeguarding the Concept of Public Service and the Global Public Interest in Telecommunications' (2001)5 *Sing. J. Int. & Comp.* L. 71.

An International Regulator for Space Systems

A huge step that would gather together and solve some of the above would be a world licensing/regulatory authority empowered to make decisions as to the use of frequencies and orbits while taking full account of the interest of the world as a whole. Such would be one step on from giving the ITU-R Bureau power to refuse registration on 'public service' grounds. Apart from 'sovereignty', the main contra-arguments might be the actual competence of ITU-R personnel, and the length of time which its processes might require. Of these 'sovereignty' is likely to be dispositive. Nonetheless, even airing the question may cause some to consider it.

Were such a development to occur, an application for licence should be made jointly by the operator and the state which, under the Outer Space Treaty (Art. VI), will be responsible in law for the supervision of the activity. The regulator should be given discretion to decline proposals which are without substantive connection with the proposing state. It should also be able to reject proposals from states whose competence in space or radio matters is questionable.[61] In licensing the regulator should deal with technical requirements and act in the best interests of the world as a whole, taking into due account the well-being of both the developed and the less developed states. Proposed rulings should be published, and opportunity be given to interested parties, and to those with an interest in such matters (the two are not the same), to intervene. The efficient use of the radio spectrum and of orbital positions would thereby be facilitated. The regulatory body would act on a cost recovery basis for processing applications, and derive income from a suitable resource utilisation fee (q.v. *supra*). Given its standing and its proven expertise in telecommunications matters, the ITU, suitably adapted, could provide such a new regulator. (I am aware that some within the ITU would oppose it having such a role.) Its base would come from the ITU-R Bureau and the RRB. A good, though improveable, model would be the US Federal Communications Commission.

The Cape Town Convention: The Space Protocol Registry

Finally, when (or if) the Space Protocol to the Cape Town Convention on International Interests in Mobile Equipment is adopted and comes into force, a registry will have to be established. The ITU would be suitable for the purpose.

Since different legal systems have divergent concepts of the formation and enforcement of security interests, and since some do not favour non-possessory security arrangements at all, the constitution and enforcement of a security over a moveable asset moving through different jurisdictions can be problematic.[62] For

61 Cf. *supra*, 'The Rights and Duties of States'.

62 J. Carruth, 'International Secured Transactions and Insolvency', (2005) 39 *Int. L.* 363; A.M. Vassallo et al., 'Cross-Border Insolvency and Structural Reform in a Global Economy',

a number of years the International Institute for the Unification of Private Law, UNIDROIT, has worked on securities in moveables. This resulted in the adoption in 2001 at Cape Town, South Africa, of a framework Convention on International Interests in Mobile Equipment.[63] The advantage of the Cape Town Convention system is that it removes uncertainty as to the legal status of secured interests when the security asset is moved into a foreign or non-sovereign territory. It creates amongst its parties a uniform regime for the recognition of securities over a particular category of moveables which is linked to an international registry for each. The Cape Town Convention itself forms a basic spine to which is annexed protocols dealing with the regimes applicable to particular mobile assets. So far there is a Protocol on aviation assets,[64] and one on rail assets,[65] while the third, which is still under negotiation, will deal with space assets. Commercial satellite operators face unique problems in finding finance for their undertakings. The securing of a loan on the satellite element of a space system is an attractive option, but one which has particular difficulties. The satellite is a moveable but is beyond physical seizure to enforce a lien. Again there could be problems in satisfying a lender that there is no other security interest in the space object or determining where the lender might rank vis-à-vis other existing security interests. The duties of the ITU-R Bureau could well be expanded to include acting as the registry for securities over space assets. At present the Bureau possesses data in the Master International Frequency Register on satellites and their orbits. It would not be an immense step also to record security interests in satellites, in appropriate instances even before a satellite is launched.[66] Alternatively, if the operation of the registry is consigned to a commercial entity, as has been done under the Aviation Protocol, the ITU should certainly be the body to act as its supervisor.

(2001) 35 *Int'l L.* 449; S.J. Roberts et al. 'International Secured Transactions and Insolvency', (2006) 40 *Int'l L.* 381.

63 Convention on International Interests in Mobile Equipment, Cape Town, 2001, in force 1 April 2004: http://www.unidroit.org/english/conventions/mobile-equipment/main.htm; text at http://www.unidroit.org/english/conventions/mobile-equipment/mobile-equipment.pdf or via http://www.unidroit.org/english/conventions/c-main.htm. See also UN Senate Tr. Doc. 108-10; (Ireland) International Interests in Mobile Equipment (Cape Town Convention) Act 2005, 2005 No. 15. Cf. R. Goode, 'The Cape Town Convention on International Interests in Mobile Equipment: a Driving Force for International Asset-Based Financing', (2002) 7 *Uniform L. Rev.* 4-15; H. Burman, 'The Commercial Challenge in Modernizing Secured Transactions Law', (2003) 8 *Uniform L. Rev.* 347.

64 Cape Town Convention, Protocol on Aviation Assets, US Senate Tr. Doc. 108-10. Protocol at (2007) 46 ILM 662.

65 Cf. H.S. Burman, 'Introductory Note to Luxemburg Protocol on International Rail equipment', (2007) 46 ILM 658, with Protocol at 662.

66 See Lyall/Larsen, 446-58. A final draft Space Protocol is to be submitted to UNIDROIT in 2011 and, if approved, to a diplomatic conference in 2012.

Chapter 7
The Universal Postal Union: to 1964

We take 'the post' for granted. However, behind an item of mail dropping into the letter box lies a complex system of international agreements and regulations, for, as with the ITU, the arrangements for international post more or less determine national practices since it would make no sense for a state to operate a national system radically different from the international. Even such minor matters as the positioning of the address and the 'stamp' on a letter conform to international rules. The Universal Postal Union is the primary agency through which these rules are established.[1] The Acts of the Union do not derogate from the legislation of UPU members on matters not expressly provided for by those Acts, but it has to be said that the Acts dealing with particular postal services are very detailed.[2] Further, although states party to the Acts of the Union may enter into smaller 'restricted unions' and other special agreements, these are barred from providing a public postal service of a lower standard than that established by the UPU Acts.[3]

The present UPU arrangements have taken some one hundred and forty years to achieve their present form. This Chapter considers the pre-history of the international post, and then the development of the successive institutional arrangements once a world system was determined upon in 1874. It concludes with the Vienna conference of 1964 which is the base of the current arrangements. Chapter 8 will deal with the modern UPU.

Preliminary

Unlike electrical communications, where precise dates can be established for inventions and the introduction of services, the origins of postal communications are lost in the mists of time. Back then the carriage of messages was the carriage of messages either in physical form or through the memory of envoys.[4] Early evidence exists of messages carried for governmental purposes. Egypt had a government

---

1 Constitution of the Universal Postal Union, Vienna, 10 July 1964, 611 UNTS 7; 1966 UKTS 70, Cmnd. 3141; 16 UST 1291, TIAS 5881; 1964 UN Jur. YB 195, as amended. See Chapter 8.

2 Const. Art. 8, *supra*, n. 1.

3 Const. Art. 24, *supra*, n. 1.

4 Cf. Herodotus, *Histories*, V. 35-6, where for secrecy a message was written (tattooed?) on a shaven head, and the messenger sent once his hair had grown. He was instructed to tell the intended recipient to shave his head.

messaging system c. 2000 BC[5] and China had a postal system under the Chou dynasty (c. 1100 BC-255 BC) and beyond.[6] The Persian Empire is well attested to have had a messaging system which used the 'royal roads' with staging posts and accommodation for messengers.[7] The Bible makes mention of the system. Esther 3:13 and 8:14 indicate the use of mounted couriers to send messages throughout the then Persian Empire to implement and then to dismantle the attempt of Haman to eradicate the Jews. Again Ezra 5 contains transcripts of letters sent back and forth between Jerusalem and the imperial capital, Babylon, as local officials queried the lawfulness of the Jewish re-building of Jerusalem, and are instructed by the Emperor of the day. The Persian system appears to have influenced the Roman. Augustus set up a formal postal system, the *Cursus Publicus*, to serve the needs of the Emperor. The *Letters* of Pliny the Younger to and from his friends as well as the Emperor Trajan are probably the best evidence we have of the *Cursus* at work, although his correspondence with his friends is also probable evidence of the use of an official system for private purposes.[8] Another major example of informal carriage of letters at about that time is, of course, the various Pauline epistles and other later epistolators.

As time progressed the older empires crumbled but their postal arrangements remained viable to an extent in, for example, the Byzantine and the Ottoman Empires. Charlemagne had a postal service of sorts within the Holy Roman Empire. As it moved towards a monolithic structure the Roman Catholic Church

5 Codding III, 2 quotes *Les postes en Egypte* (Cairo: Ministry of Communication, 1934) at 19-20 which recounts a scribe warning his son of the dangers of the postal service, and suggesting that if he were to join that service he should first make his will. Cf. the messages in R.B. Parkinson, trans., *The Tale of Sinuhe and Other Ancient Egyptian Poems 1940-1640 BC* (Oxford: OUP, 1997).

6 Codding III, 2, n. 2 cites 'Historical Survey of the Postal Services in China' (1925) 50 *Union Postale*, 67, and C. Ruger, 'The Development of the Postal Service in China' (1940) 65 *Union Postale* 289. Marco Polo wrote of the Mongol postal relay system which consisted of both runners and horse messengers: see *The Travels of Marco Polo* (many eds.), Ch. XXVI, on the City of Cambulac (Cambuluc or Khanbali) [sc. now Beijing], 'How the Kaan's Posts and Runners are Sped through Many Lands and Provinces'.

7 Xenophon, *Cyropedia*, VII, vi; Herodotus, *Histories*, V. 52-4, and *Histories*, VIII. 98. The latter contains an observation as to the courier system: 'They say that as many days as are occupied in the whole journey, so many horses and men are posted at regular intervals, a horse and a man being stationed at each day's journey: neither snow, nor hail, nor heat nor night, prevents them from performing their appointed stage as quickly as possible.' A version of the last clause is carved on the James Farley Post Office in New York, and appears on the fictional Post Office in Ankh-Morpork in T. Pratchett, *Men at Arms* (London: Gollancz, 1993) and *Going Postal* (London: Doubleday, 2004). Cf. A.J. Silverstein, *Postal Systems in the Pre-Modern Islamic World* (Cambridge: CUP, 2007), and from modern times, J.J. DiCerto, *The Saga of the Pony Express* (Missoula, MT: Mountain Press, 2002).

8 The *Letters* of Pliny the Younger: cf. Procopius, *The Secret History*, 30.

developed a postal service for its purposes. The various monastic orders did likewise. The Templars had their own communications networks including a money-transfer system, as did such as the Medici family, particularly as they moved into international banking.[9] The universities also developed their own postal communications.[10] All these systems and services were, however, informal, and though well-used, were in a technical sense unofficial.[11]

With the emergence of modern states and the spread of writing that accompanied the invention of the press, demand for the carriage of private messages grew.[12] Steps were taken to satisfy demand. State authorities began to organise or authorise services. In the late Sixteenth century in Germany the Emperor Maximilian I gave the Thurn and Taxis family a monopoly of postal services throughout the Holy Roman Empire. At first the service was to carry mail for the various minor Hapsburgs, but was soon extended to the mail of those whom they authorised.

The Thurn und Taxis company continued to run postal services for many of the German state-lets until well into the early Nineteenth century, a general postal system coming with the creation of Germany in 1871. Beginning his career in the Prussian Post Office, Heinrich von Stephan, who was to become the German Postmaster General, was an influential figure in that development. Interested in all forms of communications, apart from the posts he was involved in both the creation of the early German telegraph arrangements and the International Telegraph Union. Prior to the Empire, von Stephan helped harmonise postal procedures and fees between the various German states. With that experience he was to be a major figure in later developments.

In other countries also the postal system became a matter of governmental concern. In England at first 'the post' was constituted as a monopoly with revenues going to the person designated to hold it and organise the service.[13] In 1516 Henry VIII created a 'Master of the Posts' to organise the carriage of official mail throughout England, a service denominated as the Royal Mail. Under Elizabeth I security considerations led to government attempts to control the carriage of letters between England and the Continent so that it was available for interception and scrutiny, but this was not very effective. In 1635 Charles I made the Royal

9 P. Strathern, *The Medici: Godfathers of the Renaissance* (London: Vintage, 2007). The Templar system in effect invented the cheque and the international money order.

10 H.C. Barnard, 'The Messageries of the University of Paris' (1955) 4 *Brit. J. Educ. Stud.* 49.

11 Codding III, 12-8.

12 Businessmen wanted to communicate, and scholars corresponded on matters that interested them, e.g. the exchange between Tycho Brahe and Johann Kepler; A. Koestler, *The Sleepwalkers, A History of Man's changing Vision of the Universe* (London: Hutchinson, 1959 (and many pb.eds.)).

13 For what follows see also G.L. Priest, 'The History of the Postal Monopoly in the United States' (1975) 18 *J. L. & Econ.* 33-80 at 34-45; A.M. Ogilvie, 'The Origin of the English Post Office' (1893) 3 *Econ. Jnl.* 443; H. Robinson, *The British Post Office: A History* (Princeton, NJ: Princeton UP, 1948).

Mail available to the public. During the 'Commonwealth' period Oliver Cromwell gave a monopoly over mail services in England to the 'Office of Postage' in 1654, and an Act of 1657 set up a postal system for England and Scotland.[14] After the 'Restoration of the Monarchy' in 1660 these arrangements continued under Charles II. The General Post Office was established by the Post Office Act, 1660 (1660, 12 Car. 2, c.35). A year later the office of Postmaster General was created, an office that in later years carried a seat within the Cabinet once the Cabinet system of government developed and the post was considered as a service to be provided by the civil authorities.[15] Within the British Empire similar arrangements were made as the Empire developed. The notion was useful. Thus, for example, an office of Postmaster General was established by the Continental Congress two years prior to the US Declaration of Independence in 1776.[16] Other states have a similar postal history.

Practical Matters

It may seem obvious, but the purpose of a postal service is the regular carriage of messages in the form of physical objects, notably letters,[17] although history shows that small packets and parcels were also carried. How is the service to be financed, and by whom? Should there be a dedicated system for their transport? As to the latter, the 'mail coach' came to be important in many countries, and additional income could be generated by allowing it to carry passengers.[18] Should mail-boats be allowed to carry passengers, or passenger boats allowed to carry mail? As to financing the service, should the sender or the recipient of a letter pay for its delivery? Is distance between sender and recipient to be considered? Should

14 This was prior to the Union of England and Scotland in 1707, but the English Parliamentary forces were at the time in control of Scotland and so the postal system could cover both countries. On early Scotland postal services see A.R.B. Haldane, *Three Centuries of Scottish Posts, an historical survey to 1836* (Edinburgh: Edinburgh UP, 1971).

15 The UK office of Postmaster General was abolished by s. 1 of the Post Office Act 1969, c. 48. The Post Office, however, continued until privatised, s. 2 of the 1969 Act providing for its operation under a Minister of Posts and Telecommunications. The Post Office was subsequently privatised in accordance with the Postal Services Act 2000, c. 26. The Postal Services Act 2011 will allow privatisation of the Royal Mail – the designated operator for deliveries.

16 G.L. Priest, *supra*, n. 13. The US Postmaster General was head of the Post Office Department and was a Cabinet office from 1829 to 1971, when the Post Office became the US Postal Service, an independent agency.

17 The postcard was patented in the US in 1861 by J.P. Charlton, a Philadelphia printer. Other countries soon took up the concept.

18 The 'post horn' signalling the arrival and departure of a mail coach was well-known, can be heard in many musical offerings (e.g. in G. Mahler, Symphony No. 3, and in the 'Post-horn Gallop'), and appears as part of the logo of many modern postal agencies.

account be taken of the size or bulk of a letter or packet? Different systems can be devised. For example, in the early stages in the UK distance (actual, not 'as the crow flies') was important, charges rising swiftly depending on the mileage between sender and recipient. For a while the recipient paid unless the sender had the privilege to 'frank' the letter. Soon, however, it was realised that payment by the sender of a missive was sensible, and it became usual for the fact of payment to be indicated on the letter or parcel by a mark.[19]

In the UK matters were transformed with the introduction of reforms proposed, and to an extent implemented, by Rowland Hill.[20] 'Franking' became regulated. As an alternative an adhesive postage stamp could be used, the stamp being cancelled by the accepting post office so that it could not be re-used.[21] Distance within the UK was ignored,[22] and a charge imposed simply depending on the weight of the material. The cost of a sending letter throughout the UK was made uniform depending on how many sheets it contained, leading to many early letters being written both vertically and horizontally so as to reduce the volume of paper required. Packets and parcels were similarly costed on a weight basis. Although implementing the new arrangements in the UK took time, these ideas swiftly spread to the postal systems of other countries, and in due course became usable in the international mail.

---

19 See *infra*, n. 22.

20 Codding III, 7-11; R. and G.B.N. Hill, *The Life of Sir Rowland Hill and the History of the Penny Black* (London: de la Rue, 1880); R.H. Coase, 'Rowland Hill and the Penny Post' (1939) 4 *Economica*, n.s., 423, and his 'The Postal Monopoly in Great Britain: An Historical Survey' in J.K. Eastham (ed.), *Essays in Commemoration of the Dundee School of Economics, 1931-1955* (London: School of Economics, Dundee, 1955) at 25. Cf. the anecdote *infra*, at n. 22.

21 The original 'stamp' was a mark stamped by hand on the letter or packet certifying that payment had been made for the 'postage' – the price for the delivery of the letter or packet – hence its name. The adhesive postage stamp was a separate piece of paper of a particular design which was pasted on to the letter or packet. The first was the famous 'Penny Black', an official black stamp bearing the head of Queen Victoria and the words 'one penny' across its bottom edge. First issued on 1 May, the Penny Black began use within the UK on 6 May 1840. A historical result or recognition of priority is that the UK is the only UPU member which is not required to put its name its stamps.

22 Studies by Hill had indicated that the major element of postal service costs was not the transport but rather the processing at sending and receiving offices. The calculation of exigible rates was arduous, and their simplification would reduce these costs. 'Editorial Comment' on the 1908 US-UK Postal Agreement (1908) 2 AJIL 850 at 851 recounts that one day at the London Post Office Rowland Hill saw a poor woman inquire for a letter for her. She was told there was a letter waiting, but that there was some two or three shillings due for its postage. She returned the letter saying she had no money. Hill asked from whom she expected the letter and offered to pay for it. She declined the offer, saying the letter was from her son in Australia. He wrote to her every month, and if a letter arrived for her she knew he was well, without having to pay for the letter. This spurred Hill who realised that postal costs were an obstruction to correspondence.

International Post Before the UPU

The earliest modern international postal agreement available in published treaty collections is the arrangement entered into between the Count of Thurn and Taxis, the Hereditary Postmaster of the Empire, and the Count of Parr on 12 February 1666.[23]

It would be wrong to say that an international postal system developed in the Eighteenth and Nineteenth centuries. There was no system. Instead there was a tangle of bilateral agreements, some of which could be extremely detailed, and many of which included provisions as to the use of the postal service of third countries. That said, the time was ripe for the development of an international system. States with a governmental structure more complex than that of former centuries now existed. They had asserted control over the posts within their boundaries, in most instances providing a national service for the purpose. They were able enter into agreements to regulate the postal connections between themselves and other states. What routes were to be used, what charges were exigible, and who paid for the postal service thus instituted were clarified on a bilateral basis. Tangles occurred when the detail of these agreements varied, as they usually (and often widely) did. A letter from state A to Z might be routed via B, H, Q and V, or through B, C, M and V, incurring different transit charges in each case and, where needed, charges for carriage by sea. On arrival in the recipient state there was a delivery charge, corresponding to the charge in the sending state for carriage to the frontier. An item might be pre-paid by the sender, or the recipient might have to pay for its delivery. In some instances postage might be paid by the sender to the frontier of the recipient state (or one earlier in the sequence) with the addressee being liable for costs thereafter. Charges might be based on the weight of an item or the distance it was to be conveyed. Different rules applied to open letters, closed letters, registered letters, pre-paid and post-paid correspondence, to packets and to manufacturing samples.

Writing, as I do, in the UK and having an interest in its history, I have read many of its postal agreements and use them to show the way in which a set of international arrangements came into being. The history of other countries may show the same features. For the UK there are initial, very basic treaties, and then a flurry of treaties begins in the 1840s revising earlier agreements. The industrial age was having an effect. Clearly the UK was trying to regularise and extend its international postal links taking account of the changes that the Rowland Hill reforms had popularised. Great Britain was an empire. Its political and commercial interests needed a good communications interface between the British Post Office and the postal systems of other empires. That seems obvious. But the location of Great Britain must also be borne in mind. As an island perched on the north-west

23 Arrangement between the Count of Thurn and Taxis (as the Hereditary Postmaster of the Empire) and the Count of Parr, Mayence, 12 February 1666, 9 CTS 1, (sourced from Lünig, Teutsches Reichs-Archiv, Pars generalis 467).

corner of Europe it had to forge satisfactory connections to its neighbours on the Continent as well as through them to other European states, and, in appropriate cases, to their empires and to their further neighbours. A whole set of agreements was therefore necessary. As will be seen the detail of these agreements was very diverse, the detail of which exposes the problems bilaterality imposed on the international post.[24] In due course patterns developed as negotiators copied previous agreements. That helped. In 1863 a Paris postal conference came up with suggestions as to how to ease some of the then current problems, and to some extent these helped.[25] Thereafter the 1865 postal conventions, which we are coming to, do to some extent show a degree of convergence, but that was all. The UK treaty history demonstrates that what was really needed was a general international system to eliminate the problems of divergent detail. With that explanation for what follows, I start with the arrangements between France and the UK because the UK/French model came to incorporate most of the elements that are to be found in other agreements.[26]

The earliest UK-France treaty available in published form is of 17 May 1802.[27] It dealt fairly extensively with postal arrangements between the two countries. Article IX specified the payments to be made in respect of correspondence that transited France,[28] showing that by that date a practice existed of sending mail through other countries sufficiently frequently for it to need regulation and charging. That payment was required shows that the mail service of France was involved in the transit. Obviously the system worked, it being given a more regular form by the introduction of an agreed mail transport between Dover and Calais in 1833.[29] The treaty set out arrangements for a regular service to operate six days each week (Art. I), leaving Calais on Sundays through Fridays and Dover on Tuesdays through Sundays, weather permitting (Art. II), although service on the seventh day was possible should either Post Office so desire (Art. III). So far as possible mail was loaded in Calais by 10 p.m., and in Dover by 11 a.m. (Art. IV). On arrival it was to be forwarded by the best possible transport available to the receiving Office (Art. IV). The vessels employed were to be state vessels, had

24 If you find the following detail tedious, feel free to skip it.

25 See *infra*, 'The Inception of the UPU'.

26 Codding III, 12-8.

27 Postal Treaty, 56 CTS 311; 1 De Clercq 576.

28 Art. IX of the May 1802 Treaty is footnoted in an 1836 treaty (*infra*, n. 32) at 24 BFSP at 424-5. Transit costs for mail to and from Turin was priced at 3.2 francs, to and from Spain and Portugal was 3.6 francs, and to and from Switzerland was 3.2 francs, as was mail to and from Turkey. Mail to and from eastern Europe, including Upper and Lower Germany, Hesse, Saxe, Hanover, Poland, Prussia, Denmark, Sweden and Prussian Poland was 1.5 francs. All these charges were for 30 grams weight of each item.

29 Postal Treaty, Great Britain and France, 83 CTS 477: Ordonnance du Roi des Français, qui prescrit la publication de la Convention, et des Articles Additionnels, conclus et signés à Londres, le 14 Juin, 1833, entre la France et la Grande Bretagne, au sujet du Service des Postes entre les deux Pays, Paris, October 7 1833; 20 BFSP 1139.

to be of sufficient power for the intended service, and were given the privileges attaching to national naval vessels (Art. V). This agreement was implemented for France by Royal Ordinance relating to letters and to printed matter.[30]

Further negotiations began almost immediately, and, though much of the 1833 arrangements were carried over into them, new arrangements were entered into in 1836. An elaborate Postal Convention was agreed in March,[31] which was supplemented by a Postage Convention in June.

Article I of the March Convention allowed the senders of ordinary letters[32] (including packets containing 'patterns of merchandise'[33] (Art. II)) to and from France and the UK the options of allowing the postage to be charged to the recipient of the letter, of paying the postage in advance to the destination, or of paying postage only as far as the frontier of the receiving country. Ordinary mail was to be carried at reduced rates set by each country (Art. III) with an additional charge for carriage within each country. The charge for a registered letter had to be paid in advance, and was the combined rates of both countries for such mail. By Art. V prices were set for the carriage of mail over various distances, these being mutually accounted for by each Post Office; these were passed on to whoever paid for the correspondence. Thus there was a charge of one franc for the carriage from Paris to the UK frontier, with a proportionate addition or reduction depending on the distance from Paris. The charge between London and the French frontier was ten pence. Such fees mounted considerably for posts going furth of France or the UK to their respective possessions and to other countries (Art. VI). Thus the charge for mail passing from the UK through Jamaica to the USA and British North America was two shillings and three pence. To and from Portugal was charged at two shillings and seven pence, with an additional penny for Madeira, the Azores and the Canaries. Mail incoming to the UK from these and passing on to France was charged at a shilling a letter. As noted above, mail was allowed to transit France to other parts of Europe subject to the payment of a charge of three francs, as had been agreed in 1820, plus the transit charges beyond France. These last were increased from those that had been set back in 1802. Thus by Art. XIII

30 Ordonnance du Roi des Français, relative au transport des Lettres de Franc pour l'Angleterre, et les Pays d'outre mer, avec lesquels l'Office des Postes Anglais entretient des communications régulières, et des Lettres d'Angleterre et desdits Pays pour France, Paris 7 October 1833, 20 BFSP 1144; Ordonnance du Roi des Français, relative au transport des Journeaux et autres Imprimés, expédiés de France en Angleterre, ou d'Angleterre en France, 7 October 1833, 20 BFSP 1147.

31 Convention between His Britannic Majesty and the King of the French, for extending the Facilities of Communication by Post between their respective Dominions, Paris, 30 March 1836; 86 CTS 57 at 58; 24 BFSP 417.

32 Newspapers were the subject of Art. VIII. UK and French newspapers were charged at four centimes per copy or its UK equivalent, had to be in the national language of the place of publication, and had to comply with local laws. Foreign newspapers passing through France to the UK were charged at four centimes per sheet.

33 I take this curious term from the BFSP text. In modern terms it is 'trade samples'.

letters to the UK from Austria and the Lombard/Venetian Kingdom of Upper Italy were charged 1.5 francs plus 1.8 francs as transit costs through Switzerland, a total of 3.3 francs for 30 grams. Similarly letters from Turkey were charged at 3 francs for French transit plus 3.2 francs for transit through Austria and Switzerland, a total of 6.2 francs. From the Ionian Islands the cost was again 3 francs for French transit plus 2.4 francs for transit through Austria and Switzerland, a total of 5.4 francs. Full accounts were to be kept, and balances settled between the parties every three months (Art. XIV). Articles X and XI dealt with misdirected letters, the forwarding of mail to recipients who had changed addresses, and with dead letters. Article XII allowed some coastal service between the Channel ports additional to the Dover-Calais services agreed in 1833. The 1836 Convention was without limit of time (Art. XVII), but six months notice had to be given should either party wish to invalidate any part of it, or generally to resile from it (Art. XVII). More importantly, it might be modified or extended by agreement of the parties (Art. XV).

Making use of the power given by Art. XV of the March Convention, the Postage Convention of 7 June 1836 is a Memorandum of Agreement that sets out more fully some of the technical detail for the UK-France postal service.[34] London and Dover were to dispatch mail every day except Sunday, to Paris, Calais and Boulogne, and those Post Offices were to send every day to Dover and London (Art. I). Mail was to be forwarded once or twice a week by the private steam-vessels plying regularly between Brighton and Dieppe, and Southampton and Hàvre, or more often if schedules permitted (Art. II). The receipt of mail was checked by a letter-bill of dispatch and an acknowledgement of receipt (Art. III), and were there to be no mail for any given sailing a blank letter-bill was sent to ensure a paper-trail existed guarding against loss (Art. IV). Charging rates were set on a weight basis for unpaid letters in both directions (Arts. VI-VII). The rate for letters carried between Channel ports was set by Art. XII at eight pence for each letter, this being shared, three pence going to France and five pence to Great Britain, which included two pence for the sea passage for which the UK paid (Art. V). Article IX set out rates for patterns of merchandise, whether pre-paid or not. The postage for which the British Post Office was to account to the French in the case of registered letters sent from the UK to France was double the postage of an ordinary letter. In the reverse direction the French were to account for two shillings and six pence in addition to the postage for an ordinary letter (Art. VIII). Registered letters transiting France for the UK were, however, not to attract any extra postal charge (Art. XI). Article XII allowed the UK to send mail to transit France, but only within limits and subject to it being charged for on the French basis of calculation. No unpaid letters for other countries were allowed to transit France (Art. XII). Articles XIII-XVI then went on to stipulate how the postage of (or due on) an item was to be signified, with provisions as to the stamp

34 Postage Convention between Great Britain and France, London, 27 June 1836, 86 CTS 56 at 69; 24 BFSP 430. Note that this was an agreement between the Post Offices.

appearing top right above the address, the colours, the currency of the stamps, and the designation of letters post-paid to destination, or only to the frontier. Finally, Arts. XVII and XVIII required the accounting of receipts and sums mutually due to be calculated monthly, based upon the 'acknowledgement of receipt' documents specified in Art. III. Calculations were made in French currency, and Art. XVIII set the rate of exchange for settlements as one décime for one penny, one franc two décimes for one shilling, and twenty-four francs for one pound sterling.

In 1843 the UK and France agreed a further Convention[35] and a set of executory Articles[36] to regulate the postal communications between their respective territories. This incorporated much of the 1836 material, providing for a 'periodical and regular exchange of correspondence ... as well as for letters, patterns of goods, newspapers, courses of exchange, prices current, and other printed papers ...' (Art. I). Exchange of mail was to take place 'On the Channel' in London, Dover, Brighton, Southampton, Jersey and Guernsey for the UK, in Paris, Calais, Boulogne, Dieppe, Hàvre, Cherbourg, Granville and St Malo for France, and 'On the Mediterranean' for Britain at the British Post Office in Alexandria, Gibraltar and Malta, and for France at Paris, Marseilles, and the French Post Office at Alexandria, Smyrna, the Dardanelles and Constantinople (Art. II). Independently of these, other offices might be established for the interchange of mail at any other place on the coasts of each where there was direct communication between the two countries (Art. III).

Chapter II (Arts. IV-XXIV) went into detail. Across the English Channel the principal interchange of correspondence was to take place in Dover and Calais, with steamboats carrying mail six days a week, France undertaking to send a steam packet from Calais to Dover on the seventh day, weather permitting (Art. IV). The Dover to Calais service was to run on Tuesdays through Sundays, with those from Calais running Sundays through Fridays (Art. V). Mail was to be collected from the Post Office agent at Dover or Calais and conveyed in sealed bags, their number being certified and that certificate being presented to the receiving office, which issued a certificate of receipt for delivery to the sending office (Art. VI). Except for government dispatches, no mail other than the certified post was to be carried, and captains were required to take care that neither crew nor any passengers were conveying unauthorised letters. Steamboats were to be of sufficient size and power for the prescribed function and were accorded the privileges of national vessels, being treated as the property of their respective governments (Art. VII). The Calais-

35 Convention between Great Britain and France, regulating the Communications by Post between their respective Dominions, London, April 3 1843, 94 CTS 265, at 266; 31 BFSP 37. This Convention is comparable with the UK-Netherlands treaty of 14 October 1843, 95 CTS 331; 31 BFSP 89, *infra*, at n. 42.

36 Articles agreed between the Post Office of Great Britain and the Post Office of France for the carrying into execution the Convention of April 3, 1843, London, 1 May 1843; 94 CTS 318; 39 BFSP 1083. For the purposes of this book suffice it to state that the Articles are extremely detailed.

Dover-Calais service was to continue even in case of a war between the parties until either government announced the discontinuance of postal communications. In that event each steam packet was to be able to return securely to its home port (Art. VIII). Passengers of any nationality might be carried, subject to the relevant national regulations as to the arrival and departure of travellers, but passengers could not carry goods, merchandise or freight (Art. IX). Mail boats had to proceed directly to their destination unless prevented by weather or damage, in which case their national authority had to be notified and steps taken to forward the mail as soon as practicable (Art. X). Apart from the designated mail-boat service private vessels might be used to carry mail (Art. XIV). Where private ships were used the French Post Office was authorised to contract with the owners for the installation of a locked mail-box on each ship, it being emptied and dealt with at the port of destination (Arts. XV-XVI). In the Mediterranean area mail interchange was to take place at least three times a month through the use of French vessels used in the Levant (Art. XVII). However, British vessels might be used in addition and arrangements were set for loss, damage and similar matters (Arts. XVIII-XXIV).

Chapter III (Arts. XXV-XLI) detailed the postage costs for international letters.[37] For ordinary correspondence postal charges each way across the Channel might be paid by the recipient or the sender (Art. XXV). The previous option of a sender paying to the frontier of the receiving country disappeared. Registered mail had to be paid in advance and was the total of the charges made by both countries for that type of mail (Art. XXVI). Arrangements were set for payment of an extra charge for unpaid letters (Art. XXIX), but for ordinary mails the laws and regulations of each country set the exigible charges (Art. XXVIII). In France a straight line between the point of sending to the point of egress from France was used to set the French charge (Art. XXXII). For the UK a charge of five pence was charged on exiting mail for a letter not exceeding half an ounce in weight, the UK having moved to the weight-based charging system (Art. XXXIII). Both countries reserved the right to cumulate their national rates to form a uniform rate for international postage (Arts. XXXVI-XXXVII). For mail exchanged in the Mediterranean area other similar charging rules applied (Arts. XXXVIII-XL).

The remaining area to be agreed was the transit of foreign correspondence through British and French territories. This was the subject of Chapter IV as to letters (Arts. XLI-LXXII) and Chapter V (Arts. LXXIII-LXXXI) as to newspapers and printed papers. In such cases much depended on the source from which the correspondence originated. An uneasy mix of the weight of each item and of distance to be carried was exigible depending on whether the origin was in France or the UK. Finally Chapter VI (Arts. LXXXII-LXXXVII) dealt with such matters as dead and undeliverable correspondence. Article LXXXVIII set the life of the Convention as five years, Art. LXXXIX maintaining the provisions of previous Conventions insofar as not contrary to the 1843 agreement. However, Arts. III

37 Article XLVIII includes provision for letters addressed to the 'States of the Church' (sc. the Papal States, which existed until 1870).

and LXXXVII permitted the two Post Offices to settle further matters of detail by mutual consent. This power was acted on by the executory Articles referred to above[38] and also by Additional Articles which were agreed in 1846.[39] Portsmouth was added as an exchange point with Hàvre (Art. I), the rules for the expenses of carriage between these points being subsumed to those for Dover-Calais, and the Convention provision as to mail-boxes on private vessels was added to for the carriage of mail between these points (Art. IV; 1843 Convention Arts. XV-XVI).

The 1843 Convention and its related regulations were replaced in 1855 and 1856 (1856, Art. XXXVII) although very many provisions from the earlier agreements persisted into the new.[40] Once more to secure the postage income in traffic between the two countries, the parties engaged 'by all means in their power' to prevent the transmission of correspondence between them through any channel other than their respective Post Offices (Art. XXXV.1). However, couriers with a single letter or newspaper might 'pass unmolested through the respective territories of both Powers' provided that in France the document was presented to the first available Post Office, where it would be taxed (Art. XXXV.2). In general, however, mail was to be organised. The regular exchange of mail between the two Post Offices was to be facilitated by means of two steam packets maintained or subsidised respectively by the UK and France on the Dover-Calais route (Art. I). These 'official carriers' could also take passengers and had various privileges (Arts. IV-X). As before the service was to continue even in case of a war between France and the UK until either government announced the discontinuance of postal communications, and in that event either steam packet was to be able to return to its home port (Art. XI). Only Post Office mail or governmental correspondence might be carried on the two packets, and their captains were to ensure that none of the crew or any passengers were conveying other correspondence (Art. XII). Routes other than Dover-Calais were allowed, and merchant ships could be used to carry mail between the two states (Art. II). Indeed, merchant ships passing between the two countries (France including Algeria for the purpose) were bound to carry any mail delivered to them by local Post Office officials (Art. III.1), and merchant ships might not leave France or Algeria for the UK without a certificate from the local postal authorities that there was no mail to be sent (Art. III.2).

38 See *supra*, n. 36.

39 Additional Articles to those agreed upon between the Post Office of Great Britain and the Post Office of France, for the carrying into execution the Convention of April 3, 1843, Paris 7 and London 30 November 1846; 100 CTS 347, 351; 34 BFSP 32.

40 Convention between Great Britain and France, relative to the reciprocal transmission of Printed Papers by Post, Paris, 10 December 1855, 114 CTS 21; 45 BFSP 35; Convention between Great Britain and France, relative to Communication by Post, Paris, 24 September 1856; 115 CTS 441; 46 BFSP 195; Detailed Regulations arranged between the Post Office of Great Britain and the Post Office of France for the execution of the Postal Convention of 24 September 1856, Paris 27 October and London 12 November 1856; 115 CTS 441; 52 BFSP 1123.

Other articles set out the postal charges exigible for conveyance between the two countries including for the purpose Algeria and Malta. Article XX was particularly important. In it France and Great Britain respectively undertook the conveyance across or through their territories of letters for other British, French or other foreign post offices, subject to the payment of transit costs which were set out in Arts. XXI-XXVIII. A free place was reserved in vehicles between Marseilles and Calais for a courier accompanying mail being carried from the East Indies to the UK, with a similar privilege granted when required to French couriers traversing UK territory (Art. XXIX). The Convention entered into force on 1 January 1857, and was supplemented by very detailed regulations which were further amended in the 1860s along with some changes to the Convention itself.[41]

Other similar British Postal Conventions can be noted. By the Eighteenth century The Netherlands had established a considerable empire in the Far East. Vis-à-vis the UK it also was a possible point of access to European states. In 1818 the British-Netherland Postal Convention provided for an exchange of mail to be carried by vessels plying between the two states. The subsequent 1843 Postal Convention between The Netherlands and Great Britain does not depart in any major way from the provisions of the UK-French treaties,[42] but are variant both in provisions as to correspondence and transit. Like the UK-France arrangements it provided for a twice-weekly service between London and Rotterdam (Arts. I and II), together with privileges and immunities for the vessels involved, as well as for charging and similar matters. Its Arts. XI-XXXIII dealt with the exchange of correspondence of all sorts, and for charges on all mail between the UK and its colonies and those of The Netherlands and its colonies, and *vice versa*. This Convention thus extended the interconnections between the different (divergent, indeed) postal systems that were operated by the empires of the time.

The 1865 Convention between the UK and Denmark also deserves to be noted, since it opened up channels between the UK and Scandinavia.[43] On the model of other agreements previously outlined, and a prior convention on a mail service between Great Britain and Hamburg of 1814,[44] Art. I provided for 'a periodical

41 Detailed Regulations arranged between the Post Office of Great Britain and the Post Office of France, for the execution of the Postal Convention of 24th September 1856, Paris 27 October and London 19 November 1856, 115 CTS 441; 52 BFSP 1123. See also 'Additional Articles' to the Detailed Regulations, London 18 and Paris 23 September 1864, 128 CTS 491; 54 BFSP 155; and further 'Additional Articles', Paris 18 and London 20 September 1865, 130 CTS 125, 323; 55 BFSP 50.

42 Convention between the General Post Office of Great Britain and the General Post Office of The Netherlands, 14 October 1843, 95 CTS 331; 31 BFSP 89. The earlier, very simple convention of 6 October 1818 is at 69 CTS 277; 39 BFSP 1311.

43 Convention between the General Post Office of Great Britain and the General Post Office of Denmark, Copenhagen 5 and London 29 September 1865, 130 CTS 125, 329; 55 BFSP 70.

44 Convention between the Post Office of Great Britain and the Post Office of Hamburgh, London 4 July 1814, 63 CTS 255; 39 BFSP 1310. The route agreed was

and regular exchange' between the UK and Denmark of correspondence 'as well for letters, book packets and patterns of merchandise' originating in each country, and 'for articles of the same nature originating in or destined for the countries the correspondence of which is forwarded through' the UK or Denmark. Transit rights were contained in Art. XVI for closed mail, and in Arts. VI and VII for open mail. Mail was to be exchanged 'via Belgium and Germany' between the General Post Office in London and the Danish Chief Post Office in Hamburg (Art. I).[45] Under Art. II the British Post Office was to make use of the right which it possessed 'under the Postal Conventions between the UK and Belgium, to exchange closed mails with the Danish Post Office through the Belgian territory', the Danish Post Office using its analogous right to exchange closed mails through the German Postal Union. The British Post Office was to pay transit postage dues to the Belgian Post Office, which were then to be reimbursed by Denmark, with Denmark paying the German transit dues which were reimbursable to Denmark by the UK. Articles III-VII set out the arrangements for payment based on weight rather than distance, including maximum weights of individual items at particular prices, prepayment, and dealing with unpaid correspondence.[46] Article IX provided for registered letters etc. passing through the UK from and to Sweden, Norway and Denmark from and to the United States of North America (including California and Oregon[47]), Liberia, the British Colonies of India, Malta, Gibraltar, Hong Kong, the British West Indies, the Cape of Good Hope, St Helena, Natal, Ceylon, Mauritius, New South Wales, Victoria, Tasmania, South Australia, Western Australia, Queensland, New Zealand, Newfoundland, Bermuda, Canada, New Brunswick, Nova Scotia, Prince Edward Island, Sierra Leone, Gambia, the Gold Coast, Lagos and the Falkland Islands.[48] By Art. X it was for either Post Office to set the additional postage required for registered materials. Article XIV provided separately for book packets carried by the UK Post Office to the countries listed in Art. IX, and included the imposition of an additional charge for the use of British mail packets or private ships using

between Harwich (UK) and Cuxhaven, with Heligoland as an alternative in winter. The packet-boats used were exempt from port costs, although required to use Hamburg, which failing Heligoland pilots, that cost being paid by the Hamburg Post Office (Arts. II-III). The British Post Office paid for the sea-transport and provided the boats (Art. II). The Preamble narrates that the signatories to the Convention, the heads of the respective Offices, had been duly authorised to act.

45 An Additional Article provided for the Danish Chief Post Office at Lübeck to be used provisionally instead of that at Hamburg.

46 By Art. XI.1 it was for the dispatching office to decide whether prepayment of postage was compulsory.

47 The separate mention of California and Oregon in brackets after the USA is strange, California having become the thirty-first US state in 1850 and Oregon the thirty-third in 1859. Perhaps it was 'for the avoidance of doubt'.

48 Tables attached to the Convention set out the charges for posts between these countries and Denmark and via Denmark. The charges varied depending on the direction of travel.

UK ports. There were also separate additional charges for the conveyance of book packets across the Isthmus of Suez and the Isthmus of Darien.[49]

Other parts of the UK-Danish Convention covered other technicalities, such as Art. XI on the ability of either Post Office to refuse the delivery of newspapers or other printed material prohibited by the country of the intended recipient. The way in which a packet could be considered to be 'open' (no cover, or open at both ends to allow inspection) was prescribed, as was the definition of a 'book packet' and its permissible content.[50] 'Patterns of merchandise' were separately provided for in Art. XII, these being not of intrinsic value or of a saleable nature (Art. XII.1). Books might be sent as 'patterns' subject to the packet being 'open', but samples of such as seeds and drugs which could not travel in an 'open' condition had to be boxed or in linen or paper bags fastened in such a way as they might be opened for inspection. Alternatively transparent bags might be used (Art. XII.3). Articles that might injure other contents of a mail-bag or a Post Office employee might not be sent as a pattern, unless so packed as to afford complete protection to the contents or employee while also allowing their inspection (Art. XII.4). Article XVII provided for correspondence that had been misdirected, or mis-sent, to be returned reciprocally without delay, for letters etc. to be sent on to recipients who changed their addresses, or, subject to an additional charge, forwarded to those who had left the country and there was a forwarding address. Undelivered ordinary mail was to be returned every week, but undeliverable registered letters were to be returned to sender as soon as possible (Art. XVIII).

The treaties so far considered involved major points of entry either to the European continent or to areas connected with them, often imperial possessions. However, similar detail can be found in other UK treaties. The 1858 Postal Convention with Haiti[51] contains very detailed provisions, many of which anticipate those of the 1865 UK-Denmark agreement. Letter post both from and to Haiti was set at the basic rate of six pence from the UK or half a dollar (paper) from Haiti up to half an ounce weight (Art. I), with a scaled progression thereafter (Art. II). Charges for newspapers were similarly regulated in units of four ounces. Its Art. IV dealt with book packets requiring these to contain only printed matter and to be open at the ends for inspection. In addition book packets were limited in size to a maximum of 'two feet British in length, width or depth' (Art. IV.4).[52]

---

49 The Suez Canal was opened in November 1869, and the Panama Canal in 1914.

50 Article XI.4. Multiple copies of books or other printed materials were allowed in one packet which could have a maximum length of two feet (UK) (Art. XI.6). No written material was allowed. Maps, prints, lithographs and photographs might be sent, the last being notable for being separately indicated as photography was in its infancy in 1865.

51 Postal Convention between the British and Haytian Governments, Port au Prince, September 9 1858, 119 CTS 491; 52 BFSP 923. This agreement was added to by Additional Articles of 8 June 1863, 127 CTS 471; 53 BFSP 264.

52 The rates for book packets were in Art. V, and were based on weight.

My last example is the 1865 Postal Convention between the UK and Austria.[53] This was an important agreement. The British Empire was expanding and the Austro-Hungarian Empire was a major international power. The effect of the Convention was to allow the UK relatively easy interchange of correspondence with a wide stretch of the Middle East and eastern Mediterranean. This UK-Austria agreement required the exchange of mail governed by it to pass exclusively through France (Art. I), the British Post Office making use of its right under the 1856 UK-France Postal Convention to exchange mail by transit through France, and Austria making use of its right to exchange mail via the German state-lets of Baden, Wurtemburg and Bavaria (Art. II). Article III provided for the UK to pay French transit charges, and Austria those of Baden, Wurtemburg and Bavaria, subject to appropriate reimbursement. The actual exchange of mail took place in London and Dover in the UK, and in Vienna and Salzburg in Austria (Art. IV). As to the Austrian use of the UK to convey mail elsewhere, Art. XII is in the same terms as Art. IX of the UK-Denmark agreement. Further, the Post Office of Trieste and the Austrian Post Office in Alexandria (Egypt) were able to exchange mail with the British Post Offices in Aden, Bombay, Calcutta, Madras, Point de Galle, Port Louis (Mauritius), Penang, Singapore, Hong Kong, King George's Sound, Adelaide, Geelong, Melbourne, Hobart Town, Launceston, Sydney, Brisbane, Auckland and Wellington.[54] For the UK the Austrian agreement opened up the Middle East, allowing the UK to send via Austria registered letters addressed to 'Botuschany, Plojeshte, Bakau, Berlad, Bucharest, Fookshau, Jassi, Piatra Roman, Tekertsch, Galatz, Giurgevom, Ibsaia, Antivarie, Durazzo, Valona, Philippopel Prevesu, Rutschuk, Sofia, Adrianope, Beyrout, Bourgas, Caïfa, Candia, Canea, Cavalla, Chio, Tchernavoda, Dardanelles, Gallipol, Jaff, Constantinpole, Kusteudje, Ineboli, Lagos, Larnaka, Mitylene, Retime, Rhodes, Salonica, Samsoun, Seres, Sinpoe, Smyrna, Sulia, Tenedos, Trebizond, Tultscha, Varna, Volo, Janina, Jerusalem, the Ionian Islands, Greece, Alexandria, Cairo, Damanour, Kaferzajat, Tanta, Birket-el-Sab, Bentra, Zagasik, Zifta, Miholla, Samamnud, Mansoura, Damietta, Suez and Porto Said'.[55]

The detail speaks for itself.

53 Postal Convention between Great Britain and Austria, London, 16 October 1865, 130 CTS 351; 55 BFSP 56.

54 In 1865 Australia and New Zealand had not become governmental units. Technically India consisted of separate states under the supervision of the (British) East India Company. Queen Victoria (UK) was proclaimed Empress of India in 1878.

55 Tables annexed to the 1865 Convention set out the various charges for various items and weights between agreed points.

The Inception of the Universal Postal Union

The transit provisions of the 1860s of the UK-French, UK-Denmark, UK-Netherlands and UK-Austria postal arrangements went a fair way to establishing an international network based on mutual recognition and cooperation. However, the detail of those arrangements show the problems earlier identified. The network worked, but for many letters there was no standard route.[56] Different routes could result in different charges. Again, although the definitions of different items such as open, closed and registered letters did show a degree of commonality, different postal authorities imposed different prices for their carriage, sometimes based on distance and sometimes on weight or bulk.[57] Another developing problem was variation in the relative exchange rates of different currencies, which could lead to problems in accounting between the various Post Offices.[58]

The harmonisation of the separate sets of national and bilateral regulations was the obvious way to cope. Citing a French source Codding III, 18 states that in 1841-2 a German economist J. von Herrfeldt had published two articles calling for reform and for an international organisation to be established for the postal system. Major cities should be connected by a daily service using the shortest possible route. Rates should be simplified and harmonised: one reform would be a uniform rate for international mail with no transit fee. Triennial congresses should discuss international problems, with a permanent international office as the intermediary between national Post Offices. Nothing happened.[59] Ten years later a London 'International and Colonial Postage Association' began to press for reform and conducted discussions with a number of European governments.[60] Cooperation and reform was in the wind. One encouragement was the existence of the German Postal Union, mentioned above in connection with the UK-Danish Convention of 1865. That Union had come into being in 1850 as a development encouraged by the abolition of custom and trade barriers between various German states and state-lets in 1834 in a customs union, the 'Zollverein'.[61] Given their

56 Note the UK-Austrian provision in its Art. I to route only through France. As will be seen below the US Post Office complained of the diversity of routes resulting in a range of possible costs for a letter that had to transit the postal systems of several countries.

57 Weight was the weight of individual items, not the total weight of a mail-bag.

58 For an extensive listing of problems arising from divergent detail see J.F. Sly, 'The Genesis of the Universal Postal Union: A Study in the Beginnings of International Organization' (1926-7) No. 233, 11 *Int. Conc.* 391 at 395-6 and 398-400.

59 Codding III, 18, citing C.J. Beelenkamp, *Les lois postales universelles* (The Hague: 1910) 521-4. I have not see Beelenkamp.

60 Codding III, 19. The Association's efforts ceased on the death in 1855 of its principal progenitor and driving force, Manuel de Ysasi, the honorary consul-general of Spain in London.

61 For the spread of the Zollverein see Treaty of Commerce and Customs between Prussia and Hesse Darmstadt and Hesse Cassel, Berlin, August 25 1831, 19 BFSP 985. Bavaria and Wirtemberg joined in 1833 (20 BFSP 472) as did Saxony (20 BFSP 487) and

diversity in postal matters the unification of the separate postal systems had made clear sense as a further aid to trade, and the administrative structure created for the Zollverein helped in the process. A Dresden conference in 1847 saw much of the negotiation, and in 1850 Prussia and Austria formed the German-Austrian Postal Union, an association to which most other German states acceded over the next few years. Procedures, charges and the basis of charge were thereby unified.[62] Finally, progress was being made in the realm of the international telegraph. The Austro-German Telegraph Union (the Eastern Telegraph Union) and the Western Telegraph Union had been in existence for some years, and progress was being made towards the formation of the International Telegraph Union in 1865. There were significant similarities between the needs of the two modes of international communication.

So far I have made little mention of the US save as the potential destination of correspondence.[63] Now the spotlight turns to it. In 1862 Montgomery Blair, then US Postmaster General, wrote to the US Secretary of State suggesting that an international conference be called to discuss common international postal problems and their solution.[64] Blair further suggested that since the matter was one of technicalities the usual form of diplomatic conference should not be used.

> The practical knowledge of details necessary and the special character of the interests involved indicate the propriety of a conference between postal representatives to arrange the propositions of improvement, rather than to submit them to the usual dilatory course of diplomacy ...[65]

The US State Department consulted other countries. Of these, sixteen considered a conference to be a good idea, France offering to act as host. So in May 1863 a Postal Conference convened in Paris.[66] Present were delegates from Austria, Belgium, Costa Rica, Denmark, France, Great Britain, the Hanseatic cities,[67]

---

the Thuringian States (20 BFSP 513). Baden joined in 1835 (37 BFSP 1218). In some ways the Zollverein is a forerunner of the concept of European free trade – the European Union being the most obvious modern manifestation of the concept.

62 Treaty between Austria and Germany on the Establishment of a German Postal Union, 6 April 1850, 104 CTS 1; 1 Neumann 161. Eventually fifteen German states joined the Austro-German Postal Union.

63 I leave it to others to examine the US postal agreements prior to the creation of the UPU.

64 Codding III, 20; Sly, *supra*, n. 58 at 397; M.A.K. Menon, 'Universal Postal Union' (1964-5) No. 552, 35 *Int. Conc.* 1.

65 Codding III, 21. It will be remembered that some of the UK postal treaties discussed above were agreements between the relevant Post Offices.

66 Codding III, 20-4.

67 The Hanseatic League comprised a number of trading cities in and around the Baltic which had treaty-making powers in matters of trade and commerce. Cf. the 'Treaty between Great Britain, Austria, Brazil, Chile, Denmark, Spain, France, Hanover, Italy,

Italy, The Netherlands, Portugal, Prussia, the Sandwich Islands (sc. the Hawaiian Islands), Spain, Switzerland and the US.[68] Based on responses from the invitees France identified some thirty-six questions for discussion, grouping these broadly into the unification of rules as to weights, the unification of rules as to rates, and the simplification of the rules as to accounting. However, all that was intended at Paris was the exchange of views, not the concluding of a binding agreement, and in fact detail does not seem to have consumed much conference time. However, to the Final Acts of the conference was attached a document entitled 'Result of the Deliberations of the International Postal Commission at Paris'. This contained thirty-one 'Principles' which summarised common (though not always best) practice among the several Post Offices represented. Many of these were thereafter adopted by states in their postal agreements, including those of the UK.

The initiative was next taken by Heinrich von Stephan. He had been a major force in the creation of the German-Austrian Postal Union, and was now to prove to be a player in the creation of the UPU. At that point as Postmaster for the North German Confederation, he had also figured in the creation of the International Telegraph Union in 1865. Following two attempts in the years after the Paris conference, in 1869 von Stephan persuaded the German postal administration to call for a binding international postal treaty to be negotiated to replace the plethora of bilateral arrangements.[69] The Franco-Prussian War (1870-1) delayed things, but on its conclusion von Stephan secured that Germany returned to the question, proposing that a postal conference be held in 1873. The conference was eventually held in Berne, Switzerland, in 1874.[70]

The Universal Postal Union

The Universal Postal Union as we know it today is, as the title of G.A. Codding's book indicates, the co-ordinator of the international mails. It does not itself provide

Oldenburg, Peru, Portugal, Prussia, Russia, Sweden and Norway, Turkey, and the Hanse Towns, on the one part, and Belgium on the other part, for the Redemption of the Scheldt Toll', Brussels, July 15 1863, 52 BFSP 8. In 1863 the League had an interest in the postal system as it affected trade in its regions.

68 Ecuador and Russia, though invited, did not attend.

69 Von Stephan had a predecessor. Menon, *supra*, n. 64, at 10, quotes from M. Rennert, 'Paul Jakob Marperger, The First Advocate of the Universal Postal Union' (1930) 55 *Union Postale* at 295. Apparently in the 1720s Marperger, Commercial Counsellor of Poland, had outlined the benefit that 'a friendly exchange of correspondence' between all countries would produce. Cf. German Wikipedia, sub. nom. Paul Jakob Marperger.

70 According to Codding III, 24, France dragged its feet, being apprehensive lest its postal receipts might drop – a matter of concern given the costs of its recovery from defeat in the 1870-1 war and of indemnities payable to Germany. Russian was also reluctant for financial reasons, and because it was not clear how or whether some of its recent postal agreements were in practice operating. Cf. Sly, *supra*, n. 58, at 402.

a mail service, but is the agency through which the procedures inherent in an international mail service are coordinated and agreed. It is for the Post Offices of the world to deliver the mail. The initial purposes of the UPU were involved with the simplification of postal rates and procedures. This was in part achieved through the invention of a 'single postal area' and moves towards commonality of regulation. Over the years it has also developed services additional to the basic mail service. All this has happened through the basic organisation as first created in 1874. In what follows I therefore deal with the initial agreements in some detail, but thereafter indicate only major developments. Thus, while the introduction of various services such as money orders and postal parcels under agreements between UPU members (but separate from the main Convention) will be noted, their development will not be dealt with.[71] The next Chapter considers the present UPU.

The Postal Congress, Berne, 1874

Meeting at the invitation of Switzerland in the former premises of the Swiss legislature in Berne, the International Postal Congress convened on 15 September 1874. Its Final Acts including a treaty were signed three weeks later on 9 October,[72] when 'Detailed Regulations' for the implementation for the treaty were also signed.[73] Twenty-one countries sent delegations, the largest, with five representatives, being that of the host. Postmaster Blair had recommended that those who conferred should have technical expertise. Of forty individuals who took part, twenty were of Postmaster General status in their countries, and a number of the others held positions of significant importance in postal matters. A problem emerged, however, when the credentials of the delegations were checked. Thirteen had full powers to conclude an agreement, five had power to negotiate but not to sign a treaty, and three had no powers whatever. Nonetheless the conference proceeded, delegations with defective credentials being asked to repair matters.[74] Rules of Procedure drafted by Switzerland were adopted, and these,

71 The later amendments to these agreements and arrangements are noted down to 1906.

72 General Postal Union: Treaty between Great Britain, Austria-Hungary, Belgium, Denmark, Egypt, France, German, Greece, Italy, Luxemburg, the Netherlands, Norway, Portugal, Roumania, Russia, Servia, Spain, Sweden, Switzerland, Turkey and the United States relative to the formation of a General Postal Union, Berne, October 9 1874, 147 CTS 136; 65 BFSP 13 (in French); 1 Bevans 29. See also http://en.wikisource.org/wiki/Treaty_of_Bern.

73 Detailed Regulations for the execution of the Treaty ... relative to the formation of a General Postal Union, Berne, October 9 1874, 147 CTS 136; 65 BFSP 23 (in French); (US) 19 Stat. 592.

74 Sly, *supra*, n. 58 at 403; Codding III, 26-7. Ultimately only the French delegation could not sign the Final Acts without permission from the French Parliament. However, the participation of France, a major junction within the embryonic international postal system,

though short, covered every eventuality.[75] A state or postal administration might be represented by one or more delegates, or by another state or administration, but a delegation might represent only one other (Art. 1). Proxy voting was permissible, but no delegation might exercise more than one additional vote (Arts. 1 and 5). Advisers might be present, but could neither speak nor vote (Art. 2). On the ground that the meeting room was small, the public and press were not admitted to the deliberations.[76] French was the language of discussion, and of any resultant agreement (Art. 3) – indeed French remains the official language of the UPU to this day, although the working languages of the International Bureau are English and French.[77] Committees might be used on particular questions (Art. 8). Only summary records were kept, though any declaration by a delegate was to be included (Art. 6). Proposals were voted on (Art. 7), as was any final document (Art. 9), with any treaty being subject to approval by governments (Art. 10).

The Berne conference took only three weeks. This speed had several explanations. Berne had the benefit of the negotiating experience of the nascent International Telegraph Union to draw on. Constituted in 1865, by 1874 the ITU had had further plenipotentiary conferences in 1868 and 1872. The German delegation included Heinrich von Stephan who had been heavily involved in those meetings. Again, while the numerous bilateral and multilateral postal agreements littering Foreign Offices, Chancelleries and Post Offices contained the divergent detail that was a major cause of the problems of the international post, these agreements shared an underlying geology. Last, Germany submitted a draft 'Original Project' which it had previously communicated to the states and administrations invited to the Berne conference.[78] Delegates therefore arrived well prepared to discuss. In practice the work of the conference was divided between a General Committee which discussed matters of principle referred to it by the plenary, and a Special Committee which worked on detailed regulations that might implement the provisions of a general convention were that to be agreed.[79]

Before turning to the result of the Berne conference, one particular matter should be highlighted in a separate paragraph. At Berne the important point was established that the UPU (as it shortly became) is a technical organisation which should, and does, so far as possible avoid political questions. Two examples show the matter. One case was that of Turkey. In Turkey other countries had by

was crucial. Accordingly a special protocol was added to the Final Acts to permit it to sign later, which it did (65 BFSP 20); Codding III, 34. As to French reluctance prior to the conference see P.S. Reinsch, 'International Unions and their Administration' (1907) 1 AJIL 579 at 586-7.

75 Sly, *supra*, n. 58, 404-5.

76 Sly, *supra*, n. 58, 403.

77 See Art. 6, Vienna Convention, 1964, and Arts. 109-110 of the General Regulations. See Chapter 8 'Languages' at n. 74.

78 Partly reproduced Sly, *supra*, n. 58, 406-7.

79 On the detail of the negotiations see Sly, *supra*, n. 58, 407-22.

treaty established branches of their national post offices. These were, however, part of the Turkish internal postal system and through them all correspondence furth of Turkey had to pass. The delegate from Turkey observed that this was abnormal and that the anomaly could be eliminated during the Berlin conference. The conference Chairman suggested that this was not a matter for the Berne conference but should be raised directly through diplomatic channels by Turkey with the relevant countries. This view was accepted, and matters were in fact so resolved, the relevant countries giving up their extra-territorial rights subsequent to diplomatic approaches by Turkey.[80] The other case was the curious example of Austro-Hungary which, though at that time technically a single entity, sent two delegations, one from Austria and one from Hungary. Each had a principal spokesman, each voted separately, and each head of delegation signed the Final Acts although the 'Hungarian' signatures followed immediately after the 'Austrian' and not in the proper alphabetic sequence. In fact this practice continued until the 1906 postal congress, at which point Austria and Hungary were formally split for UPU purposes. Nonetheless, as Codding notes, both Austria and Hungary were and are listed as separate UPU members as from the date of the coming into force of the Berne treaty on 1 July 1875. Similar arrangements were later to be made for other postal entities.[81]

The General Postal Union Treaty, Berne, 1874

The 1874 treaty created a General Postal Union, which was only four years later to be renamed the Universal Postal Union. It was a new development, but was carefully hedged. Its Article XIV stated clearly that the agreement did not involve changes to the internal postal laws of a member, or restrict the rights of members to conclude postal treaties or even establish 'more restricted unions' within which to further improve international postal relations,[82] or between themselves to arrange questions that did not concern the Union generally (Art. XIII.2).[83] Certainly the

80 Codding III, 27-8.

81 Codding III, 27, n. 8. B. Akzin, 'Membership in the Universal Postal Union' (1933) 27 AJIL 649. As at September 2010 the situation of four UN member states with regard to the UPU had not been settled. These were Andorra, the Marshall Islands, the Federated States of Micronesia and Palau. See http://www.upu.int/en/the-upu/member-countries/special-cases.html.

82 Art. XII of the Berne Convention specifically left questions of letters of declared value, and of Post Office money orders, (matters which figured in then existing bilateral agreements) to be dealt with by later bi- or multi-lateral agreements. [The Bevans translation refers to these being 'the subject of ulterior arrangements', but would seem to be a mistranslation.]

83 Cf. *infra*, Art. XXII.2 of the Madrid Postal Convention, 1920.

Berne Congress did not take up all the ideas that were aired at it.[84] But the 1874 arrangements were seminal.

Constitutional Arrangements

Under Art. I of the Berne Treaty the parties formed the General Postal Union to operate under agreed principles and provisions.[85] Apart from the residual power of members to enter into more restricted Unions under Art. XIV mentioned above, the Berne treaty replaced all international postal agreements between the parties in so far as they were at variance with it (Art. XX.1). The Treaty came into force on 1 July 1875 for a period of three years, but was 'indefinitely prolonged' thereafter, subject to the right of a party to withdraw on one year's notice (Art. XIX). That, however, did not freeze its arrangements for the international postal system. Article XVIII called for a congress of plenipotentiaries of the parties to be held at least every three years 'with a view of perfecting the system of the Union, of introducing into it necessary improvements and of discussing common affairs' (Art. XVIII.1), unless one third of the members called for an earlier meeting (Art. XVIII.6).[86] At a congress every country was to have one vote (Art. XVIII.2), and might be represented by one or more delegates or by the delegation of another country (Art. XVIII.3), although a single delegation might represent only two countries (Art. XVIII.4). A country 'beyond the sea' might join the Union provided no existing member objected. It had to apply to the Administration supervising the International Office,[87] having first reached an understanding with the countries with which it had postal or direct relations. An application would be circulated among members, and if no objection was received within six weeks the applicant was deemed to have acceded to the Treaty (formal adhesion taking place thereafter by a diplomatic act), and existing members were so notified (Art. XVII).[88]

The Single Postal Territory

Apart from constituting the Union itself, Art. I of the Berne treaty established a simple and fundamental principle or regime which has continued throughout the

84 The 'Summary of the Work of the Universal Postal Union since 1874' annexed at 439-40 to Sly, *supra*, n. 58, notes that at Berne (1874) von Stephan suggested what was to become the International Reply Coupon, but this was not taken up at Berne. It was finally introduced by Art. 11.2 of the Rome Convention of 1906, *infra*, n. 130.

85 Treaty cited *supra*, n. 72. By Art. XIII the arrangements include the Detailed Regulations. See *infra*, 'Detailed Regulations'.

86 Art. XVIII.5 called for the next meeting to be held in Paris in 1877.

87 See *infra*, 'The International Bureau'.

88 Cf. Declaration between Great Britain and Switzerland regarding the Adhesion of British India to the General Postal Union of October 9, 1874, Berne, July 1 1876; 67 BFSP 48; and the Declaration of Accession of Persia to the Universal Postal Union of 1 June, 1878, Berne, 15 August 1878, 69 BFSP 276.

existence of the UPU. By it the countries[89] that became members of the Union formed 'a single postal territory' within which correspondence is reciprocally exchanged by their post offices. Putting this the other way around, the separate jurisdictions of the member states and their post offices were subsumed into a single jurisdiction, thus eliminating many of the barriers between them which international post had to go through, and significantly reducing the possibilities for conflict between them. Article II, however, carefully restricted the items to which the Convention applied to 'letters, post-cards, books, newspapers and other printed papers, patterns of merchandise and legal and commercial documents originating in one of the countries of the Union and intended for another of those countries.' It was also to be applied to the same types of items if exchanged between countries of the Union and non-Union countries where the exchange took place through (transited) at least two Union countries.

The reference to the 'single postal territory' remains in Art. 1 of the present UPU Convention, that of 1964. However, when you examine the concept as a matter of law there is less to it than appears. The Convention did eliminate many barriers, but the implication of a 'single postal territory' would be that there would be a single postal administration which would provide the postal service for the territory and issue the stamps necessary to finance its services. Apparently, in 1934 at the Cairo Congress, Lithuania, a relative newcomer to the Union, suggested that the words be eliminated from the Convention because the implication was erroneous, but this was not accepted. It was, however, agreed that the words were figurative, implicitly recognising a will to harmonise procedures, a willingness to handle incoming and outgoing international mail as equivalent to domestic post, and an intention to equalise the charges for international mail. As Codding observes, that remains the major aim of the Union. Its attainment depends on such matters as postage rates and the ability of mail easily to transit other countries, matters which were to engage the attention of successive congresses down through the years.[90] The function of the Union was and is the facilitating of that attainment.

Rates

A postal service needs to be financed. At one extreme it can be provided as a public service, free to its users and paid for through general taxation. At the other extreme its users pay the full costs through postage charges. Usually a national system is mixed. However, the international postal service uses some facilities

89 Apparently von Stephan argued for the insertion of the phrase 'and the Administrations' after the word 'States' in Art. I and elsewhere, and this was agreed by the conference. However, the eventual document used the bald French term 'pays'. There were precedents in earlier bilateral arrangements where agreements were concluded between postal administrations, but this was not followed at Berne. Cf. Sly, *supra*, n. 58, 407.

90 Codding III, 73-4. The figurative nature of the expression 'single postal territory' is acknowledged in the official IB commentary to Art. 1 of the current Convention.

which, as far as the sender is concerned, are in a foreign country. At first thought a uniform postal rate and freedom of transit within the new single postal territory might appear to make sense. Second thoughts showed that to be impossible. Post offices in each member country varied in the area they served and in the volume of international mail which they processed. Adjustments were required to ensure that each national post office would derive financial benefit, or at least not suffer loss, from the 'single postal territory'. Much of the debate at Berne therefore concerned two matters, postage rates and the allocation of the costs of transit services. This was difficult because under Art. IX.2 neither the sender nor the addressee of the international mail covered by the Berne arrangements would be required to pay, whether in the country of origin, or of destination, any tax or postal duty other than those specified in the treaty.

In the case of postage rates, only the official correspondence of the postal service was exempt from payment, franking was abolished, and no reduction of postage was formally allowed (Art. VI). However, while Art. III.1 fixed the general rate of postage within the Union for a single prepaid letter not exceeding 15 grams at 25 centimes, and doubling every 15 grams or part of 15 grams (Art. III.3), a Union member might vary that charge, but only within the range 20-32 centimes 'in order to suit its monetary or other requirements'. Postcards had to be prepaid and were charged at half the rate for a paid letter, fractions being rounded off (Art. III.5). Unpaid letters were charged double the rate for prepaid letters as applied within the country of destination (Art. III.4). Where an item had to be transported more than 300 nautical miles within the 'single postal territory' an additional charge not exceeding half the letter rate might be applied (Art. III.6). Within the Union 'legal and commercial documents, patterns of merchandise, newspapers, stitched or bound books, pamphlets, music, visiting cards, catalogues, prospectuses, announcements and notices of various kinds, whether printed, engraved, lithographed or autographed, as well as for photographs' were to be charged at seven centimes for each packet not exceeding 50 grams and doubling thereafter every 50 or part-50 grams (Art. IV.3), with a permissible variation in the range three to eleven centimes (Art. IV.3), and with the option of an extra one-half charge for transport over 300 nautical miles (Art. IV.4). The maximum weight of a packet of patterns of merchandise was fixed at 250 grams, and 1000 grams for all other packets (Art. IV.6).[91] Any Art. III item might be registered, subject to an additional charge set as that imposed for registration within the state of origin, with a maximum 50 francs recompense for loss except in the case of *vis major* (Art. V.1,3,4,5,7). Registered packets had to be pre-paid (Art. V.2). Unpaid letters were charged at double that levied on prepaid letters in the country of destination (Art. III.4). Postal items were to be forwarded as necessary within one country without additional charge (Art. VII.1) but redirection into the service of another country could attract a further charge (Art. VI.2). Unpaid or insufficiently paid

91 In the case of the Art. IV materials, a member might refuse carriage or delivery if the conditions for their publication or circulation had not been observed.

newspapers and printed papers were not forwarded (Art. VI.2). Last, as a sensible concession to geography as opposed to sovereign boundaries, Art. XIII.2 allowed adjacent countries to settle between themselves how international correspondence was exchanged, the conditions for the exchange of post office money orders and declared value letters, and, intriguingly, 'the determination of radii in adjacent countries in which a lower rate of postage might be applied'.[92]

How might the prepayment of postal items be evidenced? Prepayment of postage was possible only by the affixing of postage stamps or the use of stamped or franked envelopes valid in the country of origin (Art. VI.1). Article III of the 'Detailed Regulations' (DR) annexed to the basic Convention standardised how stamps were to be used within the new single postal territory, provisions which establish why letters now look the way they do. A stamp was to be placed above the address indicating the place and date of posting (DR Art. III.1).[93] Postal items that were unpaid (i.e. to be paid for by the recipient) or items carrying insufficient postage were to be marked 'T' (tax to pay) (DR Art. III.3). In the absence of a 'T' mark, items were to be considered as sufficiently stamped for carriage to their destination (DR Art. III.5). Insufficiently stamped items were further marked, the difference to be made up being indicated in black stamps (DR Art. V.1). Foreign stamps invalid in the country where the items were posted were to be marked with a zero ('0') (DR Art. V.2). In all cases where a letter or other item was insufficiently or invalidly stamped the post office of destination was to collect from the recipient the postage due plus the ordinary charge within that country for delivery of an item of the same weight (DR Art. V.3). Special or national frankings were to be accepted (DR Art. III.3),[94] but their existence and nature was to be notified to other national Post Offices through the International Bureau (*infra*) thus assuring their being recognised (DR Art. III.4).

Transit

Transit was a separate matter. It involved a grant of rights rather than of revocable privileges, but also, crucially, it involved payment for the service used. The right of transit throughout the 'entire territory of the Union' was guaranteed (Art. X.1), allowing both open and closed mails to be sent through intermediate countries (Art. X.2) by 'the most rapid routes at the command of the postal administrations concerned' (Art. X.3). Where several routes allowed the same transit speed the

92 The radius was set at 30 km for the delivery of express letters by Art. XIV.2 of the Paris Convention of 1878, and applied to all post by that Article as modified by Art. X of the Additional Act of Lisbon, 1885. For an example see the Convention between France and Switzerland respecting the Postal Services on the Frasne-Vallorbe and Pontarlier Railway Lines and the international Station at Vallorbe, 220 CTS 159; 10 Martens (3rd) 871.

93 Usually this stamp is also used to cancel the postage stamp to prevent its re-use.

94 Special frankings had long existed in many countries, agencies (notably governments) and on occasion individuals being given the privilege to use them.

dispatching administration could choose which should be used (Art. X.4).[95] Closed mails (i.e. enclosed in special mail bags) were to be used when the number of items might otherwise hinder efficiency in the transmitting office (Art. X.5). But transit was not free. The dispatching office was to pay the administration providing transit services two francs per kilogram for letters, and 25 centimes per kilogram for Art. IV items, both at net weight, for both open and closed mails (Art. X.6). This could be increased respectively to four francs and 50 centimes where the transit required was over 750 kilometres within a country (Art. X.7) except where the transit was already free or established at a lower rate (Art. X.8). This last was to forestall an existing transit rate being increased and relevant post offices securing a windfall. Where transit was by sea in excess of 300 kilometres within a district of the Union the carrying office had a right to payment for the service (Art. X.9). In such cases the relevant member was to seek to reduce costs, and payment might not exceed 6.5 francs per kilogram for letters and 50 centimes per kilogram for Art. IV items, both at net weight (Art. X.10). In no case might these sums be increased beyond existing rates, again to prevent windfall benefit (Art. X.11). All this did not mean, however, that every piece of mail in transmit was to be weighed. Transit mail was to be sampled by weight over a two week period agreed between the members concerned and the result was subject to revision at yearly intervals, or if the direction of flow of the mail changed greatly (Art. X.12-3). The sample was to be used to estimate the sums reciprocally due.

Delivery

Delivery was different. As noted above, by Art. IX.2 the charges specified under Arts. III-VII were the only postage charges that might be imposed on the senders or receivers of international mails sent within the single postal territory governed by the agreement.[96] The system of international postage charges within the Union was therefore settled. But how were the proceeds to be divided? As we have seen, previous bilateral arrangements had provided for the regular settlement of accounts between the parties, the accounts being based on a careful count of the correspondence concerned. Article IX.1 cut the Gordian knot. Each administration was to keep the entire sums collected under Arts. III-VII. It was considered that the postal costs from A to B would be more or less balanced by traffic in the other direction. Accordingly 'there will be no necessity on this head for any accounts between the several administrations of the Union.' Transit charges, specified under Art. X, were different and accounting remained for these. Posts going outwith the countries of the Union were also different. These remained governed by existing

95 Art. X.1-4 did not apply to the India mail, or to mail conveyed across the US by rail between New York and San Francisco. These services remained governed by existing or subsequent agreements (Art. X.14). Cf. Postal Agreement between Great Britain and the United States, Washington, 6 October 1876, 67 BFSP 49.

96 As to mail going outwith the Union territories see *infra*.

or future agreements (Art. XI.1), and the postage rates for the segment of the conveyance of the correspondence beyond the Union were determined by them and were to be added to the relevant Union rate (Art. XI.2). That rate was to be apportioned, the relevant dispatching office within the Union keeping the whole of the postage for prepaid correspondence addressed to foreign countries, the relevant receiving office of the Union keeping the whole of the Union rate for unpaid correspondence originating in a foreign country, and the office of the Union exchanging closed mail with foreign countries keeping the whole of the Union rate for paid correspondence from foreign countries and for unpaid correspondence addressed to foreign countries (Art. XI.3). However, in this case any relevant Union office was not entitled to charge transit costs through its territory, these being regulated by Art. X.

The Detailed Regulations (DR)

The participants at Berne accepted that the new international arrangements would need to be spelled out in greater detail than was possible in the Convention itself, and a Special Committee met to formulate Regulations for the purpose. These, technically an agreement between postal administrations, were authorised by Art. XIII of the Berne treaty, and were signed along with its Final Acts on 9 October 1874.[97] Unlike the Treaty, the Detailed Regulations could be altered by the common consent of the postal administrations of the Union (Art. XIII.1). They entered into force along with the Treaty and were to share its duration unless modified by the common accord of the interested parties (DR Art. XXX).

Of the thirty Articles of the Detailed Regulations DRs I-XXVI concerned technicalities. DR Art. XXVIII had to do with the use of the French language, and DR XXIX specified certain additional territories which were to be considered as part of the postal area of a member of the General Postal Union.[98] DRs XXVII-XXVIII dealt with the International Bureau, to which I now turn.

97 Detailed Regulations for the execution of the Treaty ... relative to the formation of a General Postal Union, Berne, October 9 1874, 147 CTS 136; 65 BFSP 23 (in French); (US) 19 Stat. 592. [There is an error in the French text as reproduced in the BFSP version. Its initial paragraph refers to Art XII of the Treaty. It should be to Art. XIII.]

98 DR Art. XXIX specified that the Union single postal territory was to include The Faroës as part of Denmark, the Balearic and Canary Islands together with the Spanish African possessions and the Spanish postal stations on the west coast of Morocco as parts of Spain, Algeria as part of France, Malta as part of the UK, Madeira and the Azores as parts of Portugal, and the Grand Duchy of Finland as part of Russia.

The International Bureau[99]

Given all the technicalities of the new international system and the need that the postal administrations of the members of the Union should exchange information, and be sent information relevant to the improvement of the international service, some sort of central agency was necessary.[100] Article XV of the Berne Treaty therefore provided for the establishment of a permanent central office. The function of the 'International Office of the General Postal Union', as it was first named, was facilitative.[101] It was to collect, publish and distribute information of every kind concerning the international postal service, to circulate proposals for modifying the DR and giving notice of any alterations that were adopted, to facilitate the operation of international accounts especially in relation to Art. X (transit fees), and 'in general' to consider and work out questions in the interest of the Postal Union (Art. XV.2). This last phrase was to give the International Bureau an important role in the development of postal agreements, the first example being the case of the 1880 agreement regarding postal parcels dealt with below.[102] The importance of the new Bureau was emphasised by its Director being given the role of advising at the sessions of subsequent postal congresses and of taking part in their discussions, albeit without vote (DR Art. XXVII.14).[103]

To help it do its work postal administrations were to send the Bureau all public documents about their internal services (DR Art. XXVII.7) and, in the first week of every year, statistical data on its operations in the previous year in a form prescribed by the Bureau (DR Art. XXVII.8). The Bureau was to serve as the distribution centre for all relevant information and was to publish a journal in English, French and German (Art. XV, DR Art. XVII.7 and 9), copies being distributed to members in proportion to the contribution each made to the expenses of the running of the Bureau (see next paragraph).

Under the Berne treaty the International Bureau was to be supervised by a postal administration to be designated by the Congress, its expenses being borne by all members of the Union (Art. XV.1). DR XXVII.1 therefore designated the Swiss Post Office as the organiser and supervisor of the International Bureau, which began operation once the Berne treaty came into force on 1 July 1875. DR Art. XXVII then went on to provide for the expenses of the International Bureau.

99 Technically this heading is wrong, but since it is used by the International Bureau itself in comment on the Berne history, it is convenient to use it. See following text. The name was changed by the Paris Convention of 1878 discussed *infra*.

100 The model of the International Bureau of the International Telegraph Union, which had existed for some years, was not irrelevant.

101 Codding III, 185-213.

102 See *infra*, 'The Postal Conference, Paris, 1880'.

103 The Director was authorised to act as proxy for a UPU member at The Postal Conference of 1876, and by the DRs from 1885 (Lisbon DRs), and was made the Deputy Chairman of Congresses from 1891.

Not including the costs of the meetings of the Postal Congress, these were not to exceed 75,000 Swiss francs per annum, although this could be varied by the unanimous consent of the relevant postal administrations (DR Art. XXVII.2). That sum was not, however, to be divided equally among the members of the Union. The expenses were to be met in terms of units, six unit classes being agreed and each member taking up a particular class. Class I was set as 25 units; Class 2, 20 units; Class 3, 15 units; Class 4, 10 units; Class 5, 5 units; and Class 6, 3 units (DR Art. XXVII.4). Subscribing to Class I were Germany, Austria-Hungary, France, Great Britain, Italy, Russia, Turkey and the US. Spain was in Class 2; Belgium, Egypt, The Netherlands, Roumania and Sweden in Class 3; Denmark, Norway, Portugal and Switzerland in Class 4; Greece and Serbia in Class 5; and Luxemburg in Class 6 (DR Art. XXVII.6).[104]

Dispute Settlement

Naturally some provision had to be made for the settlement of disputes between members. Buried within the Art. XV.2 list of the duties of the International Bureau was giving 'an opinion upon questions in dispute'. On occasion that might serve. However, further specific provision was made by Art. XVI for the arbitration of disagreements as to the interpretation of the Berne treaty. Each administration involved in the disagreement was to nominate as an arbiter another member not interested in the dispute. Decisions were by a majority and, should there be a tie between arbiters, they were to choose yet another disinterested member to determine the matter.

The Postal Conference, Berne 1876

Although it was not a conference of plenipotentiaries a meeting important for the future of the UPU was convened by the Swiss authorities on 18 January and ran to 27 January 1876. During 1875 Great Britain had applied on behalf of British India for membership of the Union.[105] Similar requests were also made by France and The Netherlands for certain of their eastern colonies and possessions. Switzerland therefore called the conference to discuss such questions and, if necessary, to settle the postal rates for the carriage of mail to these territories. The conference agreed the extension of membership of the Union, and settled appropriate rates. Great Britain immediately repeated its formal request. This was circulated to members on 29 January and no objection was raised within the six week period set by Art.

---

104 The figures indicate the monetary value of a unit was initially 201 francs, if the full 75,000 franc budget was used.

105 Codding III, 35-7. British India had been admitted to the ITU in 1871.

XVII of the Berne treaty. The accession of British India to the Union was formally perfected by a diplomatic act of 1 July 1876.[106]

The importance of the admission of non-independent entities as members of the Union should not be underestimated. Codding III, 36 notes that in 1877 applications were made by Denmark, The Netherlands, Portugal and Spain in respect of their possessions, and Great Britain applied in respect of The Bermudas, Ceylon, British Guinea, Hong Kong, Jamaica, Labuan [now part of Malaysia], Mauritius, the Straits Settlement [sc. Singapore] and Trinidad. This disregard of formal concepts of statehood and sovereignty in the interests of cooperation and the facilitating of the international postal service was a significant step for the Union to take. It was formalised by Art. XXI of the next postal treaty, that of 1878, and although opposed by some, usually on the ground that it increased the potential voting power of states controlling the 'additional territories', the process continued thereafter.[107] In this the Postal Union mirrored discussions and debate within the ITU.

The Universal Postal Union, Second Congress, Paris, 1878

Although Art. XVIII.5 of the Berne treaty had set Paris 1877 for the next Postal Congress, the Paris Congress did not meet until 2 May 1878, its Final Protocol, Convention and Detailed Regulations being signed on 1 June, and a final document, on Money Orders, being signed on 4 June.[108] Including the new members thirty-two countries and administrations attended the Paris congress.[109] France had hoped for an entirely new convention to be adopted, but in fact the conference confined itself largely to the modification of some details in the 1874 arrangements.

The most obvious action taken at Paris, justified by the extension or growth in membership, was to change the title of the organisation to the 'Universal Postal Union' (Art. I). Technically to change from 'General' to 'Universal' was unimportant, but it had deep significance as a statement. Changing the name of the constituent document from 'Treaty' to 'Convention' also had some resonance. In the matter of membership the decisions of the 1876 Berne conference were

106 Declaration between Great Britain and Switzerland regarding the Adhesion of British India to the General Postal Union of October 9, 1874, Berne, July 1 1876; 67 BFSP 48.

107 See also Akzin, *supra*, n. 81. Codding III, 36-7 notes that by the 1906 Congress, the last before the First Word War, some seventeen non-independent territories had been recognised as participant by the UPU. Cf. D.B. Hollis, 'Why State Consent Still Matters – Non-State Actors, Treaties, and the Changing Sources of International Law' (2005) 23 *Berk. J. Int. L.* 137.

108 Universal Postal Union, Paris, 1 June 1878, in force 1 April 1879; 152 CTS 235; 69 BFSP 210; 20 Stat. 734; 1 Bevans 51. Detailed Regulations at 69 BFSP 220.

109 Reinsch, *supra*, n. 74, at 588.

accepted, and in Art. XXI a number of entities or territories were listed as being 'considered as forming … a single country, or a single Administration as the case may be' for the purposes of the International Bureau and access to the meetings of the Union. These were British India and Canada (which signed the Final Acts separately from the UK), the Danish Colonies, the Spanish Colonies, the French Colonies, the Dutch Colonies and the Portuguese Colonies. For these the Final Acts, the Treaty and the Detailed Regulations were signed on their behalf by the relevant states.[110] Article XVIII allowed any non-member to accede on demand to the new treaty,[111] the share it was to contribute to the expenses of the International Bureau being negotiated between it and the Swiss government. The widening, and potential further widening, of the UPU to so many territories round the world was recognised by Art. VII which allowed members that did not use the French gold franc as their monetary unit to fix their postal rates to approximate those set out by the new agreements, rounding off fractions according to a Table and procedure set out in Art. IX of the new Detailed Regulations. Innovations included Art. XI which listed items that the public was forbidden to send by the international mail service. These included gold and silver, money, jewellery or precious articles, and packets containing articles that were liable to customs duties.[112] Art. XVIII of the 1874 Convention had called for the Union to meet every three years. This was considered unduly frequent, a longer interval being needed to see how any innovations and amendments were working. Accordingly the ordinary interval between congresses or administrative conferences was re-set to five years, with two-thirds (formerly one third) of the members being able to demand an earlier gathering (Art. XIX.1). New Convention articles were to require unanimity for their adoption (Art. XXVI.3.1). The possibility of the amendment of the Convention during its currency was introduced, Arts. II-VI and XIX (broadly relating to rates and transit rights) needing unanimity for their alteration (Art. XXVI.3.1), and with a two-thirds majority needed for other amendments (Art. XXVI.3.2). Only a simple majority was, however, required for an interpretation of the Convention (Art. XXVI.3.3). The International Office was renamed the International Bureau of the Universal Postal Union (Art. XVI). The work of the International Bureau had increased both with the increase in UPU membership and through an extension of the duties in research, collection of data and publication that it was required to perform. Its budget was therefore increased to 100,000 Swiss francs,[113] and a new

110 Great Britain signed for itself and for various colonies specified in Para IV of the Final Protocol, being those for which Britain had made application prior to the Berne conference of 1876.

111 The possibility of an existing member objecting to a new member contained in Art. XVII of the 1874 treaty was dropped.

112 See *infra*, 'Postal Conference, Paris, 1880'.

113 Paris, DR Art. XXVIII.1.

one unit class was added to the classes of contribution taking the number of classes to seven, which it was to remain.[114]

An important development at Paris was that some, but not all, of the Congress participants negotiated a separate Arrangement for the exchange of 'Letters of Declared Value'[115] and of postal 'Money Orders'.[116] Both had been the subject of previous bilateral agreements, but this use of the right of UPU members to enter into other agreements (Art. XV) foreshadowed a UPU practice in which a number of particular services were the subject of individual agreements. This was a sufficiently novel development to need the inclusion of an Art. XIII to authorise it. Two years later parcel post became the subject of yet another arrangement. However, it must be noted that all these multilateral Arrangements did not prevent, prohibit or replace the right of individual UPU members to agree on such matters between themselves on a more restricted basis.

The Postal Conference, Paris, 1880

The weight limits for letters and packets specified in the 1874 Convention were on the low side. At the 1878 Congress therefore Germany raised the possibility of an arrangement as to parcel post in order to deal with heavier items. This could have been analogous to the agreements on Money Orders and Letters of Declared Value arrived at between some 1878 participants as we have just seen. However, many of the delegations had not come prepared to discuss such a matter and felt that it was too complex to be dealt with by the 1878 gathering. Accordingly it was referred to the International Bureau to consider. The Bureau soon circulated a draft agreement, which was subjected to many counter-proposals and suggestions. The

114 Paris, DR Art. XXVIII.2. Montenegro was the first in this class: DR Art. XXVIII.5.

115 Arrangement between Austria-Hungary, Belgium, Denmark and the Danish Colonies, Egypt, France and the French colonies, Germany, Italy, Luxemburg, the Netherlands, Norway, Portugal and the Portuguese Colonies, Roumania, Russia, Servia, Sweden and Switzerland, for the exchange of Letters and Small Boxes of Declared Value, Paris, 1 June 1878; 152 CTS 270; 69 BFSP 245. Detailed Rules at 69 BFSP 251. The Arrangement and DR were modified in 1885: 165 CTS 159; 76 BFSP 1333; in 1891: 174 CTS 255; 19 De Clercq 156; in 1897: 185 CTS 153; 90 BFSP 1087; in 1906: 210 CTS 234; 100 BFSP 1034; in 1920: 114 BFSP 505; in 1924: 40 LNTS 249; in 1929: 6 Hudson No. 233; in 1934: 175 LNTS 5, 6 Hudson; in 1947: 148 BFSP 605.

116 Arrangement between Austria-Hungary, Belgium, Denmark, Egypt, France and the French colonies, Germany, Italy, Luxemburg, the Netherlands, Norway, Portugal, Roumania, Sweden and Switzerland, for the Exchange of Money Orders, Paris, 4 June 1878. Detailed Regulations at 69 BFSP 264. The Arrangement and DR were modified in 1885: 165 CTS 172; 76 BFSP 1326; in 1891: 174 CTS 305; 19 De Clercq 206; in 1897: 185 CTS 170; 90 BFSP 1127; in 1906: 210 CTS 313; 100 BFSP 959; in 1924: 40 LNTS 437; in 1929: 130 BFSP 358; 6 Hudson No. 225; in 1934: 175 LNTS 269; in 1947: 149 BFSP 17.

Bureau therefore concluded that an international conference was needed to deal with the matter, and approached France which agreed to convene.

According to Codding,[117] France was selected as the best venue for the postal parcel conference partly because of its size and geographic situation.[118] Another reason was that at that time parcels were usually carried by the railway and other transport services of most UPU members, not by their post office systems. France being one of these, it was felt to be advantageous that its experience would help in the discussions, and, as it happened, the major French rail companies and three French maritime countries were represented by observers.

Twenty-three UPU members sent delegates to the Paris conference, which met from 9 October to 5 November. The result was a Convention and related Detailed Regulations on which twenty of the delegations were able to agree.[119] The weight limit for postal parcels under this convention was set at three kilograms (Art. I.1) and all such parcels had to be pre-paid (Art. IV). Each parcel had to be accompanied by customs declarations for transit and destination in one of several specified formats (DR Art. I.6). In addition to postage a dispatching administration had to pay a land transit fee of 50 centimes for each country transited Art. III.1). In the case of maritime transport, each dispatching office had to pay each of the administrations whose services were used a fee of 25 centimes for transport of up to 500 'milles marins', 50 centimes for 500-1000 m-m, one franc for 1000-3000 m-m, two francs for 3000-6000 m-m and three francs for transport in excess of 6000 'milles marins' (Art. III.2). Where two sea routes were possible the average of their distances was to be used (Art. III *ad fin*). Indemnity rates and responsibility were set by Art. XI for parcels lost or stolen.

The Universal Postal Union, Third Congress, Lisbon, 1885

By the time the Third UPU Congress convened at Lisbon from 4 February to 21 March 1855, membership of the Union had grown to fifty-four. Taking advantage of the amendment provisions of the 1878 Convention the Congress

117 Codding III, 41, citing 'The Postal Conference of Paris in the Year 1880' (1880) 5 *Union Postale*, 248.

118 France was important. As noted earlier (*supra*, n. 74), special arrangements had been made to ensure that France participated in the 1874 treaty.

119 Convention between Great Britain, Austria, Hungary, Belgium, Bulgaria, Denmark, Egypt, France, Germany, Italy, Luxemburg, Montenegro, Netherlands, Norway, Portugal, Roumania, Servia, Sweden, Switzerland and Turkey for the Exchange of Postal Parcels without declaration of value, Paris, 3 November 1880; 156 CTS 130; 71 BFSP 356, 8 Martens (2d) 120. Detailed Regulations at 71 BFSP 362. The Postal Parcel Convention and DR were modified in 1885: 165 CTS147; 76 BFSP 1315; in 1891: 174 CTS 276; 19 De Clercq 177; in 1897: 185 CTS 186; 90 BFSP 1104; in 1906: 201 CTS 332; 100 BFSP 999; in 1924: 40 LNTS 307; in 1929: 6 Hudson no. 224; in 1934: 175 LNTS 269; 6 Hudson 758; in 1947: 148 BFSP 923.

confined itself to altering various of the 1878 provisions by 'Additional Acts'.[120] Alterations included that postal cards with a paid reply were added to the material covered by Art. II of the 1878 Convention (Art. I.I), rates were altered for various services (Arts. I.II-III), a new Art. V*bis* allowed the withdrawal from the post of undelivered correspondence (Art. I.IV), a new Art. VI*bis* amended the provisions as to compensation for the loss of registered items (Art. I.V), express delivery was provided for by a new Art. XIX*bis* (Art. I.VI), the rules as to forbidden articles were amended to allow the carriage of gold, silver, precious stones or jewellery, but not items subject to customs duties (Art. I.VIII). The amendments to the Detailed Regulations were minor, but fairly extensive. An innovation was a new DR Art. XXIX*bis*, specifying in more detail the statistics to be sent yearly to the International Bureau. The existing agreements as to Letters of Declared Value, Money Orders and Postal Parcels were revisited and amended. Lisbon also saw the introduction of 'cash on delivery' (COD) services,[121] and of postal identity cards,[122] although, as the relevant footnotes show, only a minority of UPU members adopted these arrangements.

The Lisbon Congress also considered the introduction of postal subscriptions for newspapers, but no agreement was possible and the matter was referred to the International Bureau, which in 1890 asked representatives of Austria, Germany, Poland and Portugal to meet in Brussels to discuss the question. The proposals of this committee were taken to the next UPU Congress in 1891.

120 Additional Act to the Convention of 1 June 1878 establishing a Universal Postal Union, Lisbon 21 March 1885, in force 1 April 1886; 165 CTS 110; 76 BFSP 21; 25 Stat. 1339; 1 Bevans 97. Additional Act modifying the Detailed Regulations of June 1, 1878 for the execution of the Convention of that date, establishing the Universal Postal Union, Lisbon, 21 March 1885; 76 BFSP 29.

121 Arrangement concerning the Service of Cash on Delivery between Germany, Austria-Hungary, Belgium, Egypt, France. Italy, Liberia, Luxemburg, Portugal and the Portuguese Colonies, Roumania and Switzerland, Lisbon, 21 March 1885, 165 CTS 162, 76 BFSP 1336. Detailed Regulations at 76 BFSP 1340. The Arrangement and Regulations were modified in 1891: 174 CTS 317; 83 BFSP 998; in 1897: 185 CTS 209; 90 BFSP 1141; in 1906: 210 CTS 373; 100 BFSP 987; in 1924: 41 LNTS 55; in 1929: 130 BFSP 359; in 1947: 149 BFSP 8.

122 Arrangement concerning Identity Cards in postal services between Argentina, Bulgaria, Egypt, Italy, Luxemburg, Mexico, Paraguay, Portugal, Switzerland, Uruguay and Venezuela, Lisbon, 21 March 1885, 165 CTS 179, 76 BFSP 1345. The Arrangement was modified in 1891: 174 CTS 328; 83 BFSP 1007; in 1897: 185 CTS 227, 90 BFSP 1151; and thereafter.

The Universal Postal Union, Fourth Congress, Vienna, 1891

From 20 May to 4 July 1891 the UPU met in Vienna. As before the Convention and the Detailed Regulations were reviewed and amended.[123] The other Arrangements for particular services that had already been agreed by some, not all, of the UPU members also came under consideration. Reply-paid postcards were added to the list of items covered by Art. II. Intriguingly a new postal problem had to be dealt with. A new Art. XVIII barred the use of counterfeit postage stamps or the re-use of genuine stamps, and engaged member states to prohibit and suppress the manufacture, sale or distribution of counterfeit or imitation stamps whether of the national state or of any other UPU member country. More mundanely the budget for the International Bureau was increased once more, this time to 125,000 Swiss francs (DR Art. XXXII.1). The Bureau was given new duties as to the settlement of accounts between UPU members (DR Art. XXVI), and was asked to produce an alphabetic dictionary of all the post offices of the world indicating specifically those that imposed special charges (DR Art. XVII.13). Apart from the Convention and Detailed Regulations, a new Arrangement was adopted for postal subscriptions to newspapers and periodicals, more or less in the terms worked out the previous year by that small working group which had met at the behest of the International Bureau.[124]

The Universal Postal Union, Fifth Congress, Washington, DC, 1897

The UPU Congress that met at Washington DC from 5 May to 15 June 1897 largely concerned itself with changes to rates and weights, usually lowering the former and increasing the latter.[125] Its main importance, however, lay in the informal discussions that took place among the delegates, laying the foundation for the debates that were to take place in Rome in 1906.

---

123 Universal Postal Union: Vienna, 4 July 1891, in force 1 July 1892; 174 CTS 170, 212; 83 BFSP 513 (Final Protocol at 540); 19 De Clerq 114; 28 Stat. 1078; 1 Bevans 188.

124 Arrangement concerning Postal Subscriptions to Newspapers and Periodical Publications between Germany, Austria-Hungary, Belgium, Brazil, Bulgaria, Colombia, Denmark, Egypt, Liberia, Luxemburg, Norway, Persia, Portugal and the Portuguese Colonies, Roumania, Sweden, Switzerland, Turkey and Uruguay, Vienna, 4 July 1891, 174 CTS 332; 83 BFSP 1013. Detailed Regulations at 83 BFSP 1017. The Arrangement and Regulations were modified in 1897: 185 CTS 219; 90 BFSP 1079; in 1906: 201 CTS 363; 100 BFSP 1079; in 1920: 116 BFSP 571; in 1924: 41 LNTS 97; in 1929: 130 BFSP 360; in 1934: 176 LNTS 55; in 1947: 149 BFSP 52; and thereafter. The service had been proposed at Lisbon, and the Bureau had been asked to study the question: see Codding III, 40-1.

125 Universal Postal Union: Washington, DC, 15 June 1897, in force 1 January 1899; 185 CTS 59; 89 BFSP 65; 35 Stat. 1639; 1 Bevans 206. Detailed Regulations at 89 BFSP 85.

The Universal Postal Union, Extraordinary Congress, Berne, 1900

1900 was the twenty-fifth anniversary of the Union. At the invitation of the Swiss government an Extraordinary Congress was therefore held at Berne from 2 to 5 July. Its function was celebration, not business. The only formal decision with financial import was the payment of 200,000 Swiss francs to the Swiss Federal Council to defray the cost of a monument to the UPU.[126]

The Universal Postal Union, Sixth Congress, Rome, 1906

By the time of the Sixth Congress the Union had grown to 71 members, 54 being the usual states but another 17 postal administration areas were recognised as 'Postal Administrations and Colonies' under Art. XXVII – nearly one-third, a significant proportion of the membership.[127] The eventual final documents were largely in the previous form,[128] but transit and transit rates had been a matter of intense debate, not to say argument, and this was reflected in Art. IV.[129] In broad transit rates and the rates for marine transport were reduced, as were weight limits. An innovation in service was the introduction of the International Reply Coupon within Art. XI. By Art. XI.2, a reply coupon, exchangeable for a postage stamp of 25 centimes in value, was to be made available in all countries that allowed its use. The manufacture, supply and accounting for the coupons was made a function of the International Bureau.[130] Another minor (but soon to be much appreciated) innovation was Art. XI.4 which subsumed correspondence to and from prisoners

126 Codding III, 154.

127 The German Protectorates of Africa, and of Asia and Australasia, British India*, Canada*, Australia and British New Guinea**, British South Africa Colonies and Protectorates, all other British Colonies*, US Island possessions, all Danish Colonies*, all Spanish Colonies*, Algeria, French Colonies and Protectorates in Indo-China**, all other French Colonies*, all Italian Colonies, all Dutch Colonies*, Portuguese African Colonies, all other Portuguese Colonies*. Those marked * had been recognised by and since the 1878 Convention, those marked ** under the 1891 Convention and those unmarked are newly recognised by the 1906 Convention. All British and German colonies had been recognised for UPU purposes in 1897, and I do not know why these were modified, unless to add to voting power. The same reasoning may apply to the Portuguese split and the separate label for British South Africa, though the Boer War may have played a role there.

128 Universal Postal Union: Rome, 26 May 1906, in force 1 October 1907; 201 CTS 246; 99 BFSP 254; 35 Stat. 1639; 1 Bevans 492. Detailed Regulations at 99 BFSP 277.

129 798 proposals were made by participants to the Rome conference, many relating to transit and rates.

130 Rome Convention, Art. XI.1; DR Art. VII and Annex A. Von Stephan had suggested the concept in 1874: *supra*, n. 84.

of war into the 'official correspondence' category of the postal service, thus making it free of charge.[131]

The Universal Postal Union, Seventh Congress, Madrid, 1920

The Rome Congress had agreed that the next UPU Congress should be held in Madrid in 1912 or 1913. However, various difficulties meant that it could not be arranged to start until September 1914, by which time the First World War had begun. The War, of course, disrupted the international mail, and, when the Madrid Congress did convene in 1920, 2,248 proposals had been made for the rectification of the situation, nearly three times as many as had faced the Rome meeting. The effects of the War and the Peace Treaties had to be taken into account. The Congress took 61 days (1 October-30 November) during which it sat through 77 meetings before the new Convention and Detailed Regulations were agreed and the various Arrangements once more revised.[132]

At Madrid, while the overall structure and functioning of the Union was reaffirmed, a major problem was the matter of the financing of the international service. As a result of the War the relationship of currencies was significantly different from the pre-War situation. Commercial relations had been dislocated. A small committee was charged with finding solutions.[133] The gold franc was decided upon as the standard to which reference should generally made, and this was incorporated in Art. XII.[134] New rates were set for postage and for transit purposes, but for the latter purpose the period of averaging of statistics for the purpose of settling accounts between postal authorities was reduced from six to three years. Setting transit rates also caused much debate, countries that had a high transit traffic wishing to maintain their income, others wanting transit rates reduced and a

131 Codding III, 46 states that during the First World War Switzerland forwarded 529,161,367 letters and 92,946,096 packages. Other countries such as Sweden were also involved in POW correspondence. See also A. Pierce Higgins, 'The Treatment of Mails in Time of War' (1928) 9 BYIL 31; J.H. Spencer, 'The Franking Privilege for Postal Communications with Prisoners of War' (1941) 35 AJIL 365.

132 Universal Postal Union: Madrid, 30 November 1920, in force 1 January 1922; 114 BFSP 430; 42 Stat. 1971; 2 Bevans 282; 15 Martens (3d) 722, noted but not reproduced, 1 Hudson 520. Detailed Regulations at 114 BFSP 457; 42 Stat. 2010. F.H. Williamson, 'The International Postal Service and the Universal Postal Union' (1930) 9 *J. Royal Inst. Int. Aff.* 60.

133 See 'Summary', *supra*, n. 84, at 441.

134 Art. II of the Final Protocol states, whether or not users of the gold franc, were to fix the equivalent postal rates in their own currency in agreement with the Swiss Postal Administration. These equivalents were variable with fluctuations in the international money market, provided that they did not exceed the rates set in the Convention or fall below the rates of 1 October 1920, and in any event did not fall below the rates operative at the date when the Rome Convention had come into force (1 October 1907).

number calling, ineffectively, for transit rates to be abolished.[135] Identity cards for postal purposes were brought within the scope of the general Convention for those countries that wished to provide and recognise them (Art. IX, DR Art. 25). There were innovations. For the first time aviation was brought under the Convention. Thanks to the War aviation technology had considerably developed, and by its end aeroplanes were capable of flying long distances and of carrying substantial loads. The first airline companies were emerging and that offered the possibility of carrying mail by air more swiftly than by terrestrial transport systems. By Art. V the aerial transport of mail was therefore equated with 'extraordinary services specially established or maintained by one Administration' governed by Art. IV.6. By it the rates and conditions of the extraordinary service were to be regulated by the mutual consent of the Administrations concerned. As to other matters, for the first time it was forbidden to send narcotics by post (Art. XVIII.2.e). Also for the first time it was agreed that, while members might continue to make agreements on matters 'which do not concern the Union generally', they might do so only on the condition that 'these agreements do not infringe the present convention', a restriction not present in previous conventions (Art. XXII.2). Obviously the work and responsibilities of the International Bureau had considerably increased, and its new annual ordinary budget was set at 300,000 Swiss francs.[136]

The Universal Postal Union, Eighth Congress, Stockholm, 1924

While the Madrid Congress had done much to re-vivify the Union after the War it also made it clear that a major revision of the Convention of the Union would be desirable. This took place at the Stockholm Congress which ran from 4 July - 28 August 1924, a relatively short time after the 1920 Convention had come into force. The UPU Convention was thoroughly recast, the Detailed Regulations less so.[137] For this process a preparatory committee meeting in 1921 and 1922 was a major facilitator. Similar committees were to assist the preparations for the 1929

135 Codding III, 53, lists these last as the US and US possessions, Argentina, Bolivia, Brazil, Chile, Columbia, Cuba, Dominica, Ecuador, Guatemala, Honduras, Hungary, Mexico, Nicaragua, Panama, Paraguay, Peru, Salvador, Spain, Spanish Colonies, Uruguay and Venezuela. The presence of so many from Latin America explains why a Pan-American Postal Union was formed at Buenos Aires in 1921 with an International Office at Montevideo (30 LNTS 141; 1 Hudson 702). The Buenos Aires agreement was revised in 1926 (3 Hudson 2032). A Postal Union of the Americas and Spain was formed in Madrid in 1931 (131 LNTS 327; 5 Hudson 1104). This Postal Union is now governed by an agreement of 26 November 1971 (23-3 UST 2925, TIAS 7480), with Additional Protocols of 1976 (30-1 UST 337, TIAS 9206) and 1981.

136 The 1906 DR had set that budget at 125,000 Swiss francs.

137 Universal Postal Union: Stockholm, 28 August 1924, in force 1 October 1925; 40 LNTS 19; noted but not reproduced 2 Hudson 1372; 19 Martens (3rd) 365. Final Protocol, 40 LNTS 86; DR, 40 LNTS 92; 44 Stat. 2273. 4 Hudson 2917 reprints the 1929 DR, with

and 1934 Congresses, but the device was thereafter abandoned due to difficulties in agreeing its membership.[138]

The Stockholm Congress divided the Convention into three Parts or Titles, themselves divided into Chapters, and then into Articles, although the numbering of the Articles is consecutive throughout the whole document. Chapter I of Part I, the 'Universal Postal Union', dealt with the 'Organisation and Jurisdiction of the Union' and was of constitutional importance. Article 1 repeated the mantra of the Union forming a 'single postal territory for the exchange of correspondence' before stating for the first time the purpose of the Union. This was 'to assure the organisation and perfection of the various international postal services'.[139] Article 2 dealt with membership, while Art. 11 dealt with its termination or withdrawal from any of the supplementary Arrangements. Article 3 stated that regular mail services were governed by the Convention, although arrangements as to other services might be entered into by members *inter se*, these not binding their non-members. Article 4 authorised the existence of the Detailed Regulations. Article 5 dealt with special treaties, restricted unions and frontier zones. In this the right of members to reduce rates *inter se*, and to make agreements on matters that were not of interest to the whole of the Union, were retained, but only on the basis that such agreements did not introduce any provision less favourable than that provided by the Acts of the Union. Article 6 preserved the principle that the Acts of the Union did not affect domestic legislation in anything that was not expressly provided for in them (sc. an obligation to revise municipal law). Article 7 bound members to exchange correspondence from the Union area with non-members. Article 8 listed the non-states that were entitled to participate as members of the Union, while Art. 9 listed various post offices and territories to be considered as linked to Union members. Article 10 provided for the arbitration of disputes.

Part I, Chapter II, covered the technicalities of the holding of congresses, with conferences and with committees. Chapter III provided for proposals made by members in the interval between Congresses, their introduction (Art. 18), examination (Art. 19), the conditions of their approval (Art. 20),[140] notification of any resolution to members (Art. 21), and its being applied only after three months of its adoption (Art. 22). Part I, Chapter III, Arts. 23-4 and DR, set out the rules and responsibilities for the International Bureau. The seven classes of units of contribution were retained (Art. 24.2 and DR Art. 92.4), and the International Bureau budget was set at 350,000 Swiss francs (Dr. Art. 92.1).

changes from 1924 indicated in italics in the French text. For the Stockholm measures see Williamson, *supra*, n. 132.

138 Codding III, 50, notes that the 1921/2 committee (Zermatt and Nice) had seven members, that of 1928 (Paris) fourteen, and of 1934 (Ottawa) the same plus two observers.

139 This phrase echoes the purpose of postal congresses expressed in Art. XVIII of the 1874 Treaty.

140 The conditions as to unanimity, qualified majority and simple majority were unchanged.

In a sole Chapter, Part II contained 'Rules of General Order'. Article 25 set out a guaranteed liberty of transit except for minor restrictions as to packaging. Realistically, however, Art. 78 provided a sanction in the case of breach of Art. 25, giving administrations the right to discontinue postal service to and from any country failing to provide transit services. Article 26 enshrined the right of 'all persons' to use the services that were the subject of the Union and the Agreements. Article 27 prohibited unauthorised charges. Article 28 allowed the suspension of services in whole or in part, permanently or temporarily when an administration considered itself obliged to do so. Importantly, Article 29 refined the definition of the basic monetary unit for use in the Union agreements. This was set as 'the gold franc of 100 centimes weighing 10/31 of a gramme having a fineness of 0.900'. The next article, Art. 30, allowed rates to be fixed in the local currency but only 'at the closest possible equivalent' to the gold franc. Forms used in the international services were to be in French though interlinear translation was possible (Art. 31), and finally identity cards for postal purposes were authorised for use by countries so wishing (Art. 32).

Thereafter the four Chapters of Part III elaborated and rearranged the 'Provisions concerning Postal Correspondence'. Rates were by and large reduced,[141] and chargeable weights altered.[142] In the debates the usual divide emerged between countries that derived revenue from transit payments, they wishing rates to remain as was or even to be increased, while other countries looked for their reduction or even abolition. An expanded provision was made by Art. 74 for the new-fangled aeroplane service. As in 1920 such services were considered to be 'extraordinary services', but this time the possibility of an air service serving many states was taken into account (Art. 24.1). Basically the rate for an air service between points was to be provided by agreement between the postal administrations and the airline concerned. Transit charges for administrations using the aviation services but not paying operating expenses were to be agreed, but also to be uniform for all aviation mail services landing in a state (Art. 24.2). No transit charge was exigible simply because of overflight (Art. 24.4.3). Mail bags stored and transferred from one air service to another were to be charged for (Art. 24.3-4).

The Final Protocol made a number of other provisions, altering the effect of some of the elements of the Convention as noted. Most importantly, however, for the future of the UPU, its Para VII, headed 'Research Committee', provided for a committee of representatives of fourteen Administrations, and including the Director of the International Bureau, to investigate and study 'ways and means for simplifying and accelerating the labours of the Congresses'.

---

141 Para II of the Final Protocol allowed variation in some rates, but set limits to the extent of that variation.

142 By Para V of the Final Protocol countries not operating a metric system had the option of using the ounce, inaccurately substituting for the metric weight one ounce for 20 grams for letters, and two ounces for 50 grams for prints, commercial papers and samples. An ounce is 28.3465 grams.

The Universal Postal Union, Ninth Congress, London, 1929

Meeting in London from 10 May to 21 June, the UPU Congress of 1929 did not substantially alter the provisions of 1924 except in one respect, air mail.[143] Subsequent to the 1924 Congress the International Chamber of Commerce had suggested that the rules as to air mail should be the subject of a special UPU conference. The USSR recommended such a step to the International Bureau and, twenty-five UPU members agreeing, an Airmail Conference was held at The Hague, 1-10 September 1927. Thirty-eight postal administrations were present,[144] and, without vote, so were representatives of fourteen air transport companies,[145] the International Air Transport Association and the International Chamber of Commerce. The result was two agreements, one dealing with air mail letters and the other with air parcels.[146] These were accepted at the London Congress in 1929,[147] Para 7 to the London Final Protocol making their provisions integral to the Convention and the Regulations, but permitting their modification by special conference comprised of Administrations directly interested in air services.[148] As far as mail by air was to be concerned, however, the major developments of the next few years were the European Air Mail conferences of Brussels 1930, The

143 Universal Postal Union: London, 28 June 1929, in force 1 July 1930; 102 LNTS 245; 46 Stat, 2523; 4 Hudson 2869; 2 Bevans 867. Final Protocol 102 LNTS 312, 4 Hudson 2912. Detailed Regulations 102 LNTS 328, 46 Stat. 2579, 4 Hudson 2917. See Williamson, *supra*, n. 132, at 77-8.

144 Algeria, Austria, Belgian Congo, Belgium, British India, Canada, Chosen (Korea), Czechoslovakia, the Free City of Danzig, Denmark, Dutch Colonies in America, Dutch East Indies, Egypt, Finland, France, Germany, Great Britain, Greece, Hungary, the Italian Colonies, Italy, Japan, Japanese Dependencies, Latvia, Luxemburg, Morocco, the Netherlands, Norway, Persia, Portugal, the Saar, Spain, Sweden, Switzerland, Tunisia, Turkey, the US and USSR.

145 Companies were present from Austria, Belgium, Czechoslovakia, France, Germany, Great Britain, Italy, the Netherlands, Poland, Sweden, Switzerland and the USSR.

146 Provisions for the Transport of Postal Letters by Air, 75 LNTS 7; 3 Hudson 2117: Provisions for the Transport of Parcel Post by Air, 75 LNTS 39; 3 Hudson 2133, both The Hague, 10 September 1927.

147 Provisions concerning the Transport of Postal Letters by Air, 102 LNTS 504; 4 Hudson 2995: reproduced at 2 Bevans 907 as 'Provisions Concerning the Transportation of Regular Mails by Air'; 'Provisions for the Transport of Parcels Post by Air', 103 LNTS 223; 3 Hudson 3112, both London, 28 June 1929. These were revised at Cairo in 1934, 175 LNTS 73.

148 Over the years the extent to which states used air mail to subsidise air services became a matter of contention in both domestic and international markets. Cf. E.C. Johnston 'Separation of Air-Pay from Subsidy' (1951) 18 *J. Air Law & Comm.* 320; O.J. Lissitzyn, 'Public Aid to Foreign Airlines' (1951) 18 *J. Air Law & Comm.* 379 and (1952) 19 *J. Air Law & Comm.* 38; L. Flynn and C. Rizza, 'Postal Services and Competition Law' (2001) 24 *World Comp.* 475.

Hague and Paris in 1937 and Brussels in 1938.[149] These started by considering a European network but, thanks to developing technology and that planes had become a normal method of transport for first class mail within Europe, settled for establishing how the ordinary aviation services would be used. Such considerations were to be brought to the Eleventh Congress for consideration on a wider basis, but in fact the matter was barely discussed there, perhaps in the light of the political situation in April/May 1939.

The Universal Postal Union, Tenth Congress, Cairo, 1934

The Tenth Congress, meeting in Cairo from 1 February to 20 March 1934, made little substantial alteration to the Convention, the Detailed Regulations or to the various separate arrangements.[150] As usual much of the discussion related to rates and weights as well as to transit payments. One change, however, was the addition of postal travellers cheques to the Agreement respecting International Money Orders. Another was that, although the existing membership of non-sovereign entities was retained, the Congress agreed that the interpretation of 'country' for the purpose of adhesion to the Union would relate to sovereign states. There would be no new non-sovereign members.

The Universal Postal Union, Eleventh Congress, Buenos Aires, 1939

The Eleventh Congress met in Buenos Aires from 1 April to 23 May 1939 in the shadow of international political uncertainties. Under these circumstances it confined itself to technical matters, making small amendments to the various documents of the Union.[151] However, notwithstanding the political situation, the economic position of most UPU members had stabilised, and therefore many rates were reduced.

Shortly thereafter, however, the Second World War hampered the functioning of the UPU, but, thanks in part to the International Bureau being located in neutral Switzerland, did not stop it. Notably the free postal arrangements for prisoners of war, first introduced in 1906 and enshrined in Art. 49.2 of the 1939 Convention,

---

149 Codding III, 59-61. Cf. K. Colegrove, 'The International Aviation Policy of the United States' (1931) 4 *J. Air Law*, 447.

150 Universal Postal Union: Cairo, 20 March 1934, in force 1 January 1935; 174 LNTS 171; 6 Hudson 646; 49 Stat. 2741, 3 Bevans 163. Final Protocol, 6 Hudson 690. DR at 174 LNTS 253, 6 Hudson 695.

151 Universal Postal Union, Buenos Aires, 23 May 1939; 202 LNTS 159; 8 Hudson 303.

were complied with, at least in Europe. However, Germany did set up a regional postal organisation which for a period functioned within the occupied territories.[152]

The Universal Postal Union, Twelfth Congress, Paris, 1947

When the UN was established its relationship with existing international agencies had to be clarified. Similar questions had previously arisen in respect of the League of Nations. By Art. 24 of the League of Nations Covenant[153] international bureaux constituted prior to the existence of the League might be placed under its direction, but only if the parties to their constituent treaties so consented. This the UPU did not do, primarily because of a distrust of and impatience with the League that was common to many of the UPU members.[154] In terms of Art. 57 of the UN Charter, a fresh attempt was made in 1946 to relate the new world organisation and the 'specialised agencies' that had 'wide international responsibilities'. Charter Art. 63 indicated the procedure – agreement between the agency and ECOSOC.[155] There was argument that Art. 57 did not lay a positive obligation on existing organisations such as the UPU to enter relationship with the UN,[156] but other Articles of the Charter show the intention of the negotiators of the UN system.[157] In short, the UPU was brought within the UN 'family' of specialised

152 Agreement concerning a European Postal and Telecommunication Union, Vienna, 19 October 1942, 9 Hudson 43. Its Art. 9 maintained application of the UPU Convention except insofar as not contradictory to this Vienna agreement. See Chapter 4, at n. 83.

153 Covenant of the League of Nations, Part I (Arts. 1-26) of the Treaty of Peace, Versailles, 28 June 1919, and of the Treaty of St Germain, the Treaty of Trianon and the Treaty of Neuilly; 1 Hudson 1; http://avalon.law.yale.edu/20th_century/leagcov.asp.

154 Codding III, 214-8. Cf. Parry, *infra*, n. 156, at 402-4.

155 UN Charter, Art. 57.1: 'The various specialized agencies, established by intergovernmental agreement and having wide international responsibilities, as defined in their basic instruments, in economic, social, cultural, educational, health, and related fields, shall be brought into relationship with the United Nations in accordance with the provisions of Article 63.'

Art. 57.2: 'Such agencies thus brought into relationship with the United Nations are hereinafter referred to as specialized agencies.'

Art. 63.1: 'The Economic and Social Council may enter into agreements with any of the agencies referred to in Article 57, defining the terms on which the agency concerned shall be brought into relationship with the United Nations. Such agreements shall be subject to approval by the General Assembly.'

Art. 63.2: 'It may co-ordinate the activities of the specialized agencies through consultation with and recommendations to such agencies and through recommendations to the General Assembly and to the Members of the United Nations.'

156 See C. Parry, 'Documentary Section: Constitutions of International Organisations' (1946) 23 BYIL 394 at 400-1.

157 Cf. UN Charter Arts. 55, 58, and 62-4, the latter regarding the responsibilities of the Economic and Social Council.

agencies by its own action, Art. 2 of the 1947 Convention specifying that the Union was in relationship with the UN in terms of an Agreement appended to the Convention which had been negotiated with the UN Economic and Social Council, that Agreement being supplemented in 1949.[158] As a result the officials of the UPU became able to use the UN 'laissez-passer' and were and are accorded the usual international privileges and immunities.[159] Concomitantly the Statute of the International Bureau was revised. This, the legal constitution of the Bureau under Swiss Law, was brought into closer conformity to those then operative for the International Labour Organisation and the World Health Organisation. The result was that the privileges and immunities of the International Bureau were made more extensive than those indicated as necessary by the UN Resolution on such matters.[160]

However, the debates as to the status of the UPU as a specialised agency had revealed a curious problem. Technically, although its International Bureau continued ministerially to serve the interests and demands of its members, the UPU had no permanent organ. Where or what was the entity to 'be' the specialised agency, or indeed with what might the UN conclude an agreement and which body would secure that that agreement was complied with in the Union?[161] Formally speaking the UPU was a collection of members, coming together for its congresses. The new UPU Convention did not really solve the problem of 'existence', although, as noted above, its Art. 2 and the related Agreement coped with the question of

158 See Agreement between the United Nations and the Universal Postal Union, Paris, 14 July 1947, in force 1 July 1948, 19 UNTS 219; Additional Agreement, Paris, 13 July 1949, and Lake Success, 27 July, 1949; 43 UNTS 344. The 1947 Agreement was drafted by the UN and UPU 'postal experts' at Lake Success in 1946. For the discussions see [Parry] 'Documentary Section: Constitutions of International Organisations: II The Universal Postal Union' (1948) 25 BYIL 435 at 457-62. For the UPU Convention itself see *infra*, n. 162.

159 The UPU is the subject of Annex VIII to the Convention on the Privileges and Immunities of the Specialised Agencies of the United Nations, New York, 21 November 1947; 33 UNTS 261; 1959 UKTS 69, Cmnd 855. Cf. the General Convention on the Privileges and Immunities of the United Nations, New York, 13 February 1946, 1 UNTS 15 (with corrigendum at 90 UNTS 327); 1950 UKTS 10, Cmd. 7891; 21-2 UST 1418, TIAS 6900; 1946 UNGA Res. 22 (I) D; 9 Hudson 499. On the UPU and the UN see Codding III, 218-23.

160 See C. Parry, *infra*, n. 162, at 465. Cf. 'Resolution on the Co-ordination of the Privileges and Immunities of the United Nations and the Specialized Agencies', Part D of UNGA Res. 22 (I) of 13 Feb 1946. Cf. for contemporary discussion Parry, *supra*, n. 156, at 406-7; and his 'International Government and Diplomatic Privilege' (1947) 10 *Mod. L.R.* 97; L. Preuss, 'The International Organisations Immunities Act' (1946) 40 AJIL 332.

161 See comment by the Temporary Transport and Communications Commission of the Economic and Social Council, quoted by Parry, *infra*, n. 162, at 457.

the recognition of the UPU as a specialised agency.[162] However, the creation of the Executive and Liaison Committee, to which we are coming, served the purpose of the UPU having a permanent organ. Indeed, that was one of the requirements of the UN negotiators.

The Paris Congress convened on 7 May 1947. It had eight hundred and twenty-one proposals to consider, many fewer than, say, the 2,248 of the Madrid Congress of 1920, but it ran until 5 July 1947, only one day less than had been needed for Madrid.[163] Membership of the Union was a major question, the USSR, for example, suggesting that only sovereign states should be members.[164] That would have eliminated the additional influence (and often votes) to which the colonial empires and the US had access. Another possibility was that membership of the UN should be an avenue to membership of the UPU. Neither proposal was adopted. However there was a limited response to pressure from the UN which considered only sovereign states should be members of the specialised agencies. Article 3.1 added the word 'sovereign' before the word 'country' in its statement of the method by which a new member might be admitted to the Union, and Art. 3.3 required applications for membership to be approved by at least two-thirds of the countries forming the Union.[165] On the other hand Art. 8 continued to list various colonies, protectorates and the like 'as forming a single country or administration' within the UPU for the purpose of membership, and these appear in the list of parties in the Preamble to the Convention. As Cairo 1934 had decided, members that were not sovereign countries continued as members, but new members could be only sovereign states. It should be noted, however, that the effect of the 'two-thirds approval' hurdle of Art. 3.3 was that the UPU retained control over its membership for the time. As we will see under the current Constitution, as from 1964 any UN member can accede to the UPU Acts without any further approval by UPU members.[166] Last, by Art. 10, the extent of the jurisdiction of the Union beyond the territories of its members was stated generally to include post offices established in countries not members of the Union, and other territories which, though not

162 Universal Postal Union: Paris, 5 July 1947; in force 1 July 1948; 62 Stat. 3157, TIAS 1850; 1949 UKTS 57, Cmd. 7794; 148 BFSP 521; 4 Bevans 482; (1948) 25 BYIL 465. Not in UNTS. C. Parry, 'Documentary Section: Constitutions of International Organisations: II The Universal Postal Union' (1948) 25 BYIL 437 at 457-72.

163 Codding III, 65.

164 Parry, *supra*, n. 162, 463.

165 Previously adhesion or admission to the UPU was on demand by an applicant. In effect a country unilaterally declared itself a UPU member. Under the new procedure any request for membership was submitted to the Swiss Government, and by it to the UPU members (Art. 3.2). Countries not replying to the Swiss Government within four months were considered to have abstained (Art. 3.4). The Swiss Government was responsible for informing all members of the admission of a new member (Art. 3.5).

166 Arts. 2 and 11.1 of the Constitution of the Universal Postal Union, 1964. See Chapter 8, 'Membership'.

themselves UPU members, were 'dependent upon countries of the Union from a postal view-point'. Formerly such areas had been specifically named.[167]

The major constitutional innovation at Paris was Art. 18 which created the Executive and Liaison Committee (ELC).[168] Previously the work of the UPU had been carried through by the successive congresses, with the International Bureau providing ministerial support. On occasion special conferences were called, for example on the matter of air mail.[169] Now a permanent organ was recognised, albeit that 'in principle' it was to meet only once a year when convened by its Chairman (Art. 18.8).[170] It was to assure the continuation of the work of the UPU in the period between congresses in accordance with the Convention and related Agreements (Arts. 18.1 and 3). Specifically it was to maintain close contact with UPU members so as to improve the international postal service, to study technical questions,[171] and to make recommendations to members including proposals for the attention of congress, to keep in touch with the UN and other international organisations including sending a representative to their meetings, checking the operation of the International Bureau, and its staff, appointing the Director of the Bureau and its higher officials on the proposal of the Swiss government, approving the appointment of other personnel by the Director and authorising the employment of personnel on the proposal of the Director, and annually to report to UPU members on the operation of the Bureau (Art. 18.11.a-e). The nineteen members of the new body (Art. 18.3) were elected by Congress, with at least one half being up for election at each congress, and no country being elected by more than three successive congresses (Art. 18.4). Each member was to designate a representative who had to be a qualified official of its own Postal Administration (Art. 18.5). The Committee worked without remuneration. Its operating costs were covered by the Union but representatives were entitled to be reimbursed for the cost of a round-trip air or steamship ticket for meetings (Art. 18.7). The maximum operating cost for the ELC was set at 100,000 francs (Art. 18.8). As a matter of practice, although not provided for in the Convention, the ELC membership

167 E.g. Art. 10 of both the Buenos Aires Convention, 1939, and the Cairo Convention, 1934.

168 Codding III, 156-74; Parry, *supra*, n. 162, 464. The (1948) 25 BYIL 456-72 translation calls it the Executive and Liaison Commission. The Executive and Liaison Committee was renamed the Executive Committee by Arts. 13 and 17 of the Constitution of the Universal Postal Union, Vienna, 10 July 1964, in force 1 January 1966; 611 UNTS 64; 1966 UKTS 70, Cmnd, 3141, and then as the Council of Administration by the Seoul Congress, 1994: see Arts. II and III, Fifth Additional Protocol to the Constitution of the Universal Postal Union, Seoul, 14 September 1994, in force 1 January 1996; 2001 UKTS 7, Cm. 5040.

169 See *supra*, n. 146.

170 I take the words 'in principle' from the translation at 148 BFSP 521 and (1948) 25 BYIL 469. The Bevans translation uses the word 'generally' (4 Bevans 490-1).

171 Ten years later at Ottawa its power/duty to study technical matters was transferred to the CCPS: see *infra*, following at n. 180.

was divided on a geographic basis, Europe having nine seats, and America, Asia, Africa and Oceania each five. Each region elected from among its numbers.[172] Compared with other 'executive' organs in the other UN specialised agencies, the ELC was weak, the 'executive' element of its activity being minimal, and, as noted above, it was normally to meet only once a year. That said, over the years it found a major function in improving the efficiency of the Union, in preparing for congresses, and in undertaking studies for which the International Bureau was unsuitable.[173] In particular, in 1948 the Committee began considering the redrafting of the Convention and the various Acts. It was to propose the separation of organic provisions from those relating to the letter post.

The Universal Postal Union, Thirteenth Congress, Brussels, 1952

The thirteenth UPU Congress met in Brussels from 14 May to 11 July 1952. It revised the Constitution and related agreements.[174] Some of its sessions were taken up with the question of the composition of the ELC and voting procedures for its election. It was agreed to divide the UPU membership ELC purposes into five regions:[175] 1. Western Hemisphere (24 members); 2. Eastern Europe and Northern Asia (9 members); 3. Western Europe (20 members); 4. South-east Europe, Southern Asia and Oceania (27 members); 5. Africa (13 members). Region 1 was allocated five seats; Region 2, two; Region 3, five; Region 4, six; and Region 5, two. Further, this time the entire UPU membership elected the members of the ELC, each country being given a number of votes for each region equivalent to the number of seats there available.[176]

On the question of the Constitution the ELC presented proposals to group organic provisions separate from those on the letter post. This was rejected. Congress, however, was willing to accept improvements in the various agreements on particular services.

By 1952 the terminology of the Union had become prolix. Many terms and expressions in the Acts were increasingly subject to varied interpretations by and

172 Codding III, 164-5. The first ELC members were Argentina, Australia, Brazil, China, Colombia, Czechoslovakia, Egypt, France, India, Mexico, The Netherlands, Portugal, Sweden, Switzerland, Turkey, UK, US, USSR and Yugoslavia.

173 Codding III, 172-4.

174 Universal Postal Union, Brussels 1952; 4-1 UST 1118, TIAS 2800. DR at 4-1 UST 1178.

175 Codding III, 165 states there were four areas designated, and then lists five.

176 Codding III, 165-7. The ELC members elected were Region 1: Brazil, Chile, Uruguay, US and Venezuela; Region 2: Poland and UUSR; Region 3: Belgium, Denmark, France, Italy and Switzerland; Region 4: Australia, India, Indonesia, Japan, Pakistan and Syria; Region 5: Egypt and South Africa. Because only eight previous members were re-elected the question of a fifty per cent turnover did not arise. Cf. elections to the ITU Council, *supra*, Chapter 5.

among members as they translated the official French texts into their own languages and practices. Accordingly the 1952 Congress decided on the compilation of a volume of terms that would establish a precise and standard postal terminology. UPU members would then interpret the agreements of the Union in the same way. Over the years this volume was increasingly effective in attaining its purpose, soon mutating into the semi-official Multilingual Vocabulary of the UPU. However, it was to remain without legal standing for a further fifty years, being used simply for reference. Only in 1994 did the Congress amend the UPU Constitution and Convention and insert new articles containing formal definitions of particular important terms.[177]

The Universal Postal Union, Fourteenth Congress, Ottawa, 1957

According to Codding, the UPU Congress that met at Ottawa from 14 August to 27 September 1957 was the largest that there had been, ninety-five members sending delegations and a further six international organisations sending observers.[178] One thousand two hundred and eighty-eight proposals were considered, a good number of which were approved.[179] The resultant Convention contained a significant development, the creation of a new permanent body, the Consultative Committee on Postal Studies (CCPS) (Art. 17).[180] The remit of the new body was the technical, operational and economic aspects of postal systems, the responsibility for technical studies being transferred from the ELC (Art. 17.1). The CCPS was to consider how national systems worked, identify best practices, and draw these to the attention of UPU members through annual reports to the ELC and periodical reports to the meetings of the UPU Congress (Art. 17.7). While formally all state members were CCPS members (Art. 17.2), its work was directed and carried out by a Management Council of twenty elected by the Committee itself (Art. 17.3).[181] Questions to be studied might be suggested to it by UPU state members, or by

177 Seventh Additional Protocol to the Constitution of the Universal Postal Union, Bucharest, 2004. See Chapter 8, *infra*.

178 Codding III, 70-2. The note on the Universal Postal Union in (1966) 20 *Int. Org.* 834 indicates that in 1957 there were ninety-seven UPU members.

179 Universal Postal Union, Ottawa 27 September 1957; 1960 UKTS 79, Cmnd 1218; 10-1 UST 413, TIAS 4202.

180 Codding III, 174-84. The CCPS was renamed the Consultative Council for Postal Studies by Art. IV of the Additional Protocol to the Constitution of the Universal Postal Union, Tokyo, 1969 (810 UNTS 7; 1973 UKTS 72, Cmnd. 5358; 22 UST 345, TIAS 8231) and further as the Postal Operations Council (POC) by the Seoul Congress, 1994. See Arts. II and IV, Fifth Additional Protocol to the Constitution of the Universal Postal Union, Seoul, 1994; 2001 UKTS 7, Cm. 5040.

181 There was much argument about the size of the Management Council, Canada proposing a membership of four on grounds of efficiency, cost, and ease of interaction with the International Bureau, while suggesting its number could later be increased. The US and

the ELC (Art. 17.6). The three aspects of its work, the technical, operational and economic, were entrusted to separate sections within the Committee, each section being allowed to operate through study groups (Art. 17.5). In addition any UPU member state might at its request be added to a particular study group (Art. 17.5).

Importantly for the future history of the Union the ELC was encouraged to continue work on the revision of the UPU Constitution, discussing and setting out in some detail the principles that should be adopted. The ELC, thus encouraged, produced its recommendations in 1960 and circulated these to member countries. On the basis of their replies the ELC completed its part in the revision process and recommendations were brought to the Fifteenth Congress.

The Universal Postal Union, Fifteenth Congress, Vienna, 1964

The Fifteenth Congress had originally been scheduled to meet in 1962 in Rio de Janeiro, but for a variety of reasons this proved impossible. India, which had been an alternative, stepped in and the Congress was re-scheduled for 1963. However, that arrangement was disrupted by the Sino-Indian War of October-November 1962, and India withdrew its invitation. The Fifteenth Congress therefore did not meet until 29 May 1964, when it convened in Vienna. It lasted until 11 July. One hundred and twenty-two countries took part. As in various international gatherings of the time the presence of a delegation from South Africa caused difficulties, and on 5 June the expulsion of the delegation was approved by a vote of fifty-eight, thirty opposing, twenty-six abstaining and the remainder not present. One matter of debate was the official language of the Union. This was retained as French, it being, however, agreed that any linguistic group might ask for the documents of UPU sessions to be translated, provided that the group paid the cost. Institutionally the Congress renamed the ELC as the Executive Council (EC), and enlarged it. Since the 1957 Congress UPU membership had risen to one hundred and twenty-six. Accordingly seven members were added to the EC, bringing it up to twenty-seven, and its geographic distribution was altered. Five seats were allocated to the Americas, five to Western Europe, three to Eastern Europe and Northern Asia, seven to Southeast Europe, South Asia and Oceania, and seven to Africa.[182]

A major decision of the Fifteenth Congress was the alteration of the configuration of the basic documentation of the Union. Building on the work of the ELC that had been approved and encouraged by the Ottawa Congress in

---

others wanted a larger body. That, of course, lost the advantage of small group dynamics. See Codding III, 174-7.

182 The members elected to these seats were: Americas – Argentina, Canada, Mexico, Peru and the US; Western Europe – Austria, France, West Germany, Sweden and the UK; Eastern Europe and Northern Asia – Bulgaria, Hungary and the USSR; Southeast Europe, South Asia and Oceania – India, Kuwait, Malaysia, New Zealand, Syria and Turkey; Africa – Ethiopia, Madagascar, Nigeria, Senegal, Sudan, Tunisia and the United Arab Republic.

1957, Congress divided the basic documentation into four, the Constitution and its General Regulations, and the Convention and its Detailed Regulations (Const. Arts. 22.1-3).[183] The other Agreements of the Union remained as agreements between their parties (Const. Art. 22.4). The historic importance of this step is that from 1964 the basic Constitution has not formally been re-adopted, or required to be re-adopted, by later congresses. By its Art. 33 the Constitution came into effect on 1 January 1966 and remains in force indefinitely. However, amendments to the Constitution and to the documents which it authorises have been made by successive protocols and by decisions of the bodies that it established.[184] The next chapter considers the current (2011) state of the Union. It is therefore unnecessary here to rehearse the 1964 provisions in detail. Suffice it here to state that the Constitution is the basic Act of the Union, containing the organic rules under which the Union functions (Const. Art. 22.1).[185] Section I (Arts. 1-10) deals with general matters, Section II (Arts. 11-12), setting out the procedure for joining or withdrawing from the Union. Article 13.1 lists the organs of the Union as being the Congress, Administrative Conferences, the Executive Council, the Consultative Committee for Postal Studies, Special Committees and the International Bureau.[186] Of these the Executive Council, the Consultative Committee for Postal Studies and the International Bureau were designated as permanent (Const. Art. 13.2).[187] We return to these in the next chapter.

The Constitution provided for other agreements to be adopted, and for their status. The General Regulations of the UPU bind all member countries of the Union and embody provisions that ensure the application of the Constitution and

---

183 Art. 22, Constitution of the Universal Postal Union with Final Protocol and General Regulations and Final Protocol thereto, Vienna, 10 July 1964; 611 UNTS 7; 1966 UKTS 70, Cmnd. 3141; 16-2 UST 1291, TIAS 5581; 1964 UN Jur. YB 195. The UKTS version of the 1964 Constitution and General Regulations prints the French text and English translation (by the then UK General Post Office) on facing pages.

184 See Chapter 8, 'Preliminary'.

185 Although not provided for in 1964, no reservations may now be made to the Constitution: Const. Art. 22.1 as amended by Art. III.1, Seventh Additional Protocol to the Constitution of the Universal Postal Union, Bucharest, 2004. A number of declarations were made by various countries in 1964 at the time of the signature of the Constitution: see 611 UNTS 75-80.

186 Article 13.1 was amended in 1984 to eliminate reference to Administrative Conferences and to Special Committees, and Arts. 16 and 19 which related to them were deleted: Arts. II and III, Third Additional Protocol to the Constitution of the Universal Postal Union, Hamburg, 1984; 1415 UNTS 7; 1991 UKTS 81, Cm. 1748.

187 As noted *supra*, nn. 168 and 180, the Executive Council and the successor of the Consultative Committee for Postal Studies were respectively renamed the Council on Administration (CA) and the Postal Operations Council (POC) by the Seoul Congress in 1994.

the working of the Union (Const. Art. 22.2).[188] As far as particular services are concerned, the rules that operated throughout the international postal service, and the provisions on the letter post and parcel post services, were contained in Universal Postal Convention and now bind all member countries (Const. Art. 22.3).[189] The Agreements of the Union on services other than the letter and parcel post, together with their Detailed Regulations, were to apply only to those members of the Union that were parties to them, but not to UPU members that have not acceded to them (Const. Art. 22.4). By Const. Art. 22.5 the Regulations applicable to these Agreements were to be drawn up by the postal administrations of the countries concerned with each Agreement and bind these countries only, Const. Art. 22.6 allowing for the validity of the reservations that may be made in respect of the particular Agreements and their Detailed Regulations through their incorporation in any relevant Final Acts.

Subsequently the Acts of the UPU, the Constitution, the Convention, the Agreements and the Regulations both General and Detailed, have been revised by successive Protocols. In particular the legislative processes of amendment to Regulations have changed. These, and the current arrangements, are considered in the next chapter.

188 General Regulations of the Universal Postal Union, 611 UNTS 86; 1966 UKTS 70, Cmnd. 3141, 51-73; 16-2 UST 1310-31, TIAS 5581; 1964 UN Jur. YB 195. Although not so provided in 1964 no reservations may now be made to the General Regulations: Conv. Art. 22.2 as amended by Art. III.2, Seventh Additional Protocol to the Constitution of the Universal Postal Union, Bucharest, 2004. By their Art. 129 the 1964 General Regulations were to remain in force until the coming into force of the Acts of the next Congress. The current (2010) General Regulations remain in force indefinitely: see their Art. 135.

189 Universal Postal Union Convention, with Final Protocol; 16-2 UST 1328-72, and Regulations of Execution, 16-2 UST 1373-1448, with Annexes of Forms 16-2 UST 1449-1615.

Chapter 8
The Modern Universal Postal Union

Preliminary

The last chapter concluded with the Fifteenth Congress of the Universal Union held in Vienna in 1964 and the Constitution, General Regulations and Convention it adopted.[1] The 1964 reorganisation of the UPU documentation was not the end of mutation and development. The Const., Conv. and GR have undergone amendment since then at successive Congresses, as have the Agreements respecting particular services. The documentation varies.[2] Congresses have been held at Tokyo in 1969,[3] Lausanne in 1974,[4] Rio de Janeiro in 1979,[5] Hamburg in 1984,[6] Washington in

---

1 Constitution of the Universal Postal Union, with Final Protocol, General Regulations and Final Protocol thereto, Vienna, 10 July 1964; 611 UNTS 7; 1966 UKTS 70, Cmnd. 3141; 16-2 UST 1291, TIAS 5581; 1964 UN Jur. YB 195; with GR at 611 UNTS 86-99; 1966 UKTS 70 at 49-75; 16-2 UST 1310-27, TIAS 5581: UPU Convention, with Final Protocol; 16-2 UST 1328-72, and Regulations of Execution, 16-2 UST 1373-1448, with Annexes of Forms 16-2 UST 1449-1615.

2 The citations to follow give references to the UN and official state publication series of the Additional Protocols and revisions to the GR where this is known. The Additional Protocols are also available from the UPU website at http://www.upu.int/en/the-upu/acts/acts-in-force-indefinitely.html. The UNTS also contains revisions of the Postal Parcels Agreement, the Money Orders Agreement, the Giro Agreement and the Cash-on-Delivery Agreement.

3 Additional Protocol to the Constitution of the Universal Postal Union, Tokyo, 14 November 1969 (Sixteenth Congress); 810 UNTS 7, with GR at 25, Conv. at 53 and DR at 95; 1973 UKTS 72, Cmnd. 5358; 22 UST 345, TIAS 8231.

4 Second Additional Protocol to the Constitution of the Universal Postal Union, Lausanne, 5 July 1974 (Seventeenth Congress); 1005 UNTS 7, GR at 23, Conv. at 53; 1976 UKTS 56, Cmnd. 6539; 27 UST 345, TIAS 8231.

5 The General Regulations of the Universal Postal Union (Eighteenth Congress), Rio de Janeiro, 26 October 1979, 1239 UNTS 17, Conv. at 55. This Congress did not adopt any Additional Protocol amending the Constitution.

6 Third Additional Protocol to the Constitution of the Universal Postal Union, Hamburg, 27 July 1984 (Nineteenth Congress); 1415 UNTS 7, GR at 11 and Conv. at 65; 1991 UKTS 81, Cm. 1748.

1989,[7] Seoul in 1994,[8] Beijing in 1999,[9] Bucharest in 2004,[10] and Geneva in 2008 (in force 1 January 2010).[11] The next congress is scheduled for 2012.

Apart from other changes brought about by the Additional Protocols adopted by the UPU Congress, it should be noted that the location of the power to amend many UPU agreements has been altered since 1964. Thus the power to revise the Detailed Regulations (now the General Regulations (GR)) for the implementation of the Convention and the subsidiary Agreements was transferred from Congress to the Postal Operations Council (POC) by the Twenty-first Congress, Seoul, 1994, albeit that in its work the Council was to act 'bearing in mind' the decisions of Congress.[12] The Twenty-third Congress, Bucharest, 2004, resulted in the Convention now containing only fundamental or intergovernmental provisions that require to be dealt with by congresses, other matters being transferred to the Regulations.[13] The Bucharest Congress also inserted an Art. 1*bis* in the Constitution and revised Conv. Art. 1, both now comprising a list of terms and defining their meanings for UPU purposes. The Twenty-fourth Congress, Geneva, 2008, took on board the problems emergent through the privatisation of postal services together with the activities of private commercial operators engaged in postal and quasi-postal activities.[14] The Eighth Additional Protocol it adopted added to the terms in the Constitution the definition of a 'designated operator': 'any governmental or non-governmental entity officially designated by the member country to operate postal services and to fulfil the related obligations arising out of the Acts of the Union on its territory' (Art. 1.7).

Finally, what follows is mainly based on the UPU documentation as at 1 January 2010, the date at which the Eighth Additional Protocol, Geneva, 2008, and other measures of the Twenty-fourth Congress came into force. It also makes use of the Commentary by the International Bureau on the various Acts of the Union.[15]

---

7 Fourth Additional Protocol to the Constitution of the Universal Postal Union, Washington DC, 14 December 1989 (Twentieth Congress); 1687 UNTS 7, GR at 99 and Conv. at 181; 2001 UKTS 6, Cm. 5039.

8 Fifth Additional Protocol to the Constitution of the Universal Postal Union, Seoul, 14 September 1994 (Twenty-first Congress); 2001 UKTS 7, Cm. 5040.

9 Sixth Additional Protocol to the Constitution of the Universal Postal Union, Beijing, 15 September 1999 (Twenty-second Congress), 2010 UK Misc. No. 4, Cm. 7970.

10 Seventh Additional Protocol to the Constitution of the Universal Postal Union, Bucharest, 5 October 2004 (Twenty-third Congress), 2010 UK Misc. No. 5, Cm. 7969.

11 Eighth Additional Protocol to the Constitution of the Universal Postal Union, Geneva, 12 August 2008 (Twenty-fourth Congress), 2010 UK Misc. No. 3, Cm. 7968. See also the US Delegation Report, http://www.state.gov/p/io/ipp/117467.htm.

12 Art. VI.5 of the Fifth Additional Protocol, *supra*, n. 8.

13 Acts of the Twenty-third Congress of the UPU, Bucharest, 2004, *supra*, n. 10.

14 Art. I.7 of the Eighth Additional Protocol, *supra*, n. 11.

15 See the consolidated documentation published by the UPU, available through its website at http://www.upu.int/en/the-upu/acts/about-acts.html. The *Constitution, General Regulations, Resolutions and Decisions, and Legal Status of the UPU* were published

Purpose

As originally adopted the Preamble to the 1964 Constitution of the Union made a simple statement:

> With a view to developing communications between peoples by the efficient operation of the postal services, and to contributing to the attainment of the noble aims of international collaboration in the cultural, social and economic fields, the plenipotentiaries of the contracting countries have, subject to ratification, adopted this Constitution.

For many that would suffice. However the Bucharest Congress of 2004 added a mission statement:

> The mission of the Union is to stimulate the lasting development of efficient and accessible universal postal services of quality in order to facilitate communication between the inhabitants of the world by:
> – guaranteeing the free circulation of postal items over a single postal territory composed of interconnected networks;
> – encouraging the adoption of fair common standards and the use of technology;
> – ensuring cooperation and interaction among stakeholders;
> – promoting effective technical cooperation;
> – ensuring the satisfaction of customers' changing needs.[16]

Article 1 of the Constitution specifies some other elements of the UPU 'mission', Art. 1.2 speaking of the aim of the Union being the securing of the organisation, improvement of the postal service and the promotion of international collaboration, and Art. 1.3 of taking part, 'as far as possible, in postal technical assistance sought by its member countries'.

A further statement is contained in Art. 3 of the UPU Convention:

> 1. In order to support the concept of the single postal territory of the Union, member countries shall ensure that all users/customers enjoy the right to a universal postal service involving the permanent provision of quality basic postal services at all points in their territory, at affordable prices.

---

together in 2010. The Rules of Procedure were included in the previous publication of 2008. The 'Acts in four volumes' (http://www.upu.int/en/the-upu/acts/acts-in-four-volumes.html) brings together the relevant materials of the Constitution and GR on Letter Post (including the Conv.), on Parcel Post and on Postal Payment Services in the form of Manuals for each.

16 Note the reference to 'stakeholders' and to 'customers' changing needs'. 'Mission statements' were fashionable fripperies invented by bureaucrats and spin-doctors in the later Twentieth century. Their actual effect remains obscure. However, see also the 'UPU Postal Operators Statement of Values' (Recommendation C 108/199).

2. With this aim in view, member countries shall set forth, within the framework of their national postal legislation or by other customary means, the scope of the postal services offered and the requirement for quality and affordable prices, taking into account both the needs of the population and their national conditions.

3. Member countries shall ensure that the offers of postal services and quality standards will be achieved by the operators responsible for providing the universal postal service.

4. Member countries shall ensure that the universal postal service is provided on a viable basis, thus guaranteeing its sustainability.

Of this the right of all users or customers to a permanent affordable universal postal service of quality (Conv. Art. 3.1) should be noted, as should the duty on UPU members to provide such (Conv. Art. 3.2).

The Union is the specialised agency for postal matters within the UN family of specialised agencies, its relationship with the UN being set out in the Agreements annexed to the Constitution (Const. Art. 9).[17] In carrying out its functions the UPU also cooperates with other international organisations that have relevant postal interests (Const. Art. 10).[18]

Membership, Application of the UPU Acts, Withdrawal and Expulsion

Membership

Sovereign countries are the members of the UPU. The former possibility under which a non-state postal entity could be a UPU member has disappeared.[19] By Const. Art. 2 the members of the UPU are those countries which were members when the 1964 Constitution came into force on 1 January 1966 together with countries admitted under the procedures of Const. Art. 11. By Art. 11.1 all members of the UN may accede to the Union. For these a formal declaration of accession is made to the Swiss Government; intimation of this is given by that Government to the existing members and takes effect from that notification (Const. Arts. 11.3 and 5). Sovereign countries that are not UN members may apply for admission to the

17 On the negotiation with the UN see Chapter 7, 'Universal Postal Union: Twelfth Congress, Paris, 1947', at n. 153ff.

18 These contacts and arrangements are made through the Council of Administration (GR Art. 102.6.19), the Director General of the IB acting as intermediary (GR Art. 112.1.12). As to these see *infra*, 'Bodies'. See also L. Chaubert, *L'Union postale unverselle* (Berne: Lang & Cie, 1970) 68-78.

19 Postal entities are now 'designated operators'. See *infra*, 'Designated Operators', following n. 57.

Union through the Swiss Government (Const. Arts. 11.2 and 3). The application for membership has to be approved by at least two-thirds of the existing members, members which have not replied within four months to notification of the request by the Swiss Government being considered to have abstained (Const. Art. 11.4). Successful applications are notified by the Swiss Government and take effect upon that notification (Const. Art. 11.5).

As of January 2011 the UN had 192 members of which four, Andorra, the Marshall Islands, the Federated States of Micronesia and Palau, were not members of the UPU.[20] There were then 191 UPU members, of which three, the Netherlands Antilles and Aruba, the UK Overseas Territories and the Vatican, were not UN members.[21] Membership is by country: representation may alter. China became a UPU member in 1914. In April 1972 its governmental representation transferred from the Republic of China in Taipei to the People's Republic of China in Beijing in step with the change in the occupation of the 'China' seat in the UN. Palestine was granted observer status at the meetings of various UPU bodies and committees by Res. C 115/1999 of the Beijing Congress, but is not a member of the UPU. Nothing similar exists for such as the Taiwan 'Republic of China' which lost its UPU status in 1972 as indicated above, nor for states that are not widely recognised such as the 'Turkish Republic of Northern Cyprus' or Kosovo.

Membership of the Union does not preclude membership of 'restricted unions'. These are regional arrangements between groups of UPU members or their designated operators and may have a relationship with the Union including through the sending observers to UPU Congress and the two UPU Councils, the Council of Administration (CA) and the Postal Operations Council (POC) discussed *infra*. Membership of a Restricted Union by a UPU member must not result in the provision of services less favourable to users than those secured by the relevant Acts of the Union to which the member is party (Const. Art. 8.1).[22]

20 The UPU website lists these four as 'Special cases: UN members whose situation with regard to the UPU has not yet been settled'. Notwithstanding, they all possess an International Standardisation (ISO) country code, and mail services to and from them occur.

21 Aruba seceded from the Netherlands Antilles in 1996, becoming a constituent independent country within the Kingdom of the Netherlands. In October 2010 the Netherlands Antilles was dissolved, Curacao and Sint Maarten becoming, like Aruba, separate countries within the Kingdom. The other islands of the Antilles (Bonaire, Sint Eustatius and Saba) joined The Netherlands itself as separate municipalities, but without the status of 'province'. The resultant position vis-à-vis the UPU has not yet been settled.

The Charter for the Kingdom of the Netherlands regulates the political and legal relationship of the countries that form the Kingdom. It is contained in the Act of 28 October 1954, as amended. The current version, published by the Ministry of Foreign Affairs, The Hague, September 2002, is available through standard search engines.

22 See Appendix II 'Restricted Unions' for a current list, including their membership.

Application of the UPU Acts

Membership requires that the member country applies the Acts of the Union within its territory insofar as it is a party to them.[23] Any member may also at any time declare to the Director General of the IB that its acceptance of the Acts of the Union includes all, or only certain, of the territories for whose international relations it is responsible (Const. Art. 23.1-2).[24] A declaration may be withdrawn, withdrawal taking effect only one year after its date (Const. Art. 23.3). In addition, the jurisdiction of the Union and the application of relevant Acts extends to post offices set up by member countries in territories not in the Union (e.g. international areas) and territories which, from the postal point of view, are dependent on member countries (Const. Art. 3.b-c). Further, where a designated operator (q.v. *infra*) of a member country provides a service to a territory not part of the Union, it is required to provide transit services for the postal services of other members and apply the Acts of the Union (Const. Art. 4).

Withdrawal

A member country may by notice to the Director General of the IB denounce the Constitution, its withdrawal taking effect one year from the date of receipt of the denunciatory notice (Const. Art. 12.1-2). It may also denounce a declaration that it has made in respect of a territory for whose international relations it is responsible (Const. Art. 23.3). Withdrawal under Arts. 12 or 23 does not occur when the status of a member country changes, e.g. by annexation, merger or dissolution.[25] When a member withdraws it remains liable for its financial contribution for the year in which its withdrawal takes effect (GR Art. 128.7).

---

23 See *infra*, 'Acts of the Union'. Some Acts are binding on all members; others (the Agreements) only on the parties to them.

24 To avoid territorial disputes from spilling over into the UPU, Const. Art. 23.5 provides that the 'declaration' procedure does not apply to territories which have the status of a member of the Union and for whose international relations a member country is responsible. Potential examples might be certain of the UK Overseas Territories for which the UK has been responsible within the UPU since 1877, those for which France has been responsible since 1876, and those for which the USA has been responsible since 1875. See the 'General List' of UPU member countries and of territories included in the Union in the commentary in the most recent version of the Constitution and GR, available from the UPU website.

25 Perusal of the General List of member countries (*supra*, n. 24) reveals a number which were members of the Union, then dropped out because of merger etc., and have been readmitted when they re-emerged: Bosnia and Herzegovina, Croatia, Korea (Dem. Rep.), Estonia, Latvia, Lebanon, Lithuania, Serbia (twice), Slovakia, Slovenia, South Africa, Surinam and Syria.

Expulsion

There is no provision within the UPU Constitution for the expulsion of a member. However, Res. C 7 of the Nineteenth Congress, Hamburg 1984, reaffirmed the exclusion of South Africa from the Union because of its adherence to apartheid.[26] This was protested as unlawful by declarations by FDR Germany, Canada, the USA, Ireland, Switzerland, Japan, New Zealand, Australia, the Netherlands, France, Luxembourg, Portugal, Israel, Guatemala, Costa Rica, the Nordic Countries, San Marino, Belgium, the UK and Chile.[27] These countries continued to maintain postal relations with South Africa, which was readmitted to the UPU in 1994 following upon its domestic changes. I am unaware of more recent cases.

Bodies: Congress, Council of Administration (CA), Postal Operations Council (POC), International Bureau (IB), Consultative Committee

Other international organisations have 'Organs': the UPU has 'Bodies'. The Bodies of the Union are the Congress, the Council of Administration (CA), the Postal Operations Council (POC) and the International Bureau (IB) (Const. Art. 13.1). Of these the latter three are permanent bodies (Const. Art. 13.2) and are based at the seat of the Union in Berne, Switzerland (Art. 5). In addition there is a Consultative Committee which is not an official 'body', but which is nonetheless provided for in the GR. It can meet with the Councils, and makes reports to Congress. The former possibility of administrative conferences, available under Art. 16 of the 1964 Convention, was removed by the 1984 Hamburg Congress.

The Congress

The Congress is the supreme body of the Union (Const. Art. 14.1). It meets every four years[28] (GR Art. 101.1), the place and time being normally set by the previous Congress, which failing by the Council of Administration (GR Art. 101.4-5). In the event of a failure of these procedures Congress meets in Geneva, Switzerland, the IB acting as host (GR Art. 101.6). Congress elects its own Chairman, but until that is done the 'Doyen' of the Congress acts. The sole function of this individual is to open the Congress and propose the Chairman of the Congress. Nominated by

26 South Africa had been excluded from the Fifteenth Congress, Vienna,1964: *supra*, n. 1.

27 See Decls. III-XVIII, XXII-XXIII, XXV, XXVIII and XXX to the Final Acts of the Hamburg Congress, 1415 UNTS 24. Swaziland, Lesotho and Botswana reserved their position (Decls. XX, XXI and XXIV).

28 The 2004 Bucharest Congress (*supra*, n. 10) reduced the interval between congresses from five to four years.

the host country the appointment as Doyen is subject to approval by the IB and the CA (Congress, Rules, Arts. 7-8.1).

Congress consists of duly authorised representatives of all member countries (Const. Art. 14.2, GR Art. 101.2). A delegation may also represent up to one other member (GR Art. 101.2). Each member country has one vote unless it has lost its right to vote as a result of failure to meet its financial obligations (GR Art. 101.3).[29]

As the supreme body of the Union, Congress has a general power to deal with all postal questions (GR Art. 101*bis*.2). Undergirded by that nebulous 'catch-all' provision, GR Art. 101*bis*.1 details the functions of the Congress. These include: setting general policy, adopting strategy, amending the Acts of the Union, setting the dates for their entry into force, adopting its own Rules of Procedure, considering reports from the Councils and others, fixing maximum expenditures (including translation costs), and electing the members of the Council of Administration and the Postal Operations Council, and the Director General of the IB and his Deputy.[30] In all this Congress acts on the basis of proposals from members, the Council of Administration and the Postal Operations Council.[31]

The Council of Administration (CA)

By Const. Art. 17 the Council of Administration (CA) ensures the continuity of the work of the Union between Congresses, acting in the name and in the interests of the Union. It is thus the descendant of the Executive and Liaison Committee (1947-64), via the Executive Committee (1964-94), which existed in part to provide a continuing body through which relations with the UN could be arranged.[32] The main function of the CA is the oversight of the working of the Union in the period between congresses (Const. Art. 17.1). Operating under GR Arts. 102-3, the CA consists of forty-one members, of which forty are elected by Congress with due regard to geographic distribution,[33] one half being elected at each congress and no member being chosen by three successive congresses (GR Art. 102.1). The forty-

29 Cf. *infra*, 'Finance'. See also GR Art. 129.1 as to automatic suspension of voting rights.

30 A list of the Resolutions and Decisions of Congress on these and other matters is contained in Part E of the 'Constitution: General Regulations; Resolutions and decisions' which the IB publishes after each congress, and is available from the UPU and its website.

31 See *infra*, 'Legislative Procedures'.

32 For the history of its membership see the CA Guide, *infra*, n. 34, at 25-7.

33 For the purpose the world is divided into five groups: Western Hemisphere, 8 seats; Eastern Europe and Northern Asia, 5 seats; Western Europe, 6 seats; Southern Asia and Oceania, 10 seats; Africa, 11 seats. Kenya is the current Chairman, so Africa has in fact 12 seats. Cf. the regional divisions adopted by the Thirteenth Congress, Brussels, 1952, *supra*, Chapter 7 at n. 175. On the use of regional allocation of representation in international organisations see J.K. Cogan, 'Representation and Power in International Organization: The Operational Constitution and its Critics' (2009) 103 AJIL 209.

first CA member is the country hosting the Congress. That country is of right the Chairman of the CA, but, should it waive its right, it remains a member of the CA and the CA elects a Chairman from the geographical group to which it belongs (GR Art. 102.2). CA members appoint a representative who is 'competent in postal matters' (GR Art. 102.4). He or she is unpaid, but the operational expenses of the CA are borne by the Union (GR Art. 102.2). The travel and subsistence expenses of a representative are the responsibility of his sending member, but those from countries recognised as developing, or least developed, by the UN have their air or rail fares reimbursed (GR Art. 102.10). In principle the CA meets at Geneva every year (GR Art. 102.8). Its work is supervised and directed by a Council of Management consisting of its Chairman, Vice-Chairman and the Chairmen of its committees (GR Art. 102.9).

Under GR Art. 102.6 the CA has extensive responsibilities.[34] These include oversight of UPU activities, compliance with Congress decisions, studying member countries' policies, taking account of international regulatory developments including as to trade in services and competition, supervision of Union finances and financial arrangements, supervising the IB, staff regulations and staffing levels, approving reports from other UPU organs, approving contacts with member countries and other international organisations, undertaking studies and suggesting studies to be undertaken by other Union elements, and accepting and drafting proposals for amendments to the Acts.[35] The CA works through two committees ('Governance Issues' and 'Finance and Administration') and two joint committees with the Postal Operation Council (POC), these being 'Development and Cooperation' and 'Strategy' and their sub-groups. Apart from joint committees the CA also interacts with the other bodies of the Union, thus, the CA Chairman represents it in the POC (POC Rules, Art. 3.3).

The Postal Operations Council (POC)

The Postal Operations Council (POC) has existed since 1994. Under Const. Art. 18 the POC is responsible for operational, commercial, technical and economic questions concerning the postal service. It is the descendant of the Consultative Committee for Postal Studies (CCPS) and its Management Committee, first provided for under GR Arts. 104-5 as adopted by the Fifteenth Congress at Vienna in 1964.[36] Now, still governed by GR Arts. 104-5, the POC consists of forty members (GR Art. 104.1) elected by Congress with due regard to geographic

34 See *Council of Administration Practical Guide* (Berne: IB, 2009), available from the UPU website, which also contains its Rules of Procedure.

35 This is a list of examples: it is not taxative. Many CA duties and responsibilities are indicated elsewhere in this text.

36 See *Postal Operations Council Practical Guide* (Berne: IB, 2009) (available from the UPU website), with history at 46-50.

distribution, one third of the membership being elected at each Congress. Twenty-four seats are reserved for developing member countries and sixteen for developed countries (GR Art. 104.2).[37] A member country so elected nominates a representative, 'who shall have responsibilities for delivering services mentioned in the Acts of the Union' (sc. someone knowledgeable in postal matters) (GR Art. 104.3). Representatives are not paid, and their expenses are met by their sending countries, with the exception that, to encourage the participation of developing countries, representatives from countries recognised by the UN as disadvantaged[38] are reimbursed the cost of an economy air fare for attendance at POC meetings other than those held during congresses (GR Art. 104.4). In principle the POC meets every year at the UPU headquarters, the meeting being arranged by the Chairman of the CA and the Director General of the IB (GR Art. 104.7).

The POC works towards the improvement, modernisation and upgrading of postal products and services. Operational, economic and commercial aspects of the post fall within its ambit. It has a Management Committee consisting of its Chairman, Vice-Chairman and the Chairmen of the four committees through which it presently works ('Letter Post', 'Parcels', 'Postal Financial Services' and 'Standards and Technology'), each of which contain subgroups. The Management Committee prepares and directs the work of each POC meeting, and carries out other tasks the POC may decide upon (GR Art. 104.8). In addition, as indicated above, the POC is part of two joint committees with the CA ('Development and Cooperation' and 'Strategy'). Five other bodies also report directly to the POC ('Postal Security', the 'Quality of Service Fund Board of Trustees',[39] the UPU 'Clearing User Group', the 'Express Mail Service Cooperative' and the 'Telematics Cooperative'[40]). These are set up under the POC Rules of Procedure which it adopts. Bodies not reporting directly to the POC Plenary are composed of qualified experts (POC Rules, Art. 15.4). For most POC meetings the working languages are English, French, Russian and Spanish, with simultaneous translation paid for in equal proportions by the actual user groups at a meeting.[41]

---

37 For the purpose the world is divided into five groups: Western Hemisphere, Eastern Europe and Northern Asia, Western Europe, Southern Asia and Oceania and Africa. Cf. the regional divisions adopted by the Thirteenth Congress, Brussels, 1952, *supra*, Chapter XX at n. 175.

38 According to the IB Commentary on GR Art. 104.4 'disadvantaged countries' may include least developed countries, landlocked developing countries, and small island developing countries, as well as countries affected by natural disasters and conflict.

39 The Quality of Service Fund funds training courses and other endeavours directed to improvement of the quality of service offered by designated operators in developing countries. For example, one of the UPU products is a manual on addressing standards and post-codes. The Fund runs courses on the development of a post-code and addressing system. The Fund has existed since 2001. Its current mandate runs to 2016.

40 See *infra*, 'Express Mail Service Cooperative' and 'Telematics Cooperative'.

41 POC Rules, Art. 17.3. Interpretation into a language other than these groups is at the expense of those requesting it (POC Rules, Art. 17.4).

GR Art. 104.9 sets out the POC functions. Apart from conducting studies on postal matters within its remit, these include making proposals to Congress, receiving and commenting on proposals to Congress by member countries, approving such elements of the IB biennial report as are relevant to the POC, fostering cooperation and encouraging good practice and technical cooperation particularly among developing countries. Most importantly within six months after a congress it revises the Regulations to reflect the congress decisions. It also revises the Regulations when necessary in the period between congresses, as indicated below, 'Legislative procedures'.

Residing within the ambit of the POC three important bodies which require notice here are the Standards Board, the Express Mail Service Cooperative, and the Telematics Cooperative.

The Standards Board

As noted above, one POC Committee deals with standards and technologies. The Standards Board operates under it.[42] Membership of this Board is voluntary and open to postal administrations interested in such matters. Members appoint as their representatives experts qualified in international postal operations and in information technology. In addition non-members and various non-UPU organisations and entities, including industry, may ask to send observers. Within the UPU strategic planning the Board develops standards that improve the efficiency and quality of the postal service (including in telematics) by way of common standards. These standards are, however, advisory not compulsory. Standards are developed by eight working groups which report to the Board. Topics range from code allocation to postal metering. The Board also interacts with the European Committee for Standardisation (CEN) and the International Organisation for Standardisation (ISO) in matters of common interest. Standards are issued in draft, and if proved useful and stable, acquire approved status.

Express Mail Service Cooperative (EMS Cooperative)

Created in 1998 the Express Mail Service Cooperative operates under the aegis of the POC.[43] As of 1 May 2009 it had 154 members rising to 162 in November 2010 (some 74% of EMS operators).[44] Its function is to facilitate the express mail service throughout the UPU service area and operates through six regional

42 A list of UPU standards from which their range can be appreciated is in *General information on UPU standards* (Berne, 2007), and data via http://www.upu.int/en/activities/standards/upu-technical-standards.html, including the *UPU Technical Standards, version history*.

43 See http://www.ems.coop/.

44 See POC Guide, *supra*, n. 36, 27-8, and currently http://www.ems.coop/members-ems-cooperative.

divisions.[45] It audits and measures the international EMS performance of both members and non-members, advises on strategies for improvement of the service, and, through workshops, provides training for postal operators introducing the service as well as for existing providers. Its Manual provides detailed information on the working of the service.

Telematics Cooperative (T Coop)

The Telematics Cooperative is a strange animal.[46] As such it represents a sterling engagement with the possibilities that have emerged through the development of the world of electrical communications. Based on resolutions of the Seoul and Beijing Congresses, T Coop operates within UPU structures, but does not have a legal structure of its own, nor is it a cooperative company within the norms of private law. The Cooperative is divided into three user groups, the 'Advanced Electronic Services User Group' (AESUG), the 'International Financial Services User Group' (IFSUG) and the 'International Mail Services User Group' (IMSUG). Not all members of the Cooperative are members of all these groups. Its members are postal operators, whether public, semi-public or private. Membership is voluntary provided that national law permits membership. As of 1 May 2009 it had one hundred and twenty-eight members.[47] Members choose a membership class, which carries with it weighted voting rights, although if possible decisions are made by consensus.

The function of the T Coop is to improve the quality of postal services through the use of new communication systems and technologies. It seeks to establish a common electronic infrastructure and implementation systems for its members, including information exchange, secure electronic payments and e-commerce between members and their customers. Operating on a non-profit and cost-sharing basis to achieve economies of scale, the T Coop seeks to involve its members in providing high quality service, optimal organisation, and cooperation in the interest of postal customers. In so doing it vests responsibility in the Postal Technology Centre of the IB.

The T Coop has a Supervisory Body, a General Assembly and a Cooperative Management Board to direct its work. Three special user groups work within T Coop, the 'International Mail Services User Group' (IMS), the 'International Financial Services User Group' (IFS) and the 'Advanced Electronic Services User Group' (AES). Its working languages are English and French.

45 See http://www.ems.coop/operators. Access to its statutes at http://www.ems.coop/ems-cooperative-statutes was denied.

46 For detail see: Statutes and Principles of Operation of the Telematics Cooperative, as approved by the [POC] General Assembly on 4 August 2008, available via the UPU website at http://www.ptc.upu.int/tc/over.shtml.

47 See POC Guide, *supra*, n. 36, 29-30.

The International Bureau (IB)

Recognising the need of the new organisation for a central body to deliver secretarial services, an International Office was established by Art. XV of the very first UPU treaty, that of 1874.[48] Its name was changed to 'International Bureau' by the 1878 Convention, and over the decades its role increased in proportion as that of the Union developed. Until 1972 the IB was overseen by the Swiss government but now is supervised by the CA (Const. Art. 20). Since the Seoul Congress of 1994 the working languages of the IB have been English and French (GR Art.109).

The functioning of the IB is provided for by Const. Arts. 13 and 20, and GR Arts. 111-121. It is 'an organ of execution, support, liaison, information and consultation' (Const. Art. 20). Its importance can be seen by the number of provisions throughout the Acts and Regulations which require processes involving the Bureau or its Director General.

Given the crucial roles of the IB, the selection and appointment of its senior officers are important. The IB Director General and Deputy Director General are elected by Congress by secret ballot and are re-electable to office only once (GR Art. 111.1).[49] Members transmit applications by their nationals for election (together with a curriculum vitae) to the IB at least seven months before each Congress, and these are circulated by the IB to members at least two months prior to the Congress (GR Art. 111.2). Should the post of Director General fall vacant the Deputy takes over to the end of the term of office of the Director, and is (should he so wish) eligible for election as Director thereafter unless he has already been re-elected once as Deputy (GR Art. 111.3). Should both posts fall simultaneously vacant the CA elects a Deputy Director General for the period up to the next Congress on the basis of the applications for the previous elections (GR Art. 111.4). Should the post of Deputy fall vacant, on the proposal of the Director the CA instructs a senior IB official to act until the next Congress.

In broad a distinction may be drawn between the duties of the Director General and those of the IB. Both sets of duties bridge the Constitution and GR and are added to by responsibilities contained in the Letter Post, Parcel Post and the Postal Payment Services Regulations.

---

48 See Art. XV, General Postal Union: Treaty between Great Britain, Austria-Hungary, Belgium, Denmark, Egypt, France, Germany, Greece, Italy, Luxemburg, the Netherlands, Norway, Portugal, Roumania, Russia, Servia, Spain, Sweden, Switzerland, Turkey and the United States relative to the formation of a General Postal Union, Berne, October 9 1874, 147 CTS 136; 65 BFSP 13 (in French); 1 Bevans 29; Art. XXVII, Detailed Regulations for the execution of the Treaty … relative to the formation of a General Postal Union, Berne, October 9 1874, 147 CTS 136; 65 BFSP 23 (in French); (US) 19 Stat. 592.

49 The Deputy Director General assists the Director General and is responsible to him. When the Director is absent or unable to act the Deputy exercises his functions (GR Art. 113).

GR Art. 112.1 sets out the responsibilities of the Director General as to staff appointments to the IB. Posts may be filled by promotion from within the Bureau, or from outside, in which case vacancies for the more senior posts are notified to member countries. The 'paramount consideration' is the efficiency of the Bureau.[50] The professional qualifications of those recommended by member countries are important, but, subsidiary to merit, regard is also to be had to an equitable representation with respect to continents, geography and languages. The most senior posts should be filled by persons from different regions and from regions other than those from which the Director General and Deputy Director General originate unless they are filled by promotion from lower grades. Where a post requires special qualifications the Director General may seek applications from outside (GR 112.1).

The Constitution, the GRs and the other UPU Acts and Agreements place many duties on the Director General. The IB Commentary on the UPU Acts contains a thirty-five paragraph summary list. In broad the Director directs the IB in its work (Art. 20), organises and administers it, and is its legal representative (GR Art. 112.1). More particular duties range from acting as Secretary General of Congress and its meetings, including taking part in debates (GR Arts. 12.1-2), to acting in the admission process of members (Const. Art. 11.3 and 5) and their withdrawals (Const. Art. 12.1). The Director has duties in the approval of the Acts by members (Const. Art. 26), in accession to Agreements (Const. Art. 27.2), and acts as depositary for the UPU Acts (GR Arts. 112.2.1 and 135). He ensures the representation of the Union (GR Art. 112.11), and acts as its intermediary with the Restricted Unions, with the UN, with other international organisations and with associations and enterprises with which the CA and POC may wish to interact (GR Art. 112.2.12). He notifies members and their designated operators of alterations to or revisions of the Agreements drawn up by the POC (GR Art 112.2.3). On the basis of reports from the Councils he prepares for the approval of the CA the draft strategy to be submitted to each Congress together with a report on the working of the strategy adopted by the previous Congress (GR Art. 112.2.9-10). He drafts the annual budget at the lowest possible level congruent with UPU requirements for submission to the CA and, when it is approved, communicates it to members (GR Art. 112.2.4). He is responsible for executing the activities requested by the Councils and acts to achieve the objectives set by the bodies of the Union within established policy and the funds available (GR Art. 112.25-6). After each Congress he submits to the POC proposals for changes to the Agreements necessitated by decisions of that Congress (GR Art. 112.2.8), and in due course notifies to members all alterations to the Acts of the Union (GR Art. 126.1).

A separate forty-three paragraph list, also in the IB Commentary to the Acts, sets out the IB duties that implement its role within the UPU as 'an organ of execution, support, liaison, information and consultation' (Const. Art. 20). These

---

50 In making appointments the Director is also subject to the Staff Regulations, and for finance related posts to the Financial Regulations adopted by the CA.

range from correcting clerical errors in minutes (GR Arts. 24.6 and 26.2-3), to preparing biennial reports on the work of the Union (GR Arts. 102.6.17-18). It consults as to the venue and dates of congresses (GR Arts. 101.5, 7-8) and, where Congress has to be held in Geneva, it acts as the host (GR Art. 101.6). It provides secretariat functions for congresses, councils and committees (Const. Arts. 14, 15, 17 and 18; GR Arts. 12.3-4 and 114) including, under a number of other GR articles, the dissemination of proposals submitted to the various committees and councils and of reactions to them. It circulates documentation and publishes information on matters of interest to members, to postal administrations, and to designated operators (GR Art. 116.2). It publishes *Union Postale*, a quarterly periodical available in Arabic, Chinese, English, French, German, Russian and Spanish (GR Art. 120). The IB collates the views of members on particular questions, the results being, however, not binding on members though they may be of practical help to them in both the international and national services (GR Art. 116.3). It may give an opinion on a matter disputed between parties or their designated operators at the request of interested parties (Art. 116.2). In arbitrations it may be asked to appoint an arbiter (GR Art. 132.2), and may itself act as a single arbitrator (GR Art. 132.3).[51] It can act as a clearing house in the settlement of accounts of all kinds relating to the postal service (GR Art. 116.4). It develops measures of technical assistance (Const. Art. 1.3, GR Art. 117) and manufactures International Reply Coupons and supplies them at cost to member countries or designated operators that order them (GR Art. 118). It checks that the terms of the Restricted Unions and special agreements do not include conditions less favourable to postal customers than those available under the UPU Acts (GR Art. 119.2).

The Consultative Committee

The Consultative Committee was an innovation of the Bucharest Congress of 2004. Set up in terms of GR Art. 106 it gives an opportunity for non-governmental agencies to contribute to UPU deliberations, perhaps providing insight into problems and introducing wider considerations than might occur to member countries.[52] It is a hybrid, having both state and non-state members. Eight member countries are designated by the CA (CA Rules, Art. 5.1) and the POC (POC Rules, Art. 5.1) (GR Art. 106.1). Non-governmental members apply for membership and are accepted through a process set up by the CA (GR Art. 102.6.32). The current members (nineteen in 2010) represent customers, other users of the postal service, philately, and suppliers of goods and services to postal operations. Only organisations that are registered in a member country may join and they appoint their own representatives (GR Art. 106.2). Individual companies, postal operators and regulators are ineligible for membership. Members of the Committee have

51 See *infra*, 'Interpretation, Argument and Dispute'.

52 See CA Guide, *supra*, n. 34, 9, and POC Guide, *supra*, n. 36, 24.

observer status at the UPU Congress and its Committees (Congress Rules, Art. 5.1). It reports annually to the CA and POC and this report goes also to members, their designated operators and to the Restricted Unions (GR Art. 107.2). In addition it makes a detailed report to Congress which is circulated to members and designated operators at least two months before the Congress opens (GR 107.3).

The Acts of the Union

The Acts of the Union are the Constitution, the General Regulations, the Convention, and the Agreements on particular services together with their Regulations (Const. Art. 22). The Constitution of the Universal Postal Union is the basic Act of the Union, and contains the organic rules of the Union (Const. Art. 22.1). The GR deal with the application of the Constitution and the working of the Union (Const. Art. 22.2).[53] Both bind all member countries, and no reservation is permitted to either (Const. Art. 22.1 and 2). They are in force indefinitely, although they may be amended by decision of the UPU Congress.[54] Beyond these, letter and parcel post are regulated by the Universal Postal Convention and the Letter Post Regulations (RL) and Parcel Post Regulations (RC) which implement its terms.[55] These, particularly the Conv., have undergone considerable change through the years. The Conv., RL and RC also bind all UPU member countries, and members are bound to ensure that their designated operators (*infra*) observe their provisions, their detail, however, being subject to any exemptions articulated in their Final Acts (Const. Art. 22.3).[56] Finally there may be Agreements with related Regulations other than for the letter and parcel post. These bind only the UPU members that are parties to them (Const. Art. 22.4). Regulations are adopted by the Postal Operations Council (Const. Art. 22.5). Reservations to the Agreements are set out in their Final Acts (Const. Art. 22.6). Reservations to the Regulations are incorporated in the Regulations themselves.[57]

53 Until the coming into force of the Sixth Additional Protocol agreed at the Beijing Congress of 1999 (*supra*, n. 9) the General Regulations were known as the 'Detailed Regulations'.

54 For the Protocols amending the Constitution (and other legislation) see *supra*, 'Preliminary'.

55 For the current Universal Postal Convention see *Decisions of the 24th Congress - 2008* (Berne: IB, 2009) at 145.

56 The Universal Postal Convention and the Letter Post and Parcel Post Regulations were substantially revised in Beijing in 1999 (*supra*, n. 9). Between 1964 and 1999 the Convention dealt only with letter post and was supplemented by the Letter Post Regulations. In 1999 the Convention was revised in some details, the Parcel Post was brought within its scope, and the Parcel Post Regulations adopted for that service. International letters and parcels are therefore now dealt with through inter-linked rules and procedures.

57 See *infra*, 'Reservations'.

Designated Operators

The obligations imposed by the Acts of the Union apply throughout the territories of the members of the Union to those agencies designated to provide the relevant postal service. As indicated above, sovereign countries are members of the Union. However, in recent years the postal services of many countries are no longer exclusively provided by a government department. The concept of a 'designated operator' has been therefore introduced to replace the terms 'postal administration' or 'member country' in appropriate instances throughout the UPU documentation.[58] Const. Art. 1*bis* defines a 'designated operator' as: 'any governmental or non-governmental entity officially designated by the member country to operate postal services and to fulfil the related obligations arising out of the Acts of the Union on its territory'. Thereafter, for example, Const. Art. 22.3 requires that compliance with the Convention and the Letter Post and the Parcel Post Regulations is imposed by member countries on their 'designated operators'.

Legislative Procedures

The legislative procedures of the UPU are in essence simple, but contain a complex set of time limits. This provides opportunity for member countries and their designated operators to consider proposed changes and, where necessary, for them to comment and, in the case of the Regulations, to try to secure opt-outs from particular provisions. This is sensible since it allows account to be taken of the fact that designated operators provide particular services within the territories of members and national legislation and conditions may have to be considered.

The procedures for the amendment of the Acts of the Union depend upon the instrument that is being considered.[59] There is a difference between changes to Acts and changes to the Regulations. Const. Art. 29 and GR Arts. 122-7 deal with the matter. Every member country has the right to propose amendments to Acts to which it is a party for consideration either at the UPU Congress or between congresses (Const. Art. 29.1). Proposals for the amendment of the Constitution or the GR may be made only to Congress, and can be adopted only by it (Const. Art. 29.2).[60] The amendment of the Regulations of the other Agreements is carried out through the Postal Operations Council (POC) (*supra*). There are rules as to the making of proposals which, in various ways, allow member countries to

58 These changes were made by the Seoul Congress in 2008: *supra*, n. 10. There seems to be no reason why a country may not designate several entities as operators within its territory.

59 What follows does not apply to the amendment of the Rules of Procedure of Congress (GR Art. 122.5).

60 Until the revisions of 1964 the UPU Convention could be amended between congresses if all members approved.

consider, reflect on and, should they so wish, comment on proposals. Subject to the following paragraph, it is virtually impossible for a proposal to be made at a Congress itself. All proposals considered by Congress are routed through the IB, and communicated by it to member countries provided that they meet the requirements of GR Arts. 122-5.

Proposals for the amendment of the Constitution or the GR must be received by the IB at least six months before a Congress. After that deadline such proposals are considered by Congress only if a two-thirds majority of countries present at the Congress so decide and the general rules as to proposals are otherwise complied with (GR Art. 122.2).

The general rules for proposals to Congress are: that normally proposals have only one aim, and that aim justifies any suggested changes to the wording of the relevant Act (GR Art. 122.3). Where a proposal has financial implications for the Union as a whole it must be accompanied by a statement as to these implications, worked out in consultation with the IB (GR Art. 122.3). Where a proposal for the amendment of Acts other than the Const. and GRs is to be considered by Congress the proposal must be communicated to the IB (GR 122.1). A proposal which relates only to a verbal amendment cannot be considered if it is received by the IB less than six months before a Congress (GR Art. 122.1.b). A proposal for a substantive amendment made more than six months before the Congress will be accepted by the Bureau for processing (GR Art. 122.1.a), but there is a cut-off for substantive proposals that are sent in late. No substantive proposals that arrive less than two months before the Congress are accepted (GR Art. 122.1.d). In the period between six and four months before the Congress a substantive proposal must be supported by at least two member countries if it is to be accepted by the IB process (GR Art. 122.1.c). Between four and two months prior to the Congress a substantive proposal requires the support of at least eight member countries (GR Art. 122.1.d). Declarations of support by member countries for either of these classes of 'late' proposal must arrive within the relevant time limit. Where an amendment is proposed, and the rules as to its making have been complied with, it is the duty of the IB to circulate its detail to member countries and their designated operators (GR Art. 114).

The Regulations (i.e. the Letter Post and the Postal Parcel Regulations supplementing the Convention and those elaborating the Postal Payment Agreement) are now dealt with by the Postal Operations Council (POC) not the UPU Congress (Const. Art. 22.5 and GR Art. 123.1). This change was made consequential on the separation of the intergovernmental provisions of the UPU Acts and the provisions affecting the services provided by the postal operators. The result is that the postal Regulations and their amendments are not subject to formal ratification by member countries. A difference is made between proposals that surround a Congress, and proposals made between congresses. The POC may initiate change to Regulations on the basis of the decision of a Congress, or on the proposal of a POC member. Proposals consequential on (or reacting to) a proposed change to the Conv. or the Postal Payment Services Agreement, must be proposed simultaneously with the proposal of the change to Congress, and are circulated one month prior to the Congress (GR Art. 123.2). Proposals to amend the Regulations alone which are to be considered by the POC in its preparation of new Regulations in the six months after Congress must be submitted at least two months prior to the Congress (GR Art. 123.3). Finally, where the POC is to draft new Regulations arising out of the decisions of Congress, proposals may be made by member countries up to two months before the opening of the POC session and are circulated to member countries and their designated operators not later than one month before the session (GR Art. 123.4). Proposals are now made direct to the POC, the IB having the duty to transmit them to other member countries and their designated operators (Art. 29.3). This allows time for comment on the matter, and on occasion a member country may successfully make a reservation to their terms.[61]

Reservations

Not all multilateral agreements permit reservations to their substantive provisions.[62] In the UPU no reservation may be made to the Constitution or to the GR (Const. Arts. 1*bis*.8 and 22.1 and 2).[63] Reservations to the other Acts of the Union are competent (Const. Arts. 1*bis*.8 and 22.3-6).

UPU rules define what can be done by way of reservation. Within the Union they provide a mechanism through which global rules can be more precisely tailored to local sensitivities although, as we will see, reservations are not effective unilaterally but require acceptance by other member countries. Const. Art. 1*bis*.8, inserted by the Bucharest Congress in 2004, defines a reservation as:

> an exemption clause whereby a member country purports to exclude or to modify the legal effect of a clause of an Act other than the Constitution and the General Regulations, in its application to that member country. Any reservation shall be compatible with the object and purpose of the Union as defined in the preamble and article 1 of the Constitution. It must be duly justified and approved by the majority required for approval of the Act concerned, and inserted in the Final Protocol thereto.

61 See *infra*, 'Reservations'.

62 Thus by Art. 309 of the Convention on the Law of the Sea, Montego Bay, 1984 (1833 UNTS 3; (1999) UKTS 81, Cm. 4524; (1982) 21 ILM 1261) no reservations and exceptions are allowed unless expressly permitted by specific articles of the Convention.

For the general rules as to reservations to multilateral treaties see Art. 2.1.d, and Arts. 19-23 of the Convention on the Law of Treaties, Vienna, 1969, 1155 UNTS 155; 1980 UKTS 58, Cmnd. 7964; 8 ILM 679; [1969] 63 AJIL 875. See also M.H. Mendelson, 'Reservations to the Constitutions of International Organizations' (1971) 45 BYIL 137.

63 Cf. the equivalent provisions of the ITU, *supra*, Chapter 5, 'Declarations and Reservations'.

As a result reservations really operate on a basis of reciprocity. A reservation may be withdrawn by its maker at any time by notice to the IB, and its withdrawal takes effect immediately.

The Bucharest Congress, 2004, adopted the procedure by which effectual reservations are now made. The effect is that no reservation can be sprung by a member on a Congress or other UPU legislative body at the time of the signing of Final Acts, or of the adoption of a new regulative provision. Instead members are given sufficient notice to allow them to consider whether to approve the proposed reservation in terms of Const. Art. 1.8. By Art. 28 of the Rules of Procedure of Congresses any reservation to Acts must be submitted as a proposal to the IB as soon as possible after the proposal of the article to which the reservation refers (Congress Rules Art. 28.1). The proposed reservation must be submitted before a deadline set by the Bureau, and any failure to do so results in the proposed reservation not being considered either by the Bureau or the relevant Congress (Congress Rules Art. 28. 2-3).

Parallel provision is made for reservations to Regulations being considered by the POC by Art. 14 of the POC Rules of Procedure.[64] For Regulations the matter is initiated by the making of a proposal. The proposal is considered by the POC in plenary meeting (POC Rules of Procedure, Art. 14.7). Reservations to measures adopted by the POC are allowed by majority vote in the POC (POC Rules, Art. 14.8). There is, however, the possibility that a reservation may be requested by a UPU member which is not a POC member. In that instance the proposal is considered by the POC at its meeting next after the final adoption of the Regulations concerned. If that meeting is held after the date of the coming into force of the new measures the POC Management Committee may adopt the proposed reservation on a provisional basis (POC Rules, Art. 14.5). Existing reservations to provisions of the Regulations carry over without the need for their re-submission unless waived by the 'beneficiary country' (POC Rules, Art. 14.6). Reservations are published in the UPU Manuals on the Agreements. Thus, Art. 5 of the Convention deals with the ownership of postal items and their withdrawal from the post (Conv. Arts. 5.1-2), the alteration or correction of address, redirection and return to sender of undeliverable items (Conv. Art. 5.3). Art. 1 of the Final Protocol to the Convention contains the reservations of a large number of countries to these provisions.[65] These are reprinted in the relevant Manuals. Again Conv. Art. 15

64 The POC Rules are available in the POC Guide, *supra*, n. 36.

65 Cf. UPU Conv. Final Protocol, Art. I.1: 'The provisions in article 5.1 and 2 shall not apply to Antigua and Barbuda, Bahrain, Barbados, Belize, Botswana, Brunei Darussalam, Canada, Hong Kong, China, Dominica, Egypt, Fiji, Gambia, United Kingdom of Great Britain and Ireland, Overseas Dependent Territories of the United Kingdom, Grenada, Guyana, Ireland, Jamaica, Kenya, Kiribati, Kuwait, Lesotho, Malawi, Malaysia, Mauritius, Nauru, New Zealand, Nigeria, Papua New Guinea, Saint Christopher and Nevis, Saint Lucia, Saint Vincent and the Grenadines, Samoa, Seychelles, Sierra Leone, Singapore, Solomon Islands, Swaziland, Tanzania (United Rep.), Trinidad and Tobago,

deals with articles prohibited from the letter post, and the Final Protocol contains a number of reservations to its provisions, usually adding to them.[66] Thus Conv. Final Protocol Art. VII reads:

> 1. Exceptionally, Dem. People's Rep. of Korea and Lebanon shall not accept registered items containing coins, bank notes, securities of any kind payable to bearer, travellers' cheques, platinum, gold or silver whether manufactured or not, precious stones, jewels or other valuable articles. They shall not be strictly bound by the provisions of the Letter Post Regulations with regard to their liability in cases of theft or damage, or where items containing articles made of glass or fragile articles are concerned.
>
> 2. Exceptionally, Bolivia, China (People's Rep.), excluding Hong Kong Special Administrative Region, Iraq, Nepal, Pakistan, Saudi Arabia, Sudan and Viet Nam shall not accept registered items containing coins, bank notes, currency notes or securities of any kind payable to bearer, travellers' cheques, platinum, gold or silver whether manufactured or not, precious stones, jewels or other valuable articles.
>
> 3. Myanmar reserves the right not to accept insured items containing the valuable articles listed in article 15.6, as this is contrary to its internal regulations.
>
> 4. Nepal does not accept registered items or insured items containing currency notes or coins, except by special agreement to that effect.
>
> 5. Uzbekistan does not accept registered or insured items containing coins, bank notes, cheques, postage stamps or foreign currency and shall accept no liability in cases of loss of or damage to such items.
>
> 6. Iran (Islamic Rep.) does not accept items containing articles contrary to the principles of the Islamic religion.
>
> 7. The Philippines reserves the right not to accept any kind of letter post (ordinary, registered or insured) containing coins, currency notes or securities of any kind payable to bearer, travellers' cheques, platinum, gold or silver, whether manufactured or not, precious stones or other valuable articles.
>
> 8. Australia does not accept postal items of any kind containing bullion or bank notes. In addition, it does not accept registered items for delivery in Australia,

Tuvalu, Uganda, Vanuatu and Zambia.' A number of other reservations to Conv. Art. 5 are set out in the other sections of Final Protocol Art. I, and its Arts. II-XV contain reservations to yet other parts of the Convention.

66 Reference point n. 88 *infra*.

or items in transit à découvert, containing valuables such as jewelry, precious metals, precious or semi-precious stones, securities, coins or any form of negotiable financial instrument. It declines all liability for items posted which are not in compliance with this reservation.

9. China (People's Rep.), excluding Hong Kong Special Administrative Region, shall not accept insured items containing coins, bank notes, currency notes or securities of any kind payable to bearer and travellers' cheques in accordance with its internal regulations.

10. Latvia and Mongolia reserve the right not to accept, in accordance with their national legislation, ordinary, registered or insured mail containing coins, bank notes, securities payable to bearer and travellers' cheques.

11. Brazil reserves the right not to accept ordinary, registered or insured mail containing coins, bank notes in circulation or securities of any kind payable to bearer.

12. Viet Nam reserves the right not to accept letters containing articles or goods.

13. Indonesia does not accept registered or insured items containing coins, bank notes, cheques, postage stamps, foreign currency, or any kind of securities payable to bearer for delivery in Indonesia, and shall accept no liability in cases of loss of or damage to such items.

14. Kyrgyzstan reserves the right not to accept letter-post items (ordinary, registered, insured, small packets) containing coins, currency notes or securities of any kind payable to bearer, travellers' cheques, platinum, gold or silver, whether manufactured or not, precious stones, jewels or other valuable articles, and shall accept no liability in cases of loss of or damage to such items.

15. Kazakhstan shall not accept registered or insured items containing coins, banknotes, credit notes or any securities payable to bearer, cheques, precious metals whether manufactured or not, precious stones, jewels and other valuable articles or foreign currency, and shall accept no liability in cases of loss of or damage to such items.

16. Moldova and the Russian Federation do not accept registered or insured items containing bank notes in circulation, securities (cheques) of any kind payable to bearer or foreign currency, and shall accept no liability in cases of loss of or damage to such items.

Most reservations to Regulations are shorter. But each is an important modification to the international service in respect of the matter with which they deal and operates as accepted by other parties. For that reason they are incorporated into the Final Protocol of the Regulations concerned and appear in the relevant Manual.

Declarations

Declarations are competent in the sense that they are not forbidden. Declarations are reactions and statements which reflect political considerations or the relationship of their makers with others. Within the Union they are without legal effect, and therefore may be made at any time.[67] For example, the Final Protocol to the Vienna Acts of 1964 contains a statement by Poland that it was 'inadmissible' to use the definition 'Germany' in an official list in relation to the Federal Republic of Germany because the Federal Republic had no right to represent the whole of Germany, or 'Viet-Nam' in relation to the South Viet-Nam government or 'China' in relation to the 'Chiang Kai-shek group' (sc. Taiwan). Most recently the Declarations made on the signing of the Acts of the Twenty-fourth Congress in Geneva, 2008,[68] include objections to obligations relating to Israel or any implication of its recognition, which was countered by Israel,[69] by Argentina in respect of the Malvinas (Falklands), South Georgia, the South Sandwich Islands and the Argentine Antarctic Sector, countered by the United Kingdom,[70] by Turkey in respect of the 'Republic of Cyprus' (Southern Cyprus), countered by the Republic of Cyprus,[71] and by Azerbaijan in respect of Nagorno Karabakh.[72] Other declarations related to considerations of mutuality and internal municipal law, although that last would seem to be covered by Const. Art. 24. UPU Declarations are redolent of the similar Declarations within the ITU processes.[73]

Languages

In a diverse institution such as the UPU where members interact regularly *inter se* and with the bodies of the Union, the language of discourse and communication is important. One might, therefore, have expected there to be a number of 'official languages'. However, the sole official language of the Union remains French (Const. Art. 6). Notwithstanding, over the years additional arrangements

---

67 See IB Commentary on Art. 22.6, at p. A.21 of the 2010 version of the Constitution and GR. For the declarations made at the 1964 Vienna conference see 611 UNTS 75ff.

68 These are available in UK 2010 Misc. No. 3, Cm.7968.

69 Declaration I, by Syria, and Declaration IV by 'a group of countries' (Bahrein, Iran, Iraq, Libya, Lebanon, Pakistan, Saudi Arabia, Tunisia, United Arab Emirates and the Yemen). Declaration XVI, by Israel.

70 Declaration II, by Argentina. Declaration XVIII, by the UK.

71 Declaration XV, by Turkey. Declaration XIX, by the Republic of Cyprus.

72 Declaration XVII, by Azerbaijan.

73 See Chapter 5 at n. 27ff.

have been sanctioned. Thus the Seoul Congress of 1994 added English to French as the working languages of the IB (GR Art. 109).[74] Additional possibilities depend on the nature of the occasion, and special arrangements may be made. UPU documentation is normally in French, English, Arabic and Spanish, but Chinese, German, Portuguese and Russian versions of the most important basic documentation may be produced,[75] and as noted *Union Postale* is produced in Arabic, Chinese, English, French, German, Russian and Spanish editions (GR Art. 120). Other languages may also be used for particular documents provided that member countries that request this service bear all the costs involved (GR Art. 110.2). For these purposes countries form language groups (GR Art. 110.2).[76] The IB publishes documents simultaneously in the different languages that may have been requested in addition to the standard languages (GR Arts. 3-4). The rules as to the verbal use of language are different. At discussions and meetings French, English, Spanish and Russian (with simultaneous translation) are admissible and as judged necessary by the IB Director General and the member countries that may be involved (GR Art. 110.9). Other languages are also admissible provided that the delegations concerned arrange and pay for simultaneous translation (GR Art. 110.10-11).[77] Finally the rules as to correspondence are different yet again. Members and their designated operators corresponding with the IB, and the IB with outside entities, may communicate in any language with which the IB can cope (GR Art. 110.5). Official correspondence between member countries and/ or designated operators may be in a language agreed between them, which failing French is to be used (GR Art. 110.13).

Finance

Since the Bucharest Congress of 2004 the UPU has operated a two-year budget cycle, this intercalating with the four-year Congress cycle. The expenditures of the Union are set by Congress though there is an ability to exceed maxima if

74 Fifth Additional Protocol, *supra*, n. 8. The costs of translation from French to English or *vice versa* are uniform and are borne by the French and the English language group.

75 Congress sets a maximum for the cost of production of documents in Chinese, German, Portuguese and Russian (GR Art. 110.6).

76 There are seven basic language groups: Arabic, Chinese, English, German, Portuguese, Russian and Spanish. Language groups divide the costs payable amongst themselves either by agreement or in proportion to their contribution to the expenses of the Union (GR Art. 110.7).

77 Again language groups divide the cost of interpretation amongst themselves either by agreement or in proportion to their contribution to the expenses of the Union, such payment being subject to the sanctions applicable to normal contributions: see *infra*, 'Finance'. However the UPU covers the cost of installing and maintaining the technical equipment (GR Art. 110.12).

circumstances so require (Const. Art. 21.1-2).[78] A Reserve Fund is operated (GR Art. 128.14) and it is possible for the Swiss government to provide short-term advances (GR Art. 128.15). Ordinarily expenditures are met by each member's selection of a contributory class (Art. 21.3-4) paid annually in advance (GR Art. 128.8). The highest contributory class is the fifty unit class, the list of selectable classes dropping by five units down to the five unit class. Below that are classes of three, one, and a half unit class, the last being reserved for least advanced countries as listed by the UN or designated by the CA (GR Art. 130.1). The class selected by a member continues until it varies it (GR Art. 130.4 *ad fin*). A country may notify its intention to contribute more than the class it has selected, either temporarily for the period between congresses, or permanently (GR Art. 130.2).[79] A member country may also reduce its contribution by a curious procedure, subject to the limit that a member may not insist on being lowered more than one class at a time (GR Art. 130.5). To accomplish a reduction, at least two months before a Congress it must send a request to the IB that it be placed in a lower contributory class. Congress adopts a non-binding opinion on the request. The member is thereafter free to decide whether to follow that opinion and, presumably, may elect that lower class even in the face of the contrary opinion of Congress (GR Art. 130.4). A member acceding to or withdrawing from the Union remains liable for its contribution for the year in which the accession or withdrawal occurs (GR Art. 128.7). Members falling more than two years in arrears may enter into arrangements with the CA to cope with the situation, including the transfer to the Union of credits due to it from other member countries (GR Art. 128.8-13). Interest is payable on contributions paid more than four months late (GR Art. 128.8), but the CA may mitigate or release that sanction if the full capital amount of arrears is paid (GR Art. 128.12-3). Ultimately, however, a member may lose its right to vote in Congress, and any membership of the Councils or voting rights therein which it may have, if measures cannot be agreed and complied with (GR 101 and 129.1-2).

Services – General

Const. Art. 1*bis* defines the postal service: 'all postal services, whose scope is determined by the bodies of the Union. The main obligations of postal services are to satisfy certain social and economic needs of member countries, by ensuring the collection, sorting, transmission and delivery of postal items'. Simply put the purpose of the UPU is the efficient operation of the international postal service. Conv. Arts. 12 and 13 set out respectively the 'basic services' and the 'supplementary

78 In the 2008 revision GR Art. 128.1 set the limit for 2009 and 2010 at 37,000,000 Swiss francs, and 37,235,000 Swiss francs for 2011 and 2012 with that limit persisting until the next congress.

79 Such additional contributions increase monies available for UPU expenditures, but do not lessen the contribution levels of other members (GR Art. 130.2 *ad fin*).

services' that are required of Members and their designated operators in dealing with letter post and postal parcels. Despite the formulation, compliance with much of both Articles is compulsory. Conv. Art. 12 deals with the letter and parcel post,[80] while Conv. Art. 13.1 sets out the mandatory provision of the registered post. Conv. Art. 13.3 covers insurance, recorded delivery, cash-on-delivery and express delivery services, these being optional as between operators that agree to provide them, and Conv. Art. 13.4 deals with services that have both mandatory and optional elements. These are the international business reply service, the offer of which is basically optional but has to be complied with by a receiving country if requested, international reply coupons which must be honoured even if a country does not itself sell them (see *infra*), and delivery advice for incoming registered and recorded delivery items if requested.

Obligations Relating to the International Service

A variety of obligations relate to the international service provided by Members and their designated operators. Although these are contained within the terms of the Constitution, their content is elaborated in the Convention,[81] the Letter Post (RL) and the Parcel Post (RC) Regulations. These last bind all UPU members, though subject to modification by reservations accepted in their Final Acts. Members are bound to ensure their designated operators fulfil the obligations they contain (Const. Art. 22.3). Additional obligations are provided for in the relevant service agreements and their regulations, which again bind all members and are bound to ensure their designated operators comply with them (Const. Art. 22.4). A distinction is made between basic services which include handling and delivery of letter post, together with parcels where that service is offered (Conv. Art. 12), and supplementary services which include registration, insurance, recorded delivery and notification of delivery, cash-on-delivery and express delivery (Conv. Art. 13).

Delivery

The obligation to deliver mail from another UPU member country is an obvious requirement (Const. Art. 1*bis*.1, Conv. Art. 12.1) although this does not apply to parcels in countries that were not part of the Postal Parcels Agreement prior to 1 January 2001, unless they have accepted the duty (Conv. Art. 12.8). International post to and from countries that are not UPU members such as the Republic of China (Taiwan and the Taiwan postal area), the Turkish Republic of Northern Cyprus, and other entities such as Palestine, is carried through neighbouring countries either under a regional agreement or by less formal arrangements.

80 See *infra*, 'Letter Post', p. 296, and 'Parcel Post', p. 297.

81 The current (2010) Universal Postal Convention is most easily accessed *seriatim* in *Decisions of the 24th Congress - 2008* (Berne: IB, 2009) at 145ff.

Dues are payable in respect of the costs incurred by a receiving country or designated operator in complying with the duty to deliver.[82]

Transit

As in its previous incarnations the UPU Constitution guarantees freedom of transit for postal items throughout the territory of the Union, this being the 'single postal territory' first agreed in 1874 (Const. Art. 1.1). Transit is also afforded to the post of non-Union countries for which UPU members provide an intermediate service (Const. Art. 4). Freedom of transit is further explicated by Conv. Art. 4.1 which requires members to ensure that their designated operators forward letter post and parcels by the quickest routes and most secure means that they use for their own postal items. Freedom of transit for postal parcels is limited to the territories of members party to the Postal Parcel Agreement (Conv. Art. 4.3).[83] Air parcels are accorded freedom of transit, but members that do not operate a postal parcel service are not required to forward air parcels by surface (Conv. Art. 4.4). Where obligations as to freedom of transit are not complied with by a country other members may discontinue their postal service with it (Conv. Art. 4.5).

Dues are payable for the transit of international mail.[84]

Security

By Conv. Art. 9 members and their designated operators 'shall adopt and implement a pro-active security strategy at all levels of postal operations' so as to boost public confidence in the postal service 'in the interest of all officials involved'. This includes the interchange of information as to practices and practicabilities. The formulation of this Article is revealing. The inclusion of 'pro-active' indicates that security is a matter of concern. It is not enough to have security; steps must be taken in advance of any problems to secure the international mails.

Prohibited Items

The prohibition of items from the international postal service appeared in bilateral agreements prior to the creation of the Union, and first turns up in the UPU in Art. XI of the Convention adopted by the Second Congress in 1878.

Correlative to the duties to accept and deliver mail, Conv. Art. 15 now contains the general rules under which items are not admitted to the international mail service.[85] It is supplemented and modified by many other detailed provisions in the

82 See *infra*, 'Dues'.

83 See *infra*, n. 95, and Arts. RC 102-3.

84 See *infra*, 'Dues'.

85 National prohibitions applying to mail services internal to a country may be different from as well as wider or narrower than the international rules.

various Regulations and in reservations made to them. Prohibited items include narcotics, psychotropic substances and illicit drugs, obscene and immoral articles, counterfeit and pirated articles, explosive, flammable or radioactive materials and dangerous goods, live animals, gold bullion, coins and bank notes and other articles of value unless in insured letter post (Conv. Art. 15.1-6). Printed papers and literature for the blind may not contain correspondence (Conv. Art. 15.7). A general listing of prohibited items is prepared and kept up to date in consultation with other relevant organisations and entities that range from the International Narcotics Control Board to the International Civil Aviation Organisation (ICAO). In addition, through the IB individual member countries inform others of particular prohibitions set by their national regulations, and the Bureau publishes a compendium based on the model commodity descriptions and coding systems issued by the World Customs Organization. This, the *List of Prohibited Articles*, is issued by the IB for the guidance of UPU members and their designated operators for use in respect of international mails. Whether a national prohibition will apply in the case of transit depends on the relevant national law. Many countries have had their reservations to the relevant Regulations for Letter and Parcel Post accepted by the POC.[86]

The prohibitions are not, however, absolute. Thus radioactive materials and infectious substances may be admitted to the post between countries that so permit (Conv. Art. 16). Bees, leeches and silkworms, parasites and destroyers of noxious insects intended to control such insects, may be exchanged between officially recognised institutions, and Drosophilidae (fruit) flies for biomedical research may be sent by letter post (Conv. Art. 15.4.2.1-3). Live animals may be sent in parcels if relevant national laws so permit (Conv. Art. 15.4).

Postal Charges

The charges for international postal and special services are set by UPU members or their designated operators depending on national arrangements and in principle relate to the costs incurred in processing them (Conv. Art. 6.1). With limited exception a designated operator retains the charges it collects (Conv. Art. 6.1). Ordinarily the prepayment of charges is required. The principles of the Convention and the Regulations are to be complied with (Conv. Art. 6.1). No charge other than those provided for in the UPU Acts may be imposed (Conv. Art. 6.6). Charges cover delivery to an addressee provided that the delivery service requested is operated in the country of destination.[87] They must at least equal internal charges

86 See Conv. Art. 15, Art. RL 144-5, Letter Post Protocol Art. VII, Arts. RC 133-4, Parcel Post Protocol Art. VIII. Cf. Res. C 37/2008 'Counterfeit and pirated items sent through the post'. See also *supra*, n. 66.

87 Some countries do not operate the full range of delivery options: see the relevant Regulations and the service *Manuals*.

for similar items but may exceed guideline charges in the Union Acts (Conv. Art. 6.3-4). Charges may vary the guideline minimum, for example by allowing reduced internal charges or preferential rates for bulk users (Conv. Arts. 4-5).

Some postal items are exempt from postal charges. These include items relating to the operation of the international postal system exchanged between member countries, designated operators and Restricted Unions, as well as letter and parcel post items from the IB (Conv. Art. 7.1.1). Certain other items or services are also exempt from prepayment charges. Letters and parcels[88] and postal financial service items sent to prisoners of war and civilian internees are free of charge (Conv. Art. 7.2). Literature for the blind (up to 7 kg: Conv. Art. 12.2.3) is exempt from charge except as to air surcharges (Conv. Art. 7.3).

A difficulty emerged through the practice of carrying letter post mail in bulk from one country to another, and re-posting back to the originating country so as to take advantage of differences in mail charges. There have been various iterations of the UPU provisions,[89] as well as court cases on the matter.[90] Conv. Art. 26 is the current relevant UPU text.[91] Under it a designated operator is not bound to forward or deliver items which residents in one country post in another for delivery in their territory in order to profit by a more favourable rate condition (Conv. Art. 26.1-2.4). The designated operator can claim from the sender the cost of returning the bulk mail, as well as any relevant terminal dues (Conv. Art. 26. 3-4).

88 Up to 5 kg in weight, or 10kg where the content cannot be split, or the parcel is sent to a camp for distribution (Conv. Art. 7.2.4).

89 See Conv. Art. 23, Hamburg, 1984, 1415 UNTS 66, becoming Conv. Art. 43, Beijing, 1999, 2010 UKTS Misc. No. 4, Cm. 7970. Now Conv. Art. 26, Geneva, 2008, 2010 UKTS Misc. No. 3, Cm. 7968.

90 *Deutsche Post AG* v. *GZS and Citicorp Kartenservice GmbH* joined cases C-147/97, C-148/97, [2000] ECR I-825; 'International Decisions' 2001 95 AJIL 430; V. Kronenberger, 'Universal Postal Service, Circumvention of Postal Monopolies and Community Competition Law' (2000) *Int. Bus. L.J.* 893; V. Ghosal, 'Competition in International Postal Markets' (2002) 25 *World Comp.* 205; D.D. Sokol, 'Express Delivery and the Postal Sector in the Context of Public Sector Anti-Competitive Practices' (2003) 23 *Nw. J. Int. L. & Bus.* 353; C.B. Harrington, 'Weather May Not Stop USPS, but Special Interests Will: The Bush Administration's GATS Offer Supports Private Express Delivery Services but Threatens to Stamp out USPS' (2003) 19 *Am. Univ. Int. L. Rev.* 431.

See also the EU Directive 97/67/EC on the improvement of the quality of service in Community postal services: http://eur-lex.europa.eu/LexUriServ/LexUriServ.do?uri=CELEX:31997L0067:EN:HTML.

Cf. the Arbitration under NAFTA, *Universal Parcel Service of America Inc.* v. *Government of Canada* [Canada Post] (2007) 46 ILM 922; D.A. Gantz, 'Introductory Note' (2007) 46 ILM 919; for earlier stages see Harrington *supra*, at 454.

91 Subject to the reservations contained in Art. XIII of the Final Protocol to the Convention.

Dues

The sums exigible for transit and for terminal dues are set by the POC (Conv. Art. 34). They are computed on the basis of sampling and averaging over various periods, and may be calculated either by volume or by weight. They are settled either bilaterally or through the IB (Arts. RL 201-233, 246-50; Arts. RC 192-3; together with applicable reservations in relevant Final Acts).

Transit Charges[92]

Charges for the transit of a country are not new. Originally these were a matter for bilateral negotiation between the originating country of the mail item and the countries through which it would have to pass to its final destination. When the global arrangements were agreed, transit charges were provided for under Art. X of the 1874 Convention.[93] They remain part of the international postal system. In brief, transit charges are remuneration for the carriage of mails across a country, whether by land, sea or air or any combination, and whether by a designated operator, another carrier, or any combination thereof (Conv. Art. 1.6).[94] Their application is governed by Arts. RC 102 and RL 102. The POC sets the various levels of charge for transit dues (Conv. Art. 34), Arts. RC 194-206 and RL 203-211 containing the rates for transit based on the method of transit (land, sea and air) as well as the weights and distances involved. Transit charges for surface mail are accounted for annually between the designated operators of the origins of mail and those of transited territories, based on the weight of the mail received in that year (Arts. RC 207-10, RL. 205-11). The transit charge for surface conveyance of airmail is borne by the designated operator of the origin of the mail and is payable to the operators of countries crossed or whose services take part in their land or sea conveyance (Art. RL 203.1.2), except that in any conveyance by sea that transit cost may be arranged between the designated operators of origin and the shipping agencies, subject to the agreement of the port of embarkation (Art. RL 203.1.4). Airmail transit costs are borne by the country of origin, and are based on total distances as set by the POC.[95]

92 There is a UPU *Compendium of Transit Information* which sets out the detail for the use of designated operators. It gives kilometric distances for the sectors for mail in transit, and the transit services provided by members for surface mail.

93 See 'Transit and delivery', Chapter 7, c. n. 95.

94 For detail see Conv. Arts. 31, 34, and Arts. RL 204 211, together with Art. RL XV of the relevant Final Protocol. See also *supra*, n. 92.

95 The whole area is complex. What is in the text above is a loose summary. See Conv. Art. 32 and Arts. RC 203 and RL 235.

Terminal Dues

Terminal Dues are sums owed by a designated operator sending postal items to the designated operator in the receiving country. They compensate for the costs that the receiving operator incurs in their processing and delivery (Conv. Art. 1.7). Under the original arrangement arrived at in Berne in 1874, it was expected that the volume of mail to and from two countries would more or less balance out, and so Art. IX.1 provided that each administration was to keep the entire postage sums paid by senders.[96] This persisted for many years.

In 1969 the Tokyo Congress allowed receiving postal administrations to require payment from sending administrations in respect of their processing costs where there was an imbalance between volumes to and from their respective countries.[97] These were named 'Terminal Dues'. At Hamburg in 1984 the basic sums involved were set at eight gold francs per kg for letter post and two gold francs for printed papers sent in bulk.[98] The Terminal Dues system was further elaborated in 1999 when the Beijing Congress introduced country-specific rates for industrialised countries, and some thirty countries adopted this 'target' system from 2001. The Beijing system reflected cost and market elements, as well as the quality of service offered in these countries. Its use of the 'industrialised' criterion made room for less-developed countries to negotiate separate arrangements. Terminal Dues, however, remained a matter of concern, with both the CA and POC continuing to study the question. A 'World Round Table' was convened in Berne in January 2008 and as a result a new methodology was adopted at the Geneva Congress in August of that year.[99] Under Conv. Art. 27.1-3, subject to exemptions members are to apply the new country specific system in accordance with targets and transitional arrangements agreed by the Council by 2013.[100] Terminal Dues will have some regard to quality of service in the receiving countries (Conv. Art. 27.5), may be wholly or partly waived by a receiving country (Conv. Art. 27.6), and are calculated in terms of weight (Conv. Art. 27.7-8). Conv. Art. 28 then provides for Terminal Dues in respect of letter flow between designated operators in the target system, referring rates and sampling mechanisms to be established in the Letter

96 General Postal Union: Treaty … relative to the formation of a General Postal Union, Berne, October 9 1874, 147 CTS 136; 65 BFSP 13 (in French); 1 Bevans 29.

97 Conv. Art. I.7: 'Terminal dues: remuneration owed to the designated operator of the country of destination to the designated operator of the dispatching country in compensation for the costs incurred in the country of destination for letter-post items received'.

98 The French gold franc has been replaced for accounting purposes by the Special Drawing Right of the International Monetary Fund, Const. Art. 7.

99 See Congress Res. 18/2008. Cf. 'The UPU global terminal dues system: Proposal' submitted to the 'Terminal Dues' - World Round Table, Berne, 21-22 January 2008, and the joint CA and POC report to the Geneva Congress, 'Terminal Dues System', 24th Cong. Doc. 19, rev. 1.

100 See 'Classification of countries and territories for terminal dues and Quality of Service Fund purposes', Res. C 18/2008.

Post Regulations.[101] Conv. Art. 29 does the same for countries in the transitional system. Both Conv. Arts. 27.6-9 and 29.3-4 set Terminal Dues rates for the years 2010 to 2013, when the decisions of the next Congress will apply. These questions are being further studied.[102] In particular they raise (or interact with) the question of international trade in services, and competition laws.[103]

Apart from Terminal Dues, the designated operator of a country of destination can ask for payment specifically related to bulk mail sent into its postal service by the same sender. A notification of an intention to apply an additional charge can be triggered on the receipt in the same mail or on a single day of 1,500 or more items from the same sender, or 5,000 or more over a period of two weeks, and the additional charge is exigible on similar bulk mail received three months after the notification (Art. RL 218.1-2). However, if the incoming mail from the same sender exceeds 3,000 items received in a single mail or in one day, or 10,000 in a period of two weeks, the additional charge can be applied immediately.

Charges, Rates and Settlement of Accounts

An international accounting system requires a referent to which national currencies can be referred to set equivalences. For much of its existence the UPU used the French gold franc for the purpose. Since the Washington Congress of 1999 the Special Drawing Right of the International Monetary Fund has been used (Const. Art. 7), it having been used in parallel with the gold franc from 1979. The matter of rates and charges are under continuous review.[104] Accounts may be settled bilaterally between members, or through the IB (GR Art. 116.4; Arts. RC 208-9, RL 247-8).

Letter Post

Letter post is a basic service (Conv. Art. 12.1) regulated by the Constitution, the GR (neither permit reservations, Const. Art. 22.1-2), the Convention (Const. Art.

---

101 See Arts. RL 212- 7.

102 'Future work on remuneration systems for letter-post items exchanged between the designated operators of UPU member countries. Coordination of work on remuneration for other types of items', Res. C 43/2008.

103 See A. Perrazzelli, 'Terminal Dues under the UPU Convention and the GATS: An Overview of the Rules and of their Compatibility' (2000) 23 *Fordham Int. L.J.* 736; D.D. Sokol, 'Express Delivery and the Postal Sector in the Context of Public Sector Anti-Competitive Practices' (2003) 23 *Nw. J. Int. L. & Bus.* 353.

104 See C 43/2008, 'Future work on remuneration systems for letter-post items exchanged between the designated operators of UPU member countries. Coordination of work on remuneration for other types of items'.

22.3), and the Letter Post Regulations (RL). The application of the Convention and RL may be subject to the reservations accepted by the other UPU members as part of the relevant Final Protocol.[105] The IB publishes a *Letter Post Manual* which brings together the relevant materials.

Letter post is classified under the RL either by its speed of treatment or its content (Conv. Art. 12.3). Letter post items other than postcards have a maximum combined length, width and depth of 900 mm, with the greatest not more than 600 mm. If in roll form, length plus diameter is limited to 1040 mm with a maximum of 900 mm, in both cases with a tolerance of 2 mm (Art. RL 122.1.1). Minima are a surface measurement of not less than 90 by 140 mm, with a tolerance of 2 mm. If in roll form length plus twice the diameter must not be less than 170 mm, with the greater dimension not less than 100 mm. Letter post items may weigh up to 2 kg, and may include small packets, and literature for the blind up to 7 kg (Conv. Art. 12.2.1-3). Special bags ('M bags') up to 30 kg containing printed matter (newspapers, books, etc.) for a single addressee are also covered (Conv. 12.2.4). However, the RL allow optional higher weight limits (Conv. Art. 4). Whether incoming letter post is put through the customs systems of receiving countries depends on national legislation (Conv. Art. 18). Military mails may be sent in closed mail bags, rates and conditions being set by the sending designated operator. Whether there are transit charges or terminal dues payable for such depends on any relevant special agreement, which failing they are payable by the sending operator (Conv. Art 19).

Parcel Post[106]

Until 1999 the Parcel Post was the subject of a separate Agreement. Amendments to Const. Art. 22 adopted by the Beijing Congress of 1999 incorporated the international arrangements as to parcels in the provisions of the Convention. The international parcel post service is therefore now governed by the Constitution, the GR (to neither of which are reservations permitted: Const. Art. 22.1-2), the Convention (Const. Art. 22) and the Parcel Post Regulations (RC). As with Letter Post the application of the Convention and RC may be subject to the reservations accepted by the other UPU members as part of the relevant Final Protocol. A *Parcel Post Manual* collects the relevant materials.

In broad the international parcel post is subject to the same rights, requirements and duties as for Letter Post indicated immediately above.[107] Following the Beijing

105 Cf. 'Reservations', *supra*, n. 62. The IB publishes a *Letter Post Compendium* which provides country-specific particulars of the implementation of the relevant rules.

106 A *Parcel Post Compendium* published by the IB provides country specific particulars of the implementation of the relevant rules.

107 The IB publishes a *Parcel Post Manual* which brings together the relevant materials.

amendments the parcel post is a basic service (Conv. Art. 12.5-6). However, by Conv. Art. 12.8 countries that did not offer a service under the previous Postal Parcels Agreement prior to 1 January 2001, the date when the Acts of the Beijing Congress came into effect, are not obliged to provide that service. Parcels of up to 20 kg are ordinarily accepted, conveyed and delivered either by means set out in the Conv., or as agreed bilaterally with other countries (Conv. Art. 12.5). Parcels weighing above 20 kg are optionally allowed for in the RC for certain categories (Conv. Art. 12.6). A country whose designated operator does not convey parcels may allow transport companies to provide a parcel service under Conv. terms, subject to any restriction as to destination or origination that it may apply (Conv. Art. 12.7). Parcels must not be smaller than the minima prescribed for letter items (as to which see *supra*) (Art. RC 115.1). Parcels must not exceed two metres in any one dimension, or three metres for the sum of length plus the greatest circumference in any other dimension (Art. RC 115.1). Alternatively, designated operators may work to 1.5 metres for any one dimension or three metres for the sum of length plus the greatest circumference in any other dimension, or 1.05 metres for any one dimension, or two metres for the sum of length plus the greatest circumference in any other dimension (Art. RC 115.2.1-2).

Quality of Service

As required by Conv. Art. 20 both the Letter Post and the Parcel Post Regulations contain provisions as to quality of service. Member countries or their designated operators are required to establish and publish delivery standards and targets for incoming mail, and measure how far these are met. The targets, with due allowance for customs clearance, are not to be less favourable than those applied to equivalent items within the domestic service.[108] Quality of Service can be taken into account in the calculation of Terminal Dues.[109] As noted above, the POC runs a Quality of Service Fund which arranges training courses.[110]

108 Art. RL 202; less detailedly Art. RC 191. Res. C/48, Bucharest 2004, instructed the POC to develop national report cards on delivery performances. For these see Appendix to the Nairobi Postal Strategy, *infra*, n. 138. The Twenty-fourth Congress, Geneva, 2008, instructed the establishment of a Global Monitoring Service (GMS) to improve the accuracy of the measurement of the quality of service in the international mail service: Res. C 45/2008, 'UPU Global Monitoring System (GMS)'.

109 'Quality of Service', *supra*, n. 108 and text following n. 100.

110 *Supra*, n. 39.

Postal Payment Services[111]

The Second Congress of the Union, Paris, 1878, saw some discussion of the use of the new organisation to transfer money securely between customers in member states. No general measures were adopted but a number of participants did enter into appropriate arrangements. Over the years these developed into separate Agreements with their own Regulations but always within the ambit of the Union.[112] The 1999 Beijing Congress merged all the then existent agreements relating to money (the 'Money Order Agreement', the 'Giro Agreement' and the 'Cash-on-Delivery Agreement') into a single Postal Payment Services Agreement to deal with all such matters for those willing to become party to it.

The current Postal Payment Service Agreement is that revised by the 2008 Geneva Congress.[113] It is more complex and detailed than can be dealt with within the wordage of this book. It contains provisions as to definitions, the designation of operators, the functions of member countries, operational functions, the ownership of the funds being dealt with, the prevention of money laundering, terrorist funding and financial crime, confidentiality, the neutrality of the technology used, general principles of the operation of the services and their quality, principles for electronic data interchange including interoperability and security, the rules for the postal payment services, inquiries, the liability of users and operators, and the financial relations of parties and operators including the settlement of accounts.[114] The settlement of accounts for the Service is carried out either through the bilateral agreement of the operators designated by members, or through a central clearing house. Calculations are made either in the currency of a destination operator or as agreed by the designated operators concerned.[115] Article 27.3 contains a complex system for the amendment of the Agreement and its Regulations. In order to facilitate the Service the Union is putting in place a global electronic financial network. This will provide a speedy cost-efficient electronic money order service that may to a large extent replace the 'well-known postal order'.

---

111 A UPU *Postal Payment Compendium* gives country-specific particulars of the implementation of the relevant rules.

112 See Chapter 7 at n. 115.

113 See *Decisions of the 24th Congress, 2008* (Berne: IB, 2009), and the *Postal Payment Service Manual* (Berne: IB, 2010) or 'Postal Payment Services Agreement' in the Eighth Additional Protocol to the Constitution of the Universal Postal Union, 2010 UK Misc. No. 3, Cm. 7968, at 103.

114 There is an extensive Table of Forms.

115 Postal Payments Agreement, *supra*, n. 113, Art. 25.

International Reply Coupons

As indicated in the previous chapter, International Reply Coupons (IRCs) were introduced by the Rome Congress of 1906. Manufactured and issued by the IB to those UPU members and designated operators that offer them for sale (GR Art. 118), they are exchangeable in all UPU countries for the prepayment of the international postage cost of letters up to a maximum weight.[116] Conv. Art. 13.4.2 indicates their optional nature and the RL, particularly Art. RL 142, gives the detail. Each designated operator sets the value of an IRC within its list of postal charges, subject to a minimum set in terms of Special Drawing Rights by the IB, and the IB notifies the value of the IRC set by the relevant designated operator to all other members (Art. RL 142.2). The use of IRCs between members is subject to mutual accounting organised through the IB, and between a designated operator and the IB in the case of their transactions. The content and basic design of the coupon is set out in Art. RL 142.5 (with specimen). The design was revised at Beijing in 1999 and again at Geneva in 2008. The validity of IRCs of the Beijing variety expired at the end of 2009 and, unless renewed, those of Geneva will expire at the end of 2013.[117]

Postage Stamps, Franking Impressions and Prepayment

The original postage 'stamp' was a mark on a postal item that showed that its transport and delivery had been paid for, or that that would be paid for by the recipient when delivered. The adhesive stamp invented by Hill took on the name because it served part of the function – showing that payment had been made. The problem, of course, was that a 'stamp' of that kind could be reused if steamed off or otherwise removed from the item. Accordingly 'cancellation' of the adhesive stamp was introduced. Soon it was usual for the cancellation itself to be stylised, bearing the place of postal receipt and the date and time, thus becoming itself a form of 'stamp'. 'Franking' is the use of embossed or similar designation to

116 UPU members and their designated operators are not obliged to sell International Reply Coupons but must accept them in payment for international postal charges (Conv. Art. 13.4.2). About 2.2 million IRCs are sold each year by countries offering the service. IRCs are not available to and from postal administrations such as those in Taiwan, which are not UPU members.

117 See also Art. RL XIX in the Final Protocol to the RL: and description InternationalReplyCouponsTheUpuCirculatesANewIrc2009En.pdf, accessible from http://www.upu.int/en/activities/international-reply-coupons/international-reply-coupons-key-documents.html. A national flag may be featured, if commissioned and paid for by the relevant designated operator.

indicate postage has been paid.[118] Members are required to 'prevent, prosecute and punish' counterfeiting or the use of counterfeits (Conv. Art. 11.2).

Postage stamps used in the international postal service are now regulated by Conv. Art. 8 and Art. RL 115 of the Letter Post Regulations.[119] The latter lays out the characteristics of stamps and of postal prepayment or franking impressions. They may be of any shape, but must be between 15 and 50 mm in dimension. They may be of any colour. Stamps may be issued only by UPU members or by their authority and in conformity with UPU rules (Conv. Art. 8.2). A stamp should show its face value expressed in the currency of the country of issue or other method (Conv. Art. 8.3.2). It should also show the name of the member issuer in roman letters (Conv. Art. 8.3.1). An exception to the latter requirement, however, is contained in a footnote to Conv. Art. 8.3.1, which states that: 'An exception shall be granted to Great Britain, the country which invented the postage stamp'.[120] Further design options now include barcoding, date of issue or expiry, the name of the designer and/or printer and a copyright symbol.

The subject or design of stamps can cause problems. Conv. Art. 8.5 stipulates that the subject and design of stamps are to be closely linked to the cultural identity of the issuing member or contribute to its dissemination, or, if commemorating figures or events not native to the issuer, have a close bearing on it. Stamps should not have a political character or be offensive to a person or country. Finally the 'content' of stamps should be of major significance to the member issuing or authorising the issue. The application of these broad rules can be contentious. For example religious representations have on occasion been objected to. Thus, on the objection of the (UK) National Council of Hindu Temples, in 2005 the UK Royal Mail agreed not to reprint a set of stamps that reproduced a Mughal painting of Jesus and his mother because Mary bore Hindu insignia.[121] In 2010 in the US the issue of four stamps bearing the images of four Hindu deities also caused

---

118 Conv. Art. 6. Thus mail from Committees of the US Senate and House of Representatives is 'franked' by a reproduction of the signature of the relevant Committee Chairman. Jacqueline Kennedy had a similar franking privilege during her life. Under Sec. 29 (166) of the ITU Rules of Procedure for Conferences members of delegations and ITU officials present at conferences have franking privileges to the extent arranged with the host government.

119 A country may adopt additional or separate rules for internal purposes. In Germany, Denmark and Sweden (so far) it is possible to text the post office and receive by return a coded number. This is valid but only within that country for one first class postage unit. The code can be copied by the user onto a letter in the usual position for a stamp, and in due course is read by the postal technology. Codes are valid for one week from issue, and their cost is collected as part of the user's mobile phone bill.

120 Under Sec. 62 of the Postal Services Act, 2011, the Secretary of State has power to require UK stamps to bear the image of the Queen. The Act allows the privatisation of Royal Mail postal services in the UK.

121 See http://news.bbc.co.uk/1/hi/uk/4420896.stm; http://www.nchtuk.org/content.php?id=307.

discussion.[122] Another field of contention relates to territorial claims. Under general international law state conduct manifesting sovereignty in relation to territory includes the provision and regulation of postal services. The portrayal of territory on stamps can exacerbate territorial disputes.[123] Subject to such considerations, in the UK on payment of a fee customers may design their own stamps valid for both domestic and international purposes which are then printed for their use by the Royal Mail in limited quantities.[124] The US Postal Service offers a similar service,[125] as do other postal operators elsewhere.

Philately

Unsurprisingly the UPU has links with the world of philately. Many UPU members (and other issuers including the UN) now derive income from the sale of stamps apart from that connected with the purchase of the postal service.[126] To foster philately the World Association for the Development of Philately was created within the POC in 1997. It monitors market trends and disseminates data and best practice in the world of stamps. Under an arrangement between it and the main UPU a World Numbering System (WNS) has been launched as a database for all authentic stamps issued on or after 1 January 2002 by UPU members or their associated territories which have joined in the Association. Stamps lawfully issued are notified to the IB which checks their provenance and registers them, giving each issue a WNS number and adding it to the WNS website. This provides a mechanism through which unlawful 'stamps' (a problem which, it will be

---

122 See http://www.deccanherald.com/content/48165/us-stamps-hindu-deities-spark.html. Cf. M.G. Toulouse, '*Christianity Today* and American Public Life: A Case Study' (1993) 35 *J. Church & St.* 241 at 264.

123 G. Fitzmaurice, 'The Law and Procedure of the International Court of Justice, 1952-4: Points of Substantive Law, Part II, I Territorial Sovereignty, Disputed Claims to Territory (The Case of the Minquiers and the Ecrechos)' (1955-6) 32 BYIL 20 at 27; R.W. Bagshawe and J. Goldup 'The Postal History of Antarctica, 1904-1949' 1951 6 *Polar Record* 45; C.C. Joyner, 'Anglo-Argentine Rivalry after the Falklands/Malvinas War: Laws, Geopolitics and the Antarctic Connection' (1984) 15 *Law Am.*, 467 at 474; T. Pierce, 'Philatelic Propaganda: Stamps in Territorial Disputes' 1996 *IBRU Boundary and Security Bulletin*, 62; Recommendation I-XI of the First Meeting of the Antarctic Treaty Parties on Postal Matters (1961-2) 166 BFSP 243 at 249 and UK statement at 252; cf. Decl. XVII by Azerbaijan to the 2008 UPU Final Acts (*ad fin*). Cf. e-book: R.G. Elliot, *Philatelic Propaganda: Border Changes in Eastern Europe, 1938-1941* at http://ebookpedia.net/Philatelic-Propaganda--Border-Changes-in-Eastern-Europe--1938-1941.html.

124 See http://www.royalmail.com/customised.

125 See http://www.usa-postage.com/ and *supra*, n. 122.

126 See 'Development of philately', Res. C 36/2008, the latest of a series. Res. C 50/2004 established an action plan for the purpose. Some small UPU members (e.g. San Marino) derive a considerable proportion of their national income from philately.

recalled, goes back to early UPU days) may be identified, and spurious 'stamps' drawn to the attention of philatelists and others. The IB has issued a number of circulars as to stamps issued after the coming into force of these arrangements. Apart from the UPU the WNS system has the support of a number of philatelic organisations and clubs.[127]

In 2008 by its Recommendation C 26/2008 the Twenty-fourth Congress again revised a nine-sectioned 'Philatelic Code of Ethics' which had first been adopted in 1989. This Code covers all philatelic products. The Code bans postal authorities from going beyond their 'postal' function in order to create or feed a market for would-be collectors. Thus it requires that postal authorities issue only stamps and other means of denoting postage payment and not products irrelevant to proper postal activities. Cancellation methods should similarly be restricted to those normal within the postal service. Postal authorities should print stamps in sufficient quantity to meet market demands. A balance is therefore to be struck. On the one hand they should refrain from under-printing or giving the impression of scarcity of a particular issue. On the other hand they should not saturate the market. Equally they should not in any way give express or implied approval or status to unofficial 'stamps', or to unofficial products that incorporate valid stamps. They should not produce stamps or other philatelic products intended to exploit customers. They should also see that their agents comply with the Code. The Code concludes that postal authorities acknowledge that the secondary value of stamps (i.e. that beyond their face value) rests only on the willingness of collectors to purchase and trade them.[128] The survival of the philatelic market depends on that willingness, which compliance with the Code may help secure.

Interpretation, Argument and Dispute

Finally we come to the question of the authoritative interpretation of the UPU Acts, their implementation, and the settlement of disputes.

The interpretation of the constitutive documents of all international organisations and the performance of obligations under their agreements may produce argument amongst their parties. The UPU is no different. That was recognised in the 1874 Convention, its Art. XV.2 providing for the IB to give 'an opinion on questions in dispute', and Art. XVI for the arbitration of disputes that could not be so settled. The present UPU adopts similar arrangements. These provisions relate only to disputes between UPU members or postal administrations, disputes arising between a postal administration and a customer not being matters for the Union.[129] They do not exclude the possibility that parties to a dispute may otherwise settle

127 The various elements are available through the website: http://www.wsnstamps.ch.

128 Cf. T. Pratchett, *Going Postal* (London: Doubleday, 2004).

129 Sometimes customers of the international postal service complain to the IB. This is always passed on to the relevant postal administration.

matters by negotiation, conciliation or mediation. Under the UPU arrangements the IB may play a major role, apart from its involvement in giving opinions on what is termed, within its commentaries on the Acts, 'non-litigious' questions. Thus at the request of members and their designated operators the IB may compile the views of other members and operators on a particular question. The result is not binding, but may be of use in solving or ameliorating problems, including those of operational procedures (GR Art. 116.3).

Const. Art. 32 is simple: 'In the event of a dispute between two or more member countries concerning the interpretation of the Acts of the Union or the responsibility imposed on a member country by the application of those Acts, the question at issue shall be settled by arbitration'. Practice has gone otherwise. Usually recourse is first had to the IB, it being asked by the parties directly concerned in a dispute to give its opinion on the interpretation of the Acts of the Union (GR Art. 116.2).[130] Such an opinion is not binding on the parties to the dispute. Ultimately a matter under contention may go to Congress if it is a matter of common interest for members. Congress may adopt a resolution, make a recommendation or reach a 'decision' (GR Art. 101*bis*.2).[131] A decision of Congress is binding on members and is considered as a clarification or authentic interpretation but not as a modification of the Acts of the Union.

The ultimate alternative in a 'litigious question' is arbitration under Const. Art. 32 and GR Art. 132. Each party to a dispute selects a member country uninvolved in the dispute except where several members make common cause, in which case they must agree on the appointment of that single arbiter (GR Art. 132.1). If one side fails so to appoint within six months of the proposal of arbitration the IB calls on it to appoint or can itself appoint an arbiter *ex officio* (GR Art. 132.2). Alternatively the parties may agree on a single arbiter, which may be the IB (GR Art. 132.3). An arbitral decision is taken by a majority (GR Art. 132.4). In the event of a tie the arbiters select another member uninvolved in the dispute to act, and, failing their agreement the IB appoints the new arbiter from among members not initially proposed by the parties (GR Art. 132.5). In the case of a dispute arising from one of the Agreements, as opposed to the Acts, the arbiters must be drawn from the parties to that Agreement (GR Art. 132.6). Since an arbitration is as to the interpretation or the implementation of duties under an international agreement, only member countries can take part in an arbitration. However, it is recognised that the real dispute may actually be between designated operators rather than between the governments of their parent states. GR 132.7 therefore provides that if a dispute has to be settled between

130 The IB commentary to GR Art. 116.2 indicates that practice is that all parties concerned must request the opinion before it will take the matter up. Further, a non-party cannot intervene.

131 See e.g. Decision C3/2008 on 'Interpretation of the term "member country" replacing "postal administration" in the Acts of the Union'; and generally *Decisions of the 24th Congress - 2008* (Berne: IB, 2009).

designated postal operators, the operators are to ask their member countries to act in accordance with GR Arts. 132.1-6. UPU procedures do not permit appeal from an arbitral decision, and that decision is binding on the parties. Arbitration is infrequent. The IB Commentary to the Acts of the Union (2010) indicates that there have been twenty-eight arbitral awards since 1874, the first being in 1877 and the most recent in 1981.[132]

The Future

The main business of the UPU remains the facilitation of the physical transport of letters and parcels between senders and recipients in different countries. The circumstances under which this activity is carried out are undergoing change. Several main aspects are clear. First, the postal service has been wholly or partially privatised in a number of countries.[133] Second, as part of that development what used to be a postal monopoly may have been split, allowing, for example, a division between the acceptance of mail, and the delivery of parcels and of letters. Third, there has been the growth of international couriers such as FedEx, UPS and DHL. Some of these may use a national postal service as the end deliverer of mail items which they collect in one country and bring to another. National systems thereby lose out on income from international postage charges, receiving only the internal tariff for the business. Fourth, in many countries the privatisation of postal services, and the permitting of private carriers, has affected the financial stability of national postal systems. Fifth, electronic communication, particularly email, has diminished the physical volume of the post. Sixth, and more generally, thanks in part to privatisation and the operation of new commercial carriers, postal services are coming to be considered by some less as a public service and more as commercial business. The 'profit' element enters in. The incursion of profit (as opposed to revenue to finance operations) raises questions of competition and the emergent area of 'trade in services'.[134] For example the rules as to handling of post, sometimes in large quantities, that is posted in a foreign country for transfer back to the country of origin so as to profit by the lower charges in force there has produced debate.[135]

---

132 *Constitution, General Regulations (etc.) with commentary by the UPU International Bureau* (Berne: IB, 2010) A27.

133 There is concern as to how this has happened, e.g. in The Netherlands delivery times have deteriorated, and the number of post offices, into which customers consign international mail, has declined. In the latter respect the UK shows a similar pattern.

134 Cf. materials cited *supra*, n. 90. See also Res. C 40/2008 'International law in the field of trade in services. WTO–UPU relations'. Cf. also the problem of 'bulk mail', *supra*, under 'Terminal Dues'.

135 See Conv. Art. 23, Hamburg, 1984, 1415 UNTS 66, becoming Conv. Art. 43, Beijing, 1999, 2010 UKTS Misc. No. 4, Cm. 7970. Now Conv. Art. 26, Geneva, 2008, 2010

National postal administrations have had to cope with these developments, and so does the Union.

The 2008 Congress instructed the setting up (with due regard to geography and levels of economic development) of a working group composed of ten members from each of the CA (one of whom to be Chairman) and the POC, together with the Chairman of the Consultative Committee.[136] The impact on the Union of new market players is being studied, as are the adjustment of the UPU mission, restructuring, extra-budgetary activities, and the role of the Restricted Unions. *Ad interim* the UPU has held short Postal Strategy conferences between the meetings of Congress to review the postal scene. Participants include governments, regulators and operators, the Restricted Unions also sending representatives,[137] the most recent of the series being held in 2009.[138] These will inform the next Congress which is scheduled for 2012.

Various questions need to be faced, or faced down.

First, do we need the UPU at all? Should the international postal system simply be left to work itself out through market forces? Surely not. The result would be a fragmentation of the international system, with the ceasing of reliable international postal interchange in many areas of the world. That would be tragic. Efficient international post is in the interests of humanity. That individuals, businesses and governments can communicate efficiently by a postal system is integral to modern society. The UPU should therefore remain and should remain as one of the UN family of specialised agencies.

Second, is the UPU unduly prescriptive, containing too much detail in its regulations? Could they be simplified? Probably not, for much the same reasons as justify the UPU's existence. The UPU is concerned with the physical transport and delivery of postal items. For the international system to work efficiently as much harmonisation as possible should be sought. That was a basic motivation in the formation of the Union. There should be uniformity across as wide a swathe of the international postal system as possible. What has been achieved should not now be unpicked. As things are reservations in the Final Protocols to the Letter and Parcel Post Regulations preserve many national quirks and differences, perhaps to an unnecessary extent. But at least these exist by the mutual agreement of members, and are known to operators through the Manuals and Compendia. The existence of the various Restricted Unions adds to the

UKTS Misc. No. 3, Cm. 7968. See also *supra,* n. 90.

136 Res. C 16/2008, 'Management of the work of the Union - Further reform of the UPU'.

137 Bucharest World Postal Strategy (BWPS). Cf. *Laying the foundation of the future UPU Postal Strategy: Report of the 2006 UPU Strategy Conference, Dubai 2006* (Berne: IB, 2007), http://www.dubaiupu2006.com.

138 *The postal sector: an essential component of the global economy. Nairobi Postal Strategy 2009-2012* Congress Doc. No. 38 (Berne, 2010); http://www.upu.int/en/the-upu/strategy-conference/2010-strategy-conference/nairobi-postal-strategy.html.

complexity, but at least the extent of that complexity is limited to their members, and by Const. Art. 8.1 their provisions should not result in a service inferior to that secured under the UPU agreements.

Third, are the voting and financial element of the UPU congruent with international realities? I raise this question because it arose in connection with the ITU. In the ITU there is the argument that voting weight of the ITU should, in at least some elements, bear a greater relationship to the financial contribution made by each state. This question appears to be without basis in the UPU. The UPU member states or their designated operators are providing actual physical services. Further, within the UPU the possibility of reservations to the Final Acts of the Conv., RC and RL allow for a degree of individuation in the actual application of UPU rules. It therefore seems unnecessary, and perhaps undesirable, that the present contributory system be departed from, or that there be any change from the principle of 'one member, one vote'.[139]

Fourth, there is the question of the stability of the basic Acts. The Constitution and General Regulations bind all members and no reservation is permitted to their terms (Const. Art. 1.1-2). Notwithstanding, successive congresses have amended them. The Final Acts containing these amendments are subject to ratification by their signatories, but ratification is not always swift and certainly is not uniform in date. It is good, therefore, that the UPU is studying whether it might be possible to adopt a more stable structure, with amendment to practical detail being confined to the revisions of the service regulations.[140] Whether this will produce results for consideration at the next Congress in 2012 remains to be seen.

Such discussions provoke the fifth question. Is the structure of the Union satisfactory in the face of modern developments? Should the differentiation between regulatory and operational matters be more clearly drawn and the powers of the CA and POC revisited? Suggestions that the Union be split to take account of the problem seem extreme. However, something certainly needs to be done somehow to incorporate or harness the new commercial carriers of international 'mail'. Otherwise the activities of the commercial carriers may distort the international postal system which is the very reason the Union exists, and the political repercussions would be significant. At present private companies are ineligible to join the Consultative Committee. Perhaps as a first step they could be made eligible because their activities are relevant to the international postal system, and thereafter their role/voice could be augmented.

Amid these possibilities it is rather to be hoped that the UPU will continue to foster good practice in both national and international postal services. In terms which they have officially sanctioned, postal operators care about the

---

139 Cf. S. Zamora, 'Voting in International Economic Organizations' (1980) 74 AJIL 566.

140 Res. C 42/2008 'Study on establishing a permanent Universal Postal Convention and Postal Payment Services Agreement'.

'single postal territory' and its implications, focusing on the needs of customers, respect for the mail carried, while taking pride in their work, and supporting international postal development.[141]

141 See the 'UPU Postal Operators Statement of Values' adopted as Rec. C 108/1999 by the Twenty-second Congress, Beijing, 1999, reproduced in *Letter Post Manual* (Berne: IB, 2009) and *Parcel Post Manual* (Berne: IB, 2010), in both cases at XXI-XXII. Cf. Res. C 38/2008 'The role of the postal sector in the Information Society'.

Appendix 1
Telecommunication Technologies

There are two modes of telecommunication. The one requires a physical connection – a wire or cable – while the other is 'wire-less'. Strictly speaking the use of flags or semaphore systems also comes within the general definition of 'telecommunication', although nowadays, and particularly when used in the plural, the term is usually reserved to denote communication which one way or another employs electromagnetism. That said, the first international definition of telecommunication, to be found in the Annex to the Madrid Convention of 1932, is: 'Any telegraph or telephone communication of signs, signals, writings, images, and sounds of any nature, by wire, radio, or other systems or processes of electric or visual (semaphore) signalling.'[1]

Visual Communication – Optical Systems

Communication by visual signalling goes a long way back into history. Beacons were used on Hadrian's Wall, the Great Wall of China and to pass to London news of the approach of The Armada. In daylight flags were used to pass commands along those Walls. In their times flags were used between the ships of the Persian, Greek and Roman navies. By the end of the Eighteenth century naval flag codes had become extremely complex,[2] and semaphore had become a normal military tool. It could also be used for private communications.[3] In the 1790s the Frenchman Claude Chappé (1763-1805) adapted the semaphore concept by using signal arms on a sequence of high gantries and this, together with a telescope at each station, allowed the creation of what he called a 'telegraph' system. Others took up the

---

1 Annex to the International Telecommunication Convention, Madrid, 1932: 151 LNTS 4; 49 Stat. 2391, TS 867; 6 Hudson 109; 3 Bevans 65.

2 T. Lynn, *An Improved System of Telegraphic Communication*, 2 vols. (London, 1818). The novelist Captain Frederick Marryat made major revisions to the British Navy flag codes before his retiral to become a full-time author. He died in 1848; the memorial tablet on the wall beside his tomb at Langham Church in Norfolk, UK, summarises the code which he introduced.

3 Art. 43 of the .International Telegraph Convention, Paris, 17 May 1865, 130 CTS 198: 56 BFSP 295, provides for the setting of rates for messages where an element of the route is semaphore to or from a ship at sea.

term.[4] By 1844 the Chappé system linked Paris with twenty-nine French cities.[5] Though useless in fog and darkness,[6] the system was reliable and efficient, but by that time its replacement, the electric telegraph, was at hand.

Wires and Cables

Coding an electric current passing down a wire allows a message to be passed from one end of the wire to the other. Invented by Baron Schilling in St Petersburg in 1832, others, including Cooke and Wheatstone, worked on the concept and soon long-distance telegraphy became possible.[7] Amongst the pioneers were D.E. Hughes[8] and Samuel Morse.[9] Separate from the question of technology, the 'Morse Code' for the encoding of messages became prominent.

---

4 Aberdeen University Library has several early discussions of long-distance communication systems, including J. Conolly, *A treatise on telegraphic communication by day and night for naval, military and commercial purposes* (London, 1808), and his *An essay on universal telegraphic communication in which a plan is laid down for reciprocal intercourse between the different nations of the world* (London, 1817); J. Macdonald, *A treatise on telegraphic communication, with some consideration on the present state of the marine code and of naval signals* (London, 1808) and his *A treatise explanatory of a new system of naval, military and political telegraphic of general application, in which a comprehensive numerical dictionary is applied to different descriptions of telegraphs* (London, 1817); J.J. Fahie, *A history of wireless telegraphy, 1838-1899: including some bare-wire proposals for subaqueous telegraphs* (Edinburgh: Blackwood,1900).

5 Cf. the 'Clacks' system on the Discworld in T. Pratchett, *The Fifth Elephant* (1999) and *Going Postal* (2004).

6 These defects as well as the system itself are important in the plot of *The Count of Monte Cristo* (1844) by Alexandre Dumas, Père.

7 G. Hubbard, *Cooke and Wheatstone and the invention of the electric telegraph* (London: Routledge and Kegan Paul, 1965).

8 D.E. Hughes patented his system in the US in 1855 and it was widely adopted in the US. It was also in use in Europe as an alternative to the Morse system and remained recognised by successive versions of the Service Regulations. The UK Cooke/Wheatstone system was not widely used except by the UK.

9 Morse (1791-1872), the son of a Puritan preacher in Massachussetts, trained as a painter and was reasonably successful, graduating from Yale University in 1810 and being admitted to the Royal Academy in London in 1811. During his time at Yale he attended lectures on electricity. In 1825, while he was in Washington DC executing a painting commission, a message carried by horse informed him that his wife had died in New Haven, Conn. This impelled him to think how long-distance communications could be improved. In 1832 an encounter with C.T. Jackson, a scientist experimenter with electricity, moved Morse to turn his attention to the possibilities of the electric wire. All else followed. On Morse's complex life see K. Silverman, *Lightning man: the accursed life of Samuel F.B. Morse* (New York: Knopf, 2003). Morse had many business struggles, including patent

The technical problems faced by long-distance electrical telegraphy included the bunching and degradation of signals due to impurities in the cabling, and attenuation of the signal merely because of distance itself. Electrical resistance was combatted by the use of high voltage, but this had its limits. However, these problems were overcome, as was the problem of effective insulation for underwater cabling. In 1850 a simple gutta-percha coated cable was laid across the English Channel connecting England and France, though it was replaced with a better insulated cable in 1851. 'Repeaters' were incorporated in long cables (including submarine cables) and this helped increase the bandwidth available for the transmission of messages.

The first trans-Atlantic telegraph cable was laid in July 1866 from southern Ireland to Newfoundland by the SS Great Eastern and soon the major European empires had linked their outposts with their respective capitals, although the original cable systems made use of land-crossing segments wherever possible.[10] As time went on problems of capacitance and induction were met. Over time the number of 'repeaters' placed in cables to reduce signal distortion was increased. However, telephony by underwater cabling was found to be impossible until the 1940s, some of the development being accelerated by the needs of the 1944 Normandy Invasion. Trans-Atlantic telephony did not come until TAT-1 (Trans-Atlantic-1) in 1956, the new cable carrying only 36 voice channels. Notwithstanding, the laying of metal cables continued elsewhere round the world.[11] However, until the coming of first, satellites, and second, the fibre-optic cable, long distance trans-maritime telephony depended on short-wave radio.

A major development in telegraphy came in the 1870s with the invention of the teletype machine. This advantage was augmented in the 1930s with the development of the telex system which provided a physical copy to both sender and receiver of a message.

Fibre-optic cables came into general use in the 1980s and soon proved invaluable in a variety of circumstances, including medicine.[12] A fibre-optic cable can be used as a wave-guide for light, and light frequencies can be modulated. Fibre-optic technology provides an enormous bandwidth, allowing it, for example, to carry television signals, in contrast to copper cabling which can carry television signals for only a short distance. TAT-8, laid in 1987/8 and becoming operational in

---

disputes. For the patent case that went to the Supreme Court see *O'Reilly* v. *Morse* (1853) 56 US (15 How.) 62.

10 Thus the first UK-India cable connection went undersea only for the final link from Aden, in Yemen, South Arabia, to Bombay (Mumbai), India.

11 H. Barty-King, *Girdle round the earth: the story of Cable and Wireless and its predecessors to mark the group's jubilee, 1929-1979* (London: Heinemann, 1979); P. Young, *Power of Speech: a history of Standard Telephones and Cables, 1883-1983* (London: Allen & Unwin, 1983).

12 In October 2009 C.K. Kao was awarded the major share of the Nobel Prize for Physics for his work on the transmission of light through glass fibres.

the latter half of that year, was the first trans-Atlantic fibre-optic cable. Fibre-optic cables now circle the globe. Unlike metal cabling, junctions (submarine branching units) can be installed in a fibre-optic system, allowing different segments to communicate without a direct connection between them. The selection of an appropriate light frequency will allow a messaging connection to be established between points A and C, while the main cabling runs between points A and B, with a shorter spur off to C.

Cable has three major problems. First, cable systems are not versatile. With the exception of the fibre-optic 'junction' option, a cable runs from point A to point B. It connects what it connects. Second, cables can break, be damaged, or be broken. A system can be shut down by lightning strike, by earthquake or avalanche, or by accident. The repair of a cable can be difficult, particularly in the case of a submarine cable. Undersea cables are regularly cut by accident as where a trawler or an ill-placed anchor breaks the cable. Further, the rupture of a cable system may be deliberate. In the First Word War both sides sought to destroy the other's cable networks, the British success in the North Sea leading to the establishment of major radio transmitters/receivers south of Berlin, and a rapid flush of invention in radio which was mirrored by the Allies. Third, the laying of cable, terrestrial or submarine, can be both difficult and expensive or even impossible. The difficulty and expense of laying a cable system varies depending on the route concerned. It has to be said that there is, of course, a basic expense of manufacture. However, this may be dwarfed by the problem of the route. Many potential trans-Africa cable routes would be difficult because of forests and mountains. A trans-Andean system would run into similar problems. A trans-Canada or trans-Russia route has to cover miles of inhospitable territory. And once any such system is in place, the later problems of a fault or breakage would provide a separate set of difficulties. A wireless or satellite connection may be more sensible.

Wireless Telecommunication

Electromagnetism was discovered by Hans Christian Ørsted (1777-1851) in 1820,[13] its theory being elaborated by Michael Faraday (1791-1867), James Clerk Maxwell (1831-1879)[14] and others. The existence of the electromagnetic spectrum (radio waves) was established by Heinrich Hertz (1857-1894), whose name

13 See F. Gregory, 'Episodes in Romantic History: Ørsted and the Discovery of Electromagnetism', http://earlyradiohistory.us/sec004.htm.

14 James Clerk Maxwell, being the junior Professor of Natural Philosophy at the time of the fusion of Marischal College and Kings College in Aberdeen, Scotland, to form the unified University of Aberdeen in 1860, was surplus to requirements and left Aberdeen, first for King's College, London and then Cambridge, where he produced his most important work.

continues in the designation of portions of that spectrum by the designation 'Hz'.[15] Others took his insights further.[16] Notwithstanding these innovators, however one computes the various claims to primacy and priority the fact remains that the Marconi system came to dominate the 'wireless' environment as it developed.

Originally the discussion of radio frequencies was conducted using 'wave lengths' expressed in metres. The 'wave length' is the distance between the peaks in the radio 'wave'. However, this nomenclature is useful only for 'long wave' through 'medium wave' and into 'short wave'. Once the 'wave length' is very short it is more convenient to speak of the 'frequency' of the radiation in the electromagnetic spectrum, hence the term 'radio frequency'.[17] The term 'kilocycles' (Kc/s) became more usual as radio usage moved from 'long wave' through 'medium' and 'short wave' to digital broadcasting which uses 'very high frequency' (VHF). This section of the spectrum is normally denominated in kilohertz (KHz, 1KHz = 1000 Hz), a term introduced in 1960. Now further advances in technology have moved the language first to 'megahertz' (MHz), and then beyond that to 'gigahertz' (GHz).[18] Very high frequencies correspond to very short (fractions of a centimetre) wavelengths. Following a conference in Prague in 1929, within the European Broadcasting Area in the medium and long wave bands spacing between channels is set at 9 KHz. Channel spacing for these wave bands in the US is in 10 KHz units.[19]

At lower frequencies radio waves are reflected by the Heaviside Layer. At the VHF level and above, radio signals are not reflected by the Earth's magnetic field, and pass out into space.[20] Signals to and from satellites (uplink and downlink) are in the higher frequency ranges. Clarity and absence of interference with the signals

15 Apparently Hertz did not realise the implications of his discoveries, considering only that in various ways they proved Maxwell right.

16 G.L. Archer, *History of radio to 1926* (American Historical Association, 1938, rep. New York: Arno Press, 1971); T.H. White, 'Personal Communication by Radio' *United States Early Radio History*: http://earlyradiohistory.us/sec004.htm. On technology see early parts of H.G.J. Aitken, *The continuous wave: technology and American radio, 1900-1932* (Princeton, NJ: Princeton UP, 1985) and his *Syntony and spark: the origins of radio* (New York:Wiley, 1976).

17 Cf. the recommendations and tabular presentations of Sub-Committee 1 on the 'General Allocation of Frequency or Wave Length Bands' and of Sub-Committee 4 on 'Problems of Marine Communication' in the (US) report *Recommendations for Regulation of Radio Adopted by the Third National Radio Conference* (Department of Commerce: US GPO, 1924), http://earlyradiohistory.us/1924conf.htm.

18 See ITU RR Art. 2, 'Nomenclature', Section 1 - 'Frequency and Wavelength Bands', § 2.1 (http://life.itu.int/radioclub/rr/art02.htm) and RR Appendix 1, Section 2, § 2.2 - 'Necessary Bandwidths' (http://life.itu.int/radioclub/rr/ap01.htm).

19 Beware of buying a radio with preset tuning or station buttons in one jurisdiction/area for use in the other.

20 Modern television requires the use of VHF and above.

are crucial for satellite operation and use.[21] The ITU is the agency through which these characteristics are attained.

---

21 See Lyall/Larsen, 199-200, 229-35.

Appendix 2
Restricted Postal Unions

In UPU terms a 'Restricted Union' must be composed of at least three member countries. They, or their Designated Operators, must conclude a convention to deal with postal questions *inter se* and include a number of provisions regarding the organisation and functioning of the Union. In general a Restricted Union has organs and procedures such as periodical conferences, and a headquarters or one Designated Operator acting as its Managing Administration. The Union must also consider itself to be a Restricted Union within the terms of UPU Const. Art. 8.[1] It is noticeable that the membership of the current Restricted Unions might also be considered to have a regional character.

As at 1 January 2011 the Restricted Unions maintaining relations with the UPU were:

1. Association of Postal and Telecommunications Operators of Portuguese-Speaking Countries and Territories (AICEP), created in 1998. Members: Angola, Brazil, Cape Verde, Guinea-Bissau, Macao, Mozambique, Portugal, Sao Tome and Principe, and Timor-Leste (Dem. Rep.).
2. Southern Africa Postal Operators Association (SAPOA), created in 2001. Members: Angola, Botswana, Dem. Rep. of the Congo, Lesotho, Madagascar, Malawi, Mauritius, Mozambique, Namibia, South Africa, Swaziland, Tanzania (United Rep.), Zambia and Zimbabwe.
3. Association of European Public Postal Operators (POSTEUROP), created in 1993 after the reorganisation of the previous CEPT. Members: Albania, Armenia, Austria, Belarus, Belgium, Bosnia and Herzegovina, Bulgaria (Rep.), Croatia, Cyprus, Czech Rep., Denmark, Estonia, Finland, France, Germany, Great Britain, Greece, Guernsey/Jersey and Isle of Man, Hungary (Rep.), Iceland, Ireland, Italy, Latvia, Liechtenstein, Lithuania, Luxembourg, Malta, Moldova, Monaco, Montenegro, Netherlands, Norway, Poland, Portugal, Romania, Russian Federation, San Marino, Serbia, Slovakia, Slovenia, Spain, Sweden, Switzerland, the former Yugoslav Republic of Macedonia, Turkey and Ukraine.
4. Arab Permanent Postal Commission (APPC), created in 1992, replacing the Arab Postal Union (UPA) which had been created in 1952. Members: Algeria, Bahrain, Comoros, Djibouti, Egypt, Iraq, Jordan, Kuwait, Lebanon, Libyan Jamahiriya, Mauritania, Morocco, Oman, Palestine, Qatar, Saudi Arabia, Somalia, Sudan, Syrian Arab Rep., Tunisia, United Arab Emirates and Yemen.

---

1 Adapted from the IB Commentary to Acts, Const. and Gen. Regs. (2010), p. A.10.

5. Regional Commonwealth in the field of Communications (RCC) created in 1991. Members: Armenia, Azerbaijan, Belarus, Georgia, Kazakhstan, Kyrgyzstan, Moldova, Russian Federation, Tajikistan, Turkmenistan, Ukraine and Uzbekistan.
6. Conference of Posts and Telecommunications of Central Africa (COPTAC), created in 1998. Members: Cameroon, Central African Rep., Chad, Congo (Rep.), Dem. Rep. of the Congo, Equatorial Guinea and Gabon.
7. European Conference of Postal and Telecommunications Administrations (CEPT), created in 1959 and reorganised in 1992. Members: Albania, Andorra, Austria, Azerbaijan, Belarus, Belgium, Bosnia and Herzegovina, Bulgaria (Rep.), Croatia, Cyprus, Czech Rep., Denmark, Estonia, Finland, France, Georgia, Germany, Great Britain, Greece, Hungary (Rep.), Iceland, Ireland, Italy, Latvia, Liechtenstein, Lithuania, Luxembourg, Malta, Moldova, Monaco, Montenegro, Netherlands, Norway, Poland, Portugal, Romania, Russian Federation, San Marino, Serbia, Slovakia, Slovenia, Spain, Sweden, Switzerland, the former Yugoslav Republic of Macedonia, Turkey, Ukraine and Vatican.
8. West African Postal Conference (WAPC), created in 2001 and comprising only postal operators charged with the universal postal service, replacing the Conference of Posts and Telecommunications Administrations of the States of West Africa (CAPTEAO). Members: Benin, Burkina Faso, Côte d'Ivoire (Rep.), Ghana, Mali, Niger, Nigeria, Senegal and Togo.
9. Pan African Postal Union (PAPU), created in 1980. Members: Algeria, Angola, Benin, Botswana, Burkina Faso, Burundi, Cameroon, Central African Rep., Chad, Comoros, Congo (Rep.), Côte d'Ivoire (Rep.), Dem Rep. of the Congo, Egypt, Eritrea, Ethiopia, Gabon, Gambia, Ghana, Guinea, Kenya, Lesotho, Liberia, Libyan Jamahiriya, Madagascar, Malawi, Mali, Mozambique, Niger, Nigeria, Senegal, Sierra Leone, Somalia, South Africa, Sudan, Swaziland, Tanzania (United Rep.), Togo, Tunisia, Uganda, Zambia and Zimbabwe.
10. African Postal Union (APU), created in 1961. Members: Burundi, Dem. Rep. of the Congo, Egypt, Ghana, Guinea, Guinea-Bissau, Liberia, Mali, Mauritania, Somalia and Sudan.
11. Baltic Postal Union (BPU), created in 1994. Members: Estonia, Latvia and Lithuania.
12. Caribbean Postal Union (CPU), created in 1998. Members: Anguilla, Aruba, Barbados, Canada, Cayman Islands, Dominica, Dominican Republic, France, Great Britain, Grenada, Haiti, Netherlands, The Netherlands Antilles, Saint Lucia, Suriname, Trinidad and Tobago, Turks and Caicos Islands and United States of America.
13. Asian-Pacific Postal Union (APPU), created in 1961. Members: Afghanistan, Australia, Bangladesh, Bhutan, Brunei Darussalam, Cambodia, China (People's Rep.), Fiji, India, Indonesia, Iran (Islamic Rep.), Japan, Korea (Rep.), Lao People's Dem. Rep., Malaysia, Maldives, Mongolia, Myanmar, Nauru, Nepal, New Zealand, Pakistan, Papua New Guinea, Philippines,

Singapore, Solomon Islands, Sri Lanka, Thailand, Tonga, Vanuatu and Viet Nam.

14. Postal Union of the Americas, Spain and Portugal (PUASP), created in 1911. Members: Argentina, Bolivia, Brazil, Canada, Chile, Colombia, Costa Rica, Cuba, Dominican Republic, Ecuador, El Salvador, Guatemala, Haiti, Honduras (Rep.), Mexico, Netherlands Antilles and Aruba, Nicaragua, Panama (Rep.), Paraguay, Peru, Portugal, Spain, Suriname, United States of America, Uruguay and Venezuela.
15. Nordic Postal Union (NPU), created in 1919. Members: Denmark, Finland, Iceland, Norway and Sweden.
16. Postal Union of EurAsia (PUEA), created in 2001. Members: Azerbaijan, Pakistan and Turkey.

In addition to the Restricted Unions other entities *de facto* fulfill much the same conditions and pursue similar aims, but for various reasons do not consider themselves (or are not considered to be) Restricted Unions, e.g. the European Postal Financial Services Commission (CSFPE), which admits banks as members but not designated operators of postal services.

Index

For Product Safety Concerns and Information please contact our EU representative GPSR@taylorandfrancis.com
Taylor & Francis Verlag GmbH, Kaufingerstraße 24, 80331 München, Germany

www.ingramcontent.com/pod-product-compliance
Ingram Content Group UK Ltd.
Pitfield, Milton Keynes, MK11 3LW, UK
UKHW020020200926
475702UK00014B/1978
9781138260870